HARVARD HISTORICAL STUDIES, 123

*Published under the auspices
of the Department of History
from the income of the
Paul Revere Frothingham Bequest
Robert Louis Stroock Fund
Henry Warren Torrey Fund*

FRENCHMEN *into* PEASANTS

Modernity and Tradition in the Peopling of French Canada

Leslie Choquette

HARVARD UNIVERSITY PRESS
Cambridge, Massachusetts
London, England
1997

LIBRARY OF CONGRESS CATALOGING-IN-PUBLICATION DATA

Choquette, Leslie.
　　Frenchmen into peasants : modernity and tradition in the peopling
of French Canada / Leslie Choquette.
　　　　p.　cm.—(Harvard historical studies ; 123)
　　Includes bibliographical references and index.
　　ISBN 0-674-32315-7 (alk. paper)
　　　1. New France—Emigration and immigration—History. 2. France—
Emigration and immigration—History—17th century. 3. France—
Emigration and immigration—History—18th century. 4. Immigrants—
New France—History. 5. Canada—History—To 1763 (New France)
6. France—History—Bourbons, 1589–1789. I. Title. II. Series:
Harvard historical studies ; v. 123.
F1030.C57　1997
304.8'71044'09032—dc21　　　　　　　　　　　　　　　　96-40089

For my parents, Phyllis and Walter Choquette,
and in memory of my grandparents

Acknowledgments

This project was conceived two decades ago in a moment of curiosity. It occurred to me that I knew nothing of the French origins of the Quebecers and Acadians, and that they would make a good thesis topic for an aspiring French historian. I never dreamed that I would be at it for so long, but the rewards of investigating the francophone societies on both sides of the Atlantic have been more than adequate compensation. Needless to say, I have incurred many debts along the way.

I would like to thank the following institutions for their financial support over the years: the Minda de Gunzburg Center for European Studies, Harvard University; the Frederick R. Sheldon Traveling Fellowship; the University Consortium for Research on North America; the Department of History, Harvard University; the government of Québec; France's Centre national de la recherche scientifique (CNRS); the government of Canada; the Charles Warren Center, Harvard University; and Assumption College.

Permission to rework previously published material and include it here was generously granted by the University of California Press, for "Recruitment of French Emigrants to Canada, 1600–1760, in *"To Make America"*: *European Emigration in the Early Modern Period*, edited by Ida Altman and James Horn (1991), and by the American Antiquarian Society, for "Frenchman into Peasants: Modernity and Tradition in the Peopling of French North America," in *Proceedings of the American Antiquarian Society*, volume 104, part 1 (1994).

It would be impossible to acknowledge fully all of the individuals whose help and support have enriched this project from beginning to end. Special mention must be made of the knowledgeable and generous staff and patrons of the Archives nationales du Québec, who make working there an extraordinary pleasure. I am particularly grateful to Serge Goudreau, who pointed me to the work of the demographer Mario Boleda; to Mary Ann LaFleur, who kindly shared with me her work on Notre-Dame-des-Anges; and to Rénald Lessard. If anyone deserves to be considered the model archivist, it is Rénald. His contribution defies a brief description, but it includes introducing me to the "Témoignages de liberté au mariage," one of my richest archival sources, and putting me in touch with the members of the Programme de recherches en démographie historique (PRDH) of the Université de Montréal.

Among scholars of New France, I have benefited greatly from the enthusiasm and erudition of Jacques Mathieu and Alain Laberge of Université Laval, Hubert Charbonneau and John Dickinson of the PRDH, and Yves Landry of the Université de La Rochelle. For the Maritimes, Naomi Griffiths of Carleton University and Barry Moody of Acadia University brought to my attention exciting new evidence about the early Acadians. My understanding of French migrations in general has been immeasurably enriched by the work of Jean-Pierre Poussou of the Université de Paris IV (Sorbonne) and the Collège de France. His interest in my research and encouragement are also greatly appreciated. A valuable comparative perspective was provided by geographers Gildas Simon, Stéphane de Tapia, and Emmanuel Ma Mung of the CNRS and the Université de Poitiers. I cannot thank them enough for the warm welcome that they extended to me in 1992 at their research center, Migrations internationales: espaces et sociétés. Like the Charles Warren Center, where I was a 1993–94 fellow, MIGRINTER provided me a most congenial environment during the arduous process of transforming an unwieldy dissertation into a coherent book.

The process of rewriting was also eased by several people who read the entire manuscript early on and gave me valuable advice. Simon Schama of Columbia University, Allan Greer of the University of British Columbia, and, most especially, Bernard Bailyn of Harvard University helped me to conceptualize my argument more clearly and separate the wheat from the chaff. At a later stage, the anonymous reader for Harvard University Press made some very helpful suggestions, particularly regarding the concluding chapter.

Finally, I owe a special debt of gratitude to Patrice Higonnet of Harvard University, who has participated in every aspect of this project since its inception. His contribution is simply incalculable.

Contents

Introduction: The Peopling of French Canada   *1*

PART I
Modernity

1 | Regional Origins: Peasants or Frenchmen?   *27*
2 | A Geography of Modernity: The Northwest   *55*
3 | A Geography of Modernity: Non-Northwesterners and Women   *77*
4 | An Urban Society: Class Structure and Occupational
     Distribution   *101*
5 | Religious Diversity: Protestants, Jews, and Catholics   *129*
6 | The Age of Adventure in an Age of Expansion   *151*

PART II
Tradition

7 | Traditional Patterns of Mobility   *181*
8 | A Traditional Movement: Northwestern Emigration to Canada   *200*
9 | A Traditional Movement: Emigration Outside the Northwest   *219*
10 | The Canadian System of Recruitment   *247*

Conclusion: Frenchmen into Peasants   *279*

Notes   *307*

Index   *389*

The deeper you penetrate into the woods, the more intelli-gent, and, in one sense, less countrified do you find the inhabitants; for always the pioneer has been a traveler, and, to some extent, a man of the world; and, as the distances with which he is familiar are greater, so is his information more general and far reaching than the villagers. If I were to look for a narrow, uninformed, and countrified mind, as opposed to the intelligence and refinement which are thought to emanate from cities, it would be among the rusty inhabitants of an old-settled country, on farms all run out and gone to seed with life-everlasting, . . . and not in the backwoods.

—Henry David Thoreau, *The Maine Woods*

Introduction: The Peopling of French Canada

Migrations were an integral part of French life under the Ancien Régime, affecting large groups of people at various points in their life cycle and assuring the economic survival of entire regions. In the years before the French Revolution, at least a million French men and women, and probably a great many more, took to the roads each year in search of jobs, spouses, knowledge, or adventure. Their temporary or permanent odysseys carried them from village to village, country to city, town to town, nation to nation, and metropolis to colony.

Unfortunately, the place of migrations in French historiography has not reflected their centrality to the experience of individuals and communities. Because of the difficulties involved in tracing migrants, who simply disappear from local records when they move, historians have tended to ignore them in favor of domiciled populations, whose behavior is easier to reconstruct. This concentration on sedentary elements has its risks, for "one may well imagine that the migrants differed noticeably from the others in their attitudes toward life."[1] It has almost certainly led to an overemphasis of the time-honored and static routines that Fernand Braudel termed "material life," and with them the most traditional aspects of early modern French society.

In the past two decades, scholars have begun to redress the balance, putting familiar sources to creative use as ways to understand migratory behavior. In their hands parish registers, hospital records, passenger lists, and contracts of marriage, apprenticeship, and indentured servitude have yielded significant information on patterns of migration and the identity of migrants. Still, most of the studies carried out so far exhibit a limited geographical scope, having been conducted at the level of individual communities. A few historians, such as Jean-Pierre Poussou, have extended their investigations to entire regions, but overall understanding of regional and national migration systems remains deficient.

Likewise, migrations beyond the frontiers of France have received less attention than have internal movements. Contemporaries, however, recognized the attraction of foreign lands for the French population. In the words of one eighteenth-century naval official, "the hope of making a small fortune and of living more comfortably, even the desire to wander, often makes Frenchmen, whom one finds established in all the countries of the world, make these sorts of resolutions."[2] Yet these movements fell swiftly into oblivion, perhaps because New France never equaled New England or New Spain, or because France's emigration in the nineteenth century paled in comparison to that of its European neighbors. Whatever the reason, the migration streams linking France with other nations and with its colonies are particularly ripe for reconsideration.

In this book I seek to continue the explorations of recent historians of French migration while moving these studies beyond the confines of a single city or region. I focus on a particular migratory movement, French emigration to Canada in the seventeenth and eighteenth centuries, in an attempt to elucidate the lesser-known colonial facet of French mobility.[3]

At least 30,000 emigrants of both sexes and possibly double that number embarked for Québec during the French Regime, and an elusive but substantial number, perhaps 7,000, made their way to French Acadia. This study deals with nearly 16,000 of these emigrants, most of them Quebecers but more than 10 percent Acadians. The work is divided into two major parts: the first on social and economic history, the second on the history of migrations. My goal throughout is to situate emigration to Canada within the broad context of social, economic, cultural, and political life under the Ancien Régime.

In Part One, "Modernity," I examine emigration to Canada from the standpoint of French economic and social life, regional as well as national. My purpose in these first six chapters is to describe the volume and composition of the movement across space and time, and to discuss these aspects in the context of France's laborious transition from "feudalism" to "capitalism." Generally speaking, emigration presupposed economic expansion and involved the beneficiaries of this expansion to a greater degree than its victims. Sectors responsible for colonization did not necessarily grow dramatically, nor in a manner disruptive to traditional social relationships. They did, however, belong increasingly to an Atlantic world whose frontiers stretched from western France to the East Indies, a domain that had little in common with the autarkic world of peasant communities too often associated with the Ancien Régime.

Although social and economic analysis is illuminating, it inevitably fails to account for French emigration to Canada in all its diversity. Migrations, as a form of cultural behavior, have a sexual, social, and geographical specificity of their own. The influence of economics is indirect, mediated through a traditional repertory of mobility. In Part Two, "Tradition," I therefore reconsider the pattern of emigration in the context of the emerging discipline of migration history. In many ways the movement toward Canada occurred as a by-product of other, more perennial movements, such as the rural exodus or interurban labor migrations. It was thus a reflection of Ancien Régime tradition, though only insofar as this tradition involved mobility rather than sedentariness.

Part Two ends with a chapter on recruitment in which I focus on how the Canadian migration stream first came into being and how it maintained itself for more than a century in the absence of mass departures from the mother country. Because of the commercial marginality of the colony, the system of Canadian recruitment developed as an uneasy partnership between private and public interests that worked separately and together to promote French overseas expansion.

Overall, emigrants to Canada belonged to an outwardly turned and mobile sector of French society, and their migration took place during a phase of vigorous Atlantic expansion. They nonetheless crossed the ocean to establish a subsistence economy and peasant society, traces of which lingered on into the twentieth century. This paradox deserves attention, not only as an illustration of France's failure to secure a more dominant position in the "modern world system," but in itself. I thus conclude with a discussion of the marginalization of French Canada within the Atlantic economy from the seventeenth to the late nineteenth century. Rather than abandon the emigrants in port, I trace their differentiation from the

Americans to the south, whom they initially resembled but subsequently could not always emulate.

THE PEOPLING of French Canada was chronicled on both sides of the Atlantic, often in sources of exceptional quality. From these records I assembled a sample of nearly 16,000 emigrants, organized around the variables of regional origin, social class, occupation, religious background, age, and date of departure. The nature of the sources, both Canadian and French, and the representativity of the sample are the subject of the balance of this introduction. Canadian administrative records, whether sacred or secular, and French exit documents provide a unique opportunity to examine an emigrant population both before and after expatriation. The population examined here, which includes most of the permanent settlers, together with a substantial number of birds of passage, is a fairly representative cross section of the different types of French people who spent time in Canada during the Ancien Régime.

Canadian Sources

"Our ancestors in the seventeenth century left anonymity behind in crossing the Atlantic."[4] Thus wrote the Canadian demographer Hubert Charbonneau in *Vie et mort de nos ancêtres*, the preliminary synthesis of a vast research project dealing with the early population of Québec. The abundance and quality of the Canadian archives are indeed astounding, particularly in comparison with their French or West Indian counterparts. Whereas in France the efforts of church and state to monitor the population through a system of obligatory registration produced mixed results, in Canada the bureaucracy proved more than adequate to the task.

In the early 1660s, when the colony received an administrative and ecclesiastical infrastructure analogous to that of metropolitan France, Québec's population stood at about 3,000. The area of settlement was compact, stretching only from Québec to Montréal, and not extending beyond the Saint Lawrence Valley. The Acadian population, while more scattered, was limited to some 300 people, and that of French Newfoundland consisted of a mere handful of fishermen established along the southern coast.

In metropolitan France, by contrast, the smallest *généralité* (Perpignan) had a population of 160,000, and the largest (Paris) over 1.5 million; the average number of inhabitants for whom one intendant was responsible was about 575,000.[5] The Canadian intendants were thus in an enviable position vis-à-vis their French counterparts; despite continued demographic growth over the following century, the population of Québec never exceeded 75,000, nor that of Acadia (what remained of it) 15,000.

Added to the relative logistic facility of administering a small and concentrated population was the privileged position enjoyed by Canada as a settlement colony. The West and East Indies were valuable as economic assets, but they never possessed the strategic importance of the colony located due north of flourishing New England. From the time of the earliest permanent settlement in 1604, the French crown viewed North American colonization in terms of its rivalry with England. If Richelieu's prohibition of Protestant settlement (though not of Protestant immigration per se) stemmed primarily from the practical consideration that religious ties could prove more binding than national ones, by the time of Louis XIV this stricture had acquired an ideological cast. New France was to compete with New England, but not on New England's terms. It was to prevail, not due to the greater greed of its merchants, but because of the innate superiority of French civilization as embodied in state and church. France, by pursuing what Henri Brunschwig termed a "politics of prestige" with regard to Canada, transformed the colony into a kind of laboratory of state-of-the-art social practices. Administrators and Catholic reform clerics extended their authority into every domain of social life; hence, the plethora of ecclesiastical, administrative, notarial, and judicial records that are such a boon to demographers and historians.[6]

Ecclesiastical Records

Ecclesiastical records are of paramount importance for an understanding of early modern French populations because, pursuant to the Ordinances of Villers-Coterets and Blois (1539–1579), the legal obligation to maintain vital records of baptism, marriage, and burial fell to the parish priests. Initially applied only to the French kingdom, and there unequally, the ordinances were subsequently extended as new territories such as Lorraine and the colonies came under French control.

For the historian of migration, the Canadian vital records of primary interest are the acts of marriage. While the acts of baptism provide insights into kinship and friendship networks among emigrants through the listings of godparents, and the acts of burial offer information about emigrants who were single or who had families in France, neither type of document deals directly with the French origins of the population. The acts of marriage, on the other hand, detail the geographical antecedents of both spouses and, episodically, their professions, those of their parents, or both. As with the acts of baptism, the presence of witnesses testifies to the extent and type of social contacts prevalent among the emigrants.

The registers of baptism, marriage, and burial are the most voluminous of the Canadian ecclesiastical resources,[7] but they are by no means the only ones of interest. Because of the crucial role played by individual and institutional proponents of the Catholic Reformation in Canadian colonization, abjuration of heresy and Catholic confirmation were strongly encouraged. The resulting lists of new converts and communicants, which identify emigrants by their diocese of origin, make it possible to trace a number of people who failed to marry in the colony, including some who had no intentions of settling permanently.[8] The lists of abjuration have an added advantage: they demonstrate that even Jesuitical zeal did not deter some Protestants from seeking their fortunes in the colony, nor from deciding that their overwhelming interest lay with conforming to Catholic practice.

Other useful ecclesiastical documents are the patient lists of the Hôtel-Dieu of Québec. The lists do not, unfortunately, date back to the founding of the facility in 1639 by the Hospitalières of Dieppe. For the period from 1689 to 1824, however, they form a continuous and remarkably well maintained series. They identify the patients by name, regional origin, age, and, particularly in the case of sailors and soldiers, profession. The presence of large numbers of sailors and soldiers in the lists makes these records especially precious to the historian who wishes to place equal emphasis on the seasonal, temporary, and permanent currents of this migratory stream.

By far the most fascinating of the church documents from the point of view of migration history are the "testimonials of freedom at marriage." Compiled between 1757 and 1820, these lists originated in the bishop's fear that the demobilization of soldiers from the four regiments sent to Canada during the Seven Years' War could lead to widespread acts of bigamy. He therefore mandated that each emigrant, before the celebration of his or her marriage, provide a sworn statement, corroborated by witnesses whenever possible, attesting to the legality of the proposed union. In fact, the statements read less as protestations of singleness than as litanies of prior migrations—migrations that are rarely captured in such detail by other sources.

Characteristic in this regard is the declaration of one Nicolas Lelat, an unfortunate whose enterprising efforts to compensate for nonexistent witnesses with forged letters earned him a categorical refusal. He described himself to the priest as "Nicolas Lelat, native of Calais, muff maker, aged twenty-eight, in Canada for two years as of September and away from his country for three, and having worked in Rouen, Caen, Angers, Nantes, La Rochelle, and Bordeaux during the space of a year and a half, and embarked for these countries."[9]

Actually, Lelat's inability to produce any witnesses was unusual, and hence was possibly viewed with suspicion. What the testimonials generally portray is a slice of popular life predicated on mobility, but in which insecurity was mitigated by a rich texture of social relationships. It is a great pity that the issue of bigamy did not begin to preoccupy the Canadian ecclesiastical establishment at an earlier date—in 1665, say, with the arrival of the Regiment of Carignan-Salières. It would be fascinating to know whether the migratory circuits and short-circuits detailed in the testimonials were characteristic of the period as a whole, rather than simply the middle years of the eighteenth century. My suspicion is that they were, and that the testimonials, in fact, provide a precious window onto a largely undocumented but ubiquitous aspect of everyday life in early modern times.

In any case, it is certain that these life-cycle migrations of the laboring poor, whatever their origins, persisted well beyond the years 1757–1820. The colorful world described in Agricol Perdiguier's *Mémoires d'un compagnon* (1854), with its deprivation and danger, its excitement and education, and its ever changing constellation of friendships made on the road, would have seemed familiar, in every respect, to the men and women who appeared before Canadian priests in hopes of putting their *Wanderjahre* behind them.

Nor would the American odyssey of these journeymen, laborers, and domestics have appeared unusual to Perdiguier. His own brother Simon, having been conscripted into the army, performed his military service in Spain. "From Spain he entered Portugal, where he was made prisoner and conducted aboard the English hulks. He went from England to North America." After eleven years of absence, Simon, "having gone to Saint-Domingue, then to Barbados, after that to Canada and other lands of America, returned to our country." Not all members of the family returned. Perdiguier wrote of his grandmother, a native of Oriol, near Marseille: "Her two American uncles, named Dumas, of whom she spoke to us so often, were never heard from again. What a pity! They were going to make our fortune."[10]

Two Dumas brothers, Alexandre and Libéral, did, in fact, emigrate to Canada during the youth of Perdiguier's grandmother, in 1752. Born in Nègrepelisse (Tarn-et-Garonne) of a long line of Protestant professionals, they drifted first to Montauban and then into the army, serving as officers. Aged seventeen and twenty-two at the time of their departure from France, they already exercised the functions of royal notary and trader. In 1760 and 1761, when they made their testimonials of freedom at marriage, both were described as "merchants in Québec."[11]

Of course, there is no guarantee that these enterprising young men were indeed the great-great-uncles of Agricol Perdiguier; for one thing, the Perdiguiers were Provençals. But commercial and human ties between the Middle Garonne and the hinterlands of Marseille were legion in the eighteenth century, to the point that the first could be described as an economic satellite of the second.[12] The identification is thus possible, and, if confirmed, would be both an amusing coincidence and an illustration of the continuity of migratory practices in the age before railroads.

Censuses

The ecclesiastics were not the only Canadian authorities to take a healthy interest in the state of the colonial population. The intendants, responsible as they were for colonization and economic development, did their best to monitor these efforts through a series of nominative censuses.[13] The early censuses appear crude by today's standards, but, as Hubert Charbonneau and Yolande Lavoie have pointed out, it was unusual for such documents to exist at all anywhere before the second quarter of the nineteenth century.[14] They are of somewhat limited use to the historian of migration because they generally fail to distinguish between emigrants and those born in the colony. If a given person is already known to be an emigrant, however, his or her appearance in a census provides information about approximate age and, from 1667 on, the extent of agricultural involvement.

The first Québec census, that of 1666, is somewhat exceptional for the attention paid to the French origins of the population. Regional origins were, to be sure, completely ignored, but the occupational qualifications of the colonists were denoted with care. Jean Talon, Canada's first intendant, was keenly interested in assessing the availability of the various skills as a prerequisite to elaborating a strategy of economic self-sufficiency. His instructions to the census takers thus involved eliciting information on all trades practiced in France, whether or not the emigrants continued to make a living by them.[15]

Marriage Contracts and Criminal Records

The corpus of notarial and judicial records also contains much material concerning the emigrants and their activities. Of particular importance are the marriage contracts, which can be used to control and supplement the information obtained from the acts of marriage.[16] In a situation unique to Canada, virtually every couple passed before the notary as well as before the priest, even when the arrangement involved little or no transfer of property on the part of either spouse. The reasons for the ubiquity of this practice, which, in France, almost never descended to the ranks of the laboring poor, remain obscure.[17] In any case, it would seem to reveal the legalistic if not litigious nature of early Canadian society. It is interesting that one or both spouses occasionally declared a different place of origin in the marriage contract than in the act of marriage itself. Since most emigrants, at least those who migrated as adults, presumably knew where they came from, these discrepancies are probable indicators of prior migrations within France.[18]

Less comprehensive than the marriage contracts but of equal interest are the criminal records of the Baillage and Conseil supérieur of Louisbourg. While persons accused of crimes are not necessarily representative of a population, the persistence of Louisbourg's judges makes it possible to construct incomparably detailed portraits of certain hapless emigrants. Particularly in the early decades of the colony, interrogations of an indicted Frenchman routinely covered "the occupation of his father and

. . . the trade of the accused in France," "why he came to this island and with whom he arrived and when," "where he was indentured and by whom," and "what obliged him to indenture himself."[19]

A SURVEY of the Canadian documents thus reveals that the mania for encyclopedic description generally associated with the French eighteenth century was already well entrenched in New France from the time of the earliest settlements. Since the sole agents of this statistical revolution were royal *commissaires* and Counter-Reformation clerics, the colonial situation illustrates, perhaps even better than that of metropolitan France, Tocqueville's paradox that the Ancien Régime was itself a herald of modernity.[20]

French Sources

The French sources on emigration to Canada are, by comparison, somewhat disappointing. Wherever they exist, French exit documents such as contracts of indentured servitude or passenger lists are tremendously useful, but their state of preservation is exceedingly haphazard. In addition, efforts to exploit fully those sources that do exist are often stymied by their dispersal. Contracts of indentured servitude, in particular, are submerged in a morass of uninventoried notarial records that, in a large port city such as Rouen or Nantes, fill thirty or more hefty volumes a year.

Fortunately, the exit documents are not the only French sources pertaining to emigration to Canada. The central repository for prerevolutionary colonial documents, the Archives des Colonies, contains both systematic and piecemeal information on the identities of many military and civilian emigrants. The personnel dossiers and emigrant lists compiled by colonial functionaries are a welcome complement to the more inaccessible registers of local port officials and notaries.

Indentures and Passenger Lists

Contracts of indentured servitude probably concerned a majority of the civilian emigrants to New France.[21] Although they varied widely depending on time and place, these contracts generally stipulated that in return for overseas passage, room and board, and some form of remuneration, an emigrant would enter into service for a period of three years.[22] Once this term expired, the emigrant was free either to return to France, sometimes at the expense of the former employer, or to prolong his or her stay in the colony. Contracts of indentured servitude usually identify emigrants according to community of origin, age, and occupation; unlike the Canadian documents, they also provide the exact date of migration.

The second significant category of documents pertaining to colonial emigration consists of passenger lists. For the historian interested in the peopling of British America, such lists are the most abundant and important source of information; in the case of Canada, however, this precious resource has been rationed far more sparsely. In theory, the French maritime commercial code mandated that passenger lists be maintained. Before setting sail, the ship's captain had to deposit a *rôle d'équipage* (crew list) with the admiralty closest to his port of departure.[23] Without this roll, which was supposed to detail the names and backgrounds of passengers as well as crew members, no exit permit could be issued, and the ship would be forced to remain in port.

In spite of this categorical injunction, which leads one to expect continuous series of considerable value, the extant passenger lists leave much to be desired. First of all, "the Archives de l'Amirauté in the great ports have suffered dreadfully."[24] The dossiers of Dieppe, destroyed by fire during the British bombardment of 1694, provide the most spectacular illustration of the problem, but whether through catastrophe or more mundane forms of negligence, registers dating from the seventeenth century are nowhere numerous. For the eighteenth century the situation with regard to passenger lists is more fortunate, but it still cannot compare with that across the Channel.[25]

A further problem with the passenger lists stems from the sloppy way in which they were often drawn up. A properly executed *rôle d'équipage* consisted of a list of crew members followed by a list of passengers, the latter divided between passengers proper (those who paid their own way) and *engagés* (indentured servants). In theory, then, a passenger list duplicated the information found in the contracts of indentured servitude.[26] Of course, in practice, this ideal situation was rarely attained. Gabriel Debien discovered that in La Rochelle the names of sailors, free passengers, and servants often appeared "one after the other, with nothing to separate them." Furthermore, the rolls were not always dated, and the destinations of the ships were sometimes left blank.[27]

Fortunately, some keepers of passenger lists were more conscientious than the norm, particularly in the Southwest. Indeed, the passenger lists of Bordeaux, Bayonne, and Saint-Jean-de-Luz are a case apart in terms of the quality of the documentation. For Bordeaux, in addition to the *rôles d'équipage* preserved among the papers of the admiralty, there is a series of passports entitled "certificates of identity and catholicity." These passports, which form a continuous series for the period 1713–1787, were delivered only to passengers who were paying their own way.[28] They are nonetheless tremendously useful to the historian of migration, since they record the voyagers' regional origins, occupations, and ages with scrupulous exactitude.[29]

The rolls from Bayonne, which have the added advantage of consistently distinguishing between paying passengers and indentured servants *(engagés)*, also provide detailed information about the emigrants' places of origin and occupational backgrounds. Port officials were primarily concerned with the place of birth, but in cases where prior migration had taken place emigrants sometimes volunteered their place of residence as well. Thus, François Desclaux, a passenger who emigrated to Ile Royale (Cape Breton Island) in 1749 with his wife, son, and three daughters, declared himself born in Sare and resident in Ciboure, where he "works in town," having "opened a store."[30]

The occupational indications often consist not only of the trade but of the level at which it was exercised. Marin Paschal thus inscribed himself as a journeyman joiner, and Michel Dubinca as a master carpenter. Even fishermen, whose trade did not come under guild organization, sometimes referred to themselves as masters or domestics; here the qualifications must relate to whether or not the emigrants possessed independent capital, perhaps in the form of a fishing boat.

More surprising still is the treatment of those individuals about whom this type of document is usually silent: women and the young. Boys who did not yet exercise a trade in their own right were apparently asked to state that of their parent or guardian; hence the twenty-two-year-old Jean Larrouset, whose late father was a tailor in Bidouze, or the eighteen-year-old Charles Bourdena of Bayonne, son of a tax clerk *(commis des Fermes)*.

Women's trades were less regularly recorded because of their episodic connection to the marketplace and their often invisible nature; nonetheless, one learns, for instance, that Maria de Bouda and Catherine Guillon, the wife and daughter of a sailor-fisherman, contributed to the family income through their work as laundresses.

The rolls from Saint-Jean-de-Luz, although they contain fewer than 50 names, are, if anything, even more informative than those from Bayonne. In addition to listing the place of birth and the occupation of all of the passengers, they include a statement of the reasons for undertaking the voyage. Officials obviously restricted themselves to certain formulaic responses when drawing up this section of the roll, but their comments are illuminating nevertheless. Of 38 passengers, 6 (2 wives, a sister-in-law, and 3 young children) were returning to Louisbourg, their place of residence. By far the largest number, 26, planned to "work at their occupations or estates," which ranged from mattress maker to hardware merchant. One woman, Marie Duhalde of Saint-Jean-de-Luz, was quoted as planning to enter domestic service, an indication that the person responsible for the list did not view such service as tantamount to working at an "estate." Four of the remaining emigrants were merchants or clerks planning to engage in commerce, and to them there should perhaps be added, albeit at a humbler level, the 4 cobbler-peddlers intending to exercise their trade.[31]

Military Records

The contracts of indentured servitude and the passenger lists are clearly the best French sources for tracing civilian emigration, but no matter how well maintained, they provide little information about a second category of emigrants to Canada, the soldiers and officers.[32] Yet beginning in 1665, military emigration was a central component of the French-Canadian migratory stream.

In the earliest years of the colony, defense was assured primarily through the private recruitment of French soldiers. After 1641 there were also local militias of able-bodied men between sixteen and sixty,[33] but even these reinforcements could not stem the Iroquois incursions, especially in the west. In 1662, therefore, Louis XIV agreed to expedite 100 regular soldiers to Canada as a first installment on a much needed infusion of troops. Three years later they were joined by four companies of the

Regiment of Carignan-Salières, whose roughly 1,200 soldiers disembarked in Québec in the summer of 1665.

After the arrival of the Regiment of Carignan, regular ground troops *(troupes de terre)* did not again reach Canada in any significant numbers until the Seven Years' War. Instead, the staffing of Canadian garrisons devolved upon the *troupes de la Marine,* independent battalions composed of 50 men each and responsible not to the minister of war but to the naval minister. The Compagnies franches de la Marine, as they were called, were at certain crucial times quite numerous; between 1683 and 1685, for example, some 1,600 troops were required to drive back the Iroquois.[34] Nonetheless, the heaviest military emigration by far occurred, ironically, in the final years of the French Regime, when more than 4,000 men from six metropolitan regiments descended upon the colony.

Because of the importance of the *troupes de la Marine* in supplying Canada with military manpower, the Archives du Ministère de la Guerre, exploited so brilliantly by André Corvisier in his study of the army of the Ancien Régime, contain little material on the soldiers dispatched to Canada. In fact, only two "embarkment accounts," containing the names of the 1,000 or so soldiers from the Sare and Royal-Roussillon regiments who arrived in 1756, have been preserved there. These rolls were, at least, well maintained, identifying the soldiers by age, height, and regional origin.

In order to obtain a more general picture of the military population of Canada, it is necessary to examine the lists preserved in the Archives de la Marine and the Archives des Colonies. The naval ministry maintained exhaustive personnel files on its officers, both military and civil, which were subsequently assembled as series C1, C2, and C7. Series C6 contains scattered lists of soldiers as well as of passengers. The Archives des Colonies, for their part, bring together a large number of detailed troop lists, including that of the Regiment of Carignan, in series D.

Official Correspondence

One other French archival source containing information on emigration to Canada remains to be discussed: the general correspondence between Canadian and French authorities throughout the period of the French Regime.[35] The primary interest of this correspondence lies in the insights it provides into demographic policy generally and methods of recruitment specifically; however, as the inventories indicate, it has the additional merit of occasionally furnishing information about individual emigrants.

In this regard, the passenger lists that made their way sporadically into the collection are disappointing. They were, for the most part, drawn up solely for purposes of accounting, since the state often agreed to defray the costs of passage for specific individuals and needed to keep track of the expenses incurred. Nominative rolls are therefore rare; officials were content to indicate the number and condition of the subsidized emigrants, together with the amount of the subsidies.[36] Passenger lists, however, are not the only exit documents in series B and C of the colonial archives. In fact, the general correspondence is the sole source of information on an entire category of emigrants: the smugglers, prisoners, and *fils de famille* (young men of means) deported to Canada in the second quarter of the eighteenth century.

Material in the correspondence referring to the actual identity of deportees is scanty. The *fils de famille,* who were never very numerous, received fairly full treatment in the documents, both in regard to their antecedents and the fates that befell them in Canada.[37] Prisoners of a commoner sort, however, attracted less attention, giving rise at best to scattered indications.

The 900 or so ordinary criminals were selected from among the much larger number who languished in French prisons, on the basis of lists drawn up by prison wardens or tax farmers. The criteria considered by the naval minister included physical condition, occupation, and marital status, so these lists, had they survived, would have been valuable. The Minister, though, chose to submit to his Canadian colleagues only the finished products of this selection process: nominative lists of those prisoners to be embarked. At best, these included a mention of where the deportees had been imprisoned. Much of our knowledge of their French background thus derives less from the lists themselves than from the impressionistic commentary that accompanies them, as well as the occasional references to specific individuals.

THE SOURCES AVAILABLE on either side of the Atlantic for describing French emigrants to Canada thus confront researchers with a certain embarrassment of riches. In spite of their fragmentary nature, particularly in France, they have the unique advantage of permitting historical study of a substantial group of migrants at the points of both arrival and departure. Canadian vital, census, and legal records, on the one hand, and French exit and administrative documents, on the other, permit the elaboration of remarkably full biographical dossiers for many of the men and women who made the journey from France to Canada during the Ancien Régime.

The Sample and Its Representativity

In Canada, the computerization of all documents bearing directly on the population of colonial Québec is currently under way. This vast collective project, carried out by the Programme de recherches en démographie historique (PRDH) of the University of Montréal under the direction of Hubert Charbonneau, will soon enable historians to construct individual dossiers based on full access to the vital records, the censuses, the registers of abjuration and confirmation, and the hospital lists.[38] Rivaling in scope the massive "investigation of past populations" being conducted in France since 1960,[39] the PRDH project has already produced a nominally indexed repertory of forty-seven volumes.[40] The data bank, though still being completed for the nineteenth century, has served as the basis for two demographic analyses of the New French population, Mario Boleda's "Trente mille Français à la conquête du Saint-Laurent" and the collaborative *Naissance d'une population: les Français établis au Canada au XVIIe siècle.*[41]

For this study I did not make use of the PRDH data bank but instead accessed the Canadian sources through an older and more artisanal type of compilation: the meticulous lists of "ancestors" assembled by several generations of French-Canadian archivists, genealogists, and historians. The Quebecers have long been a people obsessed with their origins, equating, it would seem, survivance with souvenir. For more than a century, they have combed through the parish registers and censuses, the substantial corpus of notarial and judicial records, the registers of confirmation and abjuration, and the archives of religious communities in search of knowledge about the New French population. In some cases their quest has carried them to France, where they have examined parish and notarial registers in important communities of origin going back to the middle of the sixteenth century.

The emigrant sample analyzed here thus draws upon the Canadian sources through the archival or genealogical compendiums of René Jetté, Marcel Trudel, Marcel Fournier, Father Archange Godbout, and others. Only the testimonials of freedom at marriage were incorporated directly, both in their published form and in manuscript. As for French sources, in compiling the sample I made use of contracts of indentured servitude from Normandy, Aunis, Anjou, and Perche; several Breton and Aunisian passenger lists from the seventeenth century; mid-eighteenth-century passenger lists from twenty-five French ports; and emigrant data that appeared in the general correspondence between royal officials in France and Canada.[42]

The full sample contains information on 15,810 emigrants: 2,137 women or girls and 13,673 men or boys. Only 1,692 of these emigrants traveled to Acadia, while the rest made their way to Québec.[43] One in 10 of the Acadia-bound emigrants was a woman (146 in all), as opposed to 1 in 7 (or 1,991) for Québec.

Assessing the representativity of this sample involves, at the most basic level, determining what proportion of the whole it represents. Yet the preliminary task of arriving at an overall estimate, a tall order for any Ancien Régime population, is further complicated, in the case of emigration to Canada, by the question of how emigration itself is defined. As Marcel Fournier has cautioned, "the interpretation of each historian varies considerably as to the definition of the term immigrant."[44]

Definitions of Migration

Various writers have indeed applied the term "migration" to a bewildering array of phenomena, which run the gamut from daily commutes between the suburbs and the city to moves that imply not only permanent settlement but also reproduction.[45] In the case of French emigration to Canada, one encounters definitions as diverse as those of Fournier ("the presence in New France of any person . . . whose stay in the country was in excess of two months . . . The only exception to this rule . . . is the case of th[ose] deceased on American soil"),[46] Trudel ("we eliminated . . . the people who were only passing through during the summer: the ship's captains and other members of the crew, as well as the merchants who . . . made only a brief stay here for business; if one of them happened to spend the winter, we inscribed him as an immigrant from the date of his first winter"),[47] and Normand Robert ("If one generally understands by immigrant any person who has left his or her country of origin to settle in a foreign country, it was agreed that for the elaboration of this catalog, the category . . . would bear a more restrictive meaning, and that any person having declared a place of origin in France at the time of his or her marriage ceremony, with the exception of a few families formed in France and come to settle in Canada, would be considered as an immigrant").[48]

Given the arbitrary nature of all these definitions, I relied instead on the more rigorous analysis of Abel Châtelain, a historian who devoted his working life to studying the French migrations of the last three centuries. Châtelain suggested a typology of migration based on two principal criteria: the spatial and the temporal.[49] On the temporal axis, he identified daily work migrations, weekly migrations for relaxation and leisure, seasonal migrations, temporary migrations ("pluriannual" ones of at least two years' duration), lifetime migrations (encompassing the entire working life of an individual), and, finally, definitive migrations. These last, he cautioned, "are far more rare than we usually allow."[50] The spatial axis, which I discuss in detail in Part Two, takes account of local migrations (those occurring within a radius of about ten kilometers), regional migrations, and long-distance migrations, whether national, colonial, or international.

This typology, as Châtelain himself acknowledged, by no means exhausts all the possible criteria for classification; most notably, it excludes social aspects of migration such as sex ratio, marital status, occupation, and the nature of movements as individual, familial, or collective. Functional distinctions between, say, work-related migrations, migrations of leisure, and pilgrimages also receive short shrift, as do qualitative distinctions between sending and receiving areas (mountain versus plain, country versus city, and so on). Provided that these reservations are kept in mind, however, Châtelain's typology serves as a powerful analytic tool.

Seasonal, Temporary, and Permanent Migrations to Canada

The temporal distinctions between seasonal, pluriannual, and definitive migrations proposed by Châtelain fit the Canadian example very nicely. Seasonal movements involved merchants who remained in the colony only long enough to acquire a stock of furs inexpensively and then returned to France on the same ship that had brought them; fishermen who worked under seasonal contracts off the coasts of Newfoundland or Acadia;[51] and, of course, crew members who commonly set sail for Canadian destinations in the early summer, returning home in the fall.

Châtelain's description of pluriannual migrants applies perfectly to the "thirty-six monthers," or ordinary indentured servants. While some of these men and women no doubt embarked for Canada with intentions of settling there, they must have rested easier about their proposed adventure knowing that the "custom of the land" provided for their return passage should they request it. Just how many *engagés* actually availed themselves of this option, and after what period of time, will never be known with certainty given the fragmentary nature of the documentation. Attempts to follow up discrete groups of *engagés* in Canadian records, however, suggest a return migration rate of approximately two-thirds.[52]

Like the *engagés*, the soldiers recruited to serve in Canada were divided between pluriannual and permanent migrants. Provided that "the very rapid passage of numerous vagabonds through the regiment" is excluded from consideration, the average term of service in the metropolitan troops of the period was six or seven years.[53] The Canadian troops, however, were actively encouraged to settle permanently, with the encouragements, at times, taking on the insistent ring of threats. Surely, some of those who enlisted did so in order to "realize a colonial vocation." Service in the colonial troops, after all, "provided the opportunity . . . to go and settle more or less legally in the colonies, without submitting to a veritable temporary enslavement at the beginning."[54] The colonial military could even be lucrative, since the troops were permitted to offer their various skills on the open market whenever they were not actually fighting. Able-bodied soldiers were appreciated in Canada, where labor was a scarce commodity,[55] and anywhere from 15 percent to more than four times that many chose to marry and remain in the colony.[56]

My decision, based on Châtelain's typology, not to exclude seasonal and pluriannual emigrants from this study is reinforced by the practical consideration that the boundaries of the three migratory streams shifted incessantly when considered at an individual level. A crew member or fisherman whose presence in the colony was theoretically seasonal could choose to settle there permanently, or a colonist recruited with a view toward definitive establishment could decide to abandon his or her holdings and return to France. Of the many emigrants who transgressed the theoretical distinctions in this manner, one example will suffice: Louis Hébert, an apothecary from central Paris who became the first Frenchman to settle permanently in Québec.[57]

Hébert, whose youthful wanderings had taken him no farther than the College of Coutances in Lower Normandy, was thirty-one years old, professionally established, and married with two children when, in 1606, he signed on for a seasonal stint as ship's surgeon in Acadia.[58] He enjoyed his journey sufficiently to repeat it five years later; according to one witness, this denizen of the rue Saint-Honoré took "pleasure in plowing." In 1617 the forty-two-year-old Hébert embarked for Canada with his wife, three children, and a brother-in-law in order to found a farm and "aid the savages." He died in Québec in 1627.[59]

Numerical Estimates

Unfortunately, the currently available estimates of the volume of French emigration to Canada do not deal with gross migration, whether temporary or permanent, but rather with net or even "founding migration." The term "founding migration" *(migration fondatrice)* was coined by the demographer Mario Boleda to describe those "immigrants who, for the most part, founded large families constituting what was to become the nucleus of the Québécois population."[60] The best estimate of founding migration to date, that of the PRDH, stands at 8,527.[61]

In addition, two estimates for net migration have been calculated by Boleda on the basis of demographic variables. The first estimate of net migration was derived by subtracting the natural increase of the Québec population (determined from the parish registers according to the now traditional method of Louis Henry)[62] from the overall population growth between two given dates. To obtain the second estimate, Boleda examined the age structure of the population at the beginning and end of a relevant time period, then estimated to what extent the age pyramid for the later date diverged from one projected for a static population based on survival rates by age group. The two estimates were quite consistent, particularly for the eighteenth century. According to Boleda, Québec definitively absorbed 18,000 to 19,000 French emigrants between 1660 and 1759. Assuming that a similar situation obtained prior to 1660, a period when the demographic data were too sparse to support analysis, then between

19,000 and 20,000 French men, women, and children actually settled in Québec during the French Regime.

Although Boleda did not make an independent estimate of gross migration, it is possible to derive one from his figure for net migration by applying an estimated return rate. Of the available estimates, the most broad-based posits a return rate of about 70% for the entire population of Québec in the years prior to 1663.[63] Proposed return rates for *engagés* and soldiers vary, as already noted—ranging between roughly 66% and 75% for *engagés* and about 33% and 85% for soldiers.[64] The lowest overall return rate, 30% to 50% for the population of Montréal in the seventeenth century, was probably unusually low owing to more careful recruitment.[65]

Because the estimated return rates cover such a wide spectrum, I performed four different calculations, corresponding to return rates of 50%, 60%, 70%, and 80%. Based on a net immigration of some 20,000, these rates produced estimates for gross migration of, respectively, 40,000, 50,000, 67,000, and 100,000. The third figure is perhaps preferable, since the return rate of 70% corresponds both to the most comprehensive estimate and to the average of all the various estimates of back migration.[66]

While the suggestion that perhaps 67,000 French men and women emigrated to Canada during the French Regime may seem radical, it is important to note that even this estimate is incomplete. In fact, it omits two important categories of emigrants: Acadians and seasonal workers. The omission of the Acadians is explained by the dearth of documents, which has prevented demographers from reconstructing the early population of the Maritimes. It is thus difficult to propose even a broad estimate for emigration to Acadia; although periodic census returns are available, in the absence of serviceable vital records it cannot be determined how many of those listed in the censuses were emigrants versus how many were natives.[67]

One generalization can nonetheless be made: the Acadian population, both insular and peninsular, was highly unstable in the seventeenth and eighteenth centuries. The political and economic situation of the colony favored short-term movements of population, whether of fishermen, merchants, soldiers, or building workers for the fortifications. From the earliest years, the emigration turnover rate was high, so Acadia accommodated a significant (if difficult to quantify) contingent of particularly mobile Frenchmen during the French Regime.[68]

The two categories of emigrants excluded from the estimate of gross migration thus overlap to some degree. Nonetheless, seasonal migrants also embarked for Québec, and their exclusion from the available estimates of back migration distorts the attempt to evaluate how many people passed through the colony at some point or points in their lives.[69] How much my estimate of 67,000 migrants would have to be raised to account for the seasonal flow into Québec is unclear. It is known, however, that between 1689 and the end of the French Regime, the Hôtel-Dieu of Québec treated several thousand emigrants whose presence in the colony appeared to be seasonal. If this number is added to the original estimate, it can be postulated that perhaps 70,000 French migrants reached Québec during the seventeenth and eighteenth centuries. Total gross migration to Canada is impossible to estimate accurately because of the Acadian problem, but a figure of more than 75,000 appears plausible. Thus, while French emigration to Canada could not compare with British migration to the thirteen colonies in terms of either volume or staying power, it was substantial enough to dispel the notion that the French did not travel to North America.

Representativity

Having considered the different types of French emigration to Canada and attempted an inevitably rough estimate of gross migration, it is at last possible to assess the representativity of my emigrant sample. It is least representative of migrants in the seasonal category, such as the sailors and officers who staffed the various transatlantic voyages. The inclusion of such migrants was far from comprehensive, since with rare exceptions data collected from the French exit documents pertained to passengers and *engagés* only.[70] The number of Quebecers from my sample who could be clearly designated as seasonal migrants was about 600, many of them Breton seamen whose names were compiled from the hospital registers for listing in Fournier's *Dictionnaire biographique des Bretons en Nouvelle-France*. Given the obviously unrepresentative nature of this cross section, it is important to avoid making generalizations about the regional origins of Québec's seasonal migrants based on my sample.

Subtracting the 600-odd emigrants in the sample whose visits to Québec were clearly of a seasonal nature from the 14,000 destined for the colony overall yields the figure of 13,400 pluriannual or definitive emigrants. This number represents about one-fifth of gross migration, estimated at 67,000, and perhaps two-thirds of "observable migration" *(migration observée)*, defined by Mario Boleda as the portion of gross migration that has left documentary traces.[71] By virtue of its size, my sample escapes many problems of representativity posed by less comprehensive databases. The biases inherent in it are, except in the case of seasonal migrants, largely due to imperfectly preserved sources, although they may also reflect an incomplete reading of some sources. (Particular biases are discussed in Part One in connection with the actual analysis of the sample.)

THE COLONIZATION OF French Canada generated documentation of such quality that "whether in New England, Brazil, or Spanish America, no other pioneer population could undergo such a meticulous examination, at least not for such a remote period."[72] The sample of pioneers considered here, while assembled artisanally, sheds light on nearly 16,000 people over two centuries, including a number of seasonal, temporary, and Acadian emigrants who deserve attention together with the founding families of the Saint Lawrence.

PART I
_____
Modernity

1

Regional Origins: Peasants or Frenchmen?

The regional origins of French emigrants to Canada can best be described as modern, although such a description is at odds with much of the historiographical tradition. As I shall discuss, the fundamental modernity of these "Frenchmen" was long obscured by a peasantist nostalgia that projected a mythical and idealized backwardness onto a group that was, in reality, in the vanguard of French Atlantic expansion.[1]

Both the provincial and departmental maps of emigration reveal the importance of active coastal regions and the equally busy vicinity of Paris. The comparative urban and rural distributions, with their unusually heavy emphasis on towns and cities, further emphasize the cosmopolitan roots of many of the emigrants, female as well as male. Yet for right-wing Frenchmen writing in the nineteenth and twentieth centuries, French Canadians (or those who resisted the gathering exodus to New England, at any rate) embodied the classical values of a less decadent age: *travail, famille, patrie,* and, last but not least, the Catholic Church. Such writers, in their zeal to reclaim Québec's virtuous habitants for *la France profonde,* insisted on the rural and Catholic provenance of the French-Canadian ancestors. Normandy and Brittany were good candidates (though, in fact, their economic and cultural marginalization postdated the emigration), as was Poitou (the Vendée). To cite the marquis de Chennevières (writing in 1890): "Canada, I remember that in my youth, the French province that I loved the most, after Normandy, was Canada . . . From these houses of peasants departed, two hundred years ago, the sturdiest lads and the decentest girls, called beyond the seas to the conquest of a promised land."[2]

The process of colonization, as Chennevières described it, adumbrated both the Counter-Revolution and the conquest of Algeria, but whereas such glorious exploits belonged, in France, to a happier past, in Canada they formed the stuff of everyday existence:

> Throughout the century, it was a war of surprise attacks and ambushes, . . . something like our first Algerian campaigns . . . [or] the improvised military adventures of the *chouannerie* to which the cousins of these Canadians, Percherons, Manceaux, and Bretons would soon be called with the same faith, tranquil confrontation of danger, agility in assault, and passionate attachment to the land that they plowed and fertilized . . . As for us, pursued by a shameful suicide mania, our countryside is becoming deserted and impoverished; our small towns and villages are emptying out, becoming depopulated. So much so that in a hundred years, when we want to find a valliant example of the Percheron race, one of those religious, laborious, robust, patient, modest families that remain perfect specimens of inflexible faith and nearly ideal sanctity . . . ; we will have to go find it in Canada.[3]

This historiographical tradition culminated in Louis Hamilton's *Ursprung der Französischen Bevölkerung Canadas*, published in 1920.[4] An essentially philological essay, it proposed to examine the causes behind the virtually astounding resilience of the French-Canadian population: "It was no great feat for France to found a colony of some 65,000 peasants in the space of 150 years . . . But for these 65,000 souls to have become two million in Canada, to have maintained their language, their beliefs, and their customs, to have spread beyond their borders . . . , that is one of the wonders of history."[5]

According to Hamilton, this unfathomable mystery became comprehensible only by admitting that "the French Canadians were not principally Frenchmen, but rather Germans and Celts, for it was Normandy and the surrounding areas, the eastern provinces, which have much German blood, and Brittany that provided the greatest proportion of the population."[6]

While a combination of *Blut und Boden* ideology with integral Catholicism thus underlay much of the early writing on French emigration to Canada, it would be incorrect to suggest that no scholarly examination of regional origins has taken place. The publication of Abbé Cyprien Tanguay's *Dictionnaire généalogique des familles canadiennes* between 1871 and

1890 made possible the first large-scale studies of migratory geography, those of Adjutor Rivard and Stanislas Lortie, philologists studying the development of Canadian French; Edouard-Zotique Massicotte, an archivist and historian; and Father Archange Godbout, a genealogist.[7]

More recently, the *Répertoire des actes de baptême, mariage, sépulture . . . du Québec ancien* has served as the basis for a comprehensive geographical overview of "founding immigration," that of the Programme de recherches en démographie historique. The study of the PRDH bears investigation both for its methodological rigor and because it allows comparison of the population of permanent settlers in the Saint Lawrence with the more diverse group of emigrants considered here.

Provincial Origins

As I mentioned in the introduction, the PRDH has assembled a database of 8,527 founding immigrants for Québec during the French Regime. Of these, a French-provincial origin could be ascribed to 7,656, or 89.8% (see Table 1.1).[8] The regional distribution of these emigrants breaks down as follows: Northwest, 28.1%; Center-west, 26.3%; Paris region, 14.3%; Southwest (including Languedoc), 10.5%; East, 8.2%; Loire Valley, 3.9%; North, 3.4%; Massif central, 2.9%; Midi, 1.3%; and Alps, 1.0%.

The provincial distributions derived from my emigrant sample are different because of the very broad definition of emigration I employed. The bedrock of founding immigrants certainly exists, although it is probably somewhat aleatory as far as the eighteenth century is concerned. Since the information for this period in my principal genealogical source, Godbout's various compilations, was incomplete, I supplemented it with material drawn from regional studies (see the introduction, n. 42). As a result, my tables may be somewhat skewed in favor of regions whose definitive emigrants have received separate attention. More disruptive, however, is the inclusion in the sample of roughly 1,700 emigrants to Acadia who did not fall within the purview of previous authors and whose recruitment could be somewhat different from that of emigrants to Québec.[9] Finally, the presence in my sample of significant numbers of emigrants—both Acadian and Québécois—who never settled permanently in Canada introduces a further distinction between these and previous statistics.

Table 1.1   Provincial origins of French emigrants to Canada (PRDH)

Province	No. of emigrants	% of emigrants
Normandy	1,111	14.5
Ile-de-France	1,094	14.3
Poitou	750	9.8
Aunis	679	8.9
Brittany	461	6.0
Saintonge	406	5.3
Guyenne	338	4.4
Anjou	222	2.9
Languedoc	221	2.9
Perche	217	2.8
Gascony	188	2.5
Angoumois	182	2.4
Picardy	162	2.1
Champagne	154	2.0
Maine	144	1.9
Lorraine	138	1.8
Orléanais	137	1.8
Burgundy	133	1.7
Touraine	115	1.5
Provence	98	1.3
Franche-Comté	91	1.2
Auvergne	79	1.0
Limousin	77	1.0
Dauphiné	76	1.0
Lyonnais	64	0.8
Flanders	57	0.7
Marche	48	0.6
Berry	46	0.6
Artois	39	0.5
Béarn	31	0.4
Alsace	25	0.3
Nivernais	24	0.3
Bourbonnais	21	0.3
Roussillon	19	0.2
Foix	9	0.1
Total	7,656	99.8

Note: Percentages do not total 100.0% owing to rounding.

It was possible to determine the regional origins of more than three-quarters of the emigrants in my sample: specifically, 12,050 out of 15,810.[10] This figure represents an increase of more than 30% over that of the "founders"; even excluding the Acadians, the number of emigrants considered is considerably higher. The provincial distributions, presented in Table 1.2, indicate that migration to Canada involved the major regions of France in the following proportions: Northwest, 38.6%; Center-west, 19.0%; Southwest, 10.9%; East, 9.0%; Paris region, 8.5%; Loire Valley, 3.3%; North, 3.1%; Massif central, 2.9%; Midi, 1.9%; and Alps, 1.3%.[11] The other 1.4% consisted of 171 emigrants who described themselves as foreign nationals, in spite of having embarked from French ports.[12] Clearly, there were circumstances in which Richelieu's original strictures against foreigners, like those against Protestants, went unheeded.[13]

A comparison of these results with those of the PRDH brings to light similarities as well as differences. To begin with, the tables resemble each other in two fundamental respects. First, no province of France, no matter how isolated, remained untouched by migration to Canada. The attraction of the colony certainly varied widely from place to place, increasing with proximity to the Atlantic coast, but accessibility to the ocean was by no means a prerequisite for emigration to occur. Second, in both the sample of founding immigrants and in this more diverse sample, the western seaboard provided roughly two-thirds of the emigrants—in the first case slightly less, and in the second slightly more.

These broad similarities do not preclude significant differences at the regional as well as the provincial level. The percentage of emigrants departing from the Atlantic provinces as a whole is comparable, but my sample heavily favors the Northwest at the expense of the Center-west and the Paris region. Since my data may incorporate a bias toward regions for which discrete studies of emigration exist, it is worth noting that these regions include the Northwest, but not Ile-de-France. The widened gap between the Northwest and Center-west is, however, significant, because the contribution of the Center-west to the peopling of Canada has also received considerable attention. It thus reflects the definitional broadening that enabled me to examine the overlapping categories of Acadian and temporary migrants, and suggests that prevailing patterns of temporary overseas migration differed from those exhibited by permanent colonists.[14]

This phenomenon is particularly striking in the case of Brittany, which

Table 1.2 Provincial and foreign origins of French emigrants to Canada
(my sample)

Place of origin	No. of emigrants	% of emigrants
Province		
Brittany	2,035	16.9
Normandy	1,871	15.5
Aunis	1,209	10.0
Ile-de-France	983	8.2
Poitou	620	5.2
Guyenne	513	4.3
Gascony	463	3.8
Languedoc	393	3.3
Saintonge	311	2.6
Anjou	300	2.5
Champagne	293	2.4
Perche	287	2.4
Picardy	274	2.3
Burgundy	271	2.3
Lorraine	222	1.8
Orléanais	184	1.5
Maine	163	1.4
Angoumois	144	1.2
Touraine	139	1.2
Dauphiné	133	1.1
Franche-Comté	129	1.1
Auvergne	126	1.1
Lyonnais	111	0.9
Provence	108	0.9
Limousin	91	0.8
Berry	80	0.7
Alsace	76	0.6
Flanders	61	0.5
Béarn	57	0.5
Bourbonnais	49	0.4
Artois	36	0.3
Roussillon	32	0.3
Nivernais	28	0.2
Savoy	27	0.2
Marche	24	0.2
Foix	18	0.2
Comtat	17	0.1
Monaco	1	0

Table 1.2 (continued)

Place of origin	No. of emigrants	% of emigrants
Country		
Belgium	48	0.4
Germany	34	0.3
Switzerland	23	0.2
Italy	14	0.1
Ireland	10	0
Luxembourg	9	0
Portugal	8	0
Spain	7	0
England	4	0
Isle of Jersey	4	0
Austria	3	0
Isle of Guernsey	2	0
Holland	2	0
Malta	2	0
India	1	0
Total	12,050	99.9

moves from fifth place in the PRDH's sample, with just over 6% of the emigrants, to first place in mine, with close to 17%. An integral reading of Québec's hospital registers would surely alter this finding somewhat by supplying the names of seasonal emigrants from provinces other than Brittany; nonetheless, even excluding the 545 Bretons whose presence, recorded in these registers, was probably limited to a season, the figure remains at 13% and marks Brittany's contribution as second only to that of Normandy. Normandy and other areas notable for high rates of temporary maritime emigration, such as Gascony, also figure more prominently in my sample than they do among the founding immigrants.

Departmental Origins

I supplemented the provincial tabulations with a series based on departmental information, which was available for more than 73% of French emigrants. Once again, it is clear that every corner of France contributed to the movement (see Table 1.3). Even at the departmental level, no area

Table 1.3 Departmental origins of French emigrants to Canada

Department	No. of emigrants	% of emigrants
Charente-Maritime	1,522	13.4
Seine	869	7.6
Seine-Maritime	793	7.0
Ille-et-Vilaine	759	6.7
Manche	483	4.2
Calvados	347	3.1
Loire-Atlantique	346	3.0
Côtes-du-Nord	341	3.0
Orne	317	2.8
Pyrénées-Atlantiques	288	2.5
Finistère	254	2.2
Vendée	253	2.2
Sarthe	249	2.2
Vienne	193	1.7
Indre-et-Loire	187	1.6
Gironde	181	1.6
Charente	159	1.4
Maine-et-Loire	135	1.2
Morbihan	134	1.2
Dordogne	127	1.1
Deux-Sèvres	124	1.1
Côte-d'Or	119	1.0
Haute-Garonne	112	1.0
Isère	94	0.8
Gers	93	0.8
Lot-et-Garonne	91	0.8
Eure	90	0.8
Seine-et-Oise	89	0.8
Aisne	88	0.8
Rhône	84	0.7
Somme	83	0.7
Marne	78	0.7
Puy-de-Dôme	77	0.7
Yonne	77	0.7
Haute-Vienne	76	0.7
Oise	76	0.7
Loiret	72	0.6
Eure-et-Loir	68	0.6
Moselle	66	0.6
Saône-et-Loire	66	0.6
Seine-et-Marne	66	0.6
Bas-Rhin	61	0.5
Haute-Marne	61	0.5
Nord	61	0.5

Table 1.3 (continued)

Department	No. of emigrants	% of emigrants
Hérault	60	0.5
Meurthe-et-Moselle	60	0.5
Pas-de-Calais	59	0.5
Tarn-et-Garonne	58	0.5
Bouches-du-Rhône	56	0.5
Landes	56	0.5
Lot	56	0.5
Tarn	56	0.5
Mayenne	52	0.5
Jura	50	0.4
Aube	48	0.4
Allier	47	0.4
Aude	46	0.4
Gard	43	0.4
Doubs	42	0.4
Cher	39	0.3
Loir-et-Cher	39	0.3
Vosges	38	0.3
Ardennes	34	0.3
Indre	33	0.3
Meuse	33	0.3
Var	32	0.3
Pyrénées-Orientales	31	0.3
Aveyron	30	0.3
Corrèze	28	0.3
Haute-Loire	28	0.3
Hautes-Pyrénées	28	0.3
Nièvre	28	0.3
Cantal	28	0.3
Ain	27	0.2
Ardèche	26	0.2
Haute-Saône	25	0.2
Vaucluse	25	0.2
Drôme	23	0.2
Loire	21	0.2
Ariège	18	0.2
Creuse	18	0.2
Savoie	17	0.2
Hautes-Alpes	11	0.1
Alpes-Maritimes	9	0.1
Haute-Savoie	9	0.1
Haut-Rhin	8	0.1
Lozère	6	0.1
Total	11,390	100.4

remained untouched; however, the departmental distributions also bring the patchwork quality of the recruitment into sharper focus. The large homogeneous splotch that covers much of northern and eastern France is broken by Paris and its environs, where emigration was greater by a factor of ten, and by Haut-Rhin, where it was insignificant. In the Northwest, the areas of *bocage* (hedge country) and *landes* (heaths) generally provided fewer emigrants than those devoted to more prosperous monoculture; and in the Southwest, the fertile valleys of the Garonne and the Dordogne formed a corridor of considerable movement that contrasted with the mountainous areas to the north and south. Indeed, a brief survey of the contributions to Canadian migration of the Massif central, Alps, and Pyrénées suggests an inverse correlation between entrenched habits of continental seasonal migration and the incidence of colonial departures. With the exception of Haut-Rhin, at the extremity of the Vosges, all of the departments that individually provided fewer than .2% of the emigrants in my sample fall squarely within the confines of one of the major mountain ranges.

Consideration of departmental origins also further accentuates the fundamental east-west cleavage in the geography of French emigration to Canada. While studies of the economy, demography, and culture traditionally emphasize north-south dividers such as the Loire, or imaginary lines running from Saint-Malo to Geneva or Marseille,[15] such divisions appear largely irrelevant to the cartography of Canadian migration. On the basis of the departmental distributions, I propose instead a hypothetical line from Rouen to Toulouse to distinguish an Atlantic France with strong demographic ties to the colonies from an inland France less consistently engaged in the migratory process. The only major exception to this rule of thumb is Paris; and the city's ever increasing role as the nation's decision-making and financial center suffices to explain the anomaly.[16]

Where migrations were concerned, it thus appears that the international connection represented by the Atlantic economy superseded the cultural backwardness generally attributed to southern France as a whole. To the extent that overseas mobility and modernity were associated, the highly mobile regions to the south of the Loire that fell within the orbit of La Rochelle, Bordeaux, or Bayonne belonged, regardless of their subsequent destinies, to the more privileged of *les deux France* under the Ancien Régime.

Urban/Rural Distributions and Degree of Concentration

The relative precision with which most French and Canadian officials recorded the emigrants' regional origins enables me to carry my analysis a step further and consider such questions as the urban/rural distribution and the indexes of concentration and dispersion. An identified community of origin exists for 10,538, or 66.7%, of the emigrants in my sample, a decrease of about 6% from the number to whom a department could be ascribed. Only about half of this differential arose from a failure to identify a given community owing to incomplete or erroneous information, and the remainder is attributable to emigrants who identified themselves by diocese alone. This small residual of unidentifiable communities, which compares very favorably with the 15% noted as the average by Jean-Pierre Poussou, confirms the high quality of the documents pertaining to New France.[17] One should nonetheless keep in mind that such communities were predominantly, if not entirely, rural,[18] and that my results could therefore underestimate the rural component of the sample by as much as 1.5%. With this caveat in mind, I can say that French emigrants to Canada were distributed among the different types of communities as shown in Table 1.4.[19]

Focusing first on the urban/rural distribution, one sees that fewer than a quarter of the emigrants declared themselves villagers, and that slightly over a third claimed to inhabit the countryside in villages or bourgs. Of the urban dwellers, who together made up nearly two-thirds of the overall sample, 35.5% came from towns of under 10,000, and the remaining 64.5% from large cities. These figures are eloquent, indeed shocking, in relation to the commonplaces of both French and Canadian history. *La France profonde* of the seventeenth and eighteenth centuries, as Pierre Goubert has so often noted, was overwhelmingly rural; 85% of all French women and men lived and worked in communities of fewer than 2,000 inhabitants, and perhaps 80% gained a living directly from the land. Cities of more than 10,000 were still anomalous at the end of the Ancien Régime and accounted for at most 10% of the total population.[20]

The unquestionable unrepresentativity of the emigrants with regard to communities of origin becomes even more remarkable when one considers their destinies in Canada. While it is true that settlers in the Saint Lawrence tended to cluster around the three "urban" centers of Québec,

Table 1.4 Distribution of emigrants by community type

Community type	No. of communities	No. of emigrants	% of emigrants	No. of emigrants/ community
Rural				
Village	1,756	2,600	24.7	1.5
Bourg	490	1,130	10.7	2.3
Total/average	2,246	3,730	35.4	1.7
Urban				
Large Bourg	26⎱	105⎱	22.9	3.9
Town	599⎰	2,312⎰		
City	68	4,391	41.7	64.6
Total/average	693	6,808	64.6	9.8
Overall total/average	2,939	10,538	100.0	3.6

Montréal, and Trois-Rivières, the characterization of these centers as veritable towns is disputable. At the time of the British conquest, none could boast a population of more than 8,000, and Trois-Rivières was merely a rural bourg, irremediably tied to the activities of the surrounding countryside.[21]

The situation in Acadia was even more extreme, with minuscule fishing and trading posts dotting the entire peninsula.[22] Port-Royal had only 500 inhabitants when the English acquired it in 1713, and a half century later, when the islands were ceded as well, the town of Louisbourg had 8,000, nearly half of them soldiers. Since the total populations of these areas stood, at the end(s) of the French Regime, at 75,000 for Québec, 3,000 for peninsular Acadia, and 15,000 for Cape Breton and Ile Saint-Jean (Prince Edward Island), it is clear that the urban phenomenon was, if anything, more marginal in French Canada than in the metropolis.

I will return to this double paradox of a profoundly rural nation replicating itself overseas by means of its least rural elements; for the moment, it is enough to emphasize the amplitude of the deviation from the norm. An urbanization rate of almost two-thirds and a rate for the largest cities of more than 40 percent were virtually unheard of under the Ancien Régime. In comparison with the general population of France,

French emigrants to Canada included four times as many town dwellers and residents of major urban agglomerations.[23]

Moving from the urban/rural distributions to the degree to which emigration was concentrated or dispersed, one finds that two fundamental patterns emerge (see Table 1.4). First, there was a clear distinction between the countryside and the city, with urban communities providing an average of 9.8 emigrants each to a mere 1.7 for the rural communities. Second, recruitment increased with the size of the community, whether rural or urban—and in the case of cities, the increase was dramatic. Villages overall were unable to muster even 2 emigrants apiece, an index of nearly complete dispersion. Bourgs, or rural centers, cut a somewhat better figure with 2.3; but it is only with the large cities that one sees a real takeoff—64.6 emigrants each, a factor increase of more than sixteen over towns. Recruitment densities thus present a double appearance of concentration and dispersion, with concentration correlating positively to community size. The aleatory character of emigration from the countryside contrasted sharply with the relative importance of recruitment in urban centers, and particularly in cities of more than 10,000.[24]

To the extent that the density of emigration corresponded to that of population, such results are not unexpected. They nonetheless raise questions about the mechanisms of recruitment, or the means by which knowledge of expanded migratory options was able to penetrate even the smallest villages. As I shall discuss, recruiters generally operated at the level of regional capitals and did so according to procedures that fail to explain the apparent decentralization of the flow of information. The existence among the migrants of a significant (if ultimately minority) contingent of country folk of exceedingly disparate origins points to the likelihood of some prior experience on their part with the city—if not in the form of immigration, at least as a more ephemeral presence at such times as market days.

Regional Variations

Beginning with regional divisions, and descending to the level of department, I constructed additional tables to reflect the respective levels of urbanization and communal concentration among emigrants to Canada. The regional results, presented in Table 1.5, exhibit a marked degree of

Table 1.5 Distribution of emigrants by community type and region

Region	Community type	No. of communities	No. of emigrants	% of emigrants	No. of emigrants/ community
Northwest	Village	642	1,170	28.8	1.8
	Bourg	179	493	12.1	2.8
	Town	107	798	19.6	7.5
	City	18	1,605	39.5	89.2
Center-west	Village	222	336	16.2	1.5
	Bourg	143	348	16.8	2.4
	Town	53	397	19.1	7.5
	City	5	994	47.9	198.8
Southwest	Village	266	311	27.8	1.2
	Bourg	49	132	11.8	2.7
	Town	112	367	32.8	3.3
	City	6	309	27.6	51.5
East	Village	281	351	38.2	1.3
	Bourg	25	36	3.9	1.4
	Town	106	268	29.2	2.5
	City	14	263	28.7	18.8
Greater Paris	Village	51	75	7.4	1.5
	Bourg	19	27	2.7	1.4
	Town	25	87	8.6	3.5
	City	2	821	81.3	410.5
Loire	Village	50	74	25.3	1.5
	Bourg	27	35	12.0	1.3
	Town	34	94	32.1	2.8
	City	4	90	30.7	22.5
Massif	Village	101	120	40.5	1.2
	Bourg	25	31	10.5	1.2
	Town	40	69	23.3	1.7
	City	4	76	25.7	19.0
North	Village	71	86	27.7	1.2
	Bourg	13	18	5.8	1.4
	Town	42	124	39.9	3.0
	City	8	83	26.7	10.4
South	Village	18	18	9.0	1.0
	Bourg	4	4	2.0	1.0
	Town	41	66	32.8	1.6
	City	16	113	56.2	7.1

Table 1.5 (continued)

Region	Community type	No. of communities	No. of emigrants	% of emigrants	No. of emigrants/ community
Alps	Village	47	52	38.0	1.1
	Bourg	6	6	4.4	1.0
	Town	13	42	30.7	3.2
	City	1	37	27.0	37.0
Total/average		2,890	10,426	—	3.6

Note: Data and totals do not reflect emigrants whose place of origin was outside France.

differentiation and underscore the heterogeneous nature of Canada's attraction for the French population.

With regard to urbanization, four rather unlikely regional ensembles stand out. In Ile-de-France and the Midi, emigration to Canada was primarily an urban phenomenon, with nearly nine-tenths of all recruits declaring a town or city as their place of origin.[25] In the Center-west and the North, this proportion dropped to two-thirds, and in the Massif central, to just under one-half. Everywhere else—which is to say, in regions as dissimilar as the Loire Valley, the Southwest, the Northwest, the East, and the Alps—the number of urban emigrants clustered at around 60%, forming a plateau slightly lower than the overall average.

These distributions do not, for the most part, reflect actual distributions of population between the given types of communities in the various regions. While Ile-de-France was unquestionably more urbanized than the Massif central, the relatively loose urban networks of the Center-west and Southwest did not possess more demographic weight than those of the Northwest or the Loire. The example of Canada thus confirms Poussou's observation that migrations proceed according to an inner logic only distantly related to the static configurations of either economy or demography.[26] Refraction serves as a better metaphor than reflection.

The degree of concentration, as indicated by the average number of emigrants per community, also holds some surprises when considered at the regional level. In fact, these statistics call into question the positive correlation between urbanization and concentration. While cities as a whole produced a larger number of emigrants than villages as a whole, the situation within particular regions was more complex. To be sure, the most urban emigrants, those from the Paris region, also exhibited the highest degree of concentration, and the most rural, those from the Alps and the Massif, the greatest amount of dispersion. Between these two extremes, however, the equation falls apart; the urbanized emigrants of the North and the South were widely dispersed, and the more rural northwesterners quite highly concentrated.

Upon closer examination, the regional indexes of concentration reveal a secondary correlation that attenuates that between concentration and community size. Specifically, those regions most heavily involved in emigration to Canada produced emigrants whose origins were more highly concentrated, while areas more marginal to the movement sent contingents that were geographically more diverse. The Northwest and Center-west, which together accounted for close to 60% of the emigrants, contributed greater than average numbers per community in the countryside as well as the city. In regions responsible for less than 10% of the departures, emigration was more dispersed than the average regardless of its provenance; this suggests that the recruitment of city dwellers as well as countryfolk was, to some extent, aleatory.[27]

Variations in the levels of urbanization and concentration also occurred at the level of province and department. They were particularly salient among emigrants from the Northwest and Center-west, where from a migratory point of view it is possible to isolate two geographical ensembles: one where recruitment was overwhelmingly urban and relatively concentrated, and a second where it was predominantly rural and more dispersed (see Table 1.6). In the Northwest, the first ensemble included Upper Normandy, Brittany, and part of Anjou (the Loire Valley), whereas the second covered Maine, Perche, Lower Normandy, and Anjou sarthois. In the Center-west, the urban emigrants came principally from Aunis and Upper Poitou, leaving Saintonge, Angoumois, and Lower Poitou to produce higher proportions of scattered country folk. In both the Northwest and Center-west, emigrants from the first ensemble outnumbered those from the second by just over two to one; the figures, identical for each area, are respectively 67.8% and 32.2% of the regional totals.

It is tempting to describe the dual nature of the emigration from these regions as the by-product of profound economic divisions affecting the Atlantic provinces north of the Garonne. The juxtaposition of, on the one

Table 1.6 Urban/rural distribution of emigrants (Northwest and Center-west)

Region	Community type	No. of communities	No. of emigrants	% of emigrants	No. of emigrants/ community
Ensemble 1 (Urban)					
Northwest	Village	403	688	25.0	1.7
	Bourg	68	119	4.3	1.8
	Town	67	431	15.6	6.4
	City	15	1,517	55.1	101.1
Center-west	Village	80	116	8.3	1.5
	Bourg	63	183	13.0	2.9
	Town	20	141	10.0	7.1
	City	4	966	68.7	241.5
Ensemble 2 (Rural)					
Northwest	Village	239	482	36.8	2.0
	Bourg	111	374	28.5	3.4
	Town	40	367	28.0	9.2
	City	3	88	6.7	29.3
Center-west	Village	142	220	32.9	1.6
	Bourg	80	165	24.7	2.1
	Town	33	256	38.3	7.8
	City	1	28	4.2	28.0

hand, Upper Normandy, Upper Poitou, and Aunis with, on the other hand, Lower Normandy, Lower Poitou, Maine, and Perche brings immediately to mind the perennial opposition of *plaine* (open field) and *bocage,* with its connotations of market-oriented versus subsistence agriculture. The more modern "plain"—characterized by high rates of urbanization, large cities, areas of capitalist monoculture, and commercial links to the Atlantic economy—would thus have animated migrations more massive, more concentrated, and more urban than those originating in the smaller centers and isolated farmsteads of the *bocage.*

The predominance of *plaine* over *bocage* as a source of emigrants for Canada may be accepted provided that two caveats are acknowledged. First, the cleavages outlined above do not correspond exactly to the geographical boundaries of *plaine* and *bocage.* Brittany belongs not to the second, but to the first ensemble, in spite of proverbial rural underdevelopment that persisted into the twentieth century. Likewise, Saintonge and Angoumois fall into the second category, although agriculture in these provinces, organized around the twin poles of wheat and wine, differed little from that of Aunis. Second, it is worth remembering that in absolute numbers the contribution of even the most backward areas of the North-west and Center-west was highly significant; the second ensemble alone furnished close to 2,000 emigrants to Canada, more than any other French region in its entirety.

In the Southwest, the situation was more complicated, although regions of predominantly rural or urban recruitment again coexisted. The former included Périgord, Béarn, and Agenais, the latter Gironde, Gers, Upper Languedoc, Foix, Roussillon, the Pays basque, Quercy, Rouergue, Hautes-Pyrénées, and Landes. The indexes of dispersion, however, do not correlate fully with the levels of urbanization. Whereas emigrants from the Pays basque, Bordelais, Toulousain, and Montalbanais were both urbanized and concentrated, and those from Périgord and Agenais were neither, the neo-Canadians of Quercy, Rouergue, Landes, and Hautes-Pyrénées combined a low rate of rural departures with a high degree of dispersion.

The key factors in this rather confusing pattern appear to be, on the one hand, the state of development of regional urban networks and, on the other hand, the extent to which agricultural areas tied in to the national and colonial economies via the commercialization of their products. The prevalence of town dwellers in the migration streams originating in and around Bordeaux, Bayonne, Montauban, and Toulouse comes as no surprise considering the demographic weight of these cities and, in the case of the first three, their economic links with Canada. By contrast, the urban infrastructures of Périgord, Béarn, and Agenais were significantly weaker, and the colonial connections of such cities as Périgueux and Bergerac were mediated entirely through Bordeaux.

The seeming anomaly of town-dwelling emigrants from such backwaters as Quercy, Rouergue, Landes, and Hautes-Pyrénées is resolved when attention shifts from city to country. While the emigrant-producing cities in these regions maintained, at best, peripheral relations with the Atlantic economy (this explains the essentially aleatory character of their migratory contribution), the surrounding countryside remained almost completely isolated from regional and national economic trends. The future departments of Gironde, Gers, Dordogne, and Lot-et-Garonne sent numerous villagers to Canada—as to Bordeaux and the Islands[28]—due to their prosperous agricultural landscape dotted with urbanized villages and largely open to prevailing commercial currents.[29] Village-dwelling Quercynois, Rouergats, Landais, and Pyrénéens, on the other hand, remained aloof from the movement of Atlantic colonization. This is not to say that they were sedentary, but rather that their frequently intense mobility assumed different forms and followed different routes.

With the Alps and Massif central, one again finds the simpler bifurcated pattern of the Northwest and Center-west. Recruitment was at once heavier and more urban in the least backward parts of these generally isolated areas: Lower Auvergne, Upper Limousin, Bourbonnais, and Dauphiné. In contrast, the populations of Upper Auvergne, Lower Limousin, Marche, the Massif languedocien, and Savoy remained thoroughly marginal to the process of Canadian colonization. Like the Pyrénéens, these *montagnards* were often exceedingly mobile, but here again, the ever shorthanded Canadians never succeeded in exploiting what was perhaps the mother country's largest reserve army of the underemployed.

Women's Origins

My discussion of regional origins has thus far dealt with the entire emigrant sample as an undifferentiated whole; however, it is a truism of the demographic literature that migration is sex-specific. Migratory streams are frequently segregated by sex and nearly always feature one sex more prominently than the other. For example, in early modern France, certain small or midsize towns attracted primarily women, for whom employment prospects were available in the form of domestic service or industrial work such as lace making.[30] Other forms of migration, such as those involving the temporary exercise of artisanal or commercial skills, were almost exclusively male. Male and female migration streams also tended to differ in the amount of distance covered, with men enjoying a near monopoly on long-distance movements throughout the period. (Of course, it would be incorrect to regard such distinctions as absolute; familial migration, by definition, mobilized both men and women for an identical destination, although the decision-making process may well have been male dominated.)

Emigration to Canada resembled other long-distance population movements in that it was overwhelmingly male, but it also included a small female contingent. To the extent that the 2,137 Québécoises and Acadiennes in my sample did not belong to constituted families, they defied the normal predictions about their migratory behavior. As I discuss in Part Two, many of them did indeed make the journey in their own right, rather than as mothers or daughters; moreover, recruitment practices for single men and single women differed substantially. To go beyond clichés about separate migratory spheres, one must therefore consider female emigrants separately from emigrants as a whole and compare the behavior of men and women within a single, predominantly male, migratory environment. Concentrating first on provincial and national origins, I obtained the distributions for female emigrants shown in Table 1.7.

Of course, the contrast between this pattern and that exhibited by the entire sample is striking. Women's emigration tended to be at once more concentrated and more fragmented. At one end of the spectrum, the Center-west, Northwest, and Paris region produced 28.4%, 27.5%, and 24.7% of the emigrants respectively, while at the other end, contributions fell off precipitously, with all other regions taken together garnering less than 20% of the total. In order of declining frequency, women stemmed from the East (7.3%), the Loire Valley (5.0%), the North (4.1%), the Southwest (1.5%), the South (.4%), the Massif central (.2%), and the Alps (.2%). A residual .9% declared a foreign country as their place of origin.

The provincial cartography reveals that differences in the geography of overall and female emigration were not limited to contrasting indexes of dispersion. The line from Rouen to Toulouse, which functioned as the significant divider between the principal and secondary foyers of departure for the movement as a whole, is nowhere in evidence when men are excluded from consideration. Instead, the Loire, that perennial line of demarcation, again makes its appearance, this time to distinguish between a northern France characterized by female mobility and a southern France untouched by female participation in colonial ventures. The only exceptions to this rule are, to the south of the Loire, the central-western

Table 1.7 Provincial and foreign origins of women emigrants

Place of origin	No. of women emigrants	% of women emigrants	Sex ratio
Province			
Ile-de-France	440	23.9	0.81
Aunis	357	19.4	0.42
Normandy	274	14.9	0.17
Brittany	90	4.9	0.05
Perche	87	4.7	0.44
Poitou	81	4.4	0.15
Picardy	70	3.8	0.34
Saintonge	69	3.7	0.29
Champagne	65	3.5	0.29
Orléanais	61	3.3	0.50
Anjou	41	2.2	0.16
Burgundy	39	2.1	0.17
Touraine	26	1.4	0.23
Alsace	21	1.1	0.38
Angoumois	16	0.9	0.13
Maine	15	0.8	0.10
Gascony	13	0.7	0.03
Guyenne	11	0.6	0.02
Lorraine	11	0.6	0.05
Franche-Comté	7	0.4	0.06
Berry	6	0.3	0.08
Provence	6	0.3	0.06
Lyonnais	4	0.2	0.04
Flanders	3	0.2	0.05
Nivernais	3	0.2	0.12
Auvergne	2	0.1	0.02
Béarn	2	0.1	0.04
Dauphiné	2	0.1	0.02
Limousin	1	0.1	0.01
Languedoc	1	0.1	0.00
Artois	1	0.1	0.06
Roussillon	1	0.1	0.03
Marche	1	0.1	0.04
Savoy	1	0.1	0.04
Country			
Belgium	6	0.3	0.14
Germany	5	0.3	0.17
England	3	0.2	3.00
Switzerland	1	0.1	0.05
Ireland	1	0.1	0.11
Total	1,844	100.4	—

provinces and, in the North and East, Artois, Flanders, Lorraine, and Franche-Comté.

The Center-west provided the most female emigrants of any region at all, suggesting that, in migratory matters at least, the Vienne and the Charente functioned as appendages of the Loire.[31] The far North and East, on the other hand, resembled more marginal regions such as the Alps or the Massif central insofar as female emigration was concerned.[32] Whatever their economic base—and it was sometimes very prosperous, as in the case of French-Flemish agriculture—these areas were incompletely integrated into the mainstream of French demographic life. Migration streams of single women existed there, as elsewhere in northern France, but they were generally directed outward and to the east.[33]

An examination of sex-specific patterns of migration thus qualifies my observation about the unity of the Atlantic economy in that it reveals the most outward-turned form of mobility, emigration overseas, to have been a male preserve in southern France and southern France only. Whereas the northern provinces, together with those of the Center-west, produced 1 female emigrant for every 3 men, the provinces to the south could muster only 1 in 20.[34] Women were thus, to a large extent, excluded from the burgeoning *vie de relations* characteristic of southwestern France in the century before the Revolution, with traditional gender roles serving to retard the demographic impact of economic change.[35]

Women's Departmental Origins

As with emigration overall, the departmental distributions render a more precise image of women's origins. While women's provincial affiliations were nearly as diverse as those of the men, with only Bourbonnais (and Foix, the Comtat, and Monaco) failing to produce any emigrants, extended areas of noninvolvement appear in the departmental table. As can be seen by comparing Table 1.8 with Table 1.3, twenty-four departments that figure in the table of combined emigration with at least a half dozen emigrants sent no women to Canada at all.

The empty spaces include, in the East, parts of Lorraine, Franche-Comté, Lyonnais, and, more surprisingly, Burgundy. The absence of Bourguignonnes from Ain, despite the relative importance of Burgundy as a whole, is perhaps attributable to the department's prominence as a foyer of temporary migrations.[36] Such movements often entailed an exac-

Table 1.8 Departmental origins of women emigrants

Department	No. of women emigrants	% of women emigrants	Sex ratio
Charente-Maritime	423	23.5	0.38
Seine	400	22.2	0.85
Seine-Maritime	168	9.3	0.27
Orne	84	4.7	0.36
Calvados	52	2.9	0.18
Vendée	43	2.4	0.20
Sarthe	38	2.1	0.18
Ille-et-Vilaine	37	2.1	0.05
Seine-et-Oise	36	2.0	0.68
Indre-et-Loire	33	1.8	0.21
Vienne	27	1.5	0.16
Aisne	24	1.3	0.38
Seine-et-Marne	24	1.3	0.57
Loiret	23	1.3	0.47
Côte-d'Or	22	1.2	0.23
Eure-et-Loir	22	1.2	0.48
Oise	22	1.2	0.41
Aube	20	1.1	0.71
Loire-Atlantique	20	1.1	0.06
Charente	19	1.1	0.14
Bas-Rhin	17	0.9	0.39
Manche	16	0.9	0.03
Maine-et-Loire	16	0.9	0.13
Yonne	15	0.8	0.24
Finistère	14	0.8	0.06
Loir-et-Cher	14	0.8	0.56
Eure	13	0.7	0.17
Pas-de-Calais	13	0.7	0.28
Pyrénées-Atlantiques	13	0.7	0.05
Somme	13	0.7	0.19
Côtes-du-Nord	10	0.6	0.03
Marne	10	0.6	0.03
Saône-et-Loire	9	0.5	0.16
Deux-Sèvres	8	0.4	0.07
Gironde	8	0.4	0.05
Haute-Marne	7	0.4	0.13
Moselle	7	0.4	0.12
Cher	6	0.3	0.18
Morbihan	6	0.3	0.05

Table 1.8   (continued)

Department	No. of women emigrants	% of women emigrants	Sex ratio
Jura	5	0.3	0.11
Ardennes	4	0.2	0.13
Meurthe-et-Moselle	4	0.2	0.07
Rhône	4	0.2	0.05
Nièvre	3	0.2	0.12
Nord	3	0.2	0.05
Var	3	0.2	0.10
Doubs	2	0.1	0.05
Haute-Vienne	2	0.1	0.03
Mayenne	2	0.1	0.04
Puy-de-Dôme	2	0.1	0.03
Aveyron	1	0.1	0.03
Alpes-Maritimes	1	0.1	0.13
Bouches-du-Rhône	1	0.1	0.02
Drôme	1	0.1	0.05
Gers	1	0.1	0.01
Isère	1	0.1	0.01
Haut-Rhin	1	0.1	0.14
Hérault	1	0.1	0.02
Lot	1	0.1	0.02
Lot-et-Garonne	1	0.1	0.01
Pyrénées-Orientales	1	0.1	0.03
Savoy	1	0.1	0.06
Vosges	1	0.1	0.03
Total	1,799	100.3	—

erbated sexual division of labor, with women and girls remaining home to tend to the agricultural tasks while men and boys plied their trades farther afield. Thus, established traditions of temporary migration, which (unless they were maritime in nature) could inhibit the emigration of men to Canada, could prevent that of women altogether.[37]

As if to confirm this hypothesis, virtually all the other departments that show a sex ratio of zero are located to the south of the Loire, with a preponderance in the Massif central and its Languedocian and Aquitain extensions.[38] The highest peaks of the Alps and Pyrénées remained isolated from the movement as well, leaving western Languedoc and the Gascon *landes* as the only low-lying areas to produce an all-male migratory stream.

Finally, it should be noted that although the primary division within the cartography of female emigration to Canada is incontestably between north and south, the departmental distributions reveal a secondary cleavage between east and west that is reminiscent of the pattern of the movement as a whole. Specifically, eight of the ten departments that sent more than 1.5% of the total number of women are located to the west of the Rouen-Toulouse line, with Paris and its hinterland as the one exception.

Urban/Rural Distributions and Degree of Concentration among Women

Like the provincial and departmental distributions, the indexes of urbanization change considerably when calculated for female emigrants only. A specific community of origin could be ascribed to more than 80% of the women in my sample, thus allowing a very unusual opportunity to understand women's movements better than men's. In aggregate terms, the main difference between the combined male/female and the female origins lies in the increase in town dwellers from under two-thirds to over three-quarters of the emigrant sample, a difference entirely attributable to the largest cities (see Table 1.9). Whereas the percentage of women from bourgs and small towns declines slightly, and that from villages plummets to a mere 15% of the total, the figure for the major cities rises to well over 50%. An examination of the sex ratios reveals an actual feminization of emigration with increased community size: 2 of every 10 urban emigrants were women, in contrast to 1 of every 10 in the countryside. Perhaps women, less inclined to long-distance migration than men, required a more cosmopolitan environment from which to contemplate the drastic move to Canada. They may also have been responding to adverse demographic conditions within this environment, for one of the distinguishing characteristics of urban demography under the Ancien Régime was a surplus of women—unmarried women in particular.[39]

The indexes of concentration for women, unlike the urban/rural distributions, resemble those of the sample as a whole. It thus appears that the dual pattern noted above, of intense dispersion broken by points of concentration, characterized emigrants to Canada regardless of their sex.

Table 1.9 Distribution of women emigrants by community type

Community type	No. of communities	No. of emigrants	% of emigrants	No. of emigrants/ community	Sex ratio
Rural					
Village	187	264	15.2	1.4	0.10
Bourg	89	150	8.6	1.7	0.13
Total/average	276	414	23.8	1.5	0.11
Urban					
Town	146	337	19.4	2.3	0.14
City	44	986	56.8	22.4	0.22
Total/average	190	1,323	76.2	7.0	0.19
Overall total/average	466	1,737	100.0	3.7	0.16

Further analysis of urbanization and concentration in the regional, provincial, and departmental contexts indicates that women's emigration was somewhat less differentiated than that of men (see Table 1.10). Not only did women come from a more limited geographical area than emigrants as a whole, but within that area, the rates of urbanization and concentration fluctuated less widely. The distinction noted for emigrants overall between the respective contributions of *plaine* and *bocage,* or of commercial and subsistence agriculture, blurs considerably or even disappears entirely where female emigrants are concerned. It appears that the lesser attraction of overseas migration for women in more backward areas, postulated above to explain the virtual absence of female departures south of the Charente, extended also to the pockets of traditionalism north of that boundary. Except in the *bocage* areas with very close economic and demographic ties to Canada—namely, Lower Normandy and Lower Poitou—women simply did not leave isolated hamlets to make a life in New France. To the extent that female emigrants came from such areas at all, they came from towns, either local market towns or subregional capitals, as I discuss below. The differential study of women's regional origins thus reveals that economic and cultural backwardness, while an impediment to overseas migration generally, immobilized women to an even greater degree than men.

Table 1.10 Distribution of women emigrants by community type and region

Region	Community type	No. of communities	No. of emigrants	% of emigrants	No. of emigrants/ community
Center-west	Village	29	37	7.4	1.3
	Bourg	39	60	12.0	1.5
	Town	28	90	18.0	3.2
	City	5	312	62.5	62.4
Northwest	Village	65	109	23.1	1.7
	Bourg	28	60	12.7	2.1
	Town	37	100	21.2	2.7
	City	14	202	42.9	14.4
Greater Paris	Village	20	29	6.4	1.5
	Bourg	7	9	2.0	1.3
	Town	18	30	6.6	1.7
	City	1	384	85.0	384.0
East	Village	30	41	36.3	1.4
	Bourg	3	3	2.7	1.0
	Town	19	38	33.6	2.0
	City	11	31	27.4	2.8
Loire	Village	10	12	—	—
	Bourg	3	3	—	—
	Town	11	29	—	—
	City	4	43	—	—
North	Village	20	23	—	—
	Bourg	5	5	—	—
	Town	16	29	—	—
	City	4	7	—	—
Southwest	Village	6	6	—	—
	Bourg	4	10	—	—
	Town	6	7	—	—
	City	2	3	—	—
South	Village	1	1	—	—
	Town	1	3	—	—
	City	2	2	—	—
Massif	Village	2	2	—	—
	City	1	2	—	—
Alps	Village	3	3	—	—
Total/average		455	1,725	—	3.79

Summary

Despite the long-lived stereotype of the backward French-Canadian habitant, the regional origins of French emigrants to Canada emphasized
the most outwardly turned sectors of the burgeoning Atlantic economy,
whether in the Northwest, Center-west, or Southwest, together with
greater Paris. Coastal areas characterized by high rates of seafaring, such
as Brittany, Normandy, and Gascony, also cut a good figure, although they
were less important for founding immigrants alone than for the migrants
in my diverse sample. On the other hand, the principal foyers of overland
temporary migration were far less involved in the movement toward
Canada. Perhaps a more traditional mentality on the part of migrants from
these often backward, rural areas made them reluctant to abandon customary itineraries and seasonal rhythms to embark for the unknown.

A separate examination of women's origins further emphasizes the
connection between overseas migration and modernity, in that even economic prosperity was insufficient to set women in motion in culturally
conservative southwestern France. Male emigrants stemmed, after the
Northwest, Center-west, and greater Paris, from the southwestern seaboard and the great valleys that prolong it: the Dordogne, the Garonne,
and the Gers. Secondary female departures, however, were concentrated
in the *pays de grande culture* that radiate out from the capital in all
directions: Ile-de-France, Picardy, Champagne, Burgundy, and Orléanais.
Furthermore, the proportion of urban departures was two-thirds for
emigrants as a whole but over three-quarters in the case of women. Men
and women thus exhibited fundamentally distinct patterns of recruitment,
despite their participation in a common migratory enterprise.

CHAPTER | 2

A Geography of Modernity:
The Northwest

       The essential modernity of the regional origins of French emigrants to Canada, while generally clear from the previous chapter, is both confirmed and clarified by considering the actual geography of the sending communities. The identification of local zones of greater and lesser mobility is, moreover, crucial to understanding the migratory process, for it is only at the microcosmic level that the diversity and plurality of the Ancien Régime "French mosaic" become fully apparent.[1] Thus, in this chapter and the next I consider the cartography of emigration to Canada in relation to local social and economic structures, exploring the effect of both modern and traditional arrangements on mobility. (In Part Two, I use the same cartographical patterns to anchor a comparison of emigration to Canada with other French migratory movements, internal as well as external.)[2] My regional survey begins with the Northwest, the region responsible for nearly 40 percent of emigration to Canada, and continues with the rest of France in Chapter 3, where I also focus on women emigrants.

As I have indicated, the northwestern provinces exhibited a dual pattern of emigration, which corresponded roughly to the major zones of *plaine* and *bocage*. The more prosperous open fields produced about twice as many emigrants as the more backward hedge country, and emigration from the *plaine* tended to be less rural and less dispersed. The departmental analysis, however, left questions unanswered; specifically, the fit between the areas of heavier, more urban emigration and those of economic modernity was sometimes less than perfect. Brittany, for example, defied its stereotype of near legendary backwardness to produce a

massive, concentrated, and urban emigrant contingent—an apparent paradox that can be resolved only by examining the local origins of Breton
emigrants.

Brittany

A blanket characterization of Brittany as backward actually papers over
important divisions within the province—to begin with, that between
French-speaking Upper Brittany and Celtic-speaking Lower Brittany. The
proverbial isolation of the province from the mainstream of French life
was, in fact, considerably more acute in western than in eastern Brittany,
owing to this linguistic difference. A glance at the cartography of emigration reveals the linguistic frontier to have been important; the francophone part of the province was responsible for more than 60 percent of
Breton departures for Canada. The density of emigration, however, varied
within as well as between Upper and Lower Brittany, giving the movement
a patchwork character that cannot be attributed solely to the cultural split
between French and Celtic as the primary language of the inhabitants.

In Upper Brittany, two poles of heavier recruitment stand out: one in
the southern department of Loire-Atlantique, and one in northern Ille-et-
Vilaine. Emigration from Loire-Atlantique focused on the city of Nantes,
which laid claim to 235 of the department's 333 emigrants.[3]

Despite its Breton location, Nantes was one of the principal outposts
of the Atlantic economy of the Ancien Régime; it was the leading
slave-trading port in France. Nantes's visibility as a provider of emigrants
for Canada no doubt derives from the economic ties that linked this most
important of French ports to the least important of Atlantic colonies. As
early as the 1680s, the merchants of Nantes were involved in the impor-
tation of Canadian masts, and they periodically contracted to supply
French Newfoundland with all the matériel and manpower that it required:
"Should the island need a stonecutter, a carpenter, a worker of any sort,
the shipper had to find him and send him."[4] The city's artisans were
likewise in demand in Québec; in 1740, when Québec's intendant wrote
to France for a few good journeymen carpenters, he suggested that "there
are in Nantes a great many workers of this profession, one could draw
some of them from this place."[5] The example of Nantes thus suggests

that an overlapping of commercial and demographic ties was characteristic of the migratory process.

Outside of Nantes, dispersed emigration affected many of the surrounding communities in this highly prosperous agricultural region. Heaviest to the east and southeast, where it extended to the borders of Anjou and Poitou via the Loire, the Sèvre nantaise, and the Maine, it also continued to the west between the Loire and the coast. Secondary centers such as Machecoul and Clisson produced small clusters of emigrants, while villages usually provided one emigrant apiece.

Interestingly, the recruitment of emigrants from Nantes's hinterlands did not extend to that part of the *comté nantais* situated to the north of the Loire. This oasis of subsistence agriculture appears on the map as a virtual blank, represented only by scattered communities on or near major roads. The town of Redon contributed 6 emigrants, as did several nearby villages, but owing to the fertility of the Vilaine Valley and the entrepôt functions of Redon, these parishes were a happy exception to the otherwise bleak economic situation of the "pays en-deçà de la Loire."[6] Emigration from Loire-Atlantique thus concerned the most modern sectors of the regional economy, whether rural or urban. In this department at least, the modern profile of Breton departures for Canada turns out not to be paradoxical after all.

The other area of dense emigration in Upper Brittany radiated out from the northern port complex of Saint-Malo. Together with its faubourg of Saint-Servan, Saint-Malo accounted for 431 of the 743 departures from Ille-et-Vilaine, and the rest came from a fairly narrow band of communities with decent access to the port.

Saint-Malo, like Nantes, was in the vanguard of the French economy during the Ancien Régime. In fact, in the last quarter of the seventeenth century the codfish trade combined with some judicious piracy to make it the foremost port of Brittany, if not France. Shortly after 1700, these distinctions passed respectively to Nantes and Le Havre, whose shipowners had always displayed greater initiative in the West Indian trade; however, the Malouins compensated for the shrinking of their commercial universe by multiplying their contacts with Canada.[7] Once again, the geography of migration followed that of trade.

Outside of Saint-Malo, the most significant recruitment occurred within twenty-five kilometers of the city traveling east or west, and closer to fifty kilometers toward the south. It tapered off east of Dol and south of Yvignac—in other words, at distances that could not have been covered on foot in a day or two—but it continued at a lower intensity as far away as Vitré and Rennes.

Emigration was heavier to the east of Saint-Malo, where it affected the great majority of communities, and where parishes that sent only one emigrant were exceptional. This east-west split probably reflects the linguistic divide between Upper and Lower Brittany more than it does economic divisions. Saint-Malo, as a French-speaking port, would have been a more effective magnet for redistributing the French (as opposed to the Celtic) population of its hinterland. In both commercial and demographic terms, moreover, the city maintained closer ties with the Cotentin than with Lower Brittany.

The lessening of emigration east of Dol is at first puzzling, especially since recruitment again became substantial beyond the Norman frontier. In this case the explanation is economic, for the Diocese of Dol consisted primarily of swampland, and its commercial isolation contrasted sharply with the prosperous agriculture and active industry of the Diocese of Saint-Malo.[8] In Upper Brittany as a whole, therefore, emigration occurred as the by-product of a flourishing Atlantic economy.

IN CELTIC LOWER BRITTANY, which accounted for somewhat less than 40 percent of the emigrant flow, the emigrant-producing periphery contrasted sharply with the uninvolved interior. Only a handful of emigrants originated from the vast and impoverished inland area between Morlaix, Quimper, Vannes, and Saint-Brieuc. Recruitment followed both the coastline and the province's two main roads, from Nantes to Quimper and from Rennes to Morlaix. Heavy emigration affected only the larger cities, in particular, Brest (98), Vannes (59), and Saint-Brieuc (54). Rural parishes near Brest also figured in the outflow, usually with 1 emigrant apiece. These communities, unlike most villages in Lower Brittany, had strong ties to the seaport owing to their role in billeting soldiers and sailors and supplying them with local produce. Indeed, the active commerce of Brest's *banlieue* (suburbs) rendered "this Canton, for this reason, one of the richest in the Province."[9]

The only major exception to the peripheral nature of Lower Breton emigration involves the department of Côtes-du-Nord. Like the Diocese of Saint-Malo, this area was devoted to commercial production of grain and textiles, which it marketed in both Upper and Lower Brittany through the small but active port of Saint-Brieuc. Emigration touched more communities in Côtes-du-Nord than in Loire-Atlantique, but there were fewer emigrants per community and, hence, a comparable number of departures overall. Thus, the cultural division between Upper and Lower Brittany, while important, cannot in and of itself explain the varying intensities of Breton emigration. Equal weight must be given to the economic division between "the maritime economy open to the world" and "the rural economy that remained backward,"[10] provided that the former term is construed broadly enough to include the areas of developing rural capitalism.

As MENTIONED in the introduction, Brittany holds a dominant position in the emigrant sample owing to the presence of 545 seasonal emigrants gleaned primarily from Canadian hospital records. In order to cast light on this largely ignored but numerically important group, and also to render the Breton results more comparable to those of the other provinces, I examined the origins of seasonal emigrants separately. About four-fifths of them could be associated with identifiable communities, which were distributed across the province as indicated in Table 2.1.

As compared with emigrant Bretons in general, the seasonal migrants tended to come somewhat more frequently from Upper than from Lower Brittany (70% of the seasonal migrants as opposed to 60% of all Breton emigrants) because of the increased importance of the ports of Saint-Malo and Nantes. Similarly, among Lower Bretons, Finistère cut a disproportionate figure with 59 Brestois, more than half of the port's overall total. The predominance of the great ports among seasonal emigrants was also responsible for the group's other deviations from provincial norms. More concentrated by a factor of more than two to one (13.6 as opposed to 5.5 emigrants per community), this migration exceeded even greater-Parisian or Mediterranean levels of urbanization; 95.3% of the seasonal migrants whose exact community was known hailed from urban communities, including 79.7% from cities of more than 10,000.

Table 2.1 Seasonal migration from Brittany

Upper Brittany		Lower Brittany	
Place of origin	Number	Place of origin	Number
Ille-et-Vilaine		*Finistere*	
Cities		Cities	
Saint-Malo	154	Brest	59
Rennes	22	Towns	
Saint-Servan	4	Morlaix	8
Vitré	2	Quimper	7
Towns		Saint-Pol	1
Dol	6	Villages	
Villages		Crozon	1
Pleurtuit	3	Other	
Saint-Coulomb	3	Diocese of Cournouaille	8
Saint-Briac	2	Ile de Batz	1
Cancale	1	Total	85
Miniac-Morvan	1		
Saint-Léonard	1	*Côtes-du-Nord*	
Sainte-Méloire	1	Towns	
Total	200	Saint-Brieuc	28
		Villages	
Loire-Atlantique		Plouer	2
City		Other	
Nantes	84	Diocese of Tréguier	1
Towns		Total	31
Dinan	10		
Châteaubriant	3	*Morbihan*	
Lannion	1	City	
Tréguier	1	Vannes	12
Villages		Town	
Aigrefeuille	1	Port-Louis	1
Callac	1	Total	13
Pléné-Guron	1		
Pléné-Jugon	1		
Plérin	1		
Other			
Diocese of Nantes	9		
Total	113		
Unspecified department	2	Unspecified department	6
Total Upper Brittany	315	Total Lower Brittany	135

Normandy

Norman emigration, which nearly equaled that from Brittany despite the absence of sailors from my sample, deviated from the *plaine-bocage* pattern in another respect. The Lower Norman *bocage* provided almost the same number of emigrants as the Upper Norman "plain," although the origins of the "Bocageains" were indeed more rural and more dispersed. This overrepresentation of the *bocage* was only apparent, however; closer examination reveals that Lower Norman emigration was not of one piece, and that part of the *bocage* deserves consideration together with Upper Normandy.

Irrespective of frontiers or landscapes, Norman emigration received its primary orientation from two constellations of ports, those of the northeastern and the southwestern coasts. As in Brittany, these ports conveyed an outward-turned, maritime focus to the movement as a whole, although in the northeast they drew on hinterlands far wider than those of Breton cities. In northeastern Normandy, a sharp antithesis between an animated coastline that encouraged emigration and a stagnant interior that did not failed to materialize. The appeal of overseas expansion, which had yet to penetrate *la Bretagne profonde,* already reached deeply into the heart of at least part of the Norman countryside.

The northeastern pole of Norman emigration encompassed those areas that, loosely speaking, fell within the sphere of influence of Rouen and its major satellite ports: Dieppe, Le Havre, and Honfleur.[11] Geographically speaking, this vast zone was actually bipolar, for a common maritime orientation united two regions, the "pays de Caux" and the "pays d'Auge," which were otherwise dissimilar. The pays de Caux predominated in terms of sheer numbers, largely due to the intense outflow from Rouen and Dieppe, which was unmatched by that from Le Havre and Honfleur; however, the density of emigration as measured by the number of communities touched was important in both regions.[12] Traditional distinctions between Upper and Lower Normandy, *plaine* and *bocage,* thus merged in a single northeastern migratory stream.

The pays de Caux, a fertile plain devoted to commercial wheat farming, formed an approximate triangle bordered by the port cities of Rouen, Dieppe, and Le Havre. These three communities appear to be the only true points of a sometimes remarkable concentration; the neo-Canadians in the sample included 39 Havrais, 166 Dieppois, and 299 Rouennais, who together accounted for more than two-thirds of all Cauchois.[13] No other community in the region produced more than a handful of emigrants except the small fishing port of Fécamp, with 12 departures.

The contribution of Rouen places it in the first rank of emigration centers, behind Saint-Malo but ahead of Nantes. Furthermore, this contribution has been well served by the documentation: the urban parish of origin is known for 203 out of 299 emigrants. Analysis at the level of urban geography is thus possible to see which sectors of the city participated in the demography of Atlantic expansion.

Unlike many, indeed most, cities in early modern France, Rouen was distinguished by the "precocious and intense" horizontal segregation of its population.[14] "Rouen, to look at it closely, was thus less one city than an aggregate of several cities that penetrated one another without mingling."[15] In social and economic terms, these several cities corresponded to a highly commercial southwest, a northwest populated by *robins* (members of the legal profession), and an east that, together with the faubourgs, gave shelter to the poor. Within the eastern zone, the intramural parishes of Saint-Nicaise, Saint-Vivien, and Saint-Maclou catered to a primarily artisanal populace, while the faubourgs housed an even less substantial mass of casual laborers and industrial workers. Of the faubourgs, Saint-Hilaire and Saint-Paul, the common locus of Rouen's emergent cotton manufactures, possessed the greatest social consistency.[16]

The emigrants who abandoned Rouen for Canada stemmed from virtually everywhere in the city, but the major urban zones were by no means equally represented. The commercial district came in first with 89, or 43.8% of the emigrants, followed closely by the poverty zone with 85 (41.9%). The aristocratic neighborhoods to the northwest garnered the remaining 29, a mere 14.3% of the total. Within the popular zone, emigrants from the intramural parishes outnumbered those from the faubourgs 70 to 15. The artisanal center of Saint-Maclou alone produced 46 emigrants, while, at the other end of the spectrum, the cotton-working faubourgs of Saint-Hilaire and Saint-Paul mustered but 1 apiece.

It thus appears that in Rouen, the geography of emigration to Canada reflected that of trade in general, whether international, national, or simply urban in scope. The aristocratic and industrial zones remained, by comparison, marginal to the movement; this suggests that Canada held little interest for either the most or the least traditional sectors of the urban economy.

Outside of the major ports, the pays de Caux gave rise to a dispersed but abundant emigration, especially near Dieppe and Rouen. In the Petit-Caux, a particularly prosperous subregion where monoculture in wheat and rural textile production replaced commercial polyculture during the seventeenth century, those parishes closest to Dieppe sent more than a dozen emigrants.[17] The twenty-nine communities that legally formed the *banlieue* of Rouen witnessed, for their part, 44 departures.[18] Elsewhere in the pays de Caux, emigration followed the coastline, roads, and rivers, involving numerous small towns and market centers. Except in the *banlieue* of Rouen, the Seine appears to have been less important as a vehicle for movement than the numerous roads traversing the region. Communications were clearly very easy throughout the Cauchois plain, and this attenuated the pressing need for river transport that characterized so much of early modern France.

The pays de Caux in its entirety thus exhibited a maritime orientation that enabled it to participate fully in the colonial enterprises of neighboring ports. More than any other factor, this outward-turned economy functioned as the crucial link between the Upper Norman plain and Canada under the Ancien Régime.[19]

Thanks to the proximity of Honfleur on the left bank of the Seine, the influence of Rouen radiated not only north but also south, into the *bocages* of Lower Normandy. The easternmost part of the current department of Calvados, the pays d'Auge, thus fell within the orbit of major Atlantic ports in a similar fashion to the pays de Caux. It resembled the pays de Caux in a second respect as well: the fertility and precocious commercialization of its agriculture.[20] In this case the commodities in question were not wheat and cloth but animal products; the valleys of the Dives and the Touques sustained pasturelands of a quality virtually unsurpassed anywhere else in France.

Emigration from the pays d'Auge was widespread but fairly dispersed. The points of concentration, as in the pays de Caux, were three in number: Honfleur, Touques, and Lisieux, but no one of them involved more than 20 emigrants. The pays d'Auge, although focused on the Atlantic economy, lacked a port metropolis capable of directing a large population toward the colonies. Lisieux was merely an inland cathedral town, and

Honfleur a port with a population of less than 5,000. Honfleur was too small, and its direct connection with Canada too minimal, to sustain an important migratory movement.[21]

Outside of the cities, Augeron emigrants stemmed primarily from coastal and river communities. The abundant valleys of the Dives and the Touques, together with their principal affluents, channeled the movement to a far greater degree than did roads.[22] It thus appears that while, generally speaking, communications facilitated emigration, the form of transport that predominated depended on the nature of the landscape. Roads could receive preference in areas of open field, but in the *bocage*, despite the sometimes "dense network of tracks serving fields and isolated farms," rivers tended to monopolize the immediate ties to the outside world.[23]

Beyond the pays de Caux and the pays d'Auge, emigration from northeastern Normandy decreased in intensity. The number of communities touched by departures remained relatively high only in the Lieuvin and the Roumois, those parts of the Department of Eure situated between the pays d'Auge and Rouen. Whereas the Roumois functioned, owing to its proximity to Rouen, as a left-bank counterpart of the pays de Caux, the Lieuvin served to prolong the pays d'Auge beyond the Department of Calvados. The only exception involves the Election of Bernay, a pocket of subsistence grain growing in the southern part of the Lieuvin.[24] Predictably, the *campagne* (open country) of Bernay differed from the rest of the Lieuvin in matters migratory as well as economic: it failed to produce a single emigrant for Canada.

East of Rouen, the equation linking rural capitalism and the existence of emigration begins to break down. Whether to the south or to the north of the Seine, the countryside continued to do a booming business in foodstuffs and the products of local industry,[25] but its inhabitants evinced relatively little interest for the Canadian enterprise. Emigration from this part of the Eure appears scattered, as if fortuitous. Even Evreux, the regional capital, saw the departure of only 7 emigrants. In the north, the Bray and the Vexin together managed to send some 30 emigrants from about twenty communities, all of them well served by communications. Some, like Vernon and Pontoise, were important way stations on the route to Paris.

The key to this enigmatic coexistence of decreased emigration with substantial, or even heightened, prosperity lies precisely in the increasing proximity to Paris. Unlike the pays de Caux and the pays d'Auge, or even the Lieuvin and the Roumois, the easternmost regions of Normandy fell within the sphere of influence of the capital rather than Rouen and Le Havre. One of the major supply lines for Paris passed through the Vexin,[26] where, according to an intendant, "money is more common . . . for the proximity of Paris."[27] Paris did, of course, maintain important links with Canada, but on a per capita basis, they could hardly compare with those forged by Rouen and its satellite ports. The example of northeastern Normandy thus demonstrates the interplay of geographic and economic factors that helped to determine this particular migratory stream. Participation in the market economy was necessary but not sufficent; equally crucial was the Atlantic orientation of commerce. Information about Canada could not but be better among Rouennais, for whom Canadian business constituted a major sideline, than in the capital, where it was merely one in a myriad of attractive investment possibilities.

THE SECOND, or southwestern, zone of Norman emigration radiated out from the small but flourishing seaport of Granville. Granville's connection to Canada can be traced to the sixteenth century, at which time cod fishing became the mainstay of the town's and the region's economy.[28] Initially limited to the Maritimes, particularly Newfoundland, this connection expanded in the eighteenth century to include Québec. Thirty-seven emigrants reached Canada from Granville, a significant contribution in relation to the town's size.[29]

Emigration from the communities surrounding Granville was both widespread and of limited geographic scope—a configuration familiar from my survey of the Diocese of Saint-Malo. Indeed, the sample reflects two virtually symmetrical areas of intense recruitment on both the Norman and the Breton sides of the Baie Saint-Michel. The two major zones of Norman emigration thus corresponded not to administrative but to geographical formations: the Paris Basin and the Massif armoricain, the second of which extended along the coastline with no discernible regard for provincial boundaries.[30]

Within Normandy, Armorican emigration was heaviest in the Election of Avranches, which stretched southward from Granville to the Breton border. The communities of this area, which engaged in commercial polyculture for the Norman and Breton markets, funneled the majority of their produce through Granville, Avranches, and Saint-Malo. Emigration first followed the coastline, where nearly every parish sent a small contingent, then penetrated the interior by means of roads and secondary rivers. As in the pays d'Auge, rivers outweighed roads in importance, even though none was technically navigable past its tidal basin.[31] The Sélune witnessed movement nearly as intense as did the coast, and this suggests that small-scale river transport was especially active to compensate for the inadequacy of roads through this hedge country.

To the north, in the Election of Coutances, emigration began to decline with increased distance from Granville. Economically, this area resembled the Avranchin in its emphasis on diversified market agriculture, and, except for the smaller number of communities and emigrants involved, its pattern of emigration was comparable as well. The sending communities multiplied both along the coast and in the valleys of the Sienne and the Soulle, with regional roads playing little more than a supporting role.

East of the Elections of Avranches and Coutances, emigration ceased almost completely, except in the Election of Vire, which participated marginally in the movement. Agriculturally, this whole area resembled other Norman and Breton regions that failed to produce emigrants; the terrain was "very uneven, and almost everwhere bad, yielding only buckwheat, rye, and oats." There was no commerce to speak of owing to "the difficulty of transport,"[32] except in the Election of Vire, with its brisk trade in metallurgy and sieve making.[33] Emigrants from the Election of Vire came either from small centers such as Hambye and La Lande d'Airou, or from parishes situated in the Sienne Valley.

As far as Canada was concerned, therefore, the demographic orbits of Granville and Saint-Malo extended a scant twenty-five kilometers inland from the coast, as compared with fifty to seventy-five kilometers for Rouen, Dieppe, Le Havre, and Honfleur. This narrower reach of Armorican versus Seine Valley ports can be explained in two ways. In purely demographic terms, Rouen and its satellite ports far outweighed Saint-Malo and Granville; in 1700 the combined populations of the two ensembles stood at roughly 100,000 and 25,000 respectively.[34] Since zones of urban attraction widened significantly with increased population,[35] the advantage clearly lay with the Paris Basin.

Demography is not, however, the only factor explaining the limits to urban attraction in the Massif armoricain. To some extent, the smaller size of its port complexes may even be viewed as symptom rather than cause. The dual pattern of migration characteristic of Brittany and Manche, where heavy coastal involvement contrasted sharply with interior disinterest, graphically illustrates the highly separate nature of the maritime and rural economies in these regions. The limits of the Malouin and Granvillais hinterlands were synonymous with the limits of rural capitalism, and the narrowness of both restricted the possibilities for urban development. Armorican cities "were, for the most part, turned first toward the exterior and without great influence on the hinterland"; as a consequence, "they were themselves influenced very little by the interior."[36] The distinct patterns of colonial emigration noted for northeastern and southwestern Normandy thus reflect distinct economic configurations: one truly modern in that the entire region responded to the imperatives of the Atlantic economy, and one transitional in its juxtaposition of a dynamic coastline with a stagnant interior.

Perche

Far more surprising in this context is the substantial number of emigrants from the neighboring province of Perche. This tiny region of hills and forest sandwiched between Normandy, Maine, and Beauce hardly qualified as an important outpost of the Atlantic economy in the seventeenth and eighteenth centuries. Its economy was not immune to capitalist penetration in the form of small-scale metallurgy, domestic hemp weaving, and eventually horse raising,[37] but it basically remained "a region of small-scale farming [petite culture] of northwestern France" throughout the early modern period.[38]

The Intendant of Alençon perhaps best captured the transitional situation of the province when he described it as "a region where there is almost no commerce," adding that "it is, however, true that money circulates there." Such trade as there was moved along the roads to Alençon, Paris, and Rouen, for the highways and bridges were "in fairly good shape," while the one river of the province was remarkable only in that it powered "three large mills at its source."[39] Like commerce, urbanization was also limited in scope. Three Percheron localities laid title to urban privilege—Mortagne-au-Perche, Bellême, and Nogent-le-Rotrou— but even the largest, Nogent, probably did not exceed 6,000 inhabitants in the mid-seventeenth century.[40]

Cartographically, Percheron emigration resembled that of the Pays granvillais. The sending communities formed a dense network that covered a limited geographical space, and the commoner dual pattern of concentration and dispersion gave way to a more dilute concentration affecting bourgs as well as towns. The only difference between the two movements lay in the paths they chose to follow, with roadways substituting for waterways in landlocked Perche. The post road to Paris, in fact, defined the contours of Percheron emigration. Communities directly on the route accounted for more than three-quarters of all emigrants, and the remainder came from localities within a ten-kilometer radius on either side.

The peculiarity of this migratory phenomenon did not escape contemporaries, who alluded to it with some bafflement. The turn-of-the-century reports of the intendant, which rarely referred to migrations other than the Protestant diaspora, obliquely registered this sentiment by describing Percheron settlement overseas as a brief and anomalous episode:

> In addition, the industry of the inhabitants does not go so far as to make them leave their province to earn their living. The greatest part work at plowing and cultivating the land; others are artisans, who work at the fabrication of muslins and canvases and the other mechanical arts; several exploit timber in the forests, and others work in the mines; several poor peasants work by the day for four or five francs, and still others are loafers who apply themselves to nothing at all; the women and girls of the common sort spin the hemps and wools of which the canvases and muslins are made, and each one lives thus in his canton, such that for forty years, no one has gone to the Indies, Canada, Holland, England, or to sea, though the example of ten or twelve people who went to Canada at that time, where they established themselves very well, and three or four to the Islands, where they made a reasonable profit, ought to have excited others to leave their country to sample another.[41]

The fact that this passage appeared at all belies its numerical understatement. In the middle of the seventeenth century, the Percherons collectively defied the isolation and inland orientation of their province to participate in overseas adventure, and they provided Canada with a contribution as remarkable as it was unsustained. Fortunately, the reasons for the movement appear less mysterious today than they did in 1700; Canadian enthusiasm originated with a few local notables who, having acquired lands in Québec, made a concerted effort to attract their countrymen to them. Their own involvement with Canada came about accidentally when one of their number, Robert Giffard, traveled to Québec in the capacity of naval surgeon.[42]

The recruitment of the Percherons receives fuller discussion later on, but for the moment, two points will suffice. First, directed migration worked, if only in the short term, and it worked remarkably well. The more sedentary traditions of the Percherons guaranteed their excellence as colonists; unlike so many of their fellow emigrants, they tended to settle and stay put. They thus played a disproportionate role in the formation of New French society, both figuratively and literally. Whereas only 2.4% of the emigrants in this study hailed from Perche, it has been estimated that today's Quebecers are on the order of 10% Percheron.[43]

The second point has to do more directly with the geography of emigration and what it reveals about the recruitment process. Given the directed nature of the movement, it is somewhat surprising to note the preeminence of the major communications artery. Information about Canada presumably spread through the marketplace, in Perche as elsewhere, but the grapevine must also have included *censitaires* (tenant farmers) who learned personally of the projects of their seigneurs. It would be difficult to argue that roadside communities possessed a monopoly on Canadian news, since all three major promoters held estates in rural Perche.[44] Nonetheless, the Percheron emigrants came not from these estates, but from active bourgs and towns in the economic center of the region. The migratory zone once again coincided with the zone of local capitalism, with the exception of Nogent-le-Rotrou, which apparently fell outside the promoters' sphere of influence. Giffard and his associates the Juchereau brothers thus recruited emigrants as notables but not as seigneurs. Their social prestige sufficed to mobilize local inhabitants who were well connected to the outside world, but in areas impervious to capitalist penetration, even their personal appeals failed to elicit a positive response.

Anjou and Maine

Anjou and Maine, the last northwestern provinces to be considered here, resembled Perche in their distance from the sea without sharing its inland orientation. The difference lay in a developed river system consisting of the Loire and its affluents—the Mayenne, the Sarthe, and the Loir—which provided ready access to the port of Nantes. The southwestern part of the region maintained additional ties with La Rochelle and Bordeaux,[45] and in the case of La Rochelle these ties were cultural as well as economic.[46]

As social and economic entities, both Anjou and Maine were quite complex. Indeed, they contained in microcosm virtually all the possible varieties of contemporary agriculture, from poorest to richest, and consequently produced a pattern of emigration reflective of acute subregional differences. Anjou, from an economic standpoint, could be divided into five contrasting zones: the northwest, or the Craonnais and Segréen; the southwest, or the Mauges; the Loire Valley; Central Anjou, or the Baugeois; and the "pays entre Mayenne et Loir."

Northwestern Anjou represented traditional agriculture at its worst, for once vindicating fully the stereotype of the backward *bocage*. Peasants of the Craonnais and Segréen eked out a marginal living from infertile soil and limited their market involvement to ensuring their subsistence. Cattle raising and linen manufacture were indispensable as complimentary resources, but they failed to alter either the "extreme fragility" of the economy or its fundamental isolation.[47]

Capitalism seeped into northwestern Anjou with peasants as its victims rather than its agents; the peasant linen worker was, in essence, a rural proletarian. In this respect, the Craonnais and Segréen differed completely from the *bocages* of Upper Brittany or the southern Cotentin, and even from that of Perche. In those areas, capitalist development, limited though it was, depended on the ability of local bourgeois and peasants to meet the demands of expanding markets; in northwestern Anjou, this ability was nonexistent. Of the areas considered so far, the Craonnais and Segréen resembled Lower Brittany the most closely. Their medieval economy had survived almost intact into the early modern world, and to the extent that market forces had penetrated, they had engendered exploitation rather than opportunity.

———

Given the economic similarities of Lower Brittany and northwestern Anjou, it is not surprising that their migratory patterns were similar as well. Emigration from the Craonnais and Segréen to Canada was practically nonexistent, involving only four of the several hundred Angevins. Three of them, moreover, came from Craon itself, which was a local market center and collection point for the rural textile industry.

The economic situation of the Mauges, in southwestern Anjou, was less bleak. Grain yields were typical for an area of *petite culture* but not abominable, and cattle raising had developed from an expedient into an "essential activity." The linen industry was also in full expansion from the middle of the seventeenth century, as evidenced by the doubling of the population of its center, Cholet, between 1650 and 1700. Communications were adequate in the form of roads and rivers oriented toward the Loire Valley, and a large number of bourgs maintained active commercial relations with the neighboring Pays nantais. The developing Choletais did not even confine its trading to Nantes, but already channeled a portion of its exports through La Rochelle and Bordeaux. The inhabitants of the Mauges can thus be compared with the Percherons for their acceptable living standard and at least tangential participation in a market economy. Also as in Perche, this market involvement was far more significant in the bourgs than in the villages, hamlets, and *métairies* (farms occupied by sharecroppers).[48]

Emigration from the Mauges was moderate,[49] as could be expected in a relatively productive region with second-echelon ties to the Atlantic economy. It was neither widespread nor highly concentrated, but it involved all the major bourgs except Vihiers, a local cattle market. All nine sending communities in the Mauges were bourgs of at least minor importance. Once again, this suggests a connection between emigration and the gradual commercialization of peasant agriculture.

East of the Mauges, the levels of both prosperity and emigration rose substantially. The Loire Valley from Angers to Saumur was a zone of intensive agriculture, or *grande culture*, and extensive peasant proprietorship. Industrial development was modest, but the presence of two cities of more than 10,000 inhabitants ensured the predominance of market relations in the countryside. Ninety-one emigrants abandoned this region for Canada, versus only 21 in western Anjou. As in other highly urban areas, they came in disproportionate numbers from the cities themselves;

nearly three-quarters of the Loire Valley Angevins gave Angers or Saumur as their place of origin. Emigration radiated outward from the cities along major arteries—in this case, the Loire and local roads—but dispersion prevailed beyond city limits. With the exception of Doué-la-Fontaine, a commercial center with ties to Normandy and the Antilles (5 emigrants), and La Daguenière, a prosperous farming village (3 emigrants), no one community witnessed more than a single departure for Canada.[50]

Central Anjou, or the Baugeois, resembled the northwest in its general poverty and isolation. A return to the *bocage* signified a return to *petite culture* on a terrain of forest and wasteland here, with domestic industry as an indispensable supplement. The town of Baugé coordinated local textile production, but never flourished because inadequate communications limited its export capabilities.[51] Unsurprisingly, emigration from the Baugeois was limited as well; the area produced only 4 emigrants, the same number as hailed from northwestern Anjou. As in the Craonnais and Segréen, 3 of the 4 emigrants came from the town itself, and the fourth from an adjoining parish. Contrary to the prevalent stereotypes about early modern migration, the areas most affected by rural misery appeared least affected by the movement toward Canada.[52]

The last subregion to be considered, the border area between Maine and Anjou, constitutes a partial exception to the inverse correlation noted thus far between misery and migration. The pays entre Mayenne et Loir, between Château-Gontier and Château-la-Vallière, was unquestionably more prosperous than the Craonnais and Segréen to the west or the Baugeois to the south. Fertile soils and a river system that converged on the Loire Valley favored the development of commercial polyculture, and linen manufacture flourished in the area around Château-Gontier.[53] As with the Mauges, the economic and social structures of the region marked it as intermediary between the backwardness of northwestern and the modernity of southern Anjou, but whereas the Mauges tended toward the more traditional side of the spectrum, the pays entre Mayenne et Loir tilted toward the modern. Remembering that the northwest, southwest, and south produced 4, 17, and 91 emigrants respectively, and assuming a linear relationship between emigration and prosperity, one would expect some 20 to 90 neo-Canadians to originate in the north. The actual number, however, was 130, or 158 if the neighboring Manceaux are included. As with Perche, one must once again reckon with the ability of extraneous factors to perturb, at least within certain limits, the "natural" rhythms of emigration.

In northern Anjou, the extraneous factor went by the name of the Jesuit College of La Flèche, a prestigious institution that dominated the town of 6,000 inhabitants. Father Ennemond Massé, an Acadian missionary who spent several years in La Flèche before emigrating to Québec in 1625, succeeded in transforming the college into a nursery of Canadian vocations, lay as well as religious.[54] Perhaps his most famous student was Jérôme Le Royer de La Dauversière, the town's *receveur des tailles* (tax collector), who became a foremost proponent of founding Ville-Marie (Montréal) as an apostolic enterprise. La Dauversière's recruitment efforts receive further attention in Part Two, but they are of concern here insofar as they affected the geography of Angevin emigration. Not only did they stimulate an unexpected number of departures from the pays entre Mayenne et Loir, but they did so in a way that intensifies doubt about the existence of seigneurial recruitment.

The Le Royers were prominent, if not always prosperous, landholders in northern Anjou and southern Maine. In addition to La Dauversière, they owned the seigneuries of La Motte, Chantepie, and Boistaillé, located in the parishes of Verron, Crosmières, and Malicorne.[55] Had La Dauversière appealed primarily to *censitaires* of his acquaintance, one would expect these parishes to figure prominently in the emigrant stream; and one would also expect, more generally, to find emigrants who were largely rural in origin. In fact, nothing could be farther from the case. Over half of the emigrants from northern Anjou came from the region's towns, with La Flèche alone accounting for 38. Even in the countryside, bourgs figured far more prominently than simple villages; Verron, Crosmières, and Malicorne together produced only 9 emigrants. As in Perche, the geography of emigration corresponded far better to the means of communication than to the sites of the recruiters' seigneuries.

THE NEIGHBORING PROVINCE of Maine harbored sharp economic contrasts much the same as those of Anjou, and it exhibited a similarly variegated pattern of emigration. The chief divisions affecting the province were, first of all, the one between Lower and Upper Maine and, secondarily, the one between the western and eastern parts of the Department of Sarthe. Lower Maine, as a prolongation of the Massif armoricain, was relatively backward agriculturally, although less impoverished than the Craonnais and Segréen to the south. Paul Bois has described it as a "purely peasant world" in which subsistence was generally assured; however, market relations on the part of these peasants remained rudimentary.[56] The only active commerce of the region centered on the city of Laval, which exported its domestic linens as far afield as Spanish America.[57]

It comes as little surprise to discover that Lower Maine produced a rather tepid stream of overseas migration, and that 15 of the region's 36 emigrants to Canada came from Laval itself. Only 5 of these Lower Manceaux identified themselves as villagers, and only 11 as country folk. As in Lower Brittany, the migratory pattern reveals a certain compartmentalization of rural and urban life; while the former remained mired in tradition throughout the early modern period, the latter succeeded in establishing itself on the periphery of the Atlantic world.

Upper Maine, the Sarthe mancelle, was far less homogeneous than the Department of Mayenne. Its northern and western reaches resembled the pays entre Mayenne et Loir in their social and economic base: a "prosperous peasant class" engaged in commercial polyculture. The dominant form of land tenure was leaseholding, in contrast to the sharecropping that prevailed in Lower Maine.[58] In the southeast, on the other hand, infertile soils combined with an "extraordinary weakness of peasant property" to render agriculture precarious at best. As a result, "this region was, in the entire West, one, perhaps the one, where the class of textile artisans played the most important role." The textile workers, "though scattered throughout the countryside, were not true peasants." Like their counterparts in northwestern Anjou, the rural inhabitants of southeastern Maine had already undergone a process of proletarianization at the time of the Atlantic migration.[59]

Emigration from Upper Maine to Canada was primarily derivative, in that the two areas of dense attraction prolonged movements that were centered elsewhere. Over half of the emigrants came from border communities near Perche or Anjou that fell within an extraprovincial sphere of influence. The northern parishes gravitated around two Percheron bourgs, Saint-Côme-de-Vair and Igé, and the southern ones around La Flèche. Roads and rivers were both important, among them the highway to Paris, the Sarthe, the Orne, and the Dives. By contrast, the *champagne* (open field) region between Laval and Le Mans produced a more scattered emigration, despite its economic resemblance to the two other zones. Personal recruitment efforts, or their immediate repercussions, appear once again as sources of imbalance. Provided that certain preconditions were satisfied, emigration could be boosted above expected levels by artificial stimulus.

Even near Perche and Anjou, emigration from Upper Maine did not qualify as heavy; the only real concentration occurred in Le Mans, a city of more than 10,000, and the point on which all three zones of departure converged. Nonetheless, northern and western Maine formed a stark contrast to the southeast with respect to their migratory propensities. In the impoverished triangle defined by Le Mans to the west, La Ferté-Bernard to the north, and Château-du-Loir to the south, there was no emigration whatsoever from any community. The situation in southeastern Maine was an extreme variant on that already noted in the Craonnais and Segréen, where a rural proletariat and emigration to Canada proved mutually exclusive.

On first sight, this isolation squares poorly with the standard description of the peasant weaver as "the man of markets, of distant relations." Yet the portrayal of two contrasting ways of life, that of the weavers and that of the "purely peasant milieu, more closed, more immobile," contradicts the demographic evidence.[60] The textile country of southeastern Maine, like the cotton manufacturing faubourgs of Rouen, clearly belonged to the most modern sector of the French economy, but the migratory behavior of its residents paradoxically resembled that of the most backward, traditional zones.

The examples of Maine and Rouen point to the inadequacy of considering economics in a void and to the danger of divorcing it from the context of social relations. In order to understand the absence of proto-industrial and industrial zones from the map of Canadian migration, one must go beyond generalities about the progress of capitalism and examine the actual social situation of peasants and weavers. The canonical analysis becomes relevant once again, but this time to clarify rather than confuse: "Between merchant and worker, [there was] a virtually permanent contact, so frequent was it. Periodic contact in town, if the worker confronted the trademark bureau, but especially contact in the countryside, where the merchant 'ran all year long,' establishing a professional tie that took on an appearance of dependency."[61]

Of course, the key notion here is that of dependency. For emigration to occur in northwestern France, economic development needed to accommodate, not annihilate, social independence. Emigration appeared to flourish wherever individuals avoided servitudes of either the ancient or modern type.

One may thus describe emigration as a by-product of capitalism, insofar as it concerned capitalism's beneficiaries. In making such a statement, one must obviously bear in mind the peculiarities of French capitalism, which, to a far greater degree than in England, developed "on the basis of the peasantry and the petty and middling bourgeoisie."[62] A description of the *bocage* of Anjou or the artisanal quarters of Rouen as capitalist may strike some readers as exaggerated, but it is accurate in the narrow sense of economically individualist. Whether or not early modern French capitalism was successful remains an open question, but to deny that it existed is perilous.

Summary

Throughout the Northwest, French emigration to Canada was largely the product of towns and their agricultural hinterlands, which were more or less extended depending on the degree of rural/urban integration. A maritime orientation was important, although not absolutely essential. In both Perche and Anjou, the personal efforts of a recruiter were able to compensate for a lesser familiarity with the Atlantic. Directed recruitment was not, however, seigneurial; Percheron and Angevin emigration tended to follow the geography of communications, rather than that of the recruiters' estates. Regardless of the distance from the Atlantic, the economic and social bases of northwestern emigration were consistent. Regions that participated in, and profited from, the process of economic modernization produced more emigrants than those that remained isolated, or those in which the new arrangements engendered more impoverishment than opportunity.

3

A Geography of Modernity: Non-Northwesterners and Women

Outside of the Northwest, according to my sample, the various regions of France provided more than 60% of the emigrants for Canada. About 30% came from the Center-west and Southwest, close to 25% from the *pays de grande culture* to the north of the Loire, and a residual 6% or so from the Midi, Massif central, and Alps. It is thus worthwhile to continue the "Tour de France" begun in the previous chapter, relating patterns of emigration to local social and economic structures. It is also imperative, given the evidence of gender specificity, to devote separate attention to the geography of women's emigration.

In this chapter I present data from outside the Northwest to corroborate the interpretation of emigration as a by-product of a particular avenue of capitalistic penetration, one that leaves intact small, independent units of production. The variable of gender qualifies this argument somewhat, however, by showing the extent to which cultural expectations about women's behavior could limit or prevent the expansion of their horizons, regardless of the economy, in certain regions.

The Center-west

Central-western France, or the "pays entre Loire et Gironde," produced a pattern of emigration similar to that of the Northwest. Both regions shared a common maritime orientation and "a rural civilization of the Nordic type," and both exhibited comparable levels of prosperity.[1] Contrary to the prevailing myth that the backward South commenced with the left bank of the Loire, "few regions were as active as the Pays charentais."[2] Culturally also, the Center-west was relatively privileged, at least as far as its urban elements were concerned. By the middle of the seventeenth century, the cities of the region possessed a decent network of elementary schools,[3] and in 1699 the local intendant could describe their inhabitants as "fairly polite," the populace [*peuple*] as "not as crude as elsewhere."[4]

Aunis

Central-western emigration to Canada focused first and foremost on Aunis, the tiny maritime province whose forty square kilometers formed the hinterland of La Rochelle. The port itself, an agglomeration of 20,000, produced the lion's share of emigrants, just as the comparably sized city of Saint-Malo dominated emigration from Ille-et-Vilaine.

"To a degree unmatched at other ports," John Clark has noted, "La Rochelle's economy rested almost solely on the colonial connection."[5] As early as the 1630s, the city's merchants were jockeying with Rouen for supremacy in the Canadian market, and from midcentury, when they emerged the victors in the competition, "La Rochelle was in the first rank for commerce with Canada."[6] Proportionally, the 855 Rochelais emigrants represented almost three-quarters of the Aunisian total, and in absolute numbers they marked La Rochelle as the single most important sending community in France, before Paris, Saint-Malo, and Rouen. The geography of urban emigration thus deserves attention, even though Rochelais parishes were less functionally distinct than those of Rouen.

La Rochelle was a typical early modern city in that horizontal social segregation was largely incomplete at the time of emigration to Canada.[7] Nonetheless, some economic differentiation existed, making it possible to distinguish between zones that emphasized maritime, semirural, or commercial and administrative activities. Of the 444 Rochelais who provided information on their parish of origin, the semirural parishes of Notre-Dame and Saint-Eloy garnered 178 (40.1%), the maritime parishes 151 (34.0%), and the commerical and administrative center 115 (25.9%).[8] Since each of these zones regrouped about a third of La Rochelle's population, the geography of Rochelais emigration was reasonably uniform—certainly more so than that of Rouen.[9]

This pattern is not wholly unexpected, given the more fluid nature of social segregation in the smaller city; however, the prominence of Notre-

Dame and Saint-Eloy is surprising, considering the far higher likelihood of city dwellers than country people to emigrate. Perhaps the explanation lies in the physical situation of Notre-Dame and Saint-Eloy, which bridged town and country. As a kind of buffer zone between La Rochelle and its *banlieue,* these parishes automatically received the bulk of recent immigrants from the hinterland,[10] and, as I discuss in Part Two, such zones often doubled as relays, or staging grounds, for further demographic movement. In any case, the contribution of La Rochelle's semirural zone to the peopling of Canada reveals the imprecision and permeability of town-country boundaries in the seventeenth and eighteenth centuries. "It thus seems clear," as Jean-Pierre Poussou has pointed out, "that the cities-versus-countryside opposition, so often invoked, is too simple an image."[11]

Outside of La Rochelle, Aunisian emigration was concentrated most heavily in the city's *banlieue,* a narrow wedge-shaped region sandwiched between the marshes of Poitou and Saintonge. Even in the east, where the Aunisian plain continued, the *banlieue* extended only about fifteen kilometers beyond the city, as opposed to ten kilometers in the north and south.

The exiguity of La Rochelle's hinterland stemmed from the city's location on the open ocean rather than on an estuary. Unlike Le Havre, Nantes, or Bordeaux, the port had no connection with a populous and productive river valley, and instead of penetrating the interior, "it opened onto the Atlantic."[12] The farmland of the region was "arid, poor, and stony," hence poorly suited to the production of grains. "Vines, on the contrary," to quote a contemporary, "succeed perfectly on this terrain which seems made for them."[13]

In parishes close to the city, such as Dompierre, winegrowing was already a monoculture in the seventeenth century, and in the *banlieue* as a whole, vineyards occupied 75 percent of the surface area.[14] Proprietorship of the vines fell to a multitude of small *laboureurs à bras* (cultivators without plow teams), whose operations were nonetheless fully capitalist.[15]

As expected, emigration from the *banlieue* of La Rochelle to Canada was substantial, although by no means comparable to the movement out of the city. A total of 131 persons, or 11.3 percent of the Aunisian emigrants in my sample, hailed from the area, and emigration touched thirty-one of its forty-three legally constituted communities. Only three of the *banlieue*'s twenty-nine bourgs, none of them major agglomerations, failed to produce any emigrants at all; a fourth sent a few via the intermediary of La Rochelle, and all the others participated directly. Access to the means of communication was something of a moot point, given the widespread emigration and the proximity of all of these communities to La Rochelle; however, the overrepresentation of bourgs among sending communities suggests that emigration increased with the frequency of ties to the city. Emigration was fairly concentrated throughout the *banlieue*, as indicated by the overall ratio of 3.5 emigrants per community. Two important bourgs, Dompierre and Aytré, sent more than 10 emigrants apiece, and only ten places produced merely a single emigrant.

This situation changed visibly, if not dramatically, beyond the confines of the *banlieue*. In the eastern part of the Aunisian plain, emigration affected only six of the twenty villages and seven of the twelve bourgs. The degree of concentration was also lower, with no one community producing more than a handful of emigrants.[16]

The moderate level of emigration from the eastern Aunisian plain makes sense in light of its economic and social situation. Inhabitants of the plain engaged in commercial polyculture for the urban market and maintained close business ties to La Rochelle, but they were unable to profit fully from the relationship owing to the mediocrity of their agricultural base.[17] The plain thus produced emigrants because it fell within the orbit of La Rochelle, but its activity was too limited for emigration to be truly substantial.

To the north and south, the Aunisian plain gave way to wetlands, which entrepreneurs began to drain in the first half of the seventeenth century.[18] The marshes remained thinly populated, however, and probably received more emigrants than they produced during the Ancien Régime.[19] They were also somewhat isolated, at least in comparison to the easily and often traversed plains: "A wet, opulent and unhealthy territory, . . . the marshes formed a sociological entity apart."[20]

Excluding the two cities of Marans and Rochefort, the Aunisian marshes provided Canada with only 7 emigrants, drawn from three communities. Marans played a more important role, as befitted the economic center of the northern marshes. An active trading town, Marans served as the linchpin in La Rochelle's supply line by funneling grain from the plains of Poitou into Aunis. Of the 23 emigrants from Marans,[21] at least one worked as a miller in Canada, perhaps an indication of prior involvement in the active grain trade with La Rochelle.

Rochefort, with 54 emigrants to Canada, maintained closer ties with the colony than these relatively modest numbers would indicate. From 1670 until the French Revolution, "Rochefort provided for the needs of all . . . [the] American colonies: personnel and matériel, workers and soldiers, everything left from Rochefort, and everything returned there."[22] The transformation of Rochefort, between 1666 and 1672, from an agricultural village of fewer than 600 souls into a major port complex constituted, "in the matter of employment, the major fact of the history of the Southwest in the seventeenth century." From the time of its creation, the arsenal city became "the largest hiring center, the largest industrial center, and the first immigration center" in Atlantic France south of the Loire.[23] Its mixed population of contractors, workers, and military and naval personnel was extremely unstable, fluctuating between 10,000 and 20,000 at irregular intervals.[24] Recruited from virtually everywhere in France,[25] these men may well have viewed residence in the makeshift, sexually imbalanced, and insalubrious city as a temporary expedient unworthy of documentary mention. Thus, while Rochefort's role in the transshipment of manpower from France to Canada is incontestable, the true volume of the city's contribution cannot be ascertained from the cartography.

A final contingent of Aunisians arrived in Canada from the Ile de Ré, directly off the coast from La Rochelle. The island's economy revolved around wine production and Atlantic commerce, and its limited surface area supported a city, two bourgs of more than five hundred hearths, and five ordinary bourgs. In spite of population densities that were extraordinary for the period,[26] the Ile de Ré was not overpopulated in relation to economic activity. In 1699, hardly a banner year for the French economy as a whole, the intendant of La Rochelle could state that "there is not a single poor beggar on this island, and there are twenty-five or thirty merchant families that are very rich."[27] Ninety-eight of these prosperous islanders made their way to Canada in the course of the French Regime (8.3 percent of the provincial total), of whom 80 provided information on their parish of origin. Four-fifths of these emigrants came from the island's three major agglomerations, and the remainder were distributed among all the lesser bourgs except Les Portes, the most remote.

Aunisian emigrants thus originated, in descending order, from the port of La Rochelle, lesser urban centers, and rural areas that supported a prosperous peasantry. Only the marshes were a partial exception to this rule, in that they presented favorable conditions for independent farmers yet contributed few people to the Atlantic migratory stream. Their thin population and relative inaccessibility, however, suffice to explain the anomaly.

Poitou

To the north, the province of Poitou made a significant, if far from uniform, contribution to the peopling of Canada. Once again, areas of intense recruitment juxtaposed zones of almost total noninvolvement. The departments of Lower Poitou produced, as I have noted, half again as many emigrants as those of Upper Poitou, but within Lower Poitou as well, the migratory pattern varied as a function of topographical and economic shifts between marshland, plain, and *bocage*.

Marshland dominated the coastal portion of Lower Poitou, stretching northward from Aunis to Brittany, and eastward as far as Challans and Luçon. Economically, this area resembled the Aunisian lowlands, and like them, it failed to produce a massive contingent of emigrants. In the marshland zones adjacent to Aunis, one in every five parishes witnessed an occasional departure, a proportion that declined somewhat to the north and west. The sending communities tended to be well situated with respect to the means of communication, particularly the roads leading to La Rochelle and Nantes. Multiple departures occurred only in principal towns; Les Sables, a local center of the codfish trade, sent 26 emigrants to Canada; Luçon, a market town doubling as a diocese, 14.

The *bocages* that covered the greater part of Lower Poitou, from Luçon east and Fontenay north, contributed little to the Atlantic migration despite their geographical extent.[28] Within the Diocese of La Rochelle, six Poitevin hedge parishes out of seven remained untouched by the movement, and all the sending communities together produced only 30 emigrants. In only one case did as many as 4 emigrants leave a given community: La Châtaigneraie, a regional textile center with direct ties to both La Rochelle and Canada.[29]

The lackluster performance of the Poitevin *bocages* stemmed from a distinctive feature of their economic and social landscape: the Poitevin *métairie* as it developed in the sixteenth and seventeenth centuries. The *métairie* was an agricultural exploitation of 20 to 100 hectares or more,[30] worked by a sharecropper. Throughout the *bocages*, it gradually replaced the smaller peasant farm, whose massive purchase by wealthier farmers and bourgeois marked "the true appearance of capitalism in the trade in peasant property."[31] The *métayer*, although technically "at the head of a great domain,"[32] in actuality fared no better than a simple agricultural laborer. Historians concur in describing him as a rural proletarian living at the mercy of the proprietors and enmeshed in a vicious cycle of poverty, indebtedness, and geographical instability.[33] Ironically, this instability did not translate itself into overseas migration to any significant degree. The Poitevin *métayer*, like his counterparts in western Anjou and southeastern Maine, proved far less likely to start afresh in Canada than did his more prosperous and less dependent neighbors.

The largest number of Canada-bound emigrants, in both absolute and relative terms, came from the narrow strip of plain country stretching between Luçon and Niort. This region, whose "cities, proprietors, and wheat fields" were in stark contrast to the "bourgs, nonproprietary cultivators, and weavers" of the *bocages*,[34] served as the breadbasket of La Rochelle and, to some degree, the colonies.[35] In the Diocese of La Rochelle alone, it produced more than 70 emigrants, with emigration touching, on average, one in every two communities. Fontenay and Niort, with populations of more than 10,000 and connections to the Atlantic economy,[36] sent 32 and 23 emigrants respectively.

Emigration was, however, variable within the plain itself. While most communities within the zone of Fontenay sent at least one emigrant, the zone of Niort was nearly empty except in the south. The key to this pattern lies, yet again, in the organization of agriculture. According to a report drafted by the subdélégué (intendant's subordinate) of the Election of Niort in 1716, 21 percent of householders in the hinterland of the city resided in *métairies*.[37] The zone of Niort was thus a region of transition between the plain of Fontenay and Upper Poitou, where sharecropping again predominated. The only exception was the Boutonne Valley in the south, a winegrowing area that did produce emigrants for Canada. One of the sending communities, Villeneuve-La-Comtesse, was even singled out by the subdélégué for "white wines of the same quality as those of the small *borderies* of Cognac."[38] A *borderie*, of course, was a small, peasant-owned property; in the Boutonne Valley, as in the *banlieue* of La Rochelle and the Ile de Ré, the wine industry had created a prosperous class of *bordiers*.[39]

A second difference between the zones of Fontenay and Niort involves the textile industry, which, while present in both, was far more vigorous in Niort. In the western part of the plain, notable concentrations of weavers existed only in Fontenay itself, and in parishes of its *proche banlieue* (inner suburbs) such as Charzais.[40] The peasants of the Niortais, however, were likely to exercise an industrial by-occupation, and hence to depend for their subsistence on the tender mercies of Niort's two hundred "marchands et fabricants" (merchants and manufacturers).[41]

In Upper Poitou, the cartography of emigration also reflected economic differences, but in this case they worked to minimize the contribution of the plain. Except around Poitiers, the plains of Upper Poitou resembled British moors more closely than they did the fertile lands to the west; large stretches of territory remained uncultivated, and the areas under cultivation produced little beyond the subsistence of their plowmen.[42] The system of sharecropping, as practiced in the *bocages* of Lower Poitou, made steady progress throughout this region in the sixteenth and seventeenth centuries, with the result that the peasantry became dependent as well as poor.

In keeping with the pattern noted in northwestern France and Lower Poitou, these peasants were apparently little inclined to experiment with overseas mobility, no matter how dire their economic circumstances. By far the largest number of emigrants came from Poitiers itself (88 in all),[43] or from communities within twenty-five kilometers of the city. Emigration from the *banlieue* was heavier to the north and west than to the south and east, where the *brandes* (heaths) of Poitou gave way to the even more barren Massif central. Elsewhere in the plain, it touched primarily centers like Chauvigny and Châtellerault, which circumscribed the poverty zone but were themselves located in fertile territory.[44] The only pocket of denser recruitment appeared in the northern reaches of Upper Poitou, around Thouars and Loudun. This winegrowing region shared the characteristics of other emigrant-producing zones: market-oriented agriculture and a prosperous peasantry.

Saintonge and Angoumois

The other two central-western provinces, Saintonge and Angoumois, add further detail to the picture traced thus far, without altering it significantly. In the absence of a major port complex, multiple departures were limited, touching only the *chefs-lieux d'élection* (seats of local government) and Brouage, a small port of the Charente estuary. Rural emigration was scattered but dense, and its density increased with the prosperity of the country. The fertile and active Charente Valley funneled emigrants to Canada from one end to the other, while beyond the river recruitment flourished in the wealthy countryside south of Cognac and east of Saint-Jean-d'Angély. Emigrants often departed from contiguous parishes, creating clusters or chains of sending communities.

In the center-west as a whole, therefore, emigration to Canada followed the same pattern as in the Northwest. Atlantic connections were crucial, urban areas were dominant, and, in the countryside, areas of prosperous peasant agriculture outproduced those of both subsistence farming and large-scale rural capitalism.

The Southwest

Southwestern France, the third-most-important emigrant-producing zone, was less a unified region than a mosaic of separate economies that came gradually to share a common Atlantic orientation during the eighteenth century. Crucial to this process was the economic and demographic development of Bordeaux; between 1700 and the Revolution, the city was transformed from a provincial port of 45,000 into a linchpin of the colonial economy, a metropolis of 111,000 inhabitants, and an undisputed capital of the surrounding provinces.[45]

The integration of lands as diverse as the Pays basque, the Pyrénées, the Garonne Valley, and the western Massif central into the Atlantic sphere of influence was, of course, imperfect, as Jean-Pierre Poussou has shown in his masterful study of immigration into Bordeaux. The geography of emigration to Canada confirms the existence of regional variations, and indeed reflects them with greater acuity than the geography of internal movements. As might be expected, southwestern emigrants hailed preferentially from the areas that participated fully in the economic boom of greater Aquitaine and in which some of the benefits of expansion accrued to the popular classes.

Guyenne

Bordeaux itself, as "the great French port assuring direct commerce with the Islands," became inevitably "the great port of recruitment for those who wanted to try their luck in America."[46] Perhaps 50,000 passengers and indentured servants sailed from the city in the eighteenth century,[47] most of them bound for the West Indies, but some of them for Canada as well. Canadian destinations were particularly important after 1748, when local shippers succeeded in extending their commercial supremacy from the Islands to North America.[48]

Bordeaux figures in my sample with 115 departures, making it the seventh-most-important sending community in France after Nantes and Dieppe. Except for La Rochelle, it was also the only city south of the Loire to produce more than 100 emigrants. Less than a third of these emigrants took the trouble to identify their parish of origin, an omission that is both regrettable and understandable. As I note later, many of the Bordelais in the sample were recent immigrants who, as apprentices, journeymen, or *chambrelans* (home workers), never attempted to cast down roots in the city. Of the 35 emigrants who did provide the authorities with an identifiable parish, 15 were from the waterfront, 12 from the center-city, and 8 from the adjoining faubourgs of Saint-Seurin and Sainte-Eulalie.[49]

Jean-Pierre Poussou's studies indicate that the majority of emigrants who passed through Bordeaux originated not from the city itself but from its environs: "They came essentially from Bordeaux's hinterlands, and principally from the valleys that were also the zones of heavy population, Bordeaux sending nearly a fifth of the total."[50] Emigration to Canada departs from this pattern of rural domination, for, in my sample, two-thirds of the emigrants from Bordelais and Bazadais left France as residents of Bordeaux. Emigrants who did arrive in Canada from the hinterland tended to come in clusters from communities in the Garonne Valley. In Bazadais, emigration was concentrated in the north and west, where high population and heavy river transport guaranteed active commerce, and it was sparse in the desolate and thinly populated south, except for the towns of Bazas and Casteljaloux.[51]

Emigration from the hinterlands of Bordeaux thus conforms to the expected geographical pattern. Sending communities enjoyed privileged access to the means of communication, in this case, the Garonne River and the roads between the Garonne and Dordogne, and sometimes they were centers in their own right. Their agricultural base was already intensive and speculative (the great vintages as we know them date largely from the sixteenth century),[52] and since viticulture reigned, small and middling proprietors joined large landowners in profiting from the commercialization of their crops.

THE ECONOMIC SITUATION of the Middle Garonne, comprising Agenais and Lower Quercy, was nearly as favorable as that of Bordelais. In the eighteenth century, "an era of exceptional vitality," it emerged as "one of the most prosperous and lively regions of France." It was also "one of the most open to general communications; . . . nearly half of its products were destined for the outside," and few regions could boast such a great number of fairs. An essentially speculative polyculture formed the basis not only of commerce but of industry: "It was around 1670 that the millers became flour dealers, and supplied the Americas."[53] Ports such as Moissac, Puymirol, and Montauban began to specialize in the exportation of milled flour, with Montauban nearly quadrupling its Canada-bound shipments between 1700 and 1763.[54] Other industrial specialties flourished in the valley as well. By far the most important, at least around Agen and Montauban, was the manufacture of coarse woolens for the Canadian market.[55]

Given the economic vigor and Atlantic orientation of the Middle Garonne, it comes as no surprise that emigration to Canada was fairly widespread throughout the region. Multiple departures were confined to the larger centers, especially Montauban (24), Cahors (15), and Agen (15), but bourgs or villages producing 1 or 2 emigrants were legion. The river valleys proved particularly conducive to mobility: the Garonne, the Lot, and the Tarn, to be sure, but equally, secondary valleys like the Dropt, the Baïse, and the Gimone. Beyond the valleys, emigration affected the entire fertile area between the Lot and the Dropt, but no one community figured in the sample with more than a single emigrant.

Relations with canada were far less sustained in Guyenne's semi-autonomous appendages of Upper Quercy, Rouergue, and Périgord. The situation of Rouergue typifies that of these westernmost marches of the Massif central: "at a distance from the great royal routes and the great waterways," the province found itself isolated from economic progress, the more so owing to the absence of large cities in the vicinity. Rouergat emigration to Canada was predictably sparse, and confined almost exclusively to centers. The *chefs-lieux d'élection* of the province, some of which were beginning to dabble in *le grand négoce* (overseas commerce), together sent some two dozen emigrants.[56]

Gascony

The province of Gascony united subregions at least as diverse as those of Guyenne—from Gers, where commercial polyculture flourished, to the *landes*, a zone of subsistence agriculture, to Comminges, a mountainous area devoted to animal husbandry, to the outward-turned Pays basque.[57] The geography of Canadian emigration reflects these differences more or less predictably. The Atlantic ties of the Pays basque bore demographic as well as economic fruit, as did those, more indirect, of inland Gers. The *landes* were a vast empty zone except for villages near the Pays basque and centers, and the upper Pyrénées provided only a smattering of emigrants.

In the Pays basque, communities not touched by emigration were the exception. The movement focused on the port complex of Bayonne/Saint-Esprit,[58] which, with 90 emigrants, made a proportionally greater contribution than Bordeaux.[59] Two other ports and two inland bourgs also exhibited high levels of concentration, and even the rural parishes for the most part sent more than one son to Canada. In Gers, emigration followed the Garonne or the secondary valleys that prolonged its influence, but increasing distance from the main corridor of activity meant a decreasing level of concentration; even towns like Auch, Lectoure, and Condom were unable to muster 10 emigrants apiece. Emigration affected the upper

Pyrénées only occasionally, and always by way of valleys: the Adour, the Aure, and the Garonne.

TAKEN AS A WHOLE, southwestern emigration to Canada thus provides further support for the argument linking rural departures with zones of peasant capitalism. "Within this regional ensemble," as Poussou has put it, "subsistence agriculture, economic autarky, scarcely existed; in the eighteenth century, the agriculture of the Southwest produced primarily to sell, and even where sales were only secondary, their role was not at all negligible. Furthermore, these sales were carried out largely for a distant clientele!"[60]

This commercialized rural economy was not, however, "agribusiness" as it is known today, or even as it had emerged by the eighteenth century in England, Belgium, or French Flanders. On the contrary, Poussou has pointed out, "there is even an evident contrast between the archaism of agricultural techniques and mentalities and the insertion of most of the regions considered into very vast circuits of economic or human exchanges. In particular, the production for sale did not preclude the presence of backward techniques—which to these eyes constitutes a model of real interest, whose explanatory range should not be considered at all as simply regional."[61]

To Poussou's mention of techniques and mentalities, I would add that of social structures. For in spite of large-scale agricultural investments in limited zones such as the hinterlands of great cities, the vast majority of agricultural production was assured by peasants. The example of emigration to Canada supports Poussou's intuition of the supraregional validity of his model. Whether in Normandy, Anjou, Aunis, or Guyenne, peasants had, by the eighteenth century, transcended the limits of a *comprador* economy and integrated not only their production but their migratory behavior into circuits that were Atlantic in scope.[62]

The North and East

The commercialization of the rural economy did not occur in the western provinces alone; but east of an imaginary line between Rouen and Toulouse, the overwhelming direction of commerce ceased to be Atlantic.

The importance of Atlantic migrations declined in proportion to that of commerce, with the result that this entire expanse produced fewer than a third of Canada's French immigrants. The great grain-producing regions of the North and East, which alone regrouped almost 40% of the French population in 1700,[63] were together responsible for just under a quarter of the emigration.

The migratory contribution of the North and East was nonetheless quite homogeneous. Except on the southern fringes of the Paris Basin and in the forests and mountains to the east, every department provided at least .5% of the emigrants. Likewise, this proportion exceeded 1% only at the borders of Maine and Anjou and in greater Paris, where relations with Canada were of a less casual nature.

Like the volume of emigration, the economic and social situation of these regions possessed a certain unity, one that was distinct from any considered so far. The productive capacity of the great open fields was equal or superior to that of the richest western plains, and the commercialization of agriculture was proceeding apace in the seventeenth and eighteenth centuries. The beneficiaries of agrarian capitalism, however, were fewer in number in the heart of France than on its periphery, and they were less likely to be peasants. Ironically, historians tend to associate the *pays de grande culture* with an image of the *bon laboureur,* a familiar literary stereotype since the time of Rétif de la Bretonne. Yet sturdy yeoman farmers were never more than exceptional features of the social landscape in northern and eastern France. "The dominant fact was the rarity, beyond the vineyard and the garden, of the *bon laboureur,* master of his lands, his animals, his tools, his carts, his servants, and no doubt also his destiny."[64]

The true *coqs de village,* as Georges Lefebvre has pointed out, were scarcely peasants at all, but rural "bourgeois" who derived their profits from the supervision of seigneurial estates.[65] The majority of country folk had to be content with subsistence, and in this respect they had more in common with the miserable sharecroppers of Poitou than with the enterprising *polyculteurs* (peasants engaged in mixed farming) of Normandy or the Middle Garonne. As Pierre Goubert has written,

> this countryside of grains and sheep, so pleasant in appearance, where not a lump of earth was wasted, was the very illustration of economic overpopulation. We already know that mortality was higher here than elsewhere during subsistence crises. The humble documents left by the

residents—judicial, notarial, seigneurial, and tax papers—proclaim the inadequacy of the livestock. Fewer cows than horses . . . , few or no pigs, not always or often a cow, a poorly stocked barnyard, a heavy and deficient diet, the necessity of day labor and home work (wool, linen, iron, wood, wicker) to make do . . . These regions of grains, sheep, and looms were those of overcrowding, undernourishment, and social anger. The richest of them ended up producing Babeuf.[66]

The relatively low numbers of emigrants originating from the *pays de grande culture* were thus overdetermined, in the sense that closer ties with Canada would not have altered them to any significant degree. Even in Ile-de-France, where such ties existed, and where emigration increased commensurately, the attraction of Canada made itself felt with difficulty beyond city limits. Nine-tenths of the province's emigrants were Parisians, but this made Paris, in absolute numbers, the second-most-important sending community in France.

Paris

The documents ascribe a particular parish of origin to nearly two-thirds of the Parisians in the sample (517 out of 809),[67] making it fruitful to consider the urban geography of emigration and what it implies about the movement's social selectivity. Keep in mind, however, that early modern Paris was a city "where social segregation did not exist but was developing."[68] Its division into a prosperous west and populous east dates, in its finished form, from the early nineteenth century; so many neighborhoods, particularly in the ancient and thickly settled center, cannot be neatly pigeonholed as rich or poor.[69]

Farther from the center, the situation was less ambiguous, if not in the seventeenth century, at least by the time of the Regent. Of the northwest, an observer wrote: "Since His Majesty has fixed his abode in Paris, several officers and seigneurs have found lodgings in the environs of the Louvre, Saint-Honoré, and Saint-Roch, where several *hôtels* (town mansions) have been built; which has obliged the artisans of different professions who were in and around this quarter to leave it and settle elsewhere."[70]

A similar process of gentrification occurred in the southwest, in the Faubourg Saint-Germain, while, to the east, the formerly aristocratic Marais became "parliamentary, indeed popular."[71] At the same time, the northern and eastern faubourgs grew increasingly humbler, particularly that of Saint-Marcel, which Sébastien Mercier described as the quarter of "the poorest, most restless, and most unruly rabble of Paris. There is more money," he continued, "in a single house of the Faubourg Saint-Honoré than in the whole Faubourg Saint-Marcel, or Saint-Marceau, taken collectively."[72] The popular visage of the Faubourg Saint-Antoine was, despite its subsequent notoriety, less apparent to contemporaries; a chronicler of the neighborhood described it, as late as 1738, as "a place of delights in which one tastes at one and the same time the pleasures of the city and the country."[73]

As administrative circumscriptions, the ancient parishes of Paris were virtually defunct by the seventeenth and eighteenth centuries, some of them for ecclesiastical as well as secular purposes. Municipal authorities relied instead on a system of twenty *quartiers*, which were roughly comparable in population if not in surface area; and religious life took place within the streamlined boundaries of twenty-two new or redrawn parishes.[74]

It is no surprise that emigrants rarely reported their origins in terms of *quartier*, since many of them needed to declare their previous parish affiliation in order to marry in Canada. What is strange is the discovery that they felt no compulsion to declare that affiliation accurately. Of the thirty-four parishes mentioned in the documents, only eighteen continued to exist as such in 1789; 1 in every 5 emigrants claimed to have resided in a parish where he or she could neither have been baptized nor have fulfilled subsequent religious obligations.[75] Parisians clearly identified with their neighborhoods, as symbolized by their churches; but one must wonder how meaningful this symbolic association was when the churches in question "no longer existed . . . or at least were no longer consecrated to the creed."[76]

Perhaps the forty-five or so ancient parishes simply corresponded better to the scale of urban life than did the much larger *quartiers* or newer parishes. Their number inevitably conjures up images of that most vital of municipal divisions, the revolutionary *section*, and, in fact, the map of the *sections* bears not a little resemblance to that of the older parishes. From the point of view of social relations, early modern Paris remained, to some extent, an agglomeration of villages whose inhabitants had yet to renounce *l'esprit du clocher*.[77]

The emigrants' parishes stretched the length and breadth of the city, leaving no part untouched but favoring some more than others. The most heavily populated parishes of the right bank produced about a fifth of the emigrants, while the *"ville"* as a whole (the right bank exclusive of its faubourgs) laid title to almost half. An additional fourth stemmed, on the left bank, from the Faubourg Saint-Germain, and another tenth from the Latin Quarter broadly construed. The still thickly settled islands managed a twentieth despite their small size, and the artisanal faubourgs shared the rest starting with Saint-Marcel (25 emigrants). Only 3 emigrants declared a residence in the semirural Faubourg Saint-Antoine, making it the least important of all the faubourgs except, perhaps, Saint-Honoré.[78]

The most striking feature of these distributions is the prominence of the Faubourg Saint-Germain, whose aristocratic *hôtels* and bourgeois apartments proved more conducive to emigration than the *bouges* and *garnis* (hovels and low lodgings) of neighboring Saint-Marcel. In central Paris, the findings are harder to interpret because of the prevalence of other forms of social stratification—by street or floor, for example. Nonetheless, parishes that catered to a predominantly laboring population, such as Saint-Jean-en-Grève (12 emigrants) or Saint-Nicolas-du-Chardonnay (Place Maubert, 5 emigrants), were not especially important.

It thus appears that Paris produced a mixed emigration with an important bourgeois, if not aristocratic, component—a likely scenario given that New France required administrative cadres and that the capital could be expected to provide them. In this respect, the role of the church may have been even more notable than that of the secular bureaucracy, for both the Jesuits and the Sulpicians maintained headquarters in the Faubourg Saint-Germain.

Beyond Paris

Outside of Paris, northern and eastern emigration conformed to familiar patterns. The major urban centers were the scene of limited concentration, whether in Ile-de-France (Versailles), Champagne (Reims, Troyes), or Burgundy (Dijon, Chalon-sur-Saône, Auxerre). In Lyonnais two-thirds of the emigrants (74 out of 111) came from Lyon itself: testimony to the importance and multidirectionality of the city's communications network. Secondary towns were also prominent among sending communities, even if they rarely animated mass departures. In Ile-de-France emigration favored market towns connected with Paris and, more generally, *villes-*

relais, urban way stations that linked the city to the province. In Alsace many of the emigrants named traditional "hometowns" such as La-Petite-Pierre or Neuwiller-la-Roche as their places of origin.[79]

Rural emigration, meanwhile, involved communities with ready access to transport, although the nature of that transport depended on regional topography. In Picardy the northern plain gave roads the advantage over rivers (even such rivers as the Oise and the Somme), while the Loire and its affluents prevailed, for obvious reasons, in the Loire. In Burgundy the commercially active valleys of the Yonne and Armançon contributed a string of sending communities, while in Champagne the various rivers and roads fairly bristled with secondary centers of departure. The very fertile Marne Valley stood out as the most important thoroughfare, funneling emigrants to Canada from one end to the other; but the opulent banks of several smaller rivers also cut a good figure, as did the *côte champenoise,* the wine country south of Epernay.[80]

The Center, the South, and the Alps

The remainder of French emigrants trickled into Canada from the Center, the South, and the Southeast, each of which contributed between 1% and 3% of the total emigrant flow. The relative paucity of these contributions clashes with the common image of the Mediterranean, the Alps, and the Massif central as zones of intense human mobility and points up the need to consider the relationship between internal and Atlantic migrations. As in the Pyrénées, one did not translate neatly into the other. Sustained contacts between these locales and Canada were never established, and such emigration as did occur resembled a kind of fortuitous spillover. Two constants emerge from the scattered but not patternless geography of emigration in these three areas: the limited role of concentration, even at the level of major cities; and the importance of corridors of mobility, especially valleys and coastline, in comparison with higher and more remote zones of settlement.

The urbanized South managed to send over 10 emigrants apiece from five communities (Montpellier, Marseille, Toulon, Nîmes, and Aix), while the number dwindled to 3 in the Massif central (Limoges, Clermont, and Moulins), and 2 in the Alps (Grenoble and Vienne). Elsewhere in these regions, emigration was very dispersed but rarely random. Easy communications made their mark, with the result that migrants more often stemmed from lowlands than from mountains.

Only 20 Dauphinois named the Upper Alps or Oisans as their region of origin, as opposed to 100 who indicated Lower Dauphiné. Emigrants from the province eschewed the peaks in favor of the Rhône and Isère Valleys and "the neighborhood of Lyon, traversed by so many voyagers, so many merchants, so many rumors also."[81] The same pattern prevailed in Ardèche, where emigration affected the plain and, particularly, the Rhône and Ardèche Valleys. Small centers located at the junction of mountain and plain also participated, so the configuration of sending communities resembled a *cordon sanitaire* thrown around the still isolated mountains. In Savoy, where emigration was mountainous by definition, it was also insignificant; but the dozen or so communities that did produce emigrants enjoyed access to either roads or rivers.

For the most part, emigration was so sparse throughout these regions as to betray an almost accidental character, which was only occasionally tempered by a limited clustering of the emigrants' places of origin. In Auvergne five areas of greater density stood out, three of them, predictably, in Lower Auvergne rather than mountainous Cantal. Most important was the Limagne, a fertile plain and region of passage formed by the Allier Valley around Clermont and Riom; and it was followed by the fairly fertile border area of Livradois and Velay, about fifteen kilometers north of the Loire. The Combrailles, a metalworking zone at the edge of Bourbonnais, sent a smaller cluster of emigrants, as did, in Upper Auvergne, the Dordogne Valley and the vicinity of Marvejols. This last grouping included all the emigrants from Lozère, the least generous of all departments in furnishing emigrants for Canada; however, the wider commercial connections enjoyed by these communities thanks to the fairs of Marvejols explains their anomalous behavior with regard to the rest of the proverbially isolated and backward department.[82]

The Geography of Women's Migrations

As I noted when examining regional origins at the level of province and department, aggregate statistics about the emigrants obscure crucial distinctions that existed between them on the basis of sex. Such distinctions operated at the communal level also, as even a cursory survey of the parishes sending women reveals. There existed, within the broad outlines delineated above, a geography of female emigration whose specificity was intra- as well as interregional. Rather than a single, predominantly male, migratory stream that swept a few women along in its wake, the records reveal two streams—one male and one female—that retained their individuality in coming together.

The communal origins of female emigrants were not only less varied than those of male emigrants (see Table 1.9), they were actually different in some cases. Except in the great cities, where departures involved both men and women in varying proportions, emigration was surprisingly sex-specific. Fully half of the villages and bourgs and one-fifth of the small towns that sent women to Canada sent women alone; the overall figure, including the great cities, was 36%. The strictly female places of origin accounted for only 10% of the total female emigrant flow because of the high degree of dispersion among rural and small-town emigrants regardless of sex. Outside of the large cities, however, about a quarter of women and girls came from communities whose migratory contributions were exclusively female.

Whether exclusive or not, the geography of female emigration differed strikingly from that of men. In only two provinces, Aunis and Perche, did it constitute a microcosm of the overall pattern and touch much the same communities (though with lesser intensity). The sex ratio among Aunisian and Percheron emigrants was high—only two to one in favor of males—so this example of identical migratory behavior was not numerically insignificant. The likeliest explanations are, first, familial emigration—the departure of a core of constituted families large enough to boost the sex ratio without affecting geographical provenance—and, second, unusually comparable mechanisms of recruitment for men and women.[83]

In Ile-de-France and the other provinces of the Paris Basin, another pattern emerged altogether. Although most of the women from Ile-de-France were Parisians, the 12% who were not accounted for much of the dispersed emigration in the hinterland of the city. The *grande banlieue* (outer suburbs), the valleys of the Orge, Oise, and Marne, and the *villes-relais* connecting Paris with the province produced women, and often only women, in relative abundance. The dichotomous aspect of greater-Parisian emigration, which juxtaposed urban concentration with extensive suburban scatter, derived in large part from the communal distribution of female emigrants.

In Paris itself, the origins of women resembled those of men except in one respect.[84] While the islands and the central parishes of both banks sent abroad men and women in comparable proportions, emigration from the faubourgs was more sex-specific. More than a third of the men but fewer than a fifth of the women had resided in the elegant Faubourg Saint-Germain, whereas 4% of the men but 12% of the women came from the working-class faubourgs to the north and east. The Faubourg Saint-Marcel in particular sent its daughters overseas more readily than its sons: 23 of the impoverished neighborhood's 25 emigrants for Canada were women. Once again, a distinct pattern of female recruitment seems evident.

The sex ratio among emigrants from Ile-de-France was the highest recorded for any province—nearly 1:1—yet the separate geography of female emigration argues against the idea of widespread family departures. Separate geography was also the rule elsewhere in the Paris Basin, although the sex ratio dropped outside of Ile-de-France to 1:2 in Orléanais and 1:3 in Picardy and Champagne. In Champagne female emigration was concentrated in the departments of the Seine Valley (Brie champenoise and Aube), to the detriment of the Marne and the Yonne, which were more important overall. Over half of the communities concerned produced female emigrants only, including five *villes-relais* along the routes to Paris. Nogent-sur-Seine, a bustling river town of 3,000,[85] sent 4 of its daughters but none of its sons to Canada.

In Picardy female emigration tended to follow roads, and in Orléanais, the Loire Valley, but in both provinces much of the scattered emigration was female. The Paris Basin thus supplied women for the colonies with particular ease, from the countryside and small towns as well as from the cities. The recruitment of so many women from regions not generally conducive to emigration (Paris excepted) poses a problem for later consideration.[86] It is, however, possible that many of these Briardes, Picardes, Champenoises, and Orléanaises already lived in Paris at the time of their departure, and that the capital had failed to provide them with the security they had hoped to obtain. Emigration to Canada would, in this case, have been a repeat performance—the substitution of a dream of colonial prosperity for the more familiar lure of city lights.

In the rest of the North and the East, female emigration declined precipitously, with individual provinces producing no more than .2% to 2% of the total. Its overall aspect resembled that of zones of low emigration in general: low concentration, a preference for centers, and good access to the means of communication. Nonetheless, women's movements were not merely a scaled-down version of men's, as in Aunis or Perche; fully a third of the fifty-odd sending communities produced an all-female emigrant contingent.

In the Northwest, as my departmental analysis indicated, women's emigration was far heavier in the Seine Valley than in the Massif amoricain. Women thus emigrated freely from Seine-Maritime and Calvados, though not from otherwise migrant Manche or Ille-et-Vilaine. In Upper Normandy women's departures were more circumscribed than men's, touching Rouen and Dieppe, the countryside around and between them, and scattered coastal communities, rather than the pays de Caux in its entirety. Much of the emigration from the Arques Valley connecting Dieppe with greater Rouen and the pays de Bray was uniquely female, suggesting, as in greater Paris, a separate pattern of recruitment for women.[87]

In Calvados women came from roughly the same areas as men, a congruence that became identity in the pays d'Auge, where a geographically limited example of familial migration is apparent (as I discuss in the next chapter). The pattern in Manche was very different and quite unprecedented: only 2 departures from the Avranchin—neither from an important sending community—and 3 from the Coutançais. Women hailed instead from the northern Cotentin, where, in spite of their small numbers, they comprised 20% of the emigrant pool; the corresponding figure for the rest of the department was less than 1%. In Brittany, also, a sex ratio of 1:20 in favor of males ensured a distinct profile for female emigration. It was, however, more derivative, with women stemming largely, if not entirely, from communities that also sent men.

Saintonge, Angoumois, and Poitou, like Upper Normandy, channeled women to Canada from a less far-flung network of communities than that which sent men. Its contours were again more precise, due to the greater role played by rivers and coastline. In Saintonge and Angoumois, female emigration rarely strayed from the Charente, with a clear emphasis on the river's mouth. Proximity to the ocean was also important in Poitou, where two-thirds of the female sending communities lay to the west of the road from Fontenay to Bressuire. As in Normandy and Brittany, women from these central-western provinces seem to have required a particular facility of transport in order to become emigrants.

Finally, as already noted, the regions to the south of the Charente together produced only 2 percent of the female emigrants for Canada. The discrepancy between the levels of female and male emigration was lowest in the South, where 1 in 30 emigrants was a woman; it was somewhat higher in the Southwest and the Alps (1 in 50), and was highest in the Massif central (1 in 100). The geography of these scant departures was largely random, although most of them took place within an urban context. The only cluster of sending communities was in the Pays basque, where five ports directed a combined total of 11 women to Canada.

Summary

At the end of this extensive tour of the regional geography of French emigration to Canada, several conclusions emerge. Perhaps most important is the congruence, found again and again, between zones of Atlantic capitalism and zones of emigration (provided that even the *petites gens*, those of modest means, derived some profit from the burgeoning commerce). Emigration was clearly heaviest in regions of healthy, small economies geared toward Atlantic trade, and it was lowest where neither of these criteria applied. Sending communities were often urban centers, and they usually had good access to the principal means of communication: the corridors of movement for people as well as goods. The plains, as traditional regions of passage, produced more emigrants than did the mountains, and rivers of all sizes contributed disproportionately to the migrant flow.

In certain instances this normative geography of emigration could be perturbed or distorted by an extraneous factor: the personal efforts of a recruiter. In the case of Anjou, the recruiter's influence probably did little more than accentuate a current that would have existed anyway owing to the accessibility of the Loire; but straying farther from the "natural" bases of Canadian recruitment—for example, in Perche—one must consider the extent to which this type of personal accident could actually generate a new migratory stream.

A second caveat was brought to light by separately studying women's emigration, which turned out to exhibit a widely divergent geography. Clearly, purely economic arguments could not account for all the regional variations within French emigration to Canada, since women's role in the movement fluctuated along the western seaboard between 2% and 32%, and since women and men often left from different communities. This accentuated tendency toward sexual specificity compels one to recognize once more the relative autonomy of demographic and economic phenomena.

Emigration to Canada took place within parameters defined by the economy, but the economy did not call it into being ex nihilo. In addition to an economic context, the movement possessed a cultural context that defined its relationship to particular ways of life. It developed not in a vacuum, but in accordance with traditional repertories of migratory behavior that differed from place to place, as can be seen in Part Two.

4

An Urban Society: Class Structure and Occupational Distribution

Previous historians have tended to avoid discussing the social origins of French emigrants to Canada because of the lack of hard-and-fast data,[1] and indeed, these origins are more elusive than the regional affiliations. Owing to the nature of the sources, it was impossible to ascribe a social class to more than 9,000, or 57%, of the emigrants in my sample, a proportion that rose to 59% in the case of women. An occupation of some sort could be attributed to 12,000, or three-quarters, of the emigrants—seemingly a considerable improvement. Occupational labels, however, were sometimes very vague: witness the 1,305 *filles à marier* (young unmarried women), the 913 indentured servants, or the 579 prisoners.

Nonetheless, it seems regrettable to let the considerable evidence I gathered go to waste, particularly since scholars of British migration to North America have shown a willingness to speculate to be fruitful (if not uncontroversial).[2] In this chapter I seek to show that the all too frequent silences of the documents regarding social origins constitute an obstacle to our understanding of the movement that is formidable but not insurmountable. Once again, a pattern emerges that is fully consistent with the one sketched out thus far: the class and occupational backgrounds of French emigrants to Canada disproportionately reflect the most urban and, hence, the most modern elements of Ancien Régime society.

Social Class

My sample of emigrants to Canada contained 468 nobles, 1,968 bourgeois, 613 peasants, 895 nonagricultural wage earners, 2,822 artisans, and 9,044 persons whose social status could not be determined. These numbers as they stand are not very enlightening, so my first task involved determining whether or not the three-fifths of emigrants of unknown social origin were randomly distributed. The answer, it seems, is a resounding no. The record keepers of the Ancien Régime were keenly sensitive to social distinctions, particularly to those based on wealth rather than caste. Men of substance among the emigrants could expect to receive the qualification of *sieur*, raising them above the mass of *dits* and *nommés*, even if genuine nobles could not always count on elevation above this same rank.[3] It is thus likely that the nobles and bourgeois recorded in the sample, taken together, represent the better part of those members of the French elite who participated in the migration to Canada.

Even assuming that the 9,044 unknowns belonged primarily to the popular classes, a problem of distribution remains. It is tempting to suppose, given the surprisingly small number of peasants in the sample, that the authorities took their presence for granted, underrecording them with disproportionate frequency. While perhaps true to a degree, this hypothesis becomes problematic upon closer inspection. The urban/rural distribution of the sample, after all, was based on very good evidence, and it in no way resembled the corresponding distribution within the French population.

Nearly two-thirds of the 9,044 emigrants in question left behind a precisely identified parish of origin, and of these parishes about three-fifths were urban. To be exact, at least 3,491 emigrants of unknown social origin arrived in Canada from towns or large cities—origins that lessen the possibility they were peasants. Cities and towns did, of course, include farmers among their populations, and although these men were scarcely peasants in the strictest sense of the word,[4] they did derive their living from agriculture. On the other hand, villages and bourgs always supported a number of artisans from the necessary trades, and often a rudimentary service sector as well. For purposes of rough estimation, it thus appears reasonable to classify the unknown country folk as peasants and the unknown city folk as artisans and laborers. Exceptions to each of these characterizations existed, yet they could more or less be expected to cancel each other out.

The problem of the more than 3,000 emigrants for whom neither the social class nor the parish was known still remains. Assuming, as is likely, that their urban/rural distribution was similar to that of the other, larger group of unknowns, it can be postulated that they consisted, in turn, of some 40% peasants and 60% artisans and laborers. Distinguishing between the last two groups is an even more speculative enterprise, but by applying the ratio of 3:1 that appears among the emigrants of known social class, one can at least ascribe a tentative number to each category. Together with the original figures, my adjusted estimates are shown in Table 4.1.

Aggregate information on the social structure of the early modern French population is hard to come by and is subject to a certain amount of skepticism; however, available data indicate that emigrants to Canada differed from the general population more radically than even the urban/rural distributions suggest. The most glaring discrepancy concerns the peasantry, which in 1789, after a century of gradual but progressive urbanization, still comprised 21 million out of France's 26 million inhabitants.[5] My estimate of some 4,000 agricultural emigrants reduces this sector from four-fifths to slightly over one-quarter of the total.[6] The French as a whole, it appears, were three times more likely to be peasants than the emigrants to a colony whose peasant economy would ultimately outlast France's own.

The figures for the elites are, on the contrary, inflated, particularly since they represent minimal estimates. The nobilities of robe and sword regrouped about 400,000 persons, or 1.5% of the French population on the eve of the Revolution; the bourgeoisie accounted for perhaps another 8.4%.[7] Proportionally speaking, emigrants to Canada included half again as many nobles and bourgeois as the society that produced them.

Table 4.1 Distribution of French emigrants to Canada by social class

Social class	Actual no.	Adjusted no.	Estimated %
Nobles	468	—	3.0
Bourgeois	1,968	—	12.5
Peasants	613	4,206	26.6
Laborers	895	2,255	14.3
Artisans	2,822	6,913	43.7
Total	6,766	15,810	100.1

Comparative figures for the final two categories, artisans and laborers, are nearly impossible to obtain because most historians have opted for a Marxist schema that classifies artisans as either bourgeois or proletarians according to their juridical status. Pierre Léon, for example, included journeymen in his estimate of *"ouvriers purs"* and their families,[8] while Jeffry Kaplow counted them among the "laboring poor." Only urban historians such as Jean-Pierre Poussou have begun to accord a separate place to "traditional artisans" regardless of corporate rank,[9] and their calculations do not apply to the general population.

Léon's estimate of 400,000 to 500,000 *ouvriers purs* forming, with their wives and children, a "population ouvrière" of between 1.2 million and 1.5 million persons is nonetheless telling. Including journeymen artisans, this group comprised only 5% to 6% of the French population in 1789, up from just over 1% at the beginning of the eighteenth century.[10] The proportion of laborers among emigrants to Canada, 14.3%, is more than double the later figure, in spite of both chronology and the exclusion of anyone with artisanal skills.[11] The colony thus possessed a disproportionate attraction for workers, just as it did for nobles and bourgeois.

This overrepresentation of nonagrarian wage earners comes as a surprise after my studies of Rouen and Paris, which suggested fairly low levels of purely proletarian involvement. Perhaps the reluctance to migrate applied only to ghettoized laborers, and particularly to those employed in large-scale capitalist industry of the type found in Rouen. Certainly, parishes where artisanal or commercial activities predominated also had their share of laborers: sailors, dock workers, carters, and the like. Some of these workers were "independent wage earners" who possessed little in the way of capital or skills yet contracted individually and directly with clients. Others were, of course, domestic servants. A clearer image of the laboring emigrants, or that portion of them whose identity is beyond dispute, will emerge from my examination of the occupational distributions. It is, however, clear that the cartography failed to tell the whole story and that, in an age of incipient geographical stratification, the absence of proletarian parishes was not equivalent to an absence of proletarians.

As for artisans, my maximal estimate of 44% bears a clear resemblance to the situation in large cities such as Bordeaux. There, according to Poussou, traditional artisans were the largest social group, representing roughly 45% of the population in the 1780s.[12] While remaining substantial, this proportion declined with the size of the agglomeration. Paul Bois has estimated that in Le Mans—which had 16,000 inhabitants, versus Bordeaux's 60,000, in the middle of the eighteenth century—journeymen artisans constituted about a third of the masculine population of the city.[13] Assuming a ratio of journeymen to masters of 3:1, and allowing for the wives and children of the latter, I obtain an artisanal population of about 6,500, or roughly 40% of the total. Rates in the countryside were much lower, but in a substantial bourg such as Troarn (Calvados), artisan households could account for nearly a third of the overall population.[14] An artisanal component within the sample of between 18% (my minimum estimate) and 44% was thus characteristic of a certain, essentially urban, France, although it surely had little in common with the social structure of the nation as a whole.

In spite of its speculative nature, my discussion of social class among emigrants to Canada enables me to draw two strong conclusions. First, members of every social condition participated in the movement, enabling a complete microcosm of French society to take root overseas. Second, the proportions of this microcosm were skewed in such a way as to reflect, and even exaggerate, the disproportionately urban origins of the emigrants. The overrepresentation of elites, together with that of artisans and laborers, is striking on an aggregate level, as is the underrepresentation of peasants; however, these anomalies disappear when one casts aside aggregates and concentrates on the minoritary urban sector. With all their imperfections, the data on social class both corroborate and clarify the findings of cartography. Every French region and every social class contributed to the migration stream, but they did so in proportions that presented a strangely one-sided image of the mother country.

Regional Variations

The social background of the emigrants did vary somewhat from region to region. Adjusting the regional figures in the same manner as above to eliminate the variable percentages of unknowns gives a rough idea of the regional patterns of class difference (see Table 4.2). All of the regions shared the two characteristics that marked emigration as a whole: participation of all classes, and underrepresentation of the peasantry; but these generalities also subsumed distinctions.

Table 4.2 Distribution of emigrants by social class and region

Region	Social class	Actual no.	Adjusted no.	Estimated %
Northwest	Nobles	93	—	2.0
	Bourgeois	453	—	9.7
	Peasants	220	1,356	29.2
	Laborers	439	1,076	23.1
	Artisans	675	1,672	36.0
Center-west	Nobles	40	—	1.7
	Bourgeois	233	—	10.2
	Peasants	238	541	23.6
	Laborers	183	312	13.6
	Artisans	680	1,167	50.9
Southwest	Nobles	29	—	2.4
	Bourgeois	172	—	14.1
	Peasants	28	276	22.6
	Laborers	52	104	8.5
	Artisans	323	643	52.5
Greater Paris	Nobles	75	—	7.3
	Bourgeois	192	—	18.8
	Peasants	13	71	6.9
	Laborers	24	97	9.5
	Artisans	142	589	57.5
East	Nobles	42	—	4.4
	Bourgeois	101	—	10.5
	Peasants	24	292	30.3
	Laborers	41	137	14.3
	Artisans	117	391	40.6
Loire	Nobles	27	—	6.8
	Bourgeois	43	—	10.8
	Peasants	28	106	26.6
	Laborers	15	37	9.3
	Artisans	75	186	46.6
North	Nobles	15	—	4.1
	Bourgeois	44	—	12.0
	Peasants	6	85	23.1
	Laborers	9	32	8.7
	Artisans	54	192	52.2
Massif	Nobles	8	—	2.3
	Bourgeois	45	—	13.2
	Peasants	8	112	32.8
	Laborers	10	23	6.7
	Artisans	67	154	45.0

Table 4.2   (continued)

Region	Social class	Actual no.	Adjusted no.	Estimated %
South	Nobles	12	—	5.2
	Bourgeois	36	—	15.7
	Peasants	1	18	7.9
	Laborers	9	51	22.3
	Artisans	20	112	48.9
Alps	Nobles	13	—	8.0
	Bourgeois	15	—	9.3
	Peasants	6	52	32.1
	Laborers	3	14	8.6
	Artisans	15	50	30.9

Let me first consider the balance between the elites and the popular classes. Three regions stood apart from the mean. At one end of the spectrum, the Northwest and Center-west sent comparably low numbers of nobles and bourgeois: under 12% respectively. At the other extreme, the Paris region sent more than double that figure (26%). The normal range as defined by all the other regions was between 15% and 21%, as compared with the national average of at most 10%.

The affinity between greater-Parisian elites and emigration comes as no surprise, given the capital role played by Paris in organizing the process of colonization. Indeed, I already suspected it upon discovering the gentrified geography of Parisian emigration. The relative paucity of elite departures from the Northwest and the Center-west poses more of a problem, since it seems to clash with the bourgeois and commercial dominance of cities like Rouen and La Rochelle; however, the incongruity is only apparent. These two regions produced a smaller percentage of elite emigrants because the appeal of Canada cut very deeply into their populations; nearly 60% of the emigrants in the sample stemmed from either the Northwest or the Center-west. Popular emigration was thus strongest not in regions that harbored less highly developed elites but in regions where ties to Canada were important enough for migratory behavior to percolate through all levels of the population. Had Canada not fallen to the English shortly after its commercial center of gravity shifted from the Northwest and the Center-west to Bordeaux, it is likely that the popular component of southwestern emigration would have expanded analogously.

Taking the elite classes separately, the relative plethora of nobles from all regions of the Paris Basin probably reflects the seigneurial roots of a substantial part of Canada's administrative nobility. Many prominent nobles maintained double residences in the capital and a surrounding province (for example, Louis d'Ailleboust de Coulange, an early governor of Québec who divided his time in France between the Faubourg Saint-Germain and his estates on the Champagne-Burgundy border). In the Alps, the high percentage of nobles apparently testifies to a heavy recruitment of army officers; neither there nor in the *pays de grande culture* did nobles form an especially large part of the general population.

Paris and the South provided Canada with commercial as well as administrative cadres, which explains the prominence of bourgeois as well as nobles within their emigrant contingents. In the Southwest, the bourgeois element was no doubt important thanks to Bordeaux. The unusually high rate of bourgeois emigration from the Massif central is more surprising, in that it corresponds poorly to the social and economic structures of the region; as I discuss in a later chapter, however, certain migratory traditions appealed particularly to the Massif's bourgeois—for example, the important migratory streams linking Limousin and Auvergne with Spain.

FURTHER VARIATIONS in the social structure of emigration surfaced at the level of province, department, and city, some of which again appear to have been accidents of recruitment. Thus, Brittany's emigrants to Canada included only 1% of nobles to Normandy's 3%, although the former province was "particularly rich in gentlemen."[15] The Norman figure turns out to have been inflated by the nearly 10% of noble emigrants from Calvados, an anomaly stemming from the emigration of two clans of local *hobereaux* (country gentle folk), the Le Gardeur and the Le Poutrel. They had been recruited by their curé, Jean Le Sueur, who had embarked, in turn, at the instances of a cartographer friend from Rouen.[16]

Other deviations from the norm are more easily anticipated; for example, the high proportion of laborers from Brittany (sailors), or the relative unimportance of peasant emigration in Seine-Maritime as compared with

Manche. In Rouen the proportion of elite emigrants (16.7%) approximated their distribution within the city, although the ratio of artisans to laborers (5:1) was uncharacteristic.

The same juxtaposition of representative and unrepresentative proportions affected emigration from the Center-west. La Rochelle's emigrants made up a fairly ordinary cross-section of the urban population, except perhaps for the overabundance of artisans.[17] Likewise, the social background of Rochelais from specific parishes quite precisely reflects what is known of the parish geography. Peasants came predominantly from the semirural zone of the city, where they accounted for about 20% of the population and 17% of the emigrants; elsewhere, the proportion of peasants did not exceed 5%. Elite emigrants, whether bourgeois or noble, were twice as common in the center-city as outside of it, and, in the maritime zone, artisans were especially numerous owing to the concentration of shipbuilding trades. In the Vendée, on the other hand, nobles virtually never emigrated to Canada, and bourgeois did so more frequently than in Upper Poitou, even though there were fewer of them. The emigrants of La Rochelle thus presented a fairly faithful image of the society that produced them, while those of the Vendée distorted that image significantly. A great city apparently could mobilize its entire population for overseas adventure more successfully than could the countryside.

Outside the Northwest and the Center-west, subregional variations conformed to the same binary pattern. Among emigrants from Bordeaux, these differences mirrored the social structures of the locality: fewer nobles and peasants together with more laborers and bourgeois. Farther from the Atlantic, however, in Languedoc, Auvergne, and Paris, they revealed far more about the social selectivity of emigration than about the populations from which the emigrants were drawn. Languedoc and Auvergne produced nobles with a propensity to migrate overseas; 6% to 7% of their emigrants were noble, a proportion that far exceeds both the regional averages and the weight of nobles in the provincial populations. Overrepresentation also occurred in Paris, where emigrants belonging to the nobility comprised 9% of the total. Finally, at the other end of the social scale, Parisian laborers were unattracted by the possibilities of colonial emigration. Although a great metropolis, Paris proved no more able than most rural regions to interest all of its classes equally in emigrating.[18] Outside of the great Atlantic seaports, it seems, emigration to Canada appealed primarily to the most cosmopolitan elements of a population.

The Social Class of Women

The social background of female emigrants differed from that of emigrants overall, just as the cartography of women's origins diverged from the general cartography of emigration. For women too, the margin of uncertainty was high, as 1,265 of the 2,137 female emigrants could not be classified. The remainder consisted of 70 nobles, 329 bourgeoises, 68 peasants, and 310 artisans, defined as women who belonged by birth or marriage to artisanal families. Dividing the unknowns among the last three categories based on the urban/rural distributions (3:1 in favor of towns) and the recorded ratio between artisans and laborers (also 3:1), I obtained the estimates shown in Table 4.3.

The unrepresentativity of emigrants as a whole was, once again, even more pronounced in the case of women. The probable peasant component shrank from over a quarter to under a fifth of the sample, with the difference accruing to both the urban *petit peuple* (lower class) and the noblewomen and bourgeoises. The proportion of noblewomen and bourgeoises was virtually identical to that of wealthy residents within a large city; Jean-Pierre Bardet has estimated that 19% of Rouen's inhabitants ranked above the artisan class in 1730.[19] As for women of artisanal background, their weight in the emigrant population was also comparable to that in great cities. The social origins of female emigrants were thus

Table 4.3 Distribution of women emigrants by social class

Social class	Actual no.	Adjusted no.	Estimated %
Nobles	70	—	3.3
Bourgeois	329	—	15.4
Peasants	68	384	18.0
Laborers	95	332	15.5
Artisans	310	1,022	47.8
Total	872	2,137	100.0

an extreme case of the situation already described. Characteristically urban elements predominated, and, while my estimates are subject to caution, these elements appear to have prevailed to an even greater degree than the already skewed urban/rural distributions would seem to suggest. The women who embarked for Canada were a very peculiar cross-section of the French population indeed.

Regional and subregional variations are harder to discuss in the case of women because the numbers involved were often too small to be significant. It can, however, be stated with certainty that elite emigration was highest in the Paris region and lowest in the Center-west, and that the Northwest approximated the Parisian model. Northwestern women were, as a whole, better born than northwestern men, a discrepancy that was particularly acute in Lower Normandy. While elite migrants of both sexes made up under a quarter of the total emigration from Calvados, fully half of the department's emigrant women belonged to the elites.[20] Regional migration streams of men and women could thus be socially as well as geographically distinct; the appeal of overseas migration for the different levels of society varied in part as a function of sex.

Noblewomen were concentrated more heavily in the provinces of the Paris Basin, from Normandy to Burgundy, than in the capital itself; the *damoiselles* were a class, not of urban administrators, but of *filles à marier*. Bourgeoises came in greater numbers from Paris, peasants from the Northwest, and women of the urban *petit peuple* from Poitou-Charentes. In social terms, the migrant women of the great cities tended to resemble their male counterparts.[21]

The survey of women's social origins thus essentially confirms the picture derived from geography; the primary contrast between male and female emigrants lay in the unequal importance of town and country. Acceptable migratory behavior was obviously sex-specific, as evidenced by the overall sex ratio of 1:8; and women could face severe strictures in their attempts to move to the colonies.[22] Urban women were apparently in a better position to overcome such negative attitudes than women from the countryside. Canada's first *habitantes* were drawn not from the ranks of the peasantry but rather from townsfolk of different classes, whose wider experience enabled them to engage more easily in projects as speculative as colonial migration.

Occupation

Fortunately, a study of social origins need not be restricted to more or less risky hypotheses about social class. The sources provide better information about the particular than the general, or about occupation than status. Some type of occupation could be ascribed to three-quarters of the emigrants in my sample (11,990, to be exact), up from two-fifths in the case of social class. A total of 333 different occupations or combined occupations were recorded; combined occupations were very important, accounting for fully half of the designations.

Whether simple or combined, most of the 333 occupations were too highly specialized to count more than a few emigrants apiece among their adherents. In fact, more than a third of them were sui generis, accounting for only 1 percent of the emigrants of known occupation. It therefore makes sense to aggregate the individual occupations into sectors of activity. The fifteen sectors chosen, together with their respective shares of the emigrant population, are set forth in Table 4.4.

The most striking thing to note about the table is the crucial role played by the military in maintaining the migratory flow between France and Canada. Military personnel of the various ranks and trades made up the largest occupational sector in the sample, encompassing nearly a third of emigrants whose occupations were identified and nearly a quarter of emigrants overall. Since Mario Boleda has estimated a total of 13,076 military emigrants for Québec during the French Regime, these men (excluding the Acadians) represent between a quarter and a third of the soldiers and officers who set sail for Canada. The undercounting, however, occurred mostly at the expense of the soldiers, owing to more careful recording of the officers as men of higher status. Distinguishing between officers and soldiers, my information pertains, respectively, to about four-fifths and one-quarter of Québec's military emigrants.[23]

The importance of the catchall category "Miscellaneous", representing nearly a quarter of the total, stems from its inclusion of three numerically significant but distinct groups: deportees, women for whom marital status was the sole occupational mention, and children. Other components of it were purely incidental; for example, one *page du roi*, one explorer, and one pirate. The 579 deportees represent about two-thirds of the prisoners deported to Québec and Acadia in the eighteenth century. A few of them

Table 4.4 Distribution of emigrants by occupational category

Category	No. of emigrants	% of emigrants
Military	3,655	30.5
Transport and other services	1,208	10.1
Building and woodworking	755	6.3
Maritime trades	658	5.5
Textiles and clothing	595	5.0
Church	444	3.7
Agriculture	409	3.4
Commerce	345	2.9
Metal trades	297	2.5
Food trades	292	2.4
Medicine	156	1.3
Administration and law	153	1.3
Luxury artisans	23	0.2
Diverse artisans	49	0.4
Miscellaneous	2,951	24.6
Total	11,990	100.1

were *fils de famille* whose relatives employed lettres de cachet to exile rather than imprison them, but by far the largest number consisted of wrongdoers of a commoner sort: smugglers, poachers, and deserters.[24]

The women in this category include the vast majority of female emigrants, a mere 5% of whom declared another occupation: 60 nuns, 34 servants, 4 washerwomen, 5 midwives, and 6 schoolteachers. Age and marital status were thus the defining characteristics of women who emigrated to Canada; in the estimation of contemporaries, if not in fact, the roles of child, wife, and mother subsumed most other functions that women might fulfill within or beyond the confines of the family.

Looking at these women more closely, one finds that 1,305 were prospective brides, 387 wives, 95 widows, and 228 children.[25] Taking into account that among the women "professionals" 3 servants, 1 schoolteacher, 1 washerwoman, and 2 midwives arrived in the colony as married women, then 1,440, or more than two-thirds, of the emigrant women were marriageable. Adding in the female children who in time would become so unless they entered the church, the figure rises to over three-quarters. That only 400 women accompanied or followed husbands to Canada underscores the limited place of nuclear families within the migratory stream. The number of children aged fourteen or under, 528 in all, further indicates that families that did emigrate were small. Perhaps couples preferred to move in the early stages of family formation, when they were still relatively unencumbered by children; since there were five boys for every four girls, however, it is also possible that some of the daughters chose to remain in France.[26]

The maritime and nonprofessional service sectors, with over 15% of the emigrants, were also quite diverse. Most of the occupations in the latter category carried the status of unskilled or semiskilled laborer: carter, chimney sweep, porter, domestic servant, washerwoman, and the like. More amorphous, however, was the term *engagé*, which pertained less to an occupation than to a temporary juridical arrangement. Although this term was used for classification only when nothing further could be ascertained about an emigrant's work, indentured servants accounted for 913, or more than three-quarters, of the people involved in nonprofessional services. In the maritime sector, the most common occupation was that of sailor, which marked over 400 people as members of the laboring class. The remaining emigrants were divided almost equally between those of artisanal status, notably ship's carpenters, and those of more elevated rank, such as ship's captains and navigators.

The other occupational categories were more homogeneous socially. Among the more "elevated" professions were the church, commerce, medicine, and administration and law. The contribution of the church to Canadian colonization has been estimated by the PRDH at 786: 728 priests and monks and 58 women religious.[27] Since my sample contained 444 church people, of whom 60 were women,[28] its representation of priests was somewhat better than that of soldiers. Still, the gaps in the data were not evenly distributed chronologically, but concerned the eighteenth century almost exclusively.

The commercial sector, as defined in the sample, included merchants, merchants' clerks *(commis)*, and contractors. Artisans were arbitrarily excluded, whether or not they employed the title *marchand*, but vendors such as Pierre Verpillon of Besançon, who had "traveled through France selling small wares from town to town for several years," were retained.[29] Emigrants who became *traitants*, or fur traders, shortly after their arrival in Canada also came under this category.

About 300 of the emigrants in the sample pursued medical or governmental careers; however, undercounting affected the functionaries to a greater degree than the medical personnel, particularly in the eighteenth century. Governmental service involved a broader range of emigrants than did medicine, from viceroy or governor at the top to usher or postman at the bottom. The medical sector consisted overwhelmingly of surgeons, who were just beginning to claim higher than artisanal status for their once mechanical métier. Some of them, like the Percheron Robert Giffard, doubled as pharmacists, but rare were those who possessed a university medical degree.[30] Like the surgeons, the several midwives, according to the documents, exhibited a competence that was already paraprofessional.[31]

On a less elevated plane, the agricultural component of French emigration to Canada regrouped some 400 people, or 3.5% of the sample. Of the agrarian professions mentioned by the emigrants, that of *laboureur* (plowman) was the most frequent, followed by *défricheur* (land clearer), *journalier* (day laborer), and gardener. More specialized occupations, such as vintner, occurred more rarely, in spite of the prominence of winegrowing regions among the areas of emigration.

In all the other sectors, artisanal activites predominated. Building and woodworking occupied 755 emigrants from forty-five different professions, nearly all of them artisanal. Only 18 men, mostly architects, could lay claim to bourgeois status, and only 23 described themselves additionally as *laboureurs* or *défricheurs*. Three professions alone provided almost two-thirds of the sector's overall total, with more than 100 emigrants apiece: carpenter, joiner, and mason. Coopers and stonecutters were also numberous, in contrast to less essential or more specialized trades such as plasterer or cabinetmaker.

In the textile and clothing trades, the artisanal sector garnered nearly nine-tenths of the total, to the detriment of both the capitalist sector and those who exercised rural by-occupations.[32] The most popular trades were those of shoemaker and tailor, which together accounted for almost two-thirds of the industry's emigrants. Wig makers were a distant third with 9%. The capitalist sector of the industry, or that concerned with textile manufacture, produced only 11% of the emigrants. More than two-thirds of them were weavers, with carders, drapers, dyers, and silk workers comprising the rest. Only a handful of emigrants, such as the merchant manufacturer of silk or the *marchand drapier drapant*, belonged unequivocally to the upper echelons of these trades. Perhaps by emigrating to Canada, they intended to become involved in a less specialized branch of commerce.

The Social Origins of Emigrants by Occupational Sector

Because the different occupational sectors often embraced emigrants of widely divergent backgrounds, it worth reconsidering the question of social origins in the context of these broad categories. The army was perhaps unique in the degree to which it incorporated people of very different social and professional backgrounds; but prisoners, women, and even clerics were also recruited from a variety of social milieux.[33] Artisanal emigration also deserves a second look, for the qualifications of artisans could vary considerably depending on both the trade and the stage of training.

The social origins of the military officer class suggest the existence of, if not a meritocracy, at least a meritocratic mentality on the part of administrators. In only one-third of the cases was there clear evidence of nobility, although, on the other hand, only 14 persons were revealed to be of unequivocally humbler status.[34] One suspects that the majority of officers were either nobles or bourgeois who had adopted noble ways. Although the use of titles, the only sure indication of nobility, was not widespread, the nobiliary particle was employed nearly universally.

The backgrounds of emigrant soldiers and noncommissioned officers exhibited far more variety, as Table 4.5 reflects. Nobles made up 3.4% of the men whose origins were known, and bourgeois 33.5%.[35] Comparing these figures with those André Corvisier amassed in his study of recruits serving in metropolitan France indicates that nobles and bourgeois were overrepresented among Canadian soldiers, but at the expense of peasants exclusively.[36] Laborers and artisans appeared in proportions more or less consistent with French norms.

The secondary occupations of military emigrants, like their social backgrounds, were somewhat distinct. Table 4.6, although based on a limited number of cases,[37] points to the exceptional prominence of four sectors: textiles and clothing, medicine, building and woodworking, and metal trades. The most frequent single occupations were surgeon, tailor, shoemaker, joiner, merchant, cannoneer, wig maker, *laboureur,* and mason, each of which logged 10 or more practitioners. The prominence of tailors

Table 4.5 Distribution of military emigrants by social class (officers excluded)

Social class	Canada (17th–18th c.)	France		
		1716	1737	1763
Nobles	3.4%	1.1%	1.2%	0.2%
Bourgeois	33.5	14.7	13.8	11.1
Peasants	9.7	37.9	30.5	29.7
Laborers	9.1	7.6	12.2	15.6
Artisans	44.3	38.6	42.2	43.3
Total	100.0	99.9	99.9	99.9

Table 4.6 Distribution of military emigrants by secondary occupation

Category	No. of emigrants	% of emigrants
Textiles and clothing	82	23.6
Medicine	59	17.0
Building and woodworking	48	13.8
Metal trades	36	10.4
Agriculture	20	5.8
Commerce	19	5.5
Administration and law	18	5.2
Food trades	18	5.2
Transport and other services	16	4.6
Luxury artisans	10	2.9
Maritime trades	9	2.6
Diverse artisans	9	2.6
Church	2	0.6
Miscellaneous	1	0.3
Total	347	100.1

and shoemakers accords with the findings of Corvisier, who has speculated about their particular vulnerability to economic downturns.[38] Bakers, however, whom he also cited in this regard, were not especially conspicuous among the Canadian troops.[39]

It is also interesting, although not easy, to consider the qualifications of military artisans as defined by their juridical status. Military documents tended to eschew corporate as well as caste distinctions in favor of a more functional definition of labor; the few appellations that appeared concerned trades as diverse as *laboureur*, carpenter, and musician, and referred more to capacity than corporate status. Nonetheless, my sample contained 27 masters, representing 12% of soldiers in their respective trades, 6 *compagnons* (journeymen), and 6 *garçons* (shop boys) or apprentices. This proportion of masters far exceeds that noted by Corvisier for the domestic army (2%), reflecting either a more elite recruitment policy on the part of the colonial troops or a more archaic mentality among their administrators.

THE SOCIAL ORIGINS of the other "mixed" groups of emigrants were more elusive, although scattered indications could be assembled. Among deportees, the 50-odd *fils de famille* clearly came from prosperous backgrounds. Perhaps the most illustrious among them was Charles-Antoine Ménager, chevalier de Courbuisson and a nephew of the *procureur général* of the Parlement of Paris, Joly de Fleury. Not all of them were nobles, however; the father of Daniel Portail served as the mayor of Saint-Florent-le-Vieil, an Angevin "town" of 1,000 inhabitants, and François-Joseph de Vienne was the son of a *marchand bourgeois*.[40] As for the prisoners of a commoner sort, their social antecedents could not, unfortunately, be determined from the cursory lists that survive.[41]

The social backgrounds of single women, married women, and children were difficult to compare owing to the disparate quality of the available information. A social class could be ascribed to nearly three-quarters of the wives and children, while an identical proportion of marriageable women consisted of unknowns. The proportion of elite emigrants, however, was apparently higher among the families than among the *filles à marier:* 23% as opposed to 15%. A full 4% of the wives and children were noble, nearly double the rate for the women who came to Canada in search of a husband.

Finally, the social origins of slightly more than a fifth of Canadian clerics could be determined. The one incontrovertible conclusion concerns the key role played by the nobility; 5.5% of the men and 9 of the 60 women belonged to both of the privileged orders. Bourgeois family backgrounds, or those identified with certainty, at any rate, accounted for a further 12.6% of the total. Only 7 emigrants came from indisputably humbler circumstances, most of them artisanal; but further research must determine whether or not they were atypical.

A CLOSER EXAMINATION of the backgrounds of artisanal emigrants to determine their level of qualifications was also fruitful, despite the reticence of the sources in this regard. Most of the emigrants who worked in Canadian construction possessed a general and probably versatile competence in their specialty. Carpenters could be house framers or cartwrights, just as joiners could be finish carpenters or furniture makers. Lack of specialization, however, by no means signified lack of skill, as examining the juridical ranks of the workers demonstrates.

Collectively, nearly one-quarter of the workers from fifteen different trades designated themselves as master, journeymen, or apprentice, and the first appellation numerically dwarfed the other two combined by 118 to 36. Even if all the artisans of unknown status were novices, a group of masters representing more than 15% of all builders and woodworkers was large enough to provide expert supervision and ensure the perpetuation of the various crafts.

Juridical rank was mentioned less often among maritime than among military or construction artisans, and the predominance of masters over workers was far less marked.[42] Nonetheless, the qualifications of maritime artisans were not necessarily inferior to those employed in the construction industry. Instead, the silence of the sources reflects the increasingly capitalist structure of this sector of the French economy. The Arsenal of Rochefort, from which a number of Canadian artisans were recruited, employed only 3 master carpenters to supervise the labor of up to several hundred *ouvriers charpentiers*. For the workers, "the bell regulated starting and mealtimes, resumption and quitting times."[43] Cooking fires and cabarets were forbidden at the workplace, and in 1666, a "reform" suppressed twenty traditional holidays. Wage differentials between workers and masters were enormous, with job security applying only to masters. In a word, the corporate arrangements of the Ancien Régime were already thoroughly obsolete in this sector, and with them, the need to label artisans according to their position in a discredited social order.

In the clothing and textile trades, juridical rank was mentioned rarely, although more often than in the maritime trades, and the ratio of masters to workers was quite different from any encountered so far. Only 45 clothing artisans qualified themselves as masters (less than half of the percentage for the building industry), while the count for *compagnons, garçons,* and apprentices was a hefty 44. In spite of their imperfections, these data suggest that the artisanal contribution of the clothing industry was of significantly lower quality than that encountered in building. Perhaps clothing workers emigrated more readily than wage earners in construction, owing to a more precarious economic position, or perhaps, as is equally likely, a recruitment policy favoring crucial skills artificially inflated the ranks of experienced builders. In any case, one wonders how these partly trained clothing workers fared upon arrival in Canada, for even with its elites and military, the colony seems unlikely to have provided sufficient employment for its hundreds of cobblers and tailors, its 26 tanners, or its 15 button makers.

The characteristics already discussed with regard to the building industry, on the one hand, and the clothing industry, on the other, presented themselves in the case of metals and foods in exaggerated form. Metalworkers comprised a particularly skilled portion of the emigrant workforce, while, by comparison, food workers were very poorly qualified. The most frequently mentioned trades in the two industries were blacksmith, gun smith, locksmith, and toolmaker (191 emigrants in all), and baker, miller, and cook (220 emigrants). Artisans of the first type almost certainly found a better market for their skills in Canada than those of the second.

The remaining artisanal categories, the diverse and luxury trades, did not involve large numbers of people. The unclassified artisans included mattress makers, candle makers, upholsterers, and even a sugar refiner; it is impossible to assess their individual and collective levels of skill, though it seems fair to assume that they were low. Luxury artisans, on the other hand, were highly qualified, whether engaged in clock making, sculpting, *orfèvrerie* (gold- or silversmithing), printing, or bookselling.

It is unclear whether practitioners of the *métiers d'art* felt that emigration to Canada would further their careers. The available evidence is inconclusive, although the case of the emigrant Pierre Boisseau would suggest that they did. Born in Aurillac (Cantal) in 1724, Boisseau came to Paris at the age of thirteen to learn the craft of clock making. He found work with a master on the Ile de la Cité, then the center of the luxury trades, perhaps with the assistance of a female cousin who was already established in Paris. Ten years later, when he informed his family that he intended to emigrate to Canada, he received a letter from his brother "in which he congratulates him on his future establishment."[44]

Far more ambiguous is the example of the Sevestres, a family of Parisian printers and booksellers who resided, as required by law because of their occupation, in the Faubourg Saint-Jacques. Their involvement in printing went back to 1543, when Louis Sevestre, the son-in-law of a printer, joined the master printers' guild himself. His son Thomas became the "imprimeur-libraire juré" of the University of Paris in 1586 and passed the trade on, in turn, to his son. Charles and Thomas Sevestre, who emigrated to Canada with their widowed mother in 1636, belonged to the fourth generation of master artisans.[45]

The immediate impetus for their departure was probably the publishing efforts of the *imprimeur-libraire* Louis Sevestre, which, in 1633, included *Les Voyages de la Nouvelle-France occidentale dicte Canada* by Samuel de Champlain. In addition to the *Relation* of the colony for 1631, the work contained *La Doctrine de Ledesme traduite en Canadien par le Père Brébeuf* and the *Oraison dominicale traduite en montagnard*.[46]

While the mechanism of the Sevestres' recruitment appears clear enough, their motives in actually departing remain mysterious. Continuing their trade was not possible in a colony where, in spite of widespread literacy, no printing presses existed until the English conquest.[47] If the Sevestres intended to establish one, their efforts have left no trace, and it is not even certain that they continued to engage in bookselling after their emigration.[48] General commerce and, later, legal functions occupied Charles until his death in 1657; Thomas drowned while on an expedition to the Iles de Bellechasse in 1640.

A final note on artisanal qualifications relates to agricultural emigrants, a number of whom, surprisingly, accompanied their occupation with the title of master or journeyman. Some, such as salt workers or charcoal burners, arguably possessed artisanal skills, but the rubric was also applied, on occasion, to gardeners.[49] Gardening, it turns out, was anomalous among the agricultural professions in that its practitioners often resided in suburbs or cities, belonged to "specialized and statutory corporations," and could even embark upon the Tour de France.[50]

The Regional Origins of Emigrants by Occupational Sector

Before I conclude this study of occupation, it is important to consider the regional origins of emigrants by occupational sector, for these too varied, revealing the existence of different patterns of recruitment from one profession to the next. The overall geography of emigration was, to some extent, an artificial construction; it resulted from the coming together of separate migration streams that could be professionally, as well as socially or sexually, distinct. Military emigration is a case in point, even though the sheer volume of this sector would lead one to expect a distribution approximating the overall pattern.

The geography of military recruitment, in fact, differed from that of emigration generally, although every French province provided Canada with soldiers. Relatively speaking, military emigrants came in greater numbers from the Northeast and Southwest than did civilians. The Center-west was somewhat less important for soldiers, as were Ile-de-France and Normandy, but with 15 percent of the total, Brittany remained clearly in first place.

The outlines of this geography are in striking contrast to those traced by André Corvisier in his study of domestic regiments in the eighteenth century. He found that "the West and Southwest abandoned more and more to the East and North the role of furnishing soldiers," to the point that the army practiced "insignificant recruitment in Brittany, in the Generality of La Rochelle, and in Bordelais."[51] Lower Normandy, Lower Languedoc, and Dauphiné continued to be important, but only exceptionally, the latter out of poverty and the former as a "frontier province."

Corvisier was careful to point out that his conclusions applied only to the armies recruited for service in Europe, and that the colonial troops, in particular, could be very different. In the case of Canada, military recruitment amalgamated regional traditions of military service with those of colonial emigration. Champagne, Lorraine, and Franche-Comté all played a greater role thanks to their military vocations, but, at the same time, Brittany, the Southwest, and Normandy remained important. Where the colonies were concerned, *racoleurs* (military recruiters) apparently searched in the same places as their civilian counterparts; it was easier to talk up Canada in Bordeaux than in Cambrai. Brittany's crucial role in supplying troops appears less anomalous when one recalls that between 1683 and the Seven Years' War, the navy rather than the army assured the defense of Canada, and that Brittany was a privileged zone for naval recruitment. Furthermore, the Breton aversion to military service seems not to have extended to that part of the province that produced the most emigrants, the region of Saint-Malo. Saint-Malo was, throughout the eighteenth century, an important garrison town.[52]

Comparisons of the urban geography of Canadian and domestic recruitment are harder to make, for the number of Canadian soldiers recruited in any one town was rarely impressive. Only in Paris did it exceed 100, and of that number only 63 described their residence within the city. These figures, although small, suggest that colonial and domestic *racoleurs* worked in somewhat different ways within the capital.

Corvisier described a variegated pattern of domestic troop recruitment, in which multiple small zones of activity and inactivity intertwined. The Cité, university, and aristocratic neighborhoods figured among the more dormant areas, in contrast to Châtelet–Les Halles, Saint-Paul, the Faubourg Montmartre, and the major north-south artery formed by the rues Saint-Martin and Saint-Jacques.[53] The Canadian pattern, to the extent that it is known, was far more unified. Leaving aside the 12 soldiers furnished by the various penal establishments, 32 of the 63 came from the parishes of "la ville." Parishes signaled by Corvisier as unimportant, such as Saint-Gervais and Saint-Roch, appear as frequently in my sample as, for example, Saint-Germain-l'Auxerrois. The Faubourg Montmartre, on the other hand, produced only 2 soldiers for Canada, while the aristocratic Saint-Germain captured second place with 9. The only real point of overlap was the irrelevance of the two islands, which were content to send 1 soldier apiece.

Recruiters for Canada therefore seem to have concentrated their efforts on the ancient, populous parishes of the right bank as a whole, but on none in particular. When they ventured across the river, they concerned themselves less with the older parishes than with the Faubourg Saint-Germain, a predilection that perhaps reflected the importance of the Foire

Saint-Germain as a locus of recruitment.[54] In any case, the soldiers of Saint-Germain were mostly humble folk, including 2 masons, a shoe-maker, a wig maker, and a saddle maker.

This unusual pattern of recruitment probably came about because recruiters for the colonial troops did not ordinarily concentrate on Paris but merely began there before moving on to areas on the western sea-board.[55] As a result, they could not be expected to know the capital as well as did recruiters for the domestic troops, or to have as many clearly defined itineraries within the city.

OTHER OCCUPATIONAL GROUPINGS among the emigrants also exhibited distinctive patterns of regional recruitment. The origins of the deportees, to the extent that they could be ascertained, reflected the geography of the crimes for which most of them were convicted.[56] Smuggling of salt and other contraband was a major, if clandestine, industry in parts of the North and East, notably the borders of Brittany, Flanders, Burgundy, and Dauphiné.[57] These same borders tended to produce disproportionate num-bers of deportees; Bretons, Angevins, Champenois, and Burgundians were particularly prominent within the forced-labor contingent. The largest number of deportees nonetheless hailed from Ile-de-France—evidence of the crucial role played by the capital's prisons in this particular type of colonial recruitment. Among the *fils de famille* deported by lettre de cachet, the mayor's son Portail, as a non-Parisian, was something of an exception.

The regional recruitment of women was more complex, for it varied substantially according to age and marital status. If single women were largely responsible for the overall pattern described in Chapter 3, the picture for married women and children was quite different. Although regions to the north of the Loire and the Charente continued to predomi-nate, Perche, Alsace, and Brittany gained in importance, primarily at the expense of the *pays de grande culture*.[58] Picardy, Champagne, and Or-léanais, which were major suppliers of *filles à marier*, cut a much weaker figure where families were concerned. Alone among the major sources of female recruitment, Normandy and Aunis sent streams of both single and married women to Canada. Other provinces showing a rough equilibrium between single and married women emigrants were Saintonge and Angoumois in the Center-west, and Anjou and Touraine in the Loire Valley.[59]

Thus, it was largely the Atlantic provinces that produced single and married women alike. Only emigration from the West, it seems, was massive enough to involve families as well as individual emigrants, the poor as well as the rich. Brittany and the Southwest were exceptions to this rule, in that they did not produce many single, female emigrants. As more backward societies, they must have curtailed the freedom of movement enjoyed elsewhere by single women, so that to the extent that women moved from these areas at all, they did so as members of their families.

Returning to a simpler pattern, the geography of maritime emigration was particularly specialized. Except for the Loire Valley and the Paris Basin, each of which produced small numbers of mariners, France's coastal regions dominated this occupational category. Brittany and Normandy sent the largest numbers of emigrants, followed by Aunis and Gascony; Saintonge, Poitou, and Guyenne; and, finally, the Mediterranean. The relative unimportance of Guyenne, with 3 percent of the emigrants, seems to conflict with Bordeaux's preeminent position in colonial trade in the eighteenth century. "However, the Bordelais were not mariners," and even in its heyday the city relied on the other maritime regions to complete its crews. The origins of Bordeaux's sailors, as mapped by Christian Huetz de Lemps, resemble those of the mariners who embarked for Canada; Brittany, Saintonge, Gascony, Provence, the Loire, and the Seine all complemented the Aquitain contribution, although the greater distance attenuated the supremacy of the Northwest.[60]

For ecclesiastics, the geographical distribution emphasized Paris and the Northwest, particularly Normandy and Brittany. It did not differ significantly between men and women. The Center-west, although a region of intense missionary activity, produced very few vocations for Canada. In the seventeenth century especially, its Protestant heritage remained strong, and the integral Catholicism of the Vendée lay far in the future. The Southwest also seemed marginal to clerical recruitment, particularly the Pyrénées, which, in the nineteenth century, would produce Bernadette Soubirous. Missionary zeal with regard to Canada emanated not from France's periphery but, with the exception of Brittany, from its center. As a product of the Paris Basin and the Massif armoricain, it constitutes a clear instance of the Loire's undisputed, if intermittent, function as a cultural divide.

The geographical provenance of the other "elite" groups—commercial, medical, and administrative personnel—was unique. The regional origins of commercial emigrants reflected the geography of colonial trade in general and the Canada trade in particular. The Atlantic provinces predominated with Aunis and Normandy in the forefront, followed by Gascony, Guyenne, and Brittany. Not surprisingly, Ile-de-France also cut an important figure. Medical people also came from the Atlantic seaboard, but particularly from the Southwest. The most involved province, Gascony, provided more than 10 percent of the emigrants. Legal and administrative cadres, on the other hand, were recruited mainly north of the Loire, and proximity to the Atlantic failed to produce significant migration from the Southwest. Paris was important but did not predominate; Normandy, Brittany, the Loire, and other provinces of the Paris Basin all contributed a share.

The regional recruitment of the various categories of artisans also deviated from the overall norm. Among construction workers, the province of Aunis moved from third into first place, with neighboring Poitou and Saintonge also increasing their shares. The Northwest remained in a very strong position, but the Southwest was much less important except for Gascony, which channeled Basque carpenters to Canada from the earliest years of the seventeenth century. Curiously, France's traditional reservoir of itinerant construction workers, the Massif central, made a rather modest contribution to Canada's building industry. Limousin and Marche did, it is true, quadruple their proportional shares, but to the east, those of Bourbonnais and, especially, Auvergne declined to virtually nothing. The migratory networks of Auvergnat building workers, discussed in Part Two, neither fed naturally into the Canadian migratory stream nor were tapped in a significant way by its recruiters.

The origins of clothing and textile workers were very varied, but the great textile-producing regions did not stand out with especial clarity. Maine and Anjou garnered a larger percentage, but Languedoc did not, and the proportion of emigrants from Normandy actually decreased. The explanation no doubt lies in the preponderance of artisans, who plied their trades in every province in France. In fact, the only provinces missing from my sample are the Comtat, whose clothing workers were perhaps more likely to be Jewish, and distant Alsace. At least one Alsatian tailor, Pierre Masson of Belfort, did arrive in Canada, but only after a yearlong stint as a *compagnon* in Poitiers, where, in 1750, he joined the Canadian troops together with another worker from his shop.[61]

The distribution of metalworkers bore some relation to the implantation of French forges, but the identity was by no means complete. Burgundy, Franche-Comté, Maine, and Perche increased their shares as expected; Champagne, Lorraine, Guyenne, and Berry did not.[62] In Poitou and Gascony, emigration apparently outstripped the largely unremarkable metallurgical sectors in importance. The reasons for the imperfect correspondence probably have to do again with the vagaries of recruitment. Like other emigrants, metalworkers came most readily from the Atlantic provinces, but in special cases, such as the establishment of a foundry in Trois-Rivières, recruiters enlisted them from farther afield. While Burgundy and Franche-Comté became the purveyors of choice, they need not have done so. As was pointed out in the two previous chapters, organized efforts of recruitment sometimes had a determinant influence on the geography of recruitment.

Lastly, in the food trades, the salient geographical trait was the heightened importance of the Center-west and Aquitaine, both of which regions exported wheat and flour to the colonies. In Aquitaine, moreover, the food trades were particularly receptive to immigrants and attracted people prone to mobility; Bordeaux's corporation of pastry cooks admitted large numbers of Parisian and Swiss immigrants throughout the eighteenth century.[63] This combination of greater openness with the direct tie to Canada most likely explains why the food workers of southwestern and central-western France eclipsed those of other regions among the emigrants.

Summary

The social origins of French emigrants to Canada, like their regional origins, were representative of a very particular sector of the French population. Indeed, the peculiarity was almost as much geographic as social, since the social pyramid among the emigrants resembled that within France's great cities: very few peasants, a healthy contingent of elites, and a huge number of artisans. Comparing the emigrant pool to the overall population indicates that the poor were everywhere underrepresented, especially so in rural areas and at a distance from the Atlantic seabord. The artisanal component was particularly ample, if exceedingly varied in terms of training and qualifications. Soldiers, who made up nearly a quarter of the sample, also played a disproportionate role, as could be expected in a colony that never captured the popular imagination to the same degree as other colonial or European destinations.[64] Nonetheless, currents could be traced within the overall migration stream that were occupationally and socially as well as sexually distinct. Single women, for example, came both from different regions and humbler backgrounds than their married counterparts.

The only real absentee from the movement, in relative terms at least, was the French peasant. In this most modern of migration streams, rural backgrounds accounted for merely a third of the emigrants, specifically agricultural ones for perhaps a fourth. French Canada's subsequent history as a citadel of rural traditionalism cannot be explained in reference to an influx of sturdy, pious, and backward-looking Vendéens. Such a group unquestionably emerged, but, ironically, it did so from roots that were urban, mercantile, and above all mobile.

CHAPTER | # 5

Religious Diversity: Protestants, Jews, and Catholics

Just as their regional and social origins marked French emigrants to Canada as essentially modern, so too did their religious origins, which were characterized by diversity. The presence of religious minorities in New France, while numerically small and legally tenuous, characterized the entire French Regime and presented an ongoing challenge to the monolithic conceptions of the colony's administrators. The changing ideological climate in France determined whether the Canadians actually tolerated or simply refused to acknowledge the scattered, unconverted Protestants in their midst. Unconverted Jews, on the other hand, could at no time declare their faith openly and remain in Canada.

For the most part, civil and religious authorities succeeded in obtaining conformity to Catholic practice from French emigrants regardless of their religious backgrounds, and any significance that minority backgrounds retained was probably cultural. The cultural component alone, however, justifies an examination of the emigrants whose religious antecedents distanced them from mainstream French society. For example, whether in France or the diaspora, Huguenot identity often persisted despite religious conformity.[1]

As for the Catholics, the main question concerns the roots of their subsequent history of legendary orthodoxy. Yet it does not appear that most ordinary emigrants were especially pious, and, indeed, there are several indications to the contrary. Missionary zeal seems to have been confined instead to relatively few proponents of the Catholic Reformation, most of them religious. Furthermore, even among this group, a number of women stood out for their strikingly modern notions of the irrelevance of gender to evangelical enterprise.

Protestants

Beginning in 1627, French law explicitly forbade Protestants to settle permanently in Canada. Early attempts at ecumenical colonization had raised a certain amount of havoc, particularly in Acadia, as described by Samuel de Champlain:

> I have seen the Minister and our Curé get into fistfights over the difference in religion. I do not know who was the most valiant, and who threw the best punch, but I know very well that the Minister complained sometimes to Sieur de Mons [the king's lieutenant-general, himself a Protestant] of having been beaten, and resolved the points of controversy in this fashion. I leave to you to think whether that was fair to see; the Savages were sometimes on one side, sometimes the other, and the French, mingled according to their diverse belief, said abominable things of both religions, although Sieur de Mons made peace as best he could.[2]

This particular dispute continued into the following year, 1605, when both clergymen were stricken with scurvy. They died within days of each other, and, according to Marc Lescarbot, the Picard lawyer who became the first chronicler of the colony, the sailors "put them both into the same grave, to see whether dead they would live in peace, since living they had never been able to agree."[3]

The charter of the Compagnie des Cent Associés, promulgated by Cardinal Richelieu in 1627, stipulated in article 2: "Without it being permitted, however, for the said associates and others to send any foreigners to the said places, thus to people the said colony with native French Catholics, and those who command in New France shall be enjoined to see that the present article be executed exactly as written, not suffering it to be contravened for any reason or occasion, lest they answer for it personally."[4]

This exclusion, which, it should be noted, applied to those emigrants recruited with a view toward *peopling* the colony, remained in force throughout the French Regime.[5] Richelieu put it into effect for several reasons, not least among them the internal dissensions described above. He could not but have been aware of them, for, in 1616, the Catholic hierarchy inaugurated a sustained anti-Protestant lobbying campaign complete with book burnings and vitriolic pamphlets. In 1626, for example, the Récollet Joseph Le Caron wrote that "those who say derisively that what our priests consecrate at the altar is a White John, that his Holiness is the Antichrist, that if they could get their hands on the God of the papists, they would strangle him, . . . [and] on the last monk, they would eat him, who say that the . . . antiphons we sing in honor of the Virgin Mary are hangman's songs, are not suited to execute such a design [to plant the Catholic, Apostolic, and Roman religion, plus to discover, people, build, clear, and maintain there all native Frenchmen who would like to live there]."[6]

Nonetheless, that Richelieu proved susceptible to this propaganda speaks less to his ideological commitment than to his political concerns. The charter of the Cent Associés became operative on 6 May 1627, at a time when the threat of Protestant treason weighed heavily on Richelieu's mind. Indeed, the final ratification took place outside of La Rochelle preparatory to the yearlong siege that deprived the Protestants of the last of the fortified cities granted to them by the Edict of Nantes.[7] In the case of North America, external considerations in the form of the neighboring English compounded the danger posed by potential Protestant disloyalty. Religious ties had outweighed national allegiance more than once in recent memory, and Richelieu refused to risk a mass defection of French Protestants to the thirteen colonies or, even worse, a takeover of New France engineered by the English with Protestant complicity.

The charter of the Cent Associés did not put an end to the Protestant presence in Canada, owing partly to its own ambiguity and partly to lackadaisical enforcement. Lucien Campeau has shown that the period from 1627 to 1663 witnessed the arrival in the colony of "a good many by the vessels of the company," although his qualification, "without, to our knowledge, ever having been disturbed" is more dubious.[8] One thinks, for example, of the case of Daniel Vuil, the only emigrant executed for the crime of sorcery under the French Regime. Vuil was a Huguenot miller who arrived in Canada in 1659, the same year as Bishop Laval, and who abjured his religion in order to marry an adolescent whom he had met on the voyage. The girl's parents, alleging his "bad morals," refused their consent, and shortly thereafter accused him of employing malefice to torment their daughter with demons and specters. Laval took it upon himself to investigate, and the dossier he compiled contains a revelatory "permission to inform against Vuril [*sic*], who, relapsed into heresy, nonetheless abuses the sacraments."[9]

Vuil's execution notwithstanding, Protestants continued to arrive in the colony. In 1670 Laval addressed a memorandum to the king accusing them of holding "seductive discourses," distributing books, and assembling amongst themselves "to celebrate the religion." Six years later, the Conseil supérieur de Québec remained concerned enough about the situation to promulgate a law stipulating that "Protestants do not have the right to assemble for the exercise of their religion under pain of chastisement," but adding that "Protestants can come to the colony during the summer," and even spend the winter, provided that they live "as Catholics without scandal."[10]

The Conseil's distinction between temporary and permanent migration and its willingness, however reluctant, to condone the former were implied by the original wording of the exclusion, and this interpretation of it prevailed for most of the French Regime. In the 1740s, for example, Protestant merchants from Montauban, La Rochelle, and Rouen sojourned unmolested in the colony, some for a season, others for several, and still others for many years. The Rouennais merchant house of Dugard, nominally Catholic itself, maintained two permanent factors in Québec in the decades prior to the conquest, and both of these men, François Havy and his cousin Jean Lefebvre, were Protestants from the pays de Caux.[11] Protestants also figured among the crew members who each season laid anchor in the port of Québec.[12]

The only period during which de facto toleration of temporary Protestant migration did not exist was, predictably, between 1685 and 1715. As Marc-André Bédard has pointed out, though, the hostile ideological climate did not alone account for the almost total disappearance of Protestant merchants from the colony; economic difficulties, specifically, the disruption of commerce in the wake of virtually continuous warfare, made the Canadian trade a less than attractive proposition.[13]

Protestant settlement, as alluded to above, was another matter altogether; from 1627 on, permanent residents of Québec and Acadia were required to be Catholic. Nonetheless, Protestants and emigrants of Protestant background did establish themselves during the French Regime. Bédard's research has yielded, in addition to 231 Protestant prisoners of whom little is known, 477 Protestants who settled more or less definitively in New France. Of these, some 232 were either French Huguenots or else European Protestants (Swiss and Germans primarily) who arrived as soldiers of the French army; the rest appear to have made their way to Canada, either voluntarily or under duress, from the Anglo-American colonies. The emigrant sample considered here included 110 of the 233 European expatriates mentioned by Bédard, as well as 51 others.[14] Since these last, 37 men and 14 women, also, for the most part, settled in Québec, I can estimate the domiciled Protestant population at about 300, exclusive of the Anglo-Dutch element. This number is by no means insignificant, especially when one considers that it is roughly equivalent to the number of Percheron or Angevin colonists from the same period.

THE REGIONAL ORIGINS of the Protestant emigrants in my sample do not accurately reflect the implantation of Protestantism in France as a whole. The Atlantic provinces dominated Protestant emigration as they did Catholic, and the eastern provinces sent few Protestants in spite of their strong reformed traditions. Only within the Atlantic provinces did the distribution of Protestant emigrants more or less resemble that of the religion itself.

More than three-fifths of the Protestants came from the central-western provinces of Aunis, Saintonge, and Angoumois. Curiously, the sample did not include any Poitevins, although Protestantism was important in Lower Poitou, and even more so in the Niortais.[15] Poitou's Protestants did not, in principle, refrain from emigration; of the 26 indentured servants who left Chef-Boutonne (Deux-Sèvres) for the Antilles between 1643 and 1714, 3 came from Protestant families and 2 from families that were divided along religious lines.[16] Bédard, moreover, listed 7 Poitevins in his sample, so their absence from this one may have been purely coincidental (see Table 5.1).

After the Center-west, Canada's Protestants stemmed preferentially from Normandy, Guyenne, and Languedoc. The parts of these provinces that were involved were noteworthy as Protestant strongholds, if not for their ties with Canada. Périgord and Quercy were more important than Guyenne proper, and 5 of the 7 Languedociens came from Gard or Ardèche rather than Toulousain. Generally speaking, the figures of Bédard

Table 5.1 Provincial origins of Protestant emigrants to Canada

Province	My sample	Bédard's sample
Aunis	79	80
Normandy	16	15
Saintonge	11	16
Guyenne	9	13
Languedoc	7	5
Brittany	3	3
Alsace	2	3
Angoumois	2	5
Gascony	2	1
Ile-de-France	2	5
Béarn	1	0
Comtat	1	0
Dauphiné	1	0
Foix	1	0
Poitou	0	7
Provence	0	2
Touraine	0	1
Total	137	156

were in agreement with mine. The central-western provinces claimed an even greater share of the total in his sample than in mine, but in neither did the Swiss and German border regions (as opposed to Switzerland and Germany proper) provide more than a token contribution.

The urban/rural distribution of Protestant emigrants bore even less of a resemblance to that of emigrants overall than did the provincial distribution. Of the 139 people for whom a community of origin was known,[17] only 19 came from villages or bourgs, while fully 86% were urban. Furthermore, over three-quarters of the town dwellers had abandoned cities of more than 10,000 inhabitants, first and foremost among them La Rochelle. Like emigration overall, Protestant emigration was both concentrated and dispersed, with 69 emigrants coming from La Rochelle,[18] and 1 or 2 from most other communities. Only Rouen and Marennes (Saintonge) fell somewhere in between, with 7 and 5 Protestants respectively.

The social origins of Protestants were also uncharacteristic—first of all, because they were better known. A social class could be attributed to

102, or nearly two-thirds, of the Protestants in the sample; of these, there were 9 nobles, 33 bourgeois, 4 peasants, 21 laborers, and 35 artisans. It is difficult to draw firm conclusions from such small numbers, but the one that does emerge is the relatively elevated social status of Protestants as a group. More than a quarter of all Protestants belonged to the elites, and close to a tenth were actually noble. Like their French counterparts, Canadian Protestants constituted an economically privileged, if legally disadvantaged, population.

The occupational structure of this population is fairly clear, with information available for more than four-fifths of the emigrants.[19] The most important category, soldiers and officers, accounted for a similar percentage of Protestant as of overall emigration, just under one-third. Corvisier's observation that in France "the proportion of Protestants in the army was much higher than what it was in the population" does not apply to the Canadian troops; the figure in both cases was about 1 percent. Though in some regions the army may have provided Protestants with a refuge and even facilitated their emigration, those regions clearly did not include the major source of Protestant emigration to Canada, the Center-west.[20]

Other branches of activity peopled by Protestants in my sample included commerce, carpentry, the maritime trades, and the clothing industry. Commerce did not predominate over the other options, but it might have had the sample included temporary emigrants more consistently. Regardless of the prohibition against Protestant settlement, at least 11 Protestants arrived as indentured servants. Religious controls in the exit ports must sometimes have been lax, or perhaps the demand for colonial labor provided sufficient incentive to circumvent them.

The sex ratio within this emigrant group was quite unusual: 1 in every 4 Protestants was female, as opposed to 1 in every 8 emigrants overall.[21] Most of these women emigrated as *filles à marier*, but there were also 5 married women, 2 domestic servants, and 1 child under the age of fifteen. The reasons for this enhanced female presence are not entirely clear. Perhaps, as Louis Pérouas has suggested, women were simply more amenable to conversion than men.[22] Emigrants must have been aware that residing in Canada would require outward conformity to Catholicism, at the very least; and such a prospect may well have have elicited different responses from the two sexes. A second possibility has recently been suggested by Nelson Dawson, who believes that French ecclesiastics sometimes dumped on the colony impoverished young women whom they had "saved" from Protestantism and placed in institutions. In shipping them to Canada, so the argument goes, they hoped to prevent these women from returning to their Protestant milieu, while at the same time freeing themselves from the obligation to support them.[23]

Jews

French Jews did not benefit from religious toleration, even before the revocation of the Edict of Nantes in 1685. The limited toleration promulgated by the edict applied to Protestants alone—a fact made painfully explicit by the renewed expulsion of French Jews in 1615:

> Considering that the Christian Kings, we read in Isambert, viewed with horror all enemy nations of this name and especially that of the Jews, whom they never wanted to suffer in their kingdom . . . , and since we have been informed that in contravention of the edicts and ordinances of our said predecessors, the said Jews have for several years been spreading, disguised, into several places of this our kingdom . . . We have . . . declared:
>
> > That all Jews who are in this our kingdom shall be held on pain of death and confiscation of all their property to vacate and withdraw from the same, forthwith, and this within a month's time.[24]

In actuality, the Jewish communities of Bayonne, Bordeaux, and Metz escaped the consequences of this edict, but its implications for Jewish settlement in Canada were clear. If Jews could not legally inhabit France, still less could they expect toleration in the most rigidly orthodox of French colonies.

There are only two recorded cases of emigrants who avowed their Judaism publicly during the French Regime, one in Acadia and one in Québec. The Acadian example concerns a Dutch Jew who embarked for Québec in 1752; why and for how long is unknown. His religion first came to the attention of his fellow passengers in midocean, and they responded by performing a preliminary baptism aboard ship, repeating it with due solemnity during a stopover in Louisbourg. According to Louisbourg's chaplain, the first of April of the year 1752, the man named Joseph Moïse Kel by the baptism he received on the royal frigate *La Friponne* bound for Québec, in the supplements to baptism that were solemnly supplied in the royal chapel of St. Louis . . . , was given the name of Jean Antoine Moïse, born in Mastrait [Maastricht] in Dutch Brabant, aged forty-eight years and three months, Jewish by nation. Who, after having been instructed in the truth of the Catholic, Apostolic, and Roman religion, and having recognized the falsity and horror of the Judaizing religion in which he had lived until the present, renounced this religion, and promised, by oath on these holy gospels, that he would faithfully uphold all the duties of the Catholic, Apostolic, and Roman religion for the rest of his life; in consequence of which . . . I, the undersigned, administered to him the ceremonies of baptism, and received his solemn abjuration, and absolved him of the excommunication incurred by him. He had for sponsors messire Jean Louis Comte de Raymond, chevalier, seigneur of Ayx, La Cour, and other places, brigadier in the King's armies, His Majesty's lieutenant for the town and château of Angoulême, Governor and Commander of Ile Royale, Ile Saint-Jean and their dependencies, and dame Marguerite Elizabeth de Degannes, wife of messire Louis Boisseau, chevalier of the military order of St. Louis, . . . naval lieutenant.[25]

One may surmise that this hapless Jew intended to engage in trade, particularly since the Jewish merchant firm of Abraham Gradis dominated Canadian commerce in the final years of the colony. The exceptional nature of the story nonetheless implies that Gradis would generally have employed Christian factors to handle his Canadian business. One doubts that many Jewish merchants, particularly prominent ones, would have willingly risked such scenes of forced conversion as the one described above. As for Kel himself, neither the vital records nor the hospital registers of Québec provide any indication of his passage or continuing residence there.

The other case, which preoccupied officials in both France and Québec for an entire year, has become a near legend among Canadian historians. The episode began in September of 1738, with a panicked letter from the intendant of Québec to the naval minister, asking for instructions on how to deal with a particularly troublesome emigrant. He identified the culprit as one Esther Brandeau, "about twenty years old, who embarked in the quality of passenger in boy's clothing under the name of Jacques Lafargue." According to the intendant, Esther, who claimed to be the "daughter of David Brandeau, Jewish by nation, merchant in Saint-Esprit Diocese of Dax near Bayonne," explained the circumstances surrounding her untoward arrival in the colony as follows:

> Five years ago her father and mother put her aboard a ship in the said place . . . to send her to Amsterdam to one of her aunts and her brother; . . . the ship having been lost on the Bayonne sandbar in . . . 1733, she fortunately escaped to land with one of the crew members; . . . she was taken in by . . . [a] widow living in Biarritz; . . . two weeks later she left, dressed as a man, for Bordeaux, where she embarked in the capacity of ship's cook, under the name of Pierre Mansiette, on a small boat . . . destined for Nantes; . . . she returned on the same vessel to Bordeaux, where she embarked once more in the same capacity on a Spanish vessel . . . that was leaving for Nantes; . . . upon arrival in Nantes she deserted and went to Rennes where she placed herself in the capacity of journeyman in a tailor's shop . . . , where she remained six months; . . . from Rennes she went to Clisson, where she entered into the service of the Récollet Fathers in the capacity of domestic servant and errand boy; . . . she remained for three months in this convent, which she left without warning to go to Saint-Malo, where she found asylum with a baker's wife . . . with whom she remained for five months, rendering a few services for the lady; . . . she went next to Vitré to look for a post; there she went into service . . . [with a] former infantry captain of the Queen's Regiment whom she served for ten or eleven months in the capacity of lackey; . . . she left this post because her health did not permit her to continue caring for the said gentleman . . . ; the said Esther, returning to Nantes . . . , was taken for a thief and arrested by the constabulary of the said place and led to the prison of Noisel, from which she was released after twenty-four hours because they realized their mistake; she went then to La Rochelle, where having taken the name of Jacques Lafargue, she embarked as a passenger.[26]

The French authorities ratified the intendant's decision to place Esther in the Hôpital général, but insinuated that her continued presence in the colony would be contingent on conversion. In the meantime they contacted her father, who declined to intervene, stating "that he still had eight children at home, and that his other children were dead." The matter remained unresolved until September 1739, when the intendant wrote once again to inform his superiors of Esther's refusal to cooperate and imminent deportation: "She is so flighty that she has not been able to adjust either to the Hôpital général or to several other private homes where I had her placed. The concierge of the prison took charge of her in the last instance . . . She has not conducted herself absolutely badly, but she is so flighty that she was at different times as docile as she was surly toward the instruction that zealous Churchmen wanted to give her; I have no other choice than to send her back."[27]

Esther embarked for La Rochelle in the fall of 1739, and by the following May the case was closed to everyone's satisfaction. Everyone's, that is, except Esther's. Unfortunately, nothing is known of the young woman's subsequent existence.

Esther's adventures are doubly interesting to the historian because of her unabashed defiance of two sets of norms, the religious and the sexual. Transvestism of the sort practiced by Esther was not unheard of during the Ancien Régime, and it seems to have been surprisingly successful. While the women whose stories have been preserved were, like Esther, eventually found out, many of them inhabited the male world unimpeded for considerable lengths of time. Their most daring field of endeavor was perhaps the army, in which at least 15 women enlisted and served in the eighteenth century.[28]

The rigid separation between male and female spheres of activity worked to the advantage of these transvestite women. By simply engaging in activities such as soldiering and sailoring that were reserved exclusively for men, they compelled society to view them as such. Discovery occurred only when they lost their nerve, committed sexual indiscretions, or found themselves in an environment as well policed as Canada.

Canadian officials were nearly as concerned with Esther Brandeau's unfeminine behavior as with her religion, and they asked her about it point-blank. Her explanation, however, did not allude to her sex at all, but rather presented her conduct as the result of a religious choice: "Having requested the said Esther Brandeau to tell us what reason she had to disguise her sex thus for five years, . . . she told us that having escaped the shipwreck in Bayonne, she ended up in the home of Catherine Churiau, . . . that she gave her pork to eat and other meats that are forbidden among the Jews, and that she resolved at this time never to return to her father and mother in order to enjoy the same freedom as the Christians."[29]

Esther's rebellion against the sexual roles available to her appears virtually total today, yet she herself viewed it as incidental to her true rebellion, her rejection of the constraints imposed upon her by religion.

The unequivocal refusal of administrators to sanction the presence of avowed Jews in Canada did not necessarily extend to those willing to embrace the Christian faith. The conversion of Joseph Moïse Kel presumably enabled him to continue on to Québec, and even the incorrigible Esther received a yearlong grace period in which to mend her ways. By the same token, the arrival of Marranos in the colony seems to have passed unremarked. Protestantism was the real threat to religious orthodoxy in the eyes of the authorities, and their suspicions fell upon the emigrants from La Rochelle to the exclusion of those from Bordeaux and Bayonne.

Most of the evidence about Marrano emigrants is conjectural, including any estimation of their numbers. Joseph da Silva *dit Le Portuguais,* a creditor of the New French government resident in Montréal, was almost certainly a Jew; Joseph Costes, a wine merchant from Gaillac (Tarn), and Jacob Coste (Costa) may have been as well. Genealogical research has revealed that Etienne Gélineau (Gélinas) and his son Jean, carpenters who embarked for Canada in 1658, were of Jewish origin. At the time of their departure, they resided in the hamlet of Tasdon, outside of La Rochelle, but Etienne was raised in Saint-Vivien of Pons (Saintonge), an ancient Jewish quarter. Although the family had been nominally Christian since 1558, "the Canadian Gélinases preserved numerous Jewish traditions like circumcision, the laying on of hands, the paternal blessing, and the familial Saturday evening [*sic*] supper."[30] In the words of Benjamin Sack,

> although these are isolated instances, it is nevertheless abundantly clear that the descendants of former Marranos who had renounced Judaism were to be found in Canada at various periods of French sovereignty. We are therefore led to conclude positively that even those of Jewish origin were well received in the colony, providing that they desired and were able to embrace Catholicism. Their numbers must have been quite small. It need hardly be added that in every case they lived in harmony with the other colonists and intermarried with them.[31]

Between avowed Jews, on the one hand, and Marranos on the other, there existed an intermediate category of Jews who simply remained silent about their religion. Joseph Daniel Hardiment, a French sailor who lived in Québec from at least 1758 until 1760, is the one Canadian example of an emigrant from this category. The document containing his story, an unpublished testimonial of freedom at marriage that has not before come to the attention of historians, deserves to be quoted at length.

> The second of June 1767, appeared before us Marie Joseph Fornel, or-phaned daughter of the late Joseph Fornel and Josette Pelletier, native of the seigneurie of Neuville, parish of Saint-François-de-Sales, about twenty-two years old, currently living in Saint-François on Lake Saint-Pierre; who, desiring to marry in the said place, declared to us that at the age of about thirteen, she was taken clandestinely and without the consent of her parents by a certain man whom she knew was named Joseph Daniel Hardiment, sailor by occupation, absent from this country for seven years, and this for the space of two days, but having been informed that the said man was Jewish by nation, she left him immediately and withdrew to her parents' home in Pointe-aux-Trembles; . . . she produced a document drawn up by Master Luet de Lanquinet, royal notary in Québec, dated 1 June 1767, and left in our hands, in which two men named Didier Degres and Antoine Rouillard, day laborers living in this town, attested to having known the said Daniel Hardiment well for having helped him abduct the above mentioned Marie Joseph Fornel and having heard him, the said Daniel Hardiment, tell her that he was Jewish by nation and religion, having informed the said Marie Joseph Fornel of which, she withdrew from him and went to live in Pointe-aux-Trembles . . . ; taking into account the said document and the above-mentioned declaration, we de-livered a certificate of liberty to the above-mentioned Marie Joseph Fornel and gave permission to publish the marriage bans in Québec.
> [Signed] Perrault, canon, vicar general.[32]

Hardiment clearly considered himself a Jew and opted not to conceal the fact from his lover or his two close friends. His occupation, which entailed long shipboard stays and visits to places without organized Jewish communities, must have prevented him from observing his religion, but this suspension of observance should not be equated with conversion. Hardiment's elopement differed from the prevailing Canadian pattern in that it did not involve even the semblance of a Christian ceremony. In general, illegitimate couples preferred to contract marriages "à la gau-mine"; that is, they "would go to the church in secret, accompanied by two witnesses, during the mass celebrated by the parish priest. At the solemn moment of consecration, they would loudly declare that they took each other for man and wife, without further ceremony."[33]

Hardiment's two accomplices could easily have served as witnesses, but there is no evidence that they in fact did so. Indeed, it is possible that Hardiment's confession and his subsequent estrangement from Marie Joseph Fornel were triggered by her demand for a marriage *à la gaumine* and his refusal to undergo one. All this is mere speculation; what emerges clearly from the document is that Hardiment remained in the colony unmolested for about two years following his unfortunate escapade.

Catholics

The Catholic majority of New France lived, in the seventeenth century, in an atmosphere of missionary zeal. In the eighteenth century, the attachment to Catholicism was strong enough, despite the abatement of religious enthusiasm, to survive the English conquest; and well into the twentieth century, it successfully resisted competition from secular ideologies. Yet it would be a mistake to assume that French Canadians inherited their Catholic fidelity from an idealized feudal past, rather than adopted it through historical circumstance. For among lay emigrants, neither the common folk nor the colony's leaders were particularly inclined to rigorist devotion. On the contrary, a measure of popular indifference was evident in proscribed behavior, or even outright anticlericalism, and a modern mentality was often visible among the administrative elite. Catholic zeal was thus largely confined to the missionaries, some of whom themselves espoused untraditional ideas about gender that were quite alarming to the Catholic Church.

Complaints about the religious and moral laxity of French emigrants made themselves heard throughout the French Regime. In 1664, for instance, Colbert received an anonymous memorandum claiming that "the people taken at La Rochelle are for the most part of little conscience and nearly without religion, lazy and very slack at work, and very poorly suited to settle a country, deceitful, debauched, blaspheming."[34] The memorandum's author, whom the perspicacious minister assumed to be Bishop Laval,[35] was obviously motivated by fear of Protestantism; but since fewer than a tenth of the city's emigrants were of Huguenot background, his blanket condemnation also indicted a great many Catholics.[36]

Emigrants recruited with a view toward evangelical settlement might be expected to have been different, but even here testimony is ambiguous. La Dauversière's levy in La Flèche for Ville-Marie initially gave some concern to the religious establishment; however, the secular missionary (and saint) Marguerite Bourgeoys succeeded in converting them. "Shortly after their arrival in Québec," wrote the good sister, "these hundred men were changed like the linen one puts in the wash."[37]

The baron de La Hontan, a young army officer who served in Canada in the 1680s and 1690s, did not hesitate to describe Montréal as a clerical police state. In a letter home, he wrote peevishly: "At least in Europe you have the amusements of Carnival, but here it is a perpetual Lent. We have a bigot of a pastor whose inquisition is entirely misanthropic. One must not think, under his spiritual despotism, either of games, or of seeing the ladies, or of any party of honest pleasure. Everything is scandal and mortal sin to this surly creature."[38] Particularly galling to him was the mutilation by this pastor (who had entered his room without permission) of a fine edition of Petronius.

Yet La Hontan's own writings also provide a second and quite different perspective on life in late-seventeenth-century Montréal. For one thing, there was an escape valve for men in the form of the fur trade, which took them deep into the forests and far beyond the reach of any clerical meddling. La Hontan himself spent much of the winter of 1685 with an Algonquin hunting party, reading Homer, Anacreon, and his "dear Lucian," escapees of the mishap that had befallen Petronius.[39]

Worse yet in the eyes of the clergy, the fur traders brought their untrammeled spirits back with them when they returned to the city. "They plunge up to the neck into voluptuousness," La Hontan wrote. "Good living, women, gaming, drink, everything goes."[40] Behavior was, if anything, more boisterous when Indian traders came to town; rumors of their sexual contacts with French women may well have hastened the construction of the church's Jericho Prison "for women and girls of Ill repute" in Montréal in 1686.[41]

The rapid descent of Ville-Marie into decadence is confirmed by the judicial archives. In the seventeenth century, nearly 60 percent of all morals cases were tried within the jurisdiction of Montréal. Overall, there were about 150 cases of public debauchery, seduction, rape, prostitution, solicitation, adultery, bigamy, concubinage, and sodomy in the Saint Lawrence Valley before 1700, involving some 400 men and women from some twenty-five provinces and countries.[42] Meanwhile, rates of illegitimacy and prenuptial conceptions were consistent with French norms, despite a lopsided sex ratio favoring very quick marriages.[43] Missionaries notwithstanding, the behavior of the first French Canadians was no more profoundly Catholic than their urban and commercial origins might lead one to suspect.

More surprising are the expressions of overt anticlericalism, for such challenges to spiritual authority could have capital consequences even in France, where the influence of the Counter-Reformation was less ubiquitous. La Hontan, whose pre-Enlightenment attitudes are striking, was merely a bird of passage, if a socially prominent one. On the other hand, he surely spent enough years in the colony to make his opinions known, and he surely encountered some like-minded souls among the permanent colonists. He may, for instance, have frequented the popular tavern of Anne Lamarque *dite* La Folleville, who had already publicized her religious sentiments two years before La Hontan's arrival.

La Folleville, who was one of the few women to emigrate from Bordeaux,[44] was thirty-three years old and a highly successful innkeeper when, in 1682, Montréal's pastor (the same one who would so antagonize La Hontan) demanded a criminal investigation of her enterprise. The most insistent charges against her were adultery, promiscuity, and operating a house of prostitution, but there were ancillary suggestions of sorcery, abortion, and, not least, anticlericalism.[45] In the course of her trial, it became clear that she had neglected her paschal duty for years, and that she had no use for priests, Montréal's in particular. She reportedly cried for all to hear "that the best of priests was worth nothing," and that the pastor "was not worthy to say mass and that he committed so much sacrilege, being in mortal sin, that she threatened to beat him like a dog and tear his robe."[46]

An even more shocking case occurred in Montréal a few years later, when the merchant Jean Boudor provided some unorthodox theatrical entertainment to a select group of guests.[47] His soirée—which was attended by Catherine Le Gardeur de Repentigny, the wife of the civil and criminal judge of Montréal; her daughters Catherine and Barbe d'Ailleboust, aged twenty and twenty-six; Louise Bissot de la Rivière, the daughter of a seigneur; Marie Couillard, the wife of a lieutenant; and her daughter Marie-Anne Margane de la Valtrie, aged twenty, a goddaughter of Governor de Courcelles—was carefully planned at the tavern of Mathurin Guilhet by Boudor, his wife, and several officers of the Montréal garrison. As described in the court record, it involved Boudor "having purposely and wantonly gotten his factor and clerk drunk, intoxicated, and in a state of oblivion all the better to succeed in the infidelity he wished to commit by mimicking the holy ceremonies of the Church." Specifically, Boudor had "seized his said clerk in this state of drunkenness, put him on a tray for serving beer, . . . a blanket on top for a burial shroud, six bottles around, with lit candles inside, in place of candelabra and liturgical candles, a wooden cross on the said drunken clerk, a bucket full of water for holy water, and a bottle full of wine for a censer, and with this apparatus and equipment the said Boudor and several assistants chanted the Libera and other holy prayers of the Church in mockery and derision of our holy religion." As if that were not enough, a witness noted that one member "of the company had pissed in the mouth of the said clerk."[48]

This performance was remarkable in many ways, but the strangest thing about it was not that it occurred at all, nor that it was actually rehearsed, nor even that it was staged for the ladies of the colony and their marriageable daughters. It was that Jean Boudor, like La Folleville before him, got away with it, and got away with it in Sulpician Montréal, at a time when people in France were being drawn, quartered, tortured, and burned at the stake for lesser offenses. Montréal's "bigot of a pastor" was free to inform on people, and even to force them to defend themselves in court. But their punishment depended not on him, but on royal administrators who were clearly not of the same mind. The impunity of La Folleville and Boudor was perhaps exceptional, in that they both belonged to well-connected merchant families whom officials were reluctant to antagonize. A brief survey of church-state relations in New France nonetheless suggests that the king's representatives were, from beginning to end, more likely to oppose clerical demands than indulge them.

BISHOP LAVAL'S ARRIVAL in Québec in 1659 immediately sparked a series of disputes with the governor that boded ill for the political influence of the Canadian clergy. The earliest "quarrels of precedence," in which the two men jockeyed for power over such symbolic issues as church pews, incense, the host, and kneeling cushions, are often portrayed as typical Ancien Régime slapstick; yet they also illustrate the state's determined opposition to Laval's theocratic ambitions. That the governor would retain the upper hand became clear during the more serious dispute over the Indian liquor trade, which continued despite Laval's excommunication of virtually the entire merchant elite in 1663.[49]

Clerical power ebbed yet again when Louis XIV took direct control of the colony, for Colbert disliked Laval and wanted him subservient.[50] In the 1680s and 1690s, Governor Frontenac opposed the church on a number of issues, going so far as to abolish Montréal's prison for loose women after the inhabitants complained of clerical excesses.[51]

In the eighteenth century, according to Gustave Lanctôt, "the prestige and influence of the bishop and the clergy were at such a low ebb" that the king authorized the searching of religious houses and removed religious cases from the ecclesiastical tribunal to the civil courts.[52] The situation was even more extreme in Louisbourg, a city that grew to 8,000 inhabitants without ever possessing a parish church, and whose administrators exhibited a tolerant cast of mind, as evidenced in the sacrilege trial of Yacinthe Gabriel Lebon.[53]

Lebon, unlike La Folleville or Jean Boudor, was a penniless (though educated) recent emigrant when he was charged with sacrilege in 1753. One night while extremely drunk, he had entered the military chapel and begun fumbling with one of the niches in what he later described as an urge to redecorate. Of course, he succeeded only in knocking it down, cutting himself in the process, so he took a piece of altar cloth to bind up his wound and grabbed a couple of tapers in the vain hope of making it out past the sentinels. Although he was condemned to death at his first trial, the advocate in charge of his appeal made such a strong plea for leniency that Lebon was acquitted by the Conseil supérieur in 1754.[54]

Thus, neither Canada's habitants nor its administrators gave particular satisfaction to their spiritual leaders, who would probably be shocked by their posthumous reputation of sanctity. For the clergy of New France, imposing rigorist norms was an uphill battle, and despite their commitment to their mission, some singularly advanced notions were put forward there with complete impunity.

A FINAL EXAMPLE of religious modernity comes from within the ranks of the Catholic missionaries themselves. It concerns the single women of bourgeois and aristocratic lineage who not only demanded to emigrate on their own initiative but did so in the face of suspicion or even straight-forward opposition from the religious establishment.

The eagerness of women religious to pursue their vocations in Canada was evident from the early years of the colony. "What amazes me," the Jesuit superior Paul Le Jeune wrote from Québec in 1635, "is that a great number of nuns, consecrated to our Lord, want to join the fight, sur-mounting the fear natural to their sex to come to the aid of the poor daughters and poor wives of the Savages. There are so many of them who write to us, and from so many Monasteries, . . . that you would say they are competing to see who can be the first to mock the difficulties of the Sea, the mutinies of the Ocean, and the barbary of these lands."[55]

Pious laywomen apparently shared their impatience, as illustrated by an incident that occurred in the port of La Rochelle in 1641. According to the author of *Les Véritables Motifs*, a missionary tract, "even a virtuous woman of the place was suddenly so eager to go to Montréal that, nothwithstanding the difficulty and the remonstrances that were made to her, she entered the vessel that was leaving the port by force, resolved to go serve God there."[56]

The determination of *"ces Amazones du grand Dieu,"* as Le Jeune termed them, appears less surprising today than it did to the priest and his contemporaries.[57] Women participated actively, indeed prominently, in the mystical movement that swept across Europe in the sixteenth and seventeenth centuries. Nuns like Saint Teresa of Avila and laywomen like Marie Rousseau and the controversial Madame Guyon assumed visible public roles, even to the point of serving as spiritual directors to prominent churchmen. Women's assertive behavior with regard to New France thus related to their central place within Counter-Reformation piety and their unwillingness to be excluded from one of its characteristic manifestations: the attempted conversion of Native Americans.[58]

Women met with considerable opposition in their bid to become missionaries in Canada. Mother Marie de l'Incarnation, a widow from Tours who exchanged countinghouse for convent in 1631, initially failed to convince the Jesuits of the need for Canadian Ursulines. In 1635 Le Jeune counseled her and all those like her to wait: "But in passing I must give this advice to all these good Women, that they should take great care not to hasten their departure until they have here a good House, well built and well endowed, otherwise they would be a burden to our Frenchmen and would accomplish little for these Peoples. Men manage much better with difficulties, but nuns need a good house, some cleared lands, and a good income."[59]

The women, however, persisted, and in 1639 the first Ursulines and Hospitalières embarked together with Madame de la Peltrie, a lay missionary. The latter arranged for her departure more easily than the women religious, for she managed to secure the approval of Saint Vincent de Paul and of Father Condren, the superior of the Oratoire.[60]

Even after the initial missionaries established themselves, women sometimes faced obstacles in their attempt to emigrate. The Jesuits had acquiesced to their presence, provided they were not too numerous, but families and communities continued to resist the passage of wellborn daughters to the wilds of America. When Sister Saint-Augustin, a young noblewoman from Normandy, announced her intentions to serve in Canada, her father filed suit in the Parlement of Rouen to prevent her from leaving the country.[61] The Hospitalières of La Flèche, for their part, braved a full-scale riot while en route for La Rochelle because the inhabitants refused to believe that women would willingly undertake the Canadian journey.[62]

Female missionaries continued to worry the authorities after their arrival in Canada. Le Jeune had commented four years earlier on their desire to "submit to work that is surprisingly difficult even for men," and the threat of unfeminine behavior remained a leitmotiv of his narratives.[63] Madame de la Peltrie, who, as a laywoman, was not bound by convent discipline, concerned him particularly. In 1639, the year of her arrival, he reported somewhat derisively her conversation with a group of Indians: "I have brought scarcely any workmen, but I will do what I can to aid these good people; Father, she said to me, assure them that if I could help them with my own hands, I would do it with pleasure, I will try to plant something for them. These good Savages, hearing her discourse, began to laugh, saying that grains planted by such feeble hands would be too tardy."[64]

The following year Madame de la Peltrie was beginning to learn her place. In working with the Indians, she told Le Jeune, "my principal exercise is to dress them, to comb them, and to deck them out; I am not capable of anything greater." Her dissatisfaction remained palpable, however, and in 1641 Le Jeune observed that "she speaks to them with her eyes, being unable to speak to them with her tongue, and she would speak to them much more gladly with her hands. If she could exercise the profession of mason and carpenter to build them little homes and of plowman to help them cultivate the land, she would employ herself thus with . . . ardor."[65] Madame de la Peltrie left Montréal in discouragement in 1643 and retired to the Ursulines of Québec.

Missionary women thus succeeded in embarking for the colony through their own persistence, and once there they played an influential role in its development. They did not, however, do so on their own terms, but rather within the limited sphere of autonomy that a cautious ecclesiastical establishment, prodded by their protests, reluctantly conceded to them.[66]

Summary

Thanks to the modernity and diversity of the emigrant pool, the status of religious minorities in French Canada was far more ambiguous in practice than in principle. Both Protestants and Jews could reside in the colony for extended periods or even settle there, provided that they eschewed non-Catholic forms of worship. Protestants could, at most times, identify themselves without risking deportation. Jews, however, were well advised to keep their religion a secret. The case of Daniel Hardiment is unusual in that the revelation of his origins to several of his friends did not immediately precipitate his flight.

Unlike the British colonies to the south, Canada never provided a hospitable haven to dissenters of any sort, and the few who ended up there were in no position to defy authority. Nonetheless, small numbers of non-Catholics did succeed in carving out a niche for themselves in the long or short term, and their very presence testifies to the impossibility of recruiting a completely homogeneous society from a multiethnic and multireligious metropolis.

The case of Catholic emigrants demonstrates that religious zeal was not necessarily stronger among them than it was among the Protestants and Jews who opted for outward conformity to Catholicism. The missionary élan so celebrated by later generations of clerical French Canadians was evident only within a privileged minority with ties to the Catholic Reformation, and even here, as the Amazons of the good Lord could attest, it sometimes followed untraditional paths that were unsettling to the religious hierarchy.

6

The Age of Adventure in an Age of Expansion

At this point, only the emigrants' ages and dates of arrival are needed to complete this social and economic analysis of French emigration to Canada. The age distribution provides the finishing touches to an emigrant profile composed thus far of regional, social, and religious origins, and the chronology makes it possible to go beyond this static profile, important as it is. Whereas the portrait of the emigrants provides insight into the relationship of mobility to social and economic structures, an accurate time line elucidates the equally crucial connection between emigration and economic cycles. As I detail in this chapter, French emigrants to Canada were mostly young adults not yet inserted into their milieux who were seeking adventure. They left Atlantic France at a time of economic growth and expanding horizons, conditions that gave them hopes of earning a better living or even of amassing a small fortune in Canada.

The Age Distribution

The ages of the emigrants are less well known than their regional origins but are better known than their social class. An age could be ascribed to nearly 10,000 persons, or over three-fifths of the emigrants in the sample. Not all of these ages were accurate, however; aside from the obvious problem of approximation on the part of the emigrants, the age stated in a Canadian census need not have been the actual age at emigration. Emigrants were most likely to appear in the Canadian documents after they settled in the colony, and settlement usually transpired upon expiration of a term of service. In the case of civilian emigrants, the time lag was probably around three years, the length of an average term of indentured servitude. For military emigrants, it could be even longer, since soldiers routinely signed on for stints of six to eight years.[1]

Despite the margin of error, one clear conclusion emerges from the statistics: French emigrants to Canada were not normally distributed with regard to age. The age structure of a sedentary population resembles a pyramid, tapering away from the low ages toward the high,[2] but that of the emigrants looks more like a child's top: an elongated pyramidal shape with a triangular base. The underrepresentation of both the highest and lowest ages was a consequence of the often nonfamilial nature of the movement. As an option seized upon primarily by single people, emigration to Canada tended to be dominated by young adults (see Table 6.1).

The table reveals the importance of youth, though not of childhood, among the emigrants. Even with a time lag affecting perhaps half of the sample, nearly three-quarters of the emigrants counted were under thirty. Fewer than a tenth of them, however, were children under the age of fifteen, and more than half were young people in their twenties. Emigration fell off sharply over the age of twenty-nine, but emigrants in their thirties continued to outnumber children by a large margin. At no age did emigration dwindle off into complete insignificance, which is surprising given the known rigors of the transatlantic passage. One intuitively questions whether 75 emigrants actually waited to attain the age of sixty before embarking for Canada. It seems more likely that these cases involved emigrants whose earlier existence in the colony managed to escape the vigilance of the authorities.

A consideration of the emigrants' ages by year rather than age group demonstrates clearly the expected tendency toward approximation. The modal, or most common, age was twenty-five, and multiples of five and ten were generally prominent.[3] The yearly distribution of the emigrants in the highest age group confirms the suspicion that their belated arrivals were an artifact of Canadian record keeping; more than half of them (40) were at least sixty-five, including six elders between the ages of eighty-five and 100!

The age distribution exhibited some interregional variation, due, in part, to the uneven geography of familial emigration. Nowhere, however, were the emigrants' ages spread out normally; familial or not, emigration

Table 6.1 Age distribution of French emigrants to Canada

Age group	No. of emigrants	% of emigrants
0–14	592	6.1
15–19	1,515	15.6
20–24	2,773	28.6
25–29	2,217	22.8
30–34	1,190	12.3
35–39	618	6.4
40–44	342	3.5
45–49	221	2.3
50–54	112	1.2
55–59	55	0.6
60–64	75	0.8
Total	9,710	100.2

to Canada involved certain age groups at the expense of others.[4] The overall youth of the emigrants remained constant, although children and teens below the age of fifteen came in especially large numbers from Ile-de-France and the Center-west (see Table 6.2). The extreme youth of the greater-Parisian emigrants was not a by-product of the movement of families, for more than half of the children had reached the traditional age of appenticeship, twelve to fourteen. In contrast, the children from the Center-west were much more equally divided between infants, older children, and early adolescents.

The age group fifteen to thirty-five predominated everywhere, although some regions emphasized the earlier and some the later part of this spectrum. In Ile-de-France and the Center-west, where emigrants in their late teens and early twenties outnumbered those in their late twenties and early thirties, emigration and professional formation probably occurred simultaneously. At the other extreme, represented by the Massif central and the East, the age distribution suggests a higher proportion of emigrants whose training was complete. The differences in age structure between these regions could not be reduced to global differences in social class or occupation, nor did fluctuating sex ratios provide the answer. The regional age distributions instead had a specificity of their own, one that perhaps relates to the diversity of particular migratory traditions.

The example of the Cotentin lends weight to this hypothesis of local,

Table 6.2 Distribution of emigrants by age and region

Age group	Northwest No.	%	Center-west No.	%	Southwest No.	%	Greater Paris No.	%	East No.	%
0–14	232	6.1	170	10.3	14	1.6	75	9.9	27	3.9
15–19	586	15.3	302	18.3	97	11.2	188	24.7	74	10.7
20–24	1,025	26.8	478	29.0	277	31.9	221	20.0	182	26.2
25–29	868	22.7	312	18.9	240	27.6	138	18.1	210	30.2
30–34	455	11.9	166	10.1	146	16.8	67	8.8	104	15.0
35–39	256	6.7	95	5.8	44	5.1	38	5.0	57	8.2
40–44	169	4.4	48	2.9	24	2.8	48	2.9	16	2.3
45–49	105	2.7	44	2.7	11	1.3	44	2.7	10	1.4
50–54	63	1.6	16	1.0	7	0.8	0	0	6	0.9
55–59	33	0.9	8	0.5	2	0.2	0	0	1	0.1
60 and over	35	0.9	8	0.5	7	0.8	1	0.1	8	1.2
Total	3,827		1,647		869		820		695	

Age group	Loire No.	%	North No.	%	Massif central No.	%	South No.	%	Alps (No.)	Foreigners (No.)
0–14	20	6.8	11	3.9	1	0.5	1	0.7	1	4
15–19	36	12.2	43	15.3	20	9.3	17	11.3	10	17
20–24	87	29.6	94	33.3	66	30.6	51	33.8	25	29
25–29	59	20.1	70	24.8	75	34.7	46	30.5	25	20
30–34	58	19.7	33	11.7	33	15.3	15	9.9	13	16
35–39	8	2.7	13	4.6	12	5.6	7	4.6	7	11
40–44	8	2.7	8	2.8	3	1.4	9	6.0	3	2
45–49	11	3.7	3	1.1	3	1.4	1	0.7	3	3
50–54	3	1.0	3	1.1	2	0.9	1	0.7	1	0
55–59	2	0.7	3	1.1	0	0	1	0.7	0	0
60 and over	2	0.7	1	0.4	1	0.5	2	1.3	3	0
Total	294		282		216		151		91	102

age-specific migratory streams. Emigrants from Manche were heavily rural and heavily male yet also quite young; adolescents were especially numerous, with fifteen- to nineteen-year-olds constituting over a fifth of the whole. In fact, adolescent infatuation with Canada was one of the hallmarks of a demographic regime peculiar to southwestern Normandy in the eighteenth century. According to the testimonials of freedom at marriage, dozens of sons of *laboureurs, journaliers,* or rural artisans embarked for the colony as fishermen as soon as they were old enough to be deemed independent. Etienne Malenfant, who left his father's house for Gaspé after his first communion at the age of twelve, was probably precocious; on the other hand, Julien Lorence at twenty-one seemed a bit slow. A typical case, that of Guillaume Pellerin of Val-Saint-Père, concerned a boy fifteen to sixteen years old who set sail for Canada with "several persons" of his acquaintance.[5] Instead of serving as farm servants or apprentices, the peasant boys of the Cotentin routinely became *engagés de pêche.*

Despite the importance of particular, regional traditions, emigrants from the various social classes were somewhat globally distinct in terms of age (see Table 6.3). The modal age was the same, at twenty-five, for bourgeois, peasants, and artisans, but it rose to thirty-two for nobles, and declined to twenty-two in the case of laborers. Generally speaking, elite emigrants tended to be older than emigrants who worked with their hands. About three-quarters of the peasants, laborers, and artisans whose ages were known embarked for Canada before the age of thirty; the corresponding figures for nobles and bourgeois were 62% and 71%, respectively. Either wealthier people moved at a later stage in their careers or else, as is quite likely, professional careers took longer to launch than manual ones.

The age profiles of the various occupational categories bear out the idea that the emigrants' ages increased with social status (see Table 6.4). Excluding the catchall category, the two branches of activity with the highest proportion of emigrants under thirty were textiles and clothing, with more than three-quarters, and nonprofessional services, with more than four-fifths. Those with the lowest proportions were commerce (64%), administration and law (56%), and the church (45%).[6] The modal age for service workers was only twenty-two, as opposed to twenty-four or twenty-five elsewhere. The identity of this mode with that for laborers is significant, since most of these workers consisted of indentured servants

Table 6.3 Distribution of emigrants by age and social class

Age group	Nobles		Bourgeois		Peasants		Laborers		Artisans	
	No.	%	No.	%	No.	%	No.	%	No.	%
0–14	21	7.6	112	10.1	39	9.7	40	6.2	166	9.4
15–19	38	13.7	132	11.8	71	17.6	97	15.0	264	14.9
20–24	59	21.2	272	24.4	111	27.5	208	32.1	508	28.6
25–29	54	19.4	275	24.7	92	22.8	133	20.5	381	21.5
30–34	48	17.3	157	14.1	44	10.9	70	10.8	215	12.1
35–39	24	8.6	68	6.1	25	6.2	48	7.4	107	6.0
40–44	11	4.0	45	4.0	11	2.7	22	3.4	65	3.7
45–49	13	4.7	32	2.9	7	1.7	18	2.8	36	2.0
50–54	3	1.1	12	1.1	3	0.7	6	0.9	22	1.2
55–59	2	0.7	4	0.4	1	0.2	3	0.5	6	0.3
60 and over	5	1.8	5	0.4	0	0	3	0.5	4	0.2
Total	278	100.0	1,114	99.9	404	100.0	648	100.0	1,774	99.9

whose social class could not be determined. Their relative youth suggests that their failure to state an occupation was not coincidental, but rather an indication that they did not possess one; instead, they were relying on emigration to the colonies to provide them with an "estate." This conclusion accords with the findings of David Galenson that British indentured servants of unknown profession were also, in all probability, laborers.[7] In status-conscious societies, silence about one's qualifications is rarely value-free.

Once again, the women emigrants can be looked at separately. Age was a known quantity in better than three-quarters of all cases. As their modal age of twenty-one graphically illustrates, female emigrants were younger than emigrants overall (see Table 6.5). Although the shape of the two distribution curves is very similar, that of women alone is displaced toward the lower end of the spectrum by four years. Fully four-fifths of the female emigrants arrived in Canada before their thirtieth birthday, and about half were between the ages of fifteen and twenty-five.[8]

For women, as opposed to emigrants in general, social class was largely irrelevant to age. The sample size was inconclusive for nobles, peasants, and laborers, but where bourgeois and artisanal women were concerned, the age distributions were very similar.[9] Regional distinctions were more

Table 6.4 Distribution of emigrants by age and occupational category

Age group	Military No.	Military %	Transport/services No.	Transport/services %	Maritime trades No.	Maritime trades %	Building/woodworking No.	Building/woodworking %	Textiles/clothing No.	Textiles/clothing %	Agriculture No.	Agriculture %
0–14	30	1.6	27	3.4	13	2.8	3	0.7	2	0.6	3	1.3
15–19	279	14.7	197	24.8	49	10.7	64	14.2	55	17.7	39	16.5
20–24	601	31.7	291	36.6	138	30.0	143	31.6	111	35.7	69	29.1
25–29	481	25.4	146	18.4	106	23.0	106	23.5	70	22.5	63	26.6
30–34	245	12.9	59	7.4	72	15.7	58	12.8	40	12.9	26	11.0
35–39	125	6.6	34	4.3	35	7.6	44	9.7	14	4.5	14	5.9
40–44	61	3.2	16	2.0	19	4.1	13	2.9	9	2.9	13	5.5
45–49	36	1.9	13	1.6	16	3.5	12	2.7	3	1.0	4	1.7
50 and over	39	2.1	11	1.4	12	2.6	9	2.0	7	2.3	6	2.5
Total	1,897	100.1	794	99.9	460	100.0	452	100.1	311	100.1	237	100.1

Age group	Church No.	Church %	Commerce No.	Commerce %	Food trades No.	Food trades %	Metal trades No.	Metal trades %	Admin./law (No.)	Medicine (No.)
0–14	0	0	3	1.5	2	.99	1	0.6	0	0
15–19	16	4.5	30	14.8	20	9.9	21	11.8	4	7
20–24	60	16.8	51	25.1	67	33.2	61	34.3	22	27
25–29	84	23.5	45	22.2	57	28.2	45	25.3	31	28
30–34	99	27.7	38	18.7	34	16.8	26	14.6	13	9
35–39	53	14.8	15	7.4	14	6.9	7	3.9	9	3
40–44	21	5.9	10	4.9	4	2.0	11	6.2	10	4
45–49	16	4.5	5	2.5	4	2.0	2	1.1	8	4
50 and over	8	2.2	6	3.0	0	0	4	2.2	4	4
Total	357	99.9	203	100.1	202	99.9	178	100.0	101	86

Table 6.5 Age distribution of women emigrants

Age group	No. of women emigrants	% of women emigrants
0–14	251	15.4
15–19	365	22.3
20–24	446	27.3
25–29	256	15.7
30–34	131	8.0
35–39	84	5.1
40–44	38	2.3
45–49	34	2.1
50–54	12	0.7
55–59	7	0.4
60 and over	10	0.6
Total	1,634	99.9

important, with the primary cleavage separating greater Paris from the Northwest and Center-west. The Françaises were considerably younger than the westerners; 90% rather than 77% of them were under the age of thirty. Girls, however, were less likely to be Parisians, whose greater youth was entirely attributable to women aged fifteen to twenty-five. Teenaged women were especially numerous in the Paris region regardless of class, leading once more to the conclusion that autonomous regional traditions (or specific recruitment practices) could be important in determining the age at emigration.

IN 1739 a Louisbourg charcoal burner named Claude Amiot was indicted in the assault of a Louisbourg cod salter and questioned by the judge about the circumstances of his emigration. The interrogation revealed that this twenty-four-year-old son of a winegrower and innkeeper had left his home in Champagne "through libertinage, with the intention of seeing some country."[10]

Amiot's case was probably not unique. The age distribution, the last element of the emigrant profile, confirms that the men and women who made their way to Canada during the Ancien Régime were a far-from-ordinary cross-section of the French population. As young, single adults from dynamic regions and urban backgrounds, they must have been an unusually adventurous, enterprising, even innovative group, in no way like the stereotype of the solidly ignorant and conservative habitant. Nor did they resemble the image, current since the days of Arthur Young, of the miserable, backward French peasant who only moved from his ancestral lands when chased out by hunger.

Indeed, if one considers who the emigrants were, it is tempting to write of an emigration of opportunity rather than misery, a movement of pull rather than push. But lest I go beyond the conclusions justified by the evidence, I must look more closely at the economic climate of the departures—in other words, I must pursue the story at the level of chronology.

The Chronology of Emigration

In theory, the movement of emigrants over time is as important to the historian as their movements across space. Yet no single aspect of French migrations has been more controversial than the impact of chronology—and hence economic fluctuations—on mobility. Put simply, a fundamental disagreement pits those who view emigration as a product of bad times against those who associate it with periods of prosperity.

The existing literature on French emigration to Canada has not escaped the ramifications of this debate. Using exactly the same data, historians of different persuasions have come to diametrically opposite conclusions about the economic climate of the departures. Robert Mandrou, a proponent of the bad-times hypothesis, has explained the chronology of La Rochelle's servant migrations as follows: "Emigration from La Rochelle was . . . , in very large part, due to misery: the curves of the departures for the West Indies and Canada are convincing in this regard . . . Indentured servants thus did not come voluntarily to the port of La Rochelle except in the course of difficult years."[11]

Louis Pérouas, however, has provided an alternative interpretation, focusing on the coincidence between the peaks of emigration from La Rochelle and the years of heavy immigration into the city:

A single influence was at work in both movements, the attraction of the city of La Rochelle . . . [I]f we consider, in the long term, the general movement of indentures and immigration, we must admit that their syn-chronized waves correspond to periods when La Rochelle experienced, at the same time, a moderate cost of living and an expanding maritime trade. We thus cannot entirely agree with M. Robert Mandrou when he explains the diverse pushes toward the West Indies by the incidence of troubles, famine, crisis. It turns out that it was sometimes the contrary; the colonial exodus almost acquires the status of an index of prosperity.[12]

The data on chronology in my sample were less than ideally suited to economic analysis. On the surface, they could seem excellent, with 99.9% of all emigrants associated with a date of some sort; however, that date was exact less than half of the time.[13] Furthermore, even the exact dates reflect the state of preservation of the various documents, and historians' degree of familiarity with them, rather than the actual level of gross migration. The most comprehensive chronologies established to date re-main, to some extent, at the mercy of imperfect recording and research.

Nonetheless, my graphs of exact and approximate dates do not differ markedly. The two curves are basically parallel, although, as expected, the approximate curve incorporates a certain time lag with respect to the exact. While exact emigration peaked most evidently in 1665, 1720, and the decade prior to the fall of Québec, the corresponding points in approxi-mate emigration came one to six years later, in the years 1666–1669, 1722, and 1755–1765. Of course, this last peak could not be exact, since emi-gration to Canada slowed considerably after the Battle of the Plains of Abraham and ground to a complete halt with the Treaty of Paris in 1763. For the remainder of the century, any returning Canadians or first-time emigrants had to make their way to the Saint Lawrence via London or Saint Pierre and Miquelon.

A second distinction between the exact and approximate chronologies is the less abrupt oscillation of the approximate curve. Staggered dates of settlement probably evened out some of the peaks in arrivals, but at the same time, spotty knowledge of the French exit documents could have exaggerated those peaks in the first place. The unreliability of both curves from one year to the next makes any attempt to correlate emigration to short-term economic fluctuations difficult; and the task is further compli-cated by both the geographical extension of the movement, which left no department untouched, and the social diversity of the emigrants.

The ability to discuss emigration to Canada in relation to longer-term trends such as the purported seventeenth-century crisis is less affected by the problem of approximate dates.[14] Because the exact and approximate curves are reasonably close, much of the chronological imprecision disappears when one considers emigration on a decennial rather than an annual basis. The decade-by-decade distribution of departure dates, both accurate and estimated, is presented in Table 6.6. In addition, there were 4 recorded emigrants for the early nineteenth century.

It is instructive to compare this information with previous attempts to measure the flow of French emigration to Canada, as summarized by Mario Boleda in the form of three chronological estimates. The first, compiled primarily from genealogical data, charts the arrivals of "founding immigrants," while the more broadly based second tracks all immigrants who have been "observed."[15] Most useful here is the third estimate, based on demographic evidence. By calculating the natural rate of increase of the Canadian population and subtracting it from the overall rise in population, Boleda was able to propose an independent chronology for net immigration (see Table 6.7).[16]

The difference between these estimates provokes serious questions about the accuracy of even the long-term trend lines. To give but one example, the ratio of observed to net migration declined from double in the mid-seventeenth century to less than half in the first part of the eighteenth century. The underrecording of emigrants between 1700 and 1740 was thus substantial, since net migration could not, in reality, have exceeded gross. Future efforts of historians to uncover the documentary basis of emigration on either side of the Atlantic ought perhaps to concentrate on these important but poorly understood decades.

Whatever their defects, the four proposed chronologies do have one major point in common: whichever one is chosen, any attempt to link emigration with conventional long-term periodizations of the French economy produces inconclusive results. All of the statistics allow the isolation of emigrants from the accepted period of contraction, 1660 to 1719, and the accepted period of expansion, 1720 to 1759. As the data in Table 6.8 reflect, the estimates of founding and of observed immigration give a slight edge to the period of crisis, with 56% and 54% of the totals, respectively, while those shares decline in Boleda's estimate and in mine to 47% and 41%.

The first two figures lead one to question the reliability of the sources;

Table 6.6 Chronological distribution of emigrants by decade (my sample)

Decade	No. of emigrants	% of emigrants
1600–09	5	0
1610–19	19	0.1
1620–29	29	0.2
1630–39	491	3.1
1640–49	933	5.9
1650–59	1,554	9.8
1660–69	2,313	14.7
1670–79	861	5.5
1680–89	625	4.0
1690–99	654	4.1
Total	7,484	47.4
1700–09	282	1.8
1710–19	342	2.2
1720–29	761	4.8
1730–39	907	5.7
1740–49	1,010	6.4
1750–59	4,543	28.8
1760–69	392	2.5
1770–79	29	0.2
1780–89	20	0.1
1790–99	15	0.1
Total	8,301	52.6

an enormous gap opened in the eighteenth century between founding and net immigration—they had previously approximated each other—and observed migration fell to impossibly low levels between 1700 and 1740. But even disregarding this persuasive evidence of documentary deficiencies, one need not accept that "depression" was more conducive to founding or observed emigration than "prosperity." Since the conquest cut short the second phase of the migration, the first phase extended over a longer time period, and the small superiority of the extended seventeenth century could be attributable simply to chronological asymmetry.

The opposite argument, that emigration increased with "economic growth," is not necessarily more persuasive. My data may give an advantage to the later period owing to the preservation of passenger lists

Table 6.7 Chronological distributions of emigrants (Boleda)

Years	No. of founding immigrants	No. of observed immigrants	Net no. of immigrants
1608–1639	161	1,078	—
1640–1659	873	2,416	—
1660–1679	2,509	5,377	2,870
1680–1699	1,070	3,592	2,434
1700–1719	621	1,496	3,138
1720–1739	938	1,841	3,997
1740–1759	2,355	6,927	5,520
Total	8,527	22,727	17,959

Table 6.8 Aggregate chronological distributions of emigrants

Category	1660–1719	1720–1759	Total
No. of founding immigrants	4,200	3,293	7,493
No. of observed immigrants	10,465	8,768	19,233
Net no. of immigrants	8,442	9,517	17,959
No. of emigrants in my sample	5,077	7,221	12,298

beginning in 1749. Net immigration was indeed more substantial in the eighteenth than in the seventeenth century, but that statistic proves that more emigrants settled in Canada in the later period, not that more arrived in the first place. Since it is likely that the rate of return migration declined in the course of the French Regime, as indicated by the much narrower gap between observed and net immigration in 1760 than in 1660, no clear pronouncement about the relationship between emigration to Canada and purported sea changes in the French economy can be made.

What emerges most strongly from a consideration of the available data, unsatisfactory though they often are, is the long-term stability of the migratory movement. Emigration to Canada resembled immigration into French cities like Rouen and Caen, where an overall stability of attraction defies generally accepted ideas about long-term economic trends.[17] In the short run, however, cities did witness cycles of immigration in the form of population explosions associated with traditional subsistence crises.[18] Robert Mandrou and the deficiencies of the data notwithstanding, it does not appear that the Canadian population experienced any such sudden and ephemeral shifts as a result of short-term crises in the economy.

Severe subsistence crises occurred, on the average, once per generation in seventeenth- and eighteenth-century France. The most widespread catastrophes occurred in 1630, 1662, and 1694, when epidemics compounded the ravages of hunger in an already weakened population. From the standpoint of cereals alone, several other dates loom as well: 1649, 1677, 1710, and 1741, to name only the most notorious. The geographical range of these crises tended to narrow significantly in the eighteenth century with improved productivity and better communiciations. "A last 'great' crisis appeared strongly in a few provinces (in 1741–1742), slightly in others, and not at all elsewhere."[19] Even the earlier crises affected some regions more than others, though, as could be expected in a traditional, compartmentalized economy. The famine of 1693–1694 spared the Mediterranean, whose agriculture actually profited from the wet weather that ruined grain growing elsewhere, and in 1710 the infamous *grand hyver* (great winter) had little impact on the Breton coast.

In spite of the problems with the annual curves of emigration, one could legitimately expect extreme demographic traumas to be reflected on the graph if Canada, in fact, functioned as a kind of super *ville-refuge*. The graph indicates that nothing could be further from the case. None of the crucial dates figured prominently on either the curve of exact dates or upon the combined curve of exacts and approximates. Any hypothetical link between emigration and short-term economic crisis, at least at the national level, appears as tenuous as the relationship between the departures and the so-called seventeenth-century crisis.

Extending the purview beyond the years of acute subsistence difficulties only confirms the lack of correspondence between global emigration and the annual course of grain prices. To the extent that a national market for grain was emerging in the seventeenth and eighteenth centuries, that market centered on Paris, and the prices recorded in Ile-de-France functioned as more general indicators.[20] Over the years under discussion, the curve of those prices bore virtually no resemblance to the curves of departures for Canada.[21] Fluctuating more or less abruptly depending upon the harvest, the cost of grain oscillated around a trend line that was barely concave. In keeping with the long-term periodization of boom and bust (of which it was the lead indicator), it moved slowly and steadily downward between 1640 and 1720, and just as slowly and steadily upward between 1720 and 1790.

Departures for Canada varied annually as well, but the trend they collectively shaped was far less uniform than that of prices. Emigration rose steeply between 1635 and 1665, then fell off precipitously in the following decade. After 1675 the fit between the migratory and price curves improved, with a slow rise superseding a slow decline. The rise in emigration, however, anticipated the rise in prices by nearly a decade. And the two curves again diverged after 1745, when emigration attained its highest levels to date, while prices continued on a gently inclining course. There was little apparent connection between annual price movements and the flow of emigration.

Thus, the chronology of the peopling of Canada, insofar as it can be determined, had little to do with commonly described economic trends, whether in the long or the short term. These trends, however, were based primarily on agricultural prices, which were not of equal concern to all Frenchmen. Emigrants to Canada may well have marched to a different drummer—the Atlantic, rather than the rural, economy. But before rejecting all links between emigration and price cycles, I must consider whether any existed at the level of specific regions or social classes.

Regional Chronologies

The regional chronologies of French emigration to Canada did not, for the most part, conform to the aggregate chronology outlined above. Instead, the latter was an artificial construct masking two fundamentally different patterns: one centered on the mid-seventeenth century, the other on the mid-eighteenth. The first pattern prevailed in the Paris region, the Loire Valley, and the Center-west, the second in the Southwest, South, Massif central, and Alps. Neither the Northwest nor the North were coherent ensembles; in these regions, individual provinces and departments determined the timing of emigration.

The graph of northwestern emigration resembled that of emigration overall, with the difference that the earlier peak occurred in the mid-1650s and the later one became apparent around 1735. The chronology of northwestern departures thus anticipated that of all departures combined, but mirrored it in its essentially bimodal shape. On both curves, emigration reached its highest annual levels in the mid-1750s.

Within the Northwest, areas were distinguished according to whether more emigrants departed in the seventeenth or the eighteenth century. A pattern of early emigration prevailed in a northeastern zone composed of all the Norman departments except Manche. In Upper Normandy, Calvados, and Perche departures peaked in the midst of the "seventeenth-century crisis." The movement of Percherons was particularly precocious, contrasting even with that from Upper Normandy and Calvados. While Norman emigration rose, peaked, and declined in the middle decades of the seventeenth century, Percheron emigration reached unprecedented heights in 1634, only to fall off exponentially thereafter. By 1670 it had ground to a virtual halt, with a mere 3 percent of the total number of emigrants still to set out for Canada.

The second ensemble, which included all of the Breton departments, Manche, and the Province of Maine, exhibited a very different chronological pattern. A majority of emigrants abandoned these areas after 1720, during the period of "economic growth." In Manche the contrast between the earlier and the later periods was especially clear-cut, with the later one accounting for a full 90 percent of the emigrants. Before the 1730s, which were a kind of takeoff point, Manche witnessed no more than a reasonably steady dribble of emigration amounting to at most several emigrants per year.

Breton emigration was rather idiosyncratic, at least with regard to the examples already considered. For the first fifty years of colonization, departures held steady at 10 to 20 per year, except for a peak of 40 in 1665. Emigration then reached higher levels between 1685 and 1700, and between 1715 and the conquest. At the height of the movement in the 1750s, over 100 Bretons embarked for Canada every year. The situation in Lower Brittany was similar but for the relative magnitudes of the respective peaks. In Morbihan and Finistère, the largest numbers of departures occurred not in the years prior to the Seven Years' War but between 1717 and 1720, in the midst of a long period of peace.

Analysis of northwestern emigration casts further doubt on the explanatory value of the long-term phases of economic expansion and contraction. Geographically, the Northwest was divided into two distinct entities, one of which witnessed a migration of "depression" and the other a migration of "prosperity." Yet it is not at all clear whether the respective tilt toward either the seventeenth or the eighteenth century had anything to do with the long-term movements of French grain prices. An alternative and far more obvious explanation centers on the changing structure of Franco-Canadian trade in the course of the French Regime. In 1660 this commerce revolved around the twin axes of Rouen and La Rochelle, but by 1760 it had shifted doubly southward to concentrate in Saint-Malo and Bordeaux. The reorientation of Canada-bound shipping within the Northwest from Upper Normandy to Upper Brittany provides adequate insight into the problem of changing chronology, a problem merely obscured by the reference to the "seventeenth-century crisis."

Whatever the status of migration models based on long-term economic trends, they leave the question of migratory sensitivity to short-term fluctuations unresolved. Did regional grain prices, as compiled on an annual basis, influence the local migration flows in one direction or the other? Did regional chronologies of northwestern migration bear any resemblance to the curve of grain prices as revealed in the *mercuriales* (market price lists)? A few contemporaries, at least in Canada, seemed to think that they did. A letter written by Intendant Prévost of Ile Royale in 1755, while silent on the issue of grain prices per se, describes Louisbourg as a *ville-refuge* for Upper Bretons chased from their province by hunger.

> There are many . . . who came to the colony only to wander or to keep taverns, and some others were dependent on the king from the time of their arrival, which leads me to beseech you to give orders in the ports, and particularly in Saint-Malo, to let come here only young people fit to earn their living, tradespeople and others who can be trained as sailors, fishermen, or farmers; for almost all those who come from the department are people in flight from the law, or bankrupt, or poor families, all of them considerable, who betake themselves here in the sole hope that the king will not let them die of hunger, or that they will sell wine, which brings us many paupers, vagrants, and libertines.[22]

Unfortunately, an examination of the Breton *mercuriales* does little to explain this influx of impoverished Bretons in the mid-1750s. The years from 1752 to 1756, in fact, provided a respite from the high prices that both preceded and followed them. Assuming that Prévost's concerns were not unjustified, the vagabonds and beggars whom he dreaded had not embarked in a reflexive response to the increasing cost of subsistence.

For the Ancien Régime as a whole, the annual course of Breton grain prices was just as poorly linked to the provincial flow of emigration.[23] Whether in Vannes, Saint-Brieuc, Dinan, Nantes, or Brest, the succession of points and troughs fluctuated far less widely, and out of sequence with, the peaks and valleys of the emigration curve.

What this curve did correspond to, to a far greater degree than grain prices, was the timing of efforts of recruitment. I examine the exact nature of these efforts in Part Two; suffice it to say here that they were often effective enough to increase the number of emigrants. In Brittany, the years of heavy emigration were in many cases years of stepped-up military recruitment; 1665 witnessed the departure of the Regiment of Carignan-Salières, the first contingent of publicly recruited soldiers for Canada, and the 1680s and 1690s were the heyday of the *troupes de la Marine*. The 1750s, in addition to producing the outflow of emigrants so decried by Intendant Prévost, saw the levy and transport of the largest army of the French Regime. Perhaps the vagabonds and poor families who embarked at Saint-Malo in these same years did so partly in response to the military example, as they witnessed the increased activity of shipping and the frenzy of mass departures from the port.

Civilian recruitment initiatives also made their appearance on the emigration curves. In Lower Brittany, where emigration peaked during the Regency, the impetus probably came from the Compagnie de l'Occident, later known as the Compagnie des Indes. A linchpin, with the Banque royale, of John Law's infamous "system," the company exercised proprietary rights not only over the Mississippi Valley, where its dealings received the most notoriety, but over "all the lands and mines of the New World." Although it collapsed in the wake of a speculative bubble in 1720, it had already succeeded in endowing the colonial enterprise with an "extraordinary élan."[24] The appeal of Canada in Lower Brittany, which subsequently specialized in relations with the East Indies, was never greater than during the short life of the Compagnie de l'Occident.

Other examples of civilian recruitment that have already been mentioned—Robert Giffard's and the Juchereau brothers' appeal to the Per-

cherons, and Jérôme Le Royer de la Dauversière's enrollments around La
Flèche—also stood out in the chronologies of northwestern emigration.
In Maine and Anjou, the largest contingents of the French Regime
departed in 1653, the year of La Dauversière's canvassing, and in Perche,
the flow of emigrants lasted as long as the lives of the key recruiters.

THE CENTER-WEST, consisting of Aunis, Saintonge, Poitou, and Angoumois, presented an essentially unified chronology of emigration. Since the
commercial life of the entire region revolved around La Rochelle, the
emigration curves of each of the provinces corresponded fairly closely to
that of the port city. In the seventeenth century, central-western departures
followed much the same pattern described for northwesterners and emigrants overall. The bulk of the emigration took place between 1655 and
1670, when emigrants numbered upwards of 100 per year. It then fell off
sharply to reach a nadir of zero in 1713, the year of the Treaty of Utrecht.
The two highest peaks of the seventeenth century, in 1659 and 1665,
represent two major recruitment drives, one civilian and one military. The
Regiment of Carignan embarked from La Rochelle in the summer of 1665,
and, apparently, many of the soldiers had been recruited in the environs.[25]
In 1659 the iniative lay with the Montréalistes, among them La Dauversière and Jeanne Mance of the Hôtel-Dieu. Unlike the Montréal contingent
of 1653, which originated in Sarthe and embarked from Saint-Nazaire,
that of 1659 was assembled around and transported out of La Rochelle.[26]

The similarity between the curves of central-western and overall emigration ended with the seventeenth century, which produced the lion's
share of central-western emigrants. Of the 1,500 emigrants who embarked
from the Center-west in the last century of French rule, two-thirds arrived
in Canada before 1720. Rather than speak of an emigration of misery,
however, it seems more appropriate to point out that La Rochelle, like
Rouen, played a more dominant role in the Canada trade in the earlier
century.

Eighteenth-century emigrants were not heavily concentrated in the last
years of the regime; La Rochelle had definitively abandoned its supremacy
to the Southwest and Brittany by the time of the Seven Years' War. The
1750s did witness an increase in central-western emigration everywhere

except in Lower Poitou, but, proportionally, this increase was about half as large in the Center-west as in all regions combined. The real peak of eighteenth-century emigration from the Center-west occurred around 1720, concurrent with the life span of the Compagnie de l'Ile Saint-Jean (1719–1724). This seigneurial enterprise, which operated exclusively out of La Rochelle, was designed to populate what is now Prince Edward Island in the wake of the British seizure of peninsular Acadia. In its most successful year, it succeeded in luring more than 100 central-westerners to North America.

THE SOUTHWESTERN PROVINCES, like those of the Center-west, exhibited a high degree of consistency where chronology was concerned. Presumably, this consistency derived from the commercial ascendancy of Bordeaux, which, together with Bayonne, regulated the flow of southwestern emigrants to Canada. The timing of southwestern emigration was a reversal of the pattern prevailing in the Center-west. The graph of eighteenth-century departures resembles that of departures overall, while that for the seventeenth century depicts a far less significant movement. Emigrants from the period after 1719 outnumbered those from the previous period (1660–1719) by a factor of three to one. Again, rather than belabor the issue of price trends, it makes sense to point out that Bordeaux attained its apogee as a maritime power in the eighteenth century, and that a number of its shippers began at that time to do business with Canada.

In the seventeenth century, southwestern emigration remained steady at a low level and only exceptionally exhibited discrete peaks. Some of the peaks mentioned in the above discussion of the Northwest and the Center-west did figure on the graph of southwestern departures; that of 1665 corresponded to the recruitment of the Regiment of Carignan with some 45 southwesterners, that of 1685–1700 to the era of the *troupes de la Marine*. In the civilian realm, the hiring of about a dozen Basque carpenters for Acadia caused the first small peak in southwestern emigration in 1636. As in Brittany and the Cotentin, the heaviest period of southwestern emigration was delayed until the end of the French Regime. While the recruitment of soldiers for the Seven Years' War, particularly the Regiments of Languedoc and Roussillon, contributed much to this movement, it is also likely that a heightened awareness of Canada raised the concurrent level of civilian emigration.

EASTERN EMIGRATION, as defined here, exhibited more chronological diversity than that of the Center-west or the Southwest, by virtue of the region's enormous size and varied economy. Nonetheless, discrepancies in the timing of the provincial migration streams were by no means as pronounced in the East as in the Northwest. Almost three-quarters of the eastern emigrants arrived in Canada after 1720, the same proportion as in the Southwest. Province by province, however, the percentage rose from under 60% in Champagne to a full 99% in Alsace. The remoter a province was from Paris, the more delayed the movement toward Canada tended to be.

Of the various dates that figured prominently in the history of eastern emigration, some could be easily explained by reference to recruitment. The Burgundian associate of an Acadian seigneur brought close to 20 of his countrymen to Acadia in 1636,[27] and the departure of the Regiment of Carignan was perceptible in Champagne. This second peak was prolonged, in Champagne, into the 1670s; and, as I discuss below, it reflected not only the delayed tallying of soldiers but also the actual emigration of *filles à marier.*

In the eighteenth century, the heaviest periods of emigration were the late 1730s and the middle 1750s. The first peak, which was peculiar to the East, once again resulted from recruitment policy—in this case, the choice of Burgundian ironworkers to start up a foundry in Trois-Rivières. The second peak showed up everywhere, but assumed particular importance in Lorraine. Interestingly, the previous periods of intensive military recruitment did not affect Lorraine, vindicating Corvisier's comment that the military vocation of the Northeast dated primarily from the eighteenth century.[28]

THE PARIS REGION and the Loire Valley fell squarely into the category of early emigrant producers. In both regions, about 70 percent of the emigrants from the period 1660 to the conquest reached Canada prior to

1720, and the migration streams from the period before 1660 were far from negligible. This precocity probably reflects the key role of the state in setting early colonial policy and in engineering recruitment, a role that radiated throughout the Paris Basin. In later years, the state, without relinquishing its control over policy, tended to rely more heavily on the port cities to provide the actual emigrants. Emigration peaked in the Paris Basin in the 1660s, when soldiers and *filles à marier* departed in substantial numbers, and around the time of the Seven Years' War. As in the Center-west, the second peak was proportionally much smaller than in the areas of later emigration. For its part, the curve of grain prices in Ile-de-France correlated no better to the chronology of regional departures than to that of departures overall.

The provinces of the North, like those of the Northwest, exhibited a split chronological pattern. Picardy and Artois, which bordered on Ile-de-France and Upper Normandy, produced more emigrants in the seventeenth than in the eighteenth century, but Flanders, like Lorraine, contributed the bulk of its emigrants at the time of the Seven Years' War. In Picardy, the heaviest emigration occurred in the 1660s and 1670s, as in Ile-de-France and the Loire; however, the highest annual number of departures dated from 1755.

OF THE REMAINING REGIONS, the Midi and the Alps conformed to the later pattern, producing no appreciable numbers of emigrants until the middle of the eighteenth century. The Massif central was anomalous in that, unlike the other mountainous areas, its emigrants were distributed more or less equally between the seventeenth and eighteenth centuries. Such peaks as there were tended to correspond to the periods of military recruitment, but emigration continued at a steady, if low, level throughout most of the French Regime. The evenness of this distribution probably stemmed in part from geographical position. As an area that was truly "central," the Massif partook of both major chronological trends: the later one that prevailed to the south and east, and the earlier one that dominated lands to the north and west. There was again no evidence that yearly prices of grain, on the one hand, or longer-term price cycles, on the other, serve any useful purpose in describing the chronology of this migration. My regional and provincial data, like those for the movement as a whole, were uniformly recalcitrant to the type of explanation most commonly sought after by historians of migration.

Social and Occupational Chronologies

But what of social and occupational chronologies? Did emigrants belonging to different groups respond to the short-term or long-term fluctuations of the economy in different ways?

Not necessarily, for the curves of bourgeois and artisanal emigration were similar—not only to each other, but to the aggregate curve of emigration over time. Bourgeois and artisans showed no preference for either the seventeenth or eighteenth century; their departures were divided almost equally between the two. Subsistence crises were as invisible on these two curves as on the general curve they so closely resembled.

By all appearances, bourgeois and artisans formed the dominant strands of emigration to Canada, in that together they defined its chronology. The even distribution of their departures over time suggests that the social bases of the movement remained constant in the face of important regional shifts. Whether Norman or Aunisian, Breton or Aquitain, emigrants from the bourgeoisie and *artisanat* seem to have taken the lead in determining the relative timing of emigration. It should be noted, however, that my sources discriminate less seriously against these two classes than against all others except the nobility.

The curve of noble departures concerned a much smaller number of people, but it remained consistent with the general trend. Departures were not heavily weighted toward either century, although they were somewhat more numerous in the seventeenth. The peak years of emigration generally coincided with periods of military recruitment because of the key role played by nobles in the officer corps. The year 1636, which witnessed the departures of two allied clans of Lower Norman nobles, the Le Gardeurs and the Le Poutrels, was exceptional in this regard.

Peasants and wage earners constitute a curious case of migratory chronology, owing perhaps to their sporadic appearance in the sources. Just over two-thirds of the peasants in the sample emigrated in the seventeenth century, while just under two-thirds of the workers delayed their departures until the eighteenth. One could perhaps argue that here, at last, is evidence of the sensitivity of emigration to long-term trends; when agricultural prices were low, peasants suffered and departed, and when they were high, workers, as consumers, did the same. Unfortunately, the shakiness of the data prevent the drawing of such firm conclusions, and the existence of a link between emigration and the plight of these major social classes must remain an open question.

THE VARIOUS occupational chronologies, like the regional ones, correspond to the familiar milestones in recruitment policy. Military emigration first peaked in the 1640s during the founding of Montréal, and then increased more than tenfold in 1665, with the departure of the Regiment of Carignan. As represented in the sample, the heaviest emigration by the *troupes de la Marine* occurred between 1684 and 1700, but the most important reinforcements of the regime did not arrive for another half century, when hostilities between the French and the British were once again imminent.

The different branches of the *artisanat*—or those engaged in essential activities, at least—tended to follow a specific chronological pattern. The years 1642 and 1653 marked the founding and reinforcement of the settlement of Montréal, an enterprise that required the labor of builders, metalworkers, and food workers as well as peasants. Further recruits arrived for Montréal in 1659, after which artisanal emigration stagnated until the settlement of Ile Saint-Jean around 1720. Yet another peak appeared in the final years of the regime, and it points to a possible rise in artisanal emigration concurrent with, but independent of, the recruitment of soldiers for the Seven Years' War.

Commercial, medical, and administrative or legal emigrants formed a fairly steady stream throughout the seventeenth and eighteenth centuries. As practiced in Canada, these professions did not make periodic, extraordinary demands on French labor. Emigrants from the church also fell substantially into this category, although they were somewhat fewer in number in the eighteenth century.[29]

Service workers and indentured servants of unknown profession appear to have been most numerous in the middle of the seventeenth century, but better knowledge of the eighteenth-century notarial records could conceivably alter this picture. Mariners, on the other hand, departed most willingly in the period after 1740. Assuming that this chronology is accurate and not simply the result of partial exploitation of the sources, it is perhaps attributable to the higher volume of shipping between the metropolis and the colony in the final years of the regime.

All in all, the social and occupational data hardly substantiate an analysis of migratory chronology based upon the vagaries of the economy. Long-term price cycles failed to affect the bourgeois, or even the tradesmen, among the emigrants to any degree, nor did the recurrent subsistence crises impress themselves upon the consumers. Many historians have shown that peasants habitually flocked to cities in times of dearth, but there is absolutely no evidence that they flocked to Canada in analogous circumstances. Likewise, while these same crises had the effect of inhibiting artisanal immigration into cities like Amiens and Chartres, artisanal emigration to Canada seems to have proceeded in blissful unawareness of the price of grains.[30]

The Chronology of Women's Emigration

Finally, what of women? The chronology of their emigration, like other aspects of their migratory behavior, differed from the overall pattern in important respects. Most notable was the concentration of women's departures in the middle decades of the seventeenth century. Between 1600 and 1680, the curve of female emigration rose and decayed in relative synchrony with that of men, but in the eighteenth century, despite small increases in the 1720s and 1750s, it scarcely peaked at all (see Table 6.9). Five-sixths of the women in the sample embarked for Canada before 1700, in contrast with under half of the women and men combined. While women remained a permanent part of the migration stream throughout the French Regime, the female component of the movement shrank from 24% in the seventeenth century to a mere 4% in the eighteenth.

The geographical provenance of women, primarily the Paris Basin and the Northwest and Center-west, does not fully explain the overwhelming tendency toward early departures. Region by region, the imbalance between the two centuries was consistently greater for women than it was for men. Once again, the most likely explanation centers on the process of recruitment. As I note in Part Two, state sponsorship of female emigration began and ended with Colbert's efforts to develop the colony; his successors abandoned the policy as costly and unnecessary once the population could provide an adequate number of wives through natural increase. The regional origins of women thus reflected the precocity of

Table 6.9 Chronological distribution of women emigrants by decade (my sample)

Decade	No. of emigrants	% of emigrants
1600–09	0	0
1610–19	6	0.3
1620–29	2	0.1
1630–39	106	5.0
1640–49	152	7.1
1650–59	299	14.0
1660–69	676	31.6
1670–79	394	18.4
1680–89	85	4.0
1690–99	57	2.7
Total	1,777	83.2
1700–09	34	1.6
1710–19	28	1.3
1720–29	104	4.9
1730–39	37	1.7
1740–49	29	1.4
1750–59	122	5.7
1760–69	2	0.1
1770–79	3	0.1
1780–89	0	0
1790–99	0	0
Total	359	16.8

their emigration rather than vice versa. Because women were recruited primarily in the seventeenth century, most of them stemmed from the several areas then in contact with Canada.

Once again, the peak years of female emigration had little to do with grain prices and much to do with politics. The family-oriented contingents of Percherons and Montréalistes produced the first significant points in 1636 and 1659; by comparison, the still pioneering Montréal expedition of 1653 was largely male.[31] The largest numbers of women departed in the late 1660s and early 1670s as prospective brides for the soldiers of the Regiment of Carignan, but after 1673 the level of female emigration dropped off sharply. The highest annual peak of the eighteenth century—

1720, with 36 female emigrants—was exceeded no fewer than fifteen times during the seventeenth century.

The chronologies based on marital status suggest that familial emigration tended to occur earlier in the process of Canadian settlement than did the emigration of single women. The curve of married women reached its highest levels in the 1630s, 1640s, and 1650s, then declined steadily until the final peaks of the 1720s and 1750s.[32] Single women, on the other hand, began to emigrate in earnest around 1655, and continued to do so en masse for nearly twenty years.

Summary

The chronology of French emigration to Canada, whether considered as a whole or in its constituent parts, consistently frustrates attempts to connect it with the movements of the agricultural economy. Short-term fluctuations in the price of grains sometimes influenced certain categories of migrants within France; however, they bore no relation either positive or negative to the volume of Canadian departures. Although an autonomous migration stream linked some regions of France to the colony during the French Regime, the annual variations in its size had far more to do with the system of colonial recruitment than with the fluctuations in grain prices.

This conclusion makes sense given the economic context in which emigration to Canada took place, namely, the expansion of maritime commerce in the seventeenth and eighteenth centuries. As Pierre Dardel, Alain Cabantous, and Jean-Pierre Poussou have pointed out in their respective studies of Rouen, Le Havre, and Bordeaux, this expansion occurred largely independently of fluctuations in the agricultural output and responded instead to the dictates of an international, Atlantic economy.[33]

This Atlantic dimension of emigration to Canada also helps to explain the seeming irrelevance of the standard, long-term periodization of the French economy to the chronology of the movement. Emigrants embarked for Canada in nearly equal numbers during both the seventeenth-century "crisis" and the eighteenth-century "boom," but since these categories of boom and bust are based primarily on price trends for agricultural products, their applicability to the history of overseas commerce is suspect. Contrary to the views of Pierre Chaunu, who has posited the interconnectedness of all economic indicators,[34] it is clear that in Rouen and La Rochelle, at least, Atlantic commerce was increasing throughout the seventeenth century, in defiance of the purported universal crisis.

Returning then to my initial question about the primary economic impetus for emigration—misery or prosperity?—I must certainly opt for the latter. Rare emigrants, when questioned, couched their motivations in the language of opportunity; witness Jean Galon, the son of a Norman mason and roofer, who embarked for Louisbourg "in the hope of better earning his living," or Jean-Baptiste Lascorret, a young merchant's clerk from Bayonne, who found it "more advantageous to come to this island where he was given hope of making a small fortune in a short time."[35] That is because, generally speaking, emigration to Canada was a by-product of France's steadily expanding interest in the Atlantic economy of the seventeenth and eighteenth centuries. The main fact that emerges from examining French emigrants to Canada is their modernity, as expressed through their geographic, social, and religious origins, their ages, and the general economic climate of their departures.[36]

Of course, ultimately, as shown by the impact of recruitment efforts on chronology, migratory movements proceed according to rhythms that they generate themselves; they cannot be deduced from or reduced to economics.[37] To understand emigration to Canada fully, one must consider it also on its own terms, both as a result of specific recruitment practices and as an example of long-established and slowly changing demographic traditions. Thus, Ancien Régime migratory patterns, on the one hand, and methods of recruitment, on the other, form the substance of Part Two.

PART II

Tradition

CHAPTER | 7

Traditional Patterns of Mobility

In a synthesis of the rapidly expanding scholarship on Ancien Régime migrations, Jean-Pierre Poussou emphasized the role of tradition in demographic behavior. "The study of bygone migrations," he wrote, "reveals that migratory movements have their own laws, their internal logic, indeed, their own tradition." Although Poussou himself had done invaluable research on the economic context of migrations, he recognized that migrations could be structural as well as superstructural, their relationship to economic and social phenomena determinant as well as determined.[1]

A structural approach to migrations demands that they be considered them on their own terms, as aspects not merely of economic but also of population history. Once established, migratory currents acquire a life of their own and can be surprisingly resistant to economic change. There is, in Poussou's words, an "inertia of migratory flows." On the other hand, population and economic history have one important feature in common, at least within the context of the Ancien Régime. Patterns of migration, like economic structures, varied from region to region, and, ultimately, "a regional vision of migratory movements is imperative."[2]

Until the 1960s, when historical demography first became an academic discipline, the demographic structures of the Ancien Régime received far less attention from historians than its economic and social structures. Its migratory traditions, in spite of their importance, have fared more poorly still. The difficulty of tracing migrants discouraged even the first generation of historical demographers, and only since the 1970s have the characteristics of early modern migrations become gradually more familiar. It therefore seems useful to preface my regional analysis with a discussion of those migratory patterns that transcended region under the Ancien Régime. Such a discussion, by laying the groundwork, will facilitate an understanding of the regional migration streams and the ways in which they related to French emigration to Canada.

Short-Distance Movements

The short-distance movements of the early modern population are among the best known, essentially because they are easy to study. Not surprisingly, the comings and goings of people within a twenty-kilometer radius present far fewer logistical problems to the historian than their treks across continents, or even regions. The most salient features of short-distance movements are their frequency and their ubiquity. To take the example of rural marriage, no village was too remote to witness substantial levels of local exogamy. The actual percentages varied widely, but rarely did the number of exogamous couples fall below a quarter to a third of the whole.[3] Most out-of-town spouses came from within a highly circumscribed geographical area. In Crulai, a medium-size bourg on the border between Normandy and Perche, 50% of the immigrant husbands and 58.8% of the immigrant wives hailed from an adjoining parish; 73% of the husbands and 78.6% of the wives arrived from a birthplace less than ten kilometers away. Both sexes combined, a scant tenth of the "horsins" (outsiders) made more than a three- to four-hour trek to their wedding.[4] Men ventured a little farther afield than women, but, in general, rural newlyweds remained in the immediate vicinity of their childhood home.

Population exchanges between adjacent or nearby parishes affected not only spouses but single adolescents and, in some cases, constituted families. Adolescents of both sexes frequently moved short distances to enter into service, either as domestics or apprentices. In regions of sharecropping, whole families moved on at intervals as their leases expired and their landlords sought other, equally rootless families to replace them.[5] At harvesttime, contingents of women, men, and children moved from one village to the next in a form of rural mutual aid.[6] The periodicity of short-range movements was therefore variable, ranging from the seasonal to the pluriannual or permanent.

Because all of these movements involved such a limited geographical range, some historians are loath to refer to them as migrations. Jean-Pierre Poussou has instead coined the terms "micro-mobility" and *"brassage de population"* (population mixing) to describe the multiple demographic exchanges between rural communities of comparable size and function. It is tempting to be less circumspect, for it is a truism of mobility that one move, no matter how insignificant, can often lead to other moves of a substantially bolder nature.

A number of short-distance movements have always qualified as migrations, even for the most cautious of historians. Regardless of distance, when two communities occupied different economic niches owing to their size or location, moving from one to the other entailed a change in accustomed ways of life. People who traveled from mountain to plain, from village to bourg, or from landlocked interior to river valley underwent a more fundamental transformation than those who engaged in micro-mobility per se. To distinguish between the two types of individuals, Poussou has dubbed the former "slippage migrants" *(migrants par glissement)*.[7]

Like micro-mobility, slippage migration occurred on a large scale and involved people of different sexes, ages, and professions. Sons of peasants moved to local bourgs or towns for formal training in a trade, and rural daughters placed themselves with urban families in hopes of earning a dowry. Sometimes these small-scale migrations ended after a few years with the accomplishment of their goal, the acquisition of capital, but at other times they were prolonged into permanent stays or gave rise to additional, more far-reaching moves. Either the failure or the success of an acquisitive strategy could effectively short-circuit a migrant's plans to return home.

Other slippage migrations recurred with seasonal regularity, namely, those involving agricultural or pastoral labor. Pockets of commercial agriculture attracted additional hands at fixed intervals from outlying zones of *petite culture*. The plains of Beauce, for example, received large bands of harvesters from the neighboring forests of Perche each August. In mountainous regions, well-beaten tracks and periodic runs connected not only the livestock but the people who herded it with the adjacent lowlands. Occasionally, although more rarely than in the case of pluriannual migrations, these seasonal rhythms broke down to produce a limited stream of permanent settlement.

Middle-Distance Movements

Middle-distance migrations—those involving an entire province or re-gion—also mobilized important sectors of the French population. To some extent, the patterns observed for micro-mobility and slippage mi-grations remained intact as distances increased. Seasonal migrants from the Midi-Pyrénées descended not simply to the valleys but also to the wine-producing regions of the Atlantic and Mediterranean coasts. Their counterparts in Brie, already a breadbasket of the Paris Basin, flowed in from the future departments of Aisne, Marne, Aube, Yonne, Meuse, Vosges, and Côte d'Or.[8]

Some middle-range seasonal migrants engaged in para-industrial occu-pations such as hemp combing. Hemp combers from Bugey and Savoy regularly spent the slack season in the bourgs and small towns of Bur-gundy, Bresse, and Switzerland, while the hemp fields of Poitou, Berry, and Bourbonnais were served primarily by Limousins, Marchois, and Auvergnats.[9] In comparison to the local harvest migrations, these seasonal movements and others like them exhibited a higher degree of organization. Migrants often moved in village-based bands or teams and recognized the leadership of experienced members of the group.

Whether seasonal or not, most middle-distance movements involved young men in search of work. Even when emigrants were married, as was not infrequently the case with seasonal workers, they preferred to travel without their wives and young children. The duration of the campaigns, several months at the minimum, made the participation of the entire rural community impractical.[10] Thus, the tendency already observed among short-distance migrants for men to stray farther afield than women worked, at the regional level, to limit the number of female migrants. Middle-distance migrants were clearly more homogeneous than short-dis-tance migrants, who in turn comprised a truer cross-section of the French population.

Aside from distance and migrant characteristics, middle-distance move-ments were distinguished from slippage migrations by the greater relative importance of urbanization. Whereas slippage migrations linked networks of villages with local market centers, middle-distance movements con-nected these local centers to regional capitals. Towns such as Meulan in Ile-de-France or Coutras in Guyenne functioned as *villes-relais* on the route from countryside to metropolis. Sometimes this two-stage rural exodus occurred within the lifetime of particular migrants, but perhaps more often, it took shape slowly over generations. As natives of the *ville-relais* trickled away in adolescence or young adulthood to try their luck in the great city, enterprising villagers from the surrounding countryside could be counted upon to take their place.

The steady drain of the rural population toward cities, great and small, characterized the French population for centuries prior to the industrial era. Early modern towns were unhealthy places, where death rates so exceeded birthrates as to preclude even the maintenance of existing population levels in the absence of immigration. Large cities, especially, were veritable *villes-tombeaux* (tomb cities). The demographers Louis Henry and Claude Lévy calculated that in the eighteenth century, "it was necessary for Paris, *in order not to lose population, to absorb the entire surplus of a rural area of about the same population,* that is to say, the rough equivalent of rural Seine-et-Oise and Seine-et-Marne" (their emphasis).[11] The vertiginous growth that one associates with nineteenth-century cities and the attendant devastation of the traditional countryside came not from a new migratory pattern but from what was, at most, an extension or acceleration of the old one.[12]

It is no coincidence that in calculating the base levels of Parisian immigration Henry and Lévy made reference to Seine-et-Oise and Seine-et-Marne. Even cities of unquestioned national importance such as Paris and Bordeaux drew the majority of their immigrants from the surrounding province or region. According to Poussou, "the attraction of a town is always exerted from a very marked regional base. As soon as a certain level is reached, the appeal takes on a national dimension, but whatever the size of the town, the immigrants come, in the first place, from the environs or neighboring regions. Migrants can come from beyond the zone of attraction, but theirs is a dispersed and doubtless random immigration."[13]

The actual size of this area of dense urban recruitment varies from city to city, but its outline remains extraordinarily stable over time. Examining Paris, Daniel Courgeau discovered that the immigrants' places of origin have changed little between the Revolution and the present day: "A zone of 300 kilometers surrounding the capital furnishes the majority of immigrants."[14] In Bordeaux, the privileged zone is more restricted, corresponding more closely to the definition of middle-distance migration. It too has remained basically unchanged, at least from the end of the seventeenth century to the beginning of the twentieth. According to Poussou, Bordeaux "is furnished essentially from within a zone of less than 150 to 200 kilometers, a zone that has remained, on the whole, the same across two centuries."[15] Migratory traditions, once established, are long-lived.

Long-Distance Movements

Long-distance migrations, or those that obviously overstep the bounds of region, affected a smaller but still significant portion of the French population during the Ancien Régime. Based on political considerations, one may divide them into three types—internal, colonial, and foreign—which nonetheless had several characteristics in common. Most consistent was the profile of the typical long-distance migrant: a male of working age traveling, if not alone, at least unencumbered by familial responsibilities. Even when related, traveling companions tended to be other adult males. The world of the long-distance migrant, like that of the soldier with which it often overlapped, remained closed to all but exceptionally enterprising women.

Long-distance migrations resembled slippage and middle-distance movements in that they too favored the city. Taken together, country-to-city and city-to-city moves accounted for the better part of the internal departures in this category. In cases of seasonal and temporary migration, where the urban destination was not conceived of as definitive, long-distance migrants theoretically returned to their point of departure. Despite the amplitude of these circular movements, however, individual migrants could spin off from established orbits with surprising ease.[16] All in all, "it seems that the 'return to the land' or the small town was exceptional";[17] most long-distance movements ultimately worked to the demographic advantage of the city.

Urbanization

Except for the still smaller role played by women, long-distance urbanization involved the same gamut of emigrants and activities observed in comparable short- and middle-distance movements. Important cities received, in addition to definitive rural immigrants, contingents of more mobile country folk who made seasonal or pluriannual stays. Rural masons and chimney sweeps usually emigrated for one season at a time, while tinkers and peddlers absented themselves for several years running. Different regions specialized in the export of different types of long-distance migrants. In eighteenth-century Paris, for instance, Sébastien Mercier wrote that "the Savoyards are bootblacks, floor polishers, and sawyers; the Auvergnats are almost all water carriers; the Limousins masons; the Lyonnais are ordinarily porters and sedan carriers; the Normans stonecutters, pavers, and thread merchants."[18]

The picturesque nature of these long rural migrations, which brought to the city peoples distinct in their appearance, speech, and manners, captured the imagination of observers throughout the eighteenth and nineteenth centuries.[19] By their very visibility, rural-to-urban movements thus tended to overshadow the less remarkable, although more abundant, migration streams that connected cities to other cities.

Interurban Movements

One type of interurban migration has already been explored here, that which, at a middle distance, linked together regional capitals with local market centers. At the interregional level, urban interchanges became less hierarchical, in that migrants did not simply move from cities of lesser to those of greater importance. Once a certain threshold was reached, as it generally was at a level of about 10,000 residents, cities began to secrete a particularly mobile stratum of population, the movements of which focused indiscriminately on other cities. Jean-Claude Perrot has written of the "300,000 to 350,000 residents of large cities, in constant reciprocal relations."[20] In Caen, a city of some 30,000 inhabitants, this meant that "briefly, two human networks connected the town to the outside; one was nourished by country sap, while the other, beyond rural Normandy, ran from town to town to the borders of France, and constituted the second homeland of the city folk."[21]

Interurban movements could be of various kinds, including the administrative, the commercial, and the manual. Administrators who moved at mandated intervals between the various seats of the generalities and subdelegations generally traveled with their families; merchants and artisans, on the other hand, were more likely to restrict their wanderings to

an unencumbered youth. Unlike the long-distance migrants who originated in rural areas, most of the mobile city dwellers were young,
unmarried men.

Many interurban migrations involved either one or a small number of
moves, usually undertaken for work or professional advancement. But in
addition, there were examples of what could be called interurban hypermobility; some migrants moved constantly over a period of years, remaining in a given city for weeks or months, then passing on to the next.
While hypermobility could be unstructured, for example, in the case of
an itinerant peddler, it more often conformed to timetables and routes that
were imposed by tradition. One of the most interesting forms of hypermobility was that practiced by the *compagnons du Tour de France*, young
artisans in the final stages of their training. Together with that other
"school of mobility," the army,[22] *compagnonnage* accounted for the largest
number of professional long-distance migrants in early modern France.

Compagnonnage

The term *compagnonnage* refers to three interregional confraternities of
artisans, known variously as the Enfants de Maître Jacques (Dévorants),
the Enfants de Salomon (Gavots), and the Enfants du Père Soubise (Bons
Drilles).[23] Young men joined these societies in their late teens, after
completing an apprenticeship, and provided that they did not marry, they
could remain active members until their midtwenties. During that time,
they participated in regular rituals, some of them akin to the carnivalesque
antics of local Abbayes de la Jeunesse, or bachelor societies.[24] To the
chagrin of the authorities, who always regarded these organizations of
footloose young men as dangerous, they adopted surnames that they used
among themselves, virtually to the exclusion of their given names. These
surnames, which always included a geographical component, were meant
to convey to each *compagnon* a secure regional identity just as he prepared
to set out on his travels.[25]

The heart of *compagnonnage* was the Tour de France, a voyage that
enabled the young artisan to perfect his skills, see the world, and sow his
wild oats at the same time. Studying and working would be generously
supplemented by brawling with *compagnons* from other societies (for the
three groups were bitter rivals), by drinking, and by sexual exploits. Of

necessity, the conviviality of *compagnons* was centered on inns and taverns, for their condition was defined by constant mobility.

The Tour had no fixed duration, but as a rule it lasted between three and seven years. While on the Tour, *compagnons* would move from town to town at irregular intervals, traveling by foot, stagecoach, or ferry as their budgets allowed. Upon arrival in a new town, they would descend on an inn affiliated with their society, accept the hospitality of a *mère des compagnons*, and make the acquaintance of a *rouleur*, or *compagnon* in charge of job placement. The length of their stay in any one town would vary from a few days to several months, depending on the state of the labor market in their trade and their personal whims.[26] When it came time to move on, they rarely departed alone, preferring instead the company of one or more traveling companions who might or might not have the same destination. During a single Tour, a *compagnon* could have quite an impressive number of traveling companions.

To an age nourished by ideals of introspective friendship, the interactions of migrant *compagnons* who often did not know one another's real names appear shifting and anonymous. The contacts made on the road, between workers who did not even share the same trade, may today seem particularly ephemeral, but such a view is anachronistic. The few available documents, whether autobiographical or administrative, are unanimous in proclaiming the importance of the patterns of sociability created by the Tour de France. No matter how short-lived, the acquaintances made on the Tour gave rise to vivid recollections; even such a determined and anarchic individualist as Rousseau could provide detailed descriptions decades later of the characters encountered during his youthful wanderings.[27] The fellowship of the road also created lifelong friendships, which could always be renewed at a later date. By throwing together city dwellers from all corners of the country, it fostered a cosmopolitan mentality among artisans, a mind-set that supplanted the parochial allegiance to the *petit pays*.

Despite frequent opposition from church and state, the numerical strength of the *compagnons du Tour de France* was impressive.[28] "If, at the beginning of the eighteenth century, compagnonnage could count one affiliate for every three workers, at the end, it was in a position to forbid work to nonaffiliates."[29] When Agricol Perdiguier drafted his *Mémoires d'un compagnon* in the mid-nineteenth century, he estimated that "the number of men traveling and attached, in different degrees, to *compagnonnage*, . . . and crossing France in a regular or irregular way, is composed of *two hundred thousand men*" (his emphasis).[30]

This figure, it happens, is as large as that proposed for temporary migrants from the countryside.[31] It all but guaranteed that *compagnons* would exercise some control over conditions of work, despite their internecine rivalries,[32] and it confirmed their central place in the transmission of popular culture.[33] The implantation of *compagnonnage*, however, remained uneven in spite of its numerical significance. The practice of the Tour de France was always more prevalent in some trades than others, and, geographically, *compagnons* neither came from every region nor covered every region in their habitual itineraries.

The building and clothing trades both clearly dominated the societies of *compagnons*, although this preponderance did not rule out the ancillary affiliation of trades in other branches of activity. The likeliest explanation, as Henri Hauser pointed out, centers on the unstable nature of demand in the building and clothing industries: "they are precisely those where work is subject to the greatest variations."[34] Labor mobility thus doubled as a strategy for dealing with the scarcity of employment, and by the eighteenth century it had proved reasonably effective in this regard.

The regional boundaries of *compagnonnage*, like its occupational boundaries, were clearly defined by the eighteenth century, if not before. "Although the itineraries were very variable according to the society, and also changed with the location of work, the geographical limits of the Tour de France can be represented by a line following the Seine, Saône, and Rhône Valleys, the Mediterranean coast, the Canal du Midi, and the Garonne, rejoining Nantes and the Loire Valley up to Orléans and Paris."[35] Regions east of the Rhône and north of the Seine were largely unfamiliar to the *compagnons du Tour de France*, although not to journeymen per se. At least where labor mobility was concerned, the cities of the North and East looked more toward northern and central Europe than toward France itself.[36] Also absent from traditional itineraries were regions of notorious underdevelopment such as Lower Brittany (except for Brest). The Massif central was touched only along its eastern fringes through cities such as Nevers, Moulins, and Le Puy. The legions of migrant building workers from Limousin and Marche, like the itinerant cobblers of Lorraine, were

primarily country folk who worked independently of established journeymen's organizations.

Within these geographical constraints, the *compagnons du Tour de France*
followed loosely structured itineraries that conveyed them from town to
town according to a recognizable pattern. "It seems that the ideal line
began in Lyon, [and] passed through Nîmes, Marseille, Toulouse, Agen,
Bordeaux, Rochefort, Nantes, Angers, Tours, Blois, Orléans, Paris, Auxerre, and Dijon."[37] On the northwestern fringe of this circuit, Rouen was
also an important center of *compagnonnage*.[38]

Yet the *villes de devoir*, or focal points of the Tour de France, by no
means concentrated all of the mobility of *compagnons*, as Emile Coornaert
has shown: "Before the Revolution, according to a joiner who was writing
around 1835, *compagnons* went much more readily to small towns than
afterward. . . . Under the Regency . . . [and] during the reigns of Louis
XV and Louis XVI, *compagnons* were to be found in nearly all the towns
of the kingdom, even in centers where they could not have been numerous, such as Etampes, Bar-sur-Aube, Avallon, Seurre . . ., [and] Marans."[39]

The itinerary of the journeyman glazier Jacques-Louis Ménétra, whose
Tour de France, described in his autobiography, lasted from 1757 until
1763, provides a marvelously complete view of the voyages of a *compagnon* under the Ancien Régime.[40] A Parisian by birth, Ménétra set out first
for Versailles, where he worked as a glazier to the king for about three
months. He then moved on to Orléans and, failing to find work, to
Vendôme, where his stay was cut short by an insincere promise of
marriage. His formal initiation into his society took place in Tours,
from whence he traveled to Angers. After a brawl between Gavots and
Dévorants that left seven persons dead and seventeen grievously wounded,
he abandoned Angers for Doué-la-Fontaine, then Niort.

In three more months he was on the road again, this time for Poitiers,
where he and all the other *compagnons étrangers* spent a month in jail for
a theft of wood committed by some soldiers. Upon his release, he made
his way to Saint-Malo, determined to embark on a pirate ship, and while
awaiting its departure, worked in Dinan. Five months of privateering
followed, but when they failed to earn him any money, he jumped ship
at Ile-d'Yeu. He recovered from the experience in Niort, then passed on
to Montreuil-Bellay because, in his words, "I just could not stay for such
a long time in the same town."

From Montreuil-Bellay he was called to Nantes, where he remained for eleven months as one of three *compagnons* not to observe an employee boycott; however, such work as they condescended to do amounted to a slowdown strike. After the lifting of the boycott, he moved on to La Rochelle, where he spent two weeks cutting windowpanes for the Islands, and to Rochefort, where, after hospitalization for venereal disease, he helped to fit out three ships for the royal navy.

Ménétra was then chosen by lot to work in the naval shipyards at Brest, but he returned to Rochefort to become *premier compagnon* in charge of job placement, before wanderlust and fear for his health impelled him on to Bordeaux. While en route there from Royan, he made the acquaintance of, and dined with, the linchpin of Bordeaux's Canada trade, Abraham Gradis.

Ménétra was sometimes disgusted with southern France, which he saw as a preserve of superstition and fanaticism, but he seemed to enjoy the opportunities it afforded him to display his cultural superiority as a Parisian. His southern itinerary was relatively typical: three months in Bordeaux, where he narrowly escaped military conscription, six weeks in Agen, stays of varying length in Auch and Toulouse. The sudden foreignness of his surroundings turned him, for the first time, into a tourist. He traveled from Toulouse to Saint-Jean-de-Luz with the intention of visiting Santiago-de-Compostela, but he changed his mind at the Spanish border upon encountering some returning pilgrims "in a wretched state." Unable to find work in Bayonne, he returned to Bordeaux and Toulouse via L'Isle-Jourdain, where one of his erstwhile companions had married and set himself up as a master. From Toulouse, he went on to Narbonne, Béziers, and Montpellier, making yet another detour for a *partie de plaisir* in Perpignan.

As *premier compagnon* in Montpellier, Ménétra undertook the glazing of the city's six hundred new streetlamps. He then spent five months working in Nîmes for a Protestant widow, and, making up his mind to marry her, he decided to speed up the pace of his Tour. He nonetheless found time to make two side trips from Marseille, one to Saint-Maximim-la-Sainte-Baume, a pilgrimage spot for the Enfants de Maître Jacques, and one to "the famous fair of Beaucaire." At the fair he accepted a contract to install the windows of the Carpentras Hospital; in Carpentras, forgetting his Nîmoise, he made plans to marry a Jewish woman, whose conversion would have netted him half of her family's fortune. Foiled by the family, he went on to work in Avignon and Bédoin, stopping off on the way to see Aix and the tomb of Nostradamus. He arrived in Lyon by way of Valence and Crest, where he visited his grandmother's family, and remained there long enough to refuse another offer of marriage. Deciding at last to return to Paris, he did brief stints in Dijon, Auxerre, and Montereau to reestablish his finances and arrived back in Saint-Germain-l'Auxerrois looking prosperous enough to impress his family. Six years had elapsed since his departure.[41]

Like other forms of temporary mobility, the Tour de France was vulnerable to short-circuits and could end elsewhere than at the point of departure, sometimes prematurely, sometimes after prolonging the period of mobility. The autobiography of Ménétra is illuminating in its relation of a series of close calls: offers of marriage, the lottery for military service, and, not least, an embarkment at Saint-Malo. Under other circumstances, any one of these opportunities could have disrupted the normal circularity of the Tour. Although the privateering episode was somewhat unusual, the marital and military options posed a constant threat to the normally structured itineraries of *compagnons*.

The premature sedentarization of *compagnons* through marriage occurred in virtually all of the urban relays, large and small, along the Tour de France. "Among practicing masters," Henri Hauser noted, "many had begun as *compagnons*." In Dijon the masters who served as witnesses to legal transactions in 1769 came from places as diverse as Franche-Comté, Nantes, Clisson (Loire-Atlantique), Champagne, and Saint-Aubin-en-Argonne. Not one had been born in Dijon or even, for that matter, in Burgundy.[42] Clearly, the institution of the Tour de France served not only to circulate skilled labor between France's cities and towns but also, in varying degrees, to renew the stock of the urban corporations themselves.[43]

Interruption of the Tour de France in favor of military service was a possibility as well, particularly after the institution of compulsory "militia" service in 1688.[44] *Compagnons passants* sometimes bore the brunt of this obligation, while cities chose to protect their native sons. Even where they successfully resisted,[45] however, a bridge to military service remained in the form of voluntary enrollment. I have already noted that between a third and a half of all recruits in the regular troops came from artisanal backgrounds. Not all of these artisans were *compagnons*, of course, and fewer still were *compagnons passants*, but it is clear that some *compagnons* did enlist in the course of their Tour. Hard luck seems to have played a part, at least upon occasion, for military service lacked the prestige of skilled labor among artisanal families.[46] Nonetheless, before the reign of Louis XVI military life was public, and the army was "relatively connected to the whole of society." Since a certain intimacy, or even "class solidarity," linked soldiers with "the inhabitants belonging the popular classes,"[47] it is not surprising that *compagnons* who were dissatisfied with their Tour for some reason would be willing to "prendre le parti des troupes" (decide for the troops).[48]

Military Migrations

Whether erstwhile *compagnons* or not, soldiers figured prominently among the long-distance travelers of early modern France. Although fewer than a tenth of all regular soldiers had migrated prior to their enlistment,[49] their service itself became a vehicle for mobility. A military vocation, under the conditions of the Ancien Régime, was "incompatible with a home-bound state of mind."[50] Soldiers moved almost constantly between garrison towns during the six or seven years that constituted the average term of service, and their various assignments often took them beyond the confines of province or region.

Military migrations differed from those of *compagnons* in their unstructured itineraries, which depended on momentary tactical exigencies rather than on tradition, and in their lower rate of return. While it is impossible to estimate the proportion of *compagnons* who chose to deviate from their hexagonal route, it is unlikely that it reached the three-fifths to two-thirds that it did among soldiers. On the other hand, the *compagnons* who failed to complete their Tour often settled farther afield than the *anciens soldats*. The latter, in spite of what were usually wide-ranging campaigns, tended to return to their native province. The two types of mobility did have in common the predominantly urban nature of the moves. Regardless of their origin, soldiers on active duty became familiar with towns and cities, and this familiarity made them more likely to settle ultimately in urban communities than in rural ones.[51]

Foreign and Colonial Movements

Long-distance movements carried migrants not only to French cities but beyond the frontiers of continental France. Migrations to the colonies and to areas under foreign jurisdiction were not insignificant, in spite of France's later reputation as a sedentary nation. Whether traditional or exceptional, temporary or permanent, they involved large enough numbers to alarm the populationists of eighteenth-century France. Moheau, one of the early political "arithmeticians," wrote in 1778 that "there is perhaps no State in which emigration causes more noticeable harm":

> The Frenchman bores and disgusts easily; no man is more avid for change; . . . he is the man of all countries; in almost all, his language is in use; everywhere, his society, wit, talents, and services are sought out, and what was formerly said of the Gauls by their conqueror, that there was no army in which some of them were not found, could be extended today to all the great cities of Europe: it seems that in France, expatriation is a national malady; all the arts, trades, and professions that are not necessarily attached to the soil and the state are infected with it; and the very way of life of a great number of citizens favors this emigration in that, in the great cities, there are a multitude of men who, even with a profession, have no fixed domicile.[52]

While less judgmental, the conclusions of modern demographers are not substantively different. According to Henri Bunle, "the principal point is not to underestimate French emigration to foreign lands. For the last hundred years, no doubt, it has not been as important as it was in certain periods in the great countries of emigration: United Kingdom, Russia, Italy, Germany, etc. It is, however, far from negligible, as evidenced by the number of Frenchmen settled in foreign lands and in our possessions."[53]

Migrations of work, military service, and religious refuge carried men and women, but mostly men, outside the boundaries of the French empire in the seventeenth and eighteenth centuries. Of these movements, the Protestant exodus involved the greatest number of people, more than 200,000 between 1660 and 1710, and continual, smaller contingents thereafter.[54] The range of destinations was very wide: Switzerland, Germany, England, Holland, Scandinavia, the thirteen colonies, South Africa. The range of emigrants was also impressive, though perhaps less so than the massive nature of the migration would indicate. They did come from most of the regions in France with Protestant minorities—not only regions south of the Loire, but also Normandy, Touraine, and Ile-de-France. But while they included individuals and families from all social classes, single males and artisans far outnumbered women, families, nobles, and peasants.

Service in the French army took large numbers of men abroad for stays that were in theory temporary, but sometimes became permanent. Besides the prisoners of war who eventually settled in the place of their captivity, there were soldiers who passed from one army to another, usually on account of desertion. There were also soldiers who enlisted in foreign armies in the first place, despite the risks of prosecution if they returned. The infamous Martin Guerre, a Basque peasant immortalized by an impersonator, left the way open for his double by deserting his family in the pays de Foix to serve in the Spanish army. Had he not somehow learned of his wife's infidelity and the diversion of his inheritance to an impostor, he quite likely would have remained on the south side of the Pyrénées.[55]

Traditional itineraries and work relations were also responsible for conveying French emigrants to foreign countries. Certain regions, like the Pyrénées and the Massif central, maintained privileged ties with Spain during the seventeenth and eighteenth centuries. Catalonia, Aragon, Valencia, Castille, and Andalusia all hosted communities of French nationals, who ran the gamut from peasants and unskilled laborers to artisans and merchants. Although some of these Espagnols were seasonal migrants, the length and considerable risks of the voyage generally militated in favor of longer stays. In Catalonia, at least, "definitive immigration always surpassed temporary immigration, which was often only a means to that end."[56]

In a similar spirit, French peddlers hawked their wares throughout Belgium and the Netherlands, and Savoyard *hommes de peine* (laborers) sought work in Switzerland, Germany, or northern Italy.[57] In central and eastern Europe, the sovereigns compensated for the lack of traditional demographic ties with France by an aggressive recruitment policy aimed at French peasants and artisans. Maria Theresa secured Alsatian, Lorrainer, and Dauphinois settlers for Hungary by stationing emigration agents in cities along the Rhine, and the Prussians and Russians canvassed there successfully for teachers, merchants, and soldiers. France, as "the relatively most populous country in Europe," furnished temporary or permanent labor as far afield as Sweden and Portugal in the eighteenth century.[58] According to Moheau,

> in other countries almost all the great cities have colonies of Frenchmen, and there are almost no great houses that do not have French cooks, valets, or lackeys; in all the considerable cities, one sees French surgeons, wig makers, tailors, junk dealers. Fifteen or twenty years ago, there were 30,000 Frenchmen living in London . . . The number of Frenchmen living in Spain was estimated at 8,000 . . . ; in Portugal there were 500 to 600 Frenchmen without counting the house of the Ambassador and the Jews . . . ; there are an estimated 15,000 Frenchmen living in Italy . . . Holland is full of Frenchmen, born in France or into French families . . . ; in 1738, there were 10,000 Frenchmen living in the Ottoman Empire.[59]

Emigration to the French colonies was substantial as well, contrary to traditional assumptions based on the fairly unimpressive multiplication of colonial populations. I have already mentioned that in Québec, where net immigration totaled 20,000 or so, gross immigration ran to easily triple that number. Until very recently, however, historians clung to the figure of 10,000 to 12,000, which represents little more than those individuals who founded families during the French Regime.

The standard global estimates of French colonial emigration probably need to be increased as well. Indentured servants for all the colonies numbered, by present counts, 6,000 in Nantes, 6,000 in La Rochelle, and more than 2,000 in Dieppe, for the seventeenth century alone.[60] The notarial archives of many other ports remain to be examined for this period, but it is clear that the activity of other Norman ports, at least, was far from negligible.[61] The *engagés* of the eighteenth century have been studied fully only in Bordeaux, but their numbers, some 13,000 strong, suggest that Gabriel Debien erred in assuming that the developing slave economy brought a rapid end to the system of indentured servitude.[62]

Paying passengers have garnered even less attention from historians; the only available statistics concern Nantes and Bordeaux in the eighteenth century. More than 8,000 passengers left Nantes for the Islands in that period, and they were joined by about 30,000 passengers from Bordeaux.[63] The passenger lists in the central repository of the Archives des Colonies make it possible to boost this number by a minimum of 20,000; between the various ports, they contain more than 60,000 names for the period beginning in 1749. Without even trying to be comprehensive, one arrives at a total of more than 80,000 colonial emigrants for the Ancien Régime.

An examination of colonial migrations at their points of arrival confirms that the received estimate of perhaps 90,000 emigrants is too low. Louisiana received at least 7,000 French emigrants in the eighteenth century, and French Guyana swallowed up about 15,000. Réunion, in the Indian Ocean, saw its French population rise from fewer than 1,000 at the death of Louis XIV to 10,000 at the beginning of the Revolution, by which time there were also 12,000 French people living on Ile de France and Ile de Bourbon.[64]

The poor state of the West Indian archives precludes a reconstruction of the French population along the lines of that undertaken in Québec, but it is clear that emigration occurred on a large scale throughout the period of colonization. From the very beginning, the Islands were considered the more desirable destination; 7,000 emigrants arrived there between 1635 and 1642,[65] while Québec received at most 2,400 new recruits between 1632 and 1644.[66]

By the mid-eighteenth century, this differential had increased, for, despite shrinking opportunities and a lethal environment, the Caribbean conjured up a "West Indian mirage" in sharp contrast to the Canadian image of "a few acres of snow." According to the passenger lists from La Rochelle, the years 1749–1763 witnessed an annual average of 98 departures for the Antilles, compared with 16 for Canada, 14 for Louisiana, 1 for Africa, and 3 for Guyana.[67] In Bordeaux, which was, by this time, the primary exit port for both the Islands and Canada, the corresponding figures were 548 emigrants bound for the West Indies and 34 for Canada; the highest number of passengers to leave in any one year was 124 for Canada and 1,355 for the other colonies.[68]

"Based on these fragmentary data," as Bunle observed, "it is difficult to estimate with precision the importance of French emigration to the colonies during the reigns of Louis XIV and Louis XV . . . It seems, however, that in the seventeenth and eighteenth centuries, annual French emigration to the colonies was, on the average, around 2,500 persons."[69] This figure, which was, incidentally, first proposed by Moheau in 1778, would bring the total number of French departures for the colonies to about 375,000 for the period prior to the conquest of Canada. The comparable total for England was about 300,000 for North America alone,[70] so on a per capita basis, emigration to the colonies involved between three and nine times as many English as French people.[71]

It should be remembered, however, that France was not just an Atlantic nation, but a nation divided between Atlantic and continental interests. In demographic matters, the latter seemingly prevailed to the point that fewer than a quarter of France's external migrants consisted of recruits for the colonies; for, according to Bunle, total French emigration to foreign and colonial destinations came to some 12,000 persons each year.[72] Commented Gabriel Debien: "That is not what we were taught about our countryside in the seventeenth and eighteenth centuries!"[73]

Summary

The traditional image of a sedentary France proves, for all its popularity, to be fallacious. Whether female or male, southern or northern, rural or urban, poor or rich, French people moved in the seventeenth and eighteenth centuries, and what is more, they did so on a massive scale. The fairly high rate of foreign, and even of colonial, emigration befitted what was, in absolute terms, the most populous nation in Europe; however, it was only the tip of the iceberg in comparison to the rate of internal migration. As Debien recognized many years ago, foreign or colonial emigration was really nothing more than "a lateral aspect, a derivative," of internal patterns of mobility, and particularly of the most prevalent pattern: "the rural exodus toward cities. . . . To understand it, it is necessary . . . to regard it as a particular aspect of a much more general fact: French internal migrations."[74] Region by region, then, it is necessary to reconsider the already familiar geography of French emigration to Canada—and this time to go beyond descriptions of social and economic structures and view the movement within the equally crucial context of traditions of migration.

CHAPTER 8

A Traditional Movement: Northwestern Emigration to Canada

As was indicated in the previous chapter, Ancien Régime migrations had a life of their own. While responsive to changing conditions, whether social, economic, or demographic, they were also the product of preexisting habits and traditions. When circumstances changed, migration streams ebbed and flowed, but they were unlikely to be born or disappear ex nihilo. Instead, traditional currents of migration changed course, converged, or rearranged themselves to form new migration streams. Emigration to Canada was the product of one such rearrangement and convergence.

In Northwestern France, emigration to Canada was at the confluence of several traditions of regional mobility: those of seamanship, urban immigration, and *compagnonnage*, among others. Traditions of seamanship, which included the North Atlantic by the late Middle Ages, gave rise eventually to currents of temporary and permanent migration. So did traditions of urban immigration, for, through their regional and social origins, emigrants to Canada bore a striking resemblance to immigrants of northwestern cities. The northwestern leg of the Tour de France fed directly, albeit exceptionally, into the Canadian migration stream. Traditional work migrations involving rural males did so more indirectly, in that areas noted for exporting specific kinds of labor also figure on a map of Canadian emigration, though not for the same occupational specialties. Among the elites, traditions of long-distance migration created an adventurous mentality that could work to the profit of Canada; and among middling social strata, micro-mobility indicated an availability that could be tapped, upon occasion, by Canadian recruiters. Finally, in the Northwest, emigration to the West Indies exhibited a similar profile to emigration to Canada, thereby suggesting that the whole brave new world of Atlantic colonization was built, in some measure, upon tradition.

Brittany

Studies of Breton mobility have begun to multiply in recent years, challenging the traditional assumption that Bretons remained generally immobile until the late nineteenth century.[1] The province, in fact, witnessed important currents of immigration and emigration throughout the early modern period. As elsewhere in France, immigrants directed themselves primarily toward cities, but emigration did not fit this general pattern. Preindustrial emigration from Brittany was Atlantic-based rather than continental, and, as such, it escaped the notice of earlier historians who were more concerned with the formation of the Parisian population than with provincial emigration per se. No discussion of Breton mobility would be complete, however, without mention of the population flows across the Atlantic.

Viewed within the context of Brittany's other migrations, emigration to Canada appears, first, as an extension of existing maritime traditions. Throughout the Ancien Régime, the province witnessed "very abundant recruitment of sailors for the navy and merchant marine,"[2] and northern Brittany produced not only sailors but also fishermen in abundance. Sailing, fishing, and commerce all gave rise to voyages and settlement in North America, particularly in the eighteenth century, when the economy of northern Brittany grew more dependent on Atlantic cod. Definitive emigration probably increased in proportion with the decline of Saint-Malo's traditional commerce with northern Europe;[3] that structural shift, rather than any temporary rise in grain prices, must have been responsible for the influx of Malouins decried by the Acadian intendant in 1755.[4]

Two decades earlier, Breton traditions of seamanship had already given rise to an important community on Ile Royale. An exceptionally complete census from 1734 lists every settled householder on the island, together with his or her regional origin and occupation. Over a quarter of the 229 French-born habitants were Bretons, most of them from the northern part of the province. Their stated occupations included fishing (19), navigation (10), building and metalworking (9), commerce (8), the priesthood (8), agriculture (2), the army (1), transport (1), and tailoring (1).[5] The preponderance of sailors and fishermen suggests that the expansion of Saint-Malo's relations with North America, together with the deterioration of its commerce elsewhere, resulted in the transformation of seasonal maritime activity into more or less permanent settlement in the eighteenth century.[6]

Yet Breton emigration to Canada was not solely an extension of long-established maritime traditions, for it also replicated patterns that were characteristic of interior movements. At short distances, the communities of urban demographic basins contributed to both the flow of immigrants into cities and the flow of emigrants to Canada. At middle and even long distances, the same currents that fed the growth of Breton cities also channeled emigrants through Brittany to Canada.

Cartographically, there was a link between local immigration into cities and colonial departures. In the region of Nantes, villages that sent emigrants to Canada were usually prominent on maps of rural immigration into the port. Conversely, communities without significant demographic ties to Nantes tended to be absent from the cartography of emigration.

These local patterns of immigration into Nantes explain an anomaly in the regional geography of emigration to Canada—a breach, that is, in the familiar geography of modernity. I have said that emigration from Loire-Atlantique focused on prosperous areas in close economic contact with Nantes: the southeastern part of the diocese, the Loire Valley, and the *villes-relais*.[7] There was, however, one narrow band of sending communities in the impoverished north, stretching from Riaillé through Blain to Saint-Gildas-des-Bois. At the same time, the Nantes-Rennes axis, though important economically, produced very few emigrants. These aberrations disappear when one looks beyond economics to consider migratory tradition. Nantes's demographic basin, it turns out, included not only the southeast, the Loire, and the *villes-relais*, but also, as Jacques Depauw has shown, the economically more fragile region around Blain. Likewise, the Nantes-Rennes axis, despite its economic role, channeled few immigrants into Nantes until the 1770s and 1780s, a generation after the loss of Canada.[8] In southern Brittany, the cartography of emigration to Canada bore an undeniable resemblance to that of local urban arrivals. It could not be accounted for through economic analysis alone.

It is likely that Breton emigration to Canada reproduced overall patterns of urban immigration as well as local ones. A study of 18 persons who indentured themselves in Nantes for Canada between 1725 and 1732 yielded 9 Bretons, 2 Manceaux, 2 Poitevins, 1 Orléanais, 1 Rochelais, 2 Parisians, and 1 native of "Gournay near Paris."[9] Of the Bretons, only 1 was a native of Nantes, but 7 came from the diocese, and 2 from the neighboring Dioceses of Rennes and Vannes. Half of the non-Nantais came from villages, and the other half from *villes-relais* such as Guérande, Le Croisic, and Clisson.

While there is no indication that these emigrants actually lived in Nantes at the time of their departure, it is clear that their origins matched those of the city's bona fide immigrants.[10] The same thing is true of the more than 500 Canadian emigrants who passed through Saint-Malo after 1749; this mix of Bretons, Lower Normans, and scattered individuals from far and wide was a good reflection of the currents of immigration into the "least Breton of Breton ports."[11]

The precise relationship between internal and colonial migrations is difficult to determine, for information about emigrants' prior mobility, if any, is often lacking. Overseas departures could have siphoned off a percentage of those who would otherwise have become new residents of a city, but such departures also could have occurred as an afterthought, urban immigration having already transpired. The available evidence, while too scanty to sustain firm generalizations, lends credence to the idea that colonial departures tended to succeed, rather than supersede, internal moves. A model whereby a traditional pattern of mobility could be extended or go awry seems to be valid, on an individual basis, for emigrants as different as fishermen, residents of urban environs, soldiers, and *compagnons*.

My Breton emigrant sample contained 55 persons, 3 of them women, who unquestionably lived away from their place of birth when they departed for Canada. More than half of them, 33, had moved from one place in Brittany to another, but the remaining 22 had immigrated into Brittany from a different province. Of the new arrivals, 9 came from the neighboring provinces of Normandy, Maine, Anjou, and Poitou, 2 from the Loire (Orléanais), and 3 from Paris. The others hailed from as far afield as Aunis, Champagne, Lyonnais, Franche-Comté, and the Netherlands.

The actual itineraries of the future emigrants demonstrate the importance of interurban movements and, especially, the rural exodus. Twenty of the 55 migrants had moved from one urban community to another, and in 17 cases the receiving town was the same size or larger than the sending town. Thirty-two people had made their way from the countryside to the city, and 27 in this group chose as their destination a city of more than 10,000 inhabitants. Two people had migrated from a less active to a more active rural area, and, finally, 1 nobleman had abandoned a town for a rural suburb of Nantes. All 3 of the women were Breton villagers; their respective destinations were Tréguier, Nantes, and Saint-Malo.

There were 6 cases of multiple prior migrations, most of them involving great distances, but none of them suggesting a traditional Tour de France. Repeat migrants were often soldiers, like Joseph Tourelle, a native of Franche-Comté, who had served extensively in the Low Countries before arriving in Port-Louis. One of them, Pierre Brunel, was perhaps a Protestant, for he had come to Brest via Rochefort and the Protestant strongholds of Niort and Sainte-Foye-la-Grande (Gironde).

For this small group of emigrants whose prior movements in France could be reconstructed, emigration appeared to be a further step in a migratory process that until then had been quite traditional. Soldiers enlisted for the colonies after serving in France, and city dwellers set sail for Canada after abandoning villages, *villes-relais,* or other cities for the major ports.

While none of the certified prior migrants in my sample happened to be *compagnons,* it is clear that the itineraries of Brittany's compagnons also proved flexible enough to include Canada together with more traditional destinations. Of the small number of artisans in the sample who described themselves explicitly as *garçons* or *compagnons,*[12] 5 were Breton, and a sixth departed from Nantes.[13] All of the Bretons set sail not from Nantes or Saint-Malo but from La Rochelle, an indication that they had probably embarked on a Tour de France. Two were from Nantes, 2 from the city's environs, and 1 from Finistère. In all likelihood the *compagnons* from the outskirts of Nantes had done more than simply travel along the interurban circuit from Nantes to La Rochelle; as villagers born within Nantes's demographic basin, they would also have preceded their Tour by immigrating to Nantes.[14] All 6 men practiced trades in which itinerant labor was common: joiner, cooper, edge-tool maker, tailor, wig maker, cobbler.[15] Their average age was eighteen, and their departures spanned the entire last century of the French Regime.[16]

One last Breton migratory tradition remains to be discussed in relation to emigration to Canada: emigration to the West Indies. This tradition, which emerged simultaneously with emigration to Canada, also resembled it. In fact, the origins of emigrants for the Islands recall those of both emigrants to Canada and immigrants into Breton cities. A recent study of indentured servants who embarked for the Islands in Nantes found that "one-quarter came from the *comté nantais,* nearly one-tenth from Nantes itself, the others from the West (regions of Rennes and Vannes) and the Loire Valley, but 8.4% from Paris, with small groups from the Center and East. These people were much more often town dwellers than country folk." Among paying passengers, Nantes cut a more impressive figure with 22%. "They were especially likely to be shippers, administrators, and artisans from every trade."[17] Women were rare among the individual emigrants, whether free or indentured, but the city did witness the departure of "convoys of women and girls assembled in hospices, almonries, and, later on, in general hospitals and even refuges [shelters for prostitutes]."[18] As I shall discuss, similar organized convoys made their way to Canada, though not, as it happens, from Brittany.

In 1954, Louis Merle and Gabriel Debien, studying a much smaller sample of Breton emigrants for the Islands, had already asked themselves, "Is this an original movement or a slight diversion of the very numerous moves that could be observed, at that time, from one city to another, one province to another?"[19] Today, one can confidently adopt the second proposition. In the seventeenth and eighteenth centuries, a port like Nantes or Saint-Malo was at once a home base for navigators and fishermen, a pole of attraction for rural and urban immigrants, a temporary place of residence for *compagnons* seeking a *ville de devoir,* and a port of embarkment for America.[20]

Breton emigration to Canada, in addition to being an extension of centuries-old maritime activity, was part of a larger tradition that included colonial migrations generally. Colonial migrations themselves were less independent movements than composite derivations of the diverse migration streams that converged on the city, which was a colander as well as a magnet, a "pompe aspirante et foulante" (two-way pump).[21] Thus, the parallelism between Breton emigrants for Canada and the province's other migrants was striking; Brittany's human contribution to the colony was shaped not solely by economic considerations, but also by demographic tradition.

Normandy

The demographic history of Normandy, like its economic history, varied greatly from one part of the province to another. Once again, the main division was between east and west, with the Orne as an approximate line of demarcation. In matters migratory, the two ensembles followed different trajectories in the course of the Ancien Régime. In Upper Normandy and the pays d'Auge, the rural population became gradually more sedentary, as it pioneered a modern model of family size. Western Normandy, from Caen to the Cotentin, witnessed the opposite phenomenon, with its rural inhabitants becoming increasingly mobile during the eighteenth century.

This complex migratory history adds a further dimension to an understanding of emigration to Canada, by providing insights into geography and chronology that could not always be gleaned from economic and social structures. In eastern Normandy, it clarifies the predominance of the pays de Caux over the pays d'Auge in the production of emigrants, and it better explains the decline of emigration in both regions during the eighteenth century. New conclusions about the migratory dominance of the Avranchin over the Coutançais and the greater importance of emigration in the eighteenth century also emerge from a consideration of the Lower Norman pattern.

Examined from a demographic angle, emigration from the pays d'Auge could not equal that from the pays de Caux because of the early atrophy of Augeron migrations. Except for Honfleur, whose harbor silted in the eighteenth century, and the environs of Lisieux, where some textile manu-

facturing took place, the economy of the pays d'Auge centered on capi-
tal-intensive agriculture in the form of animal husbandry. Opportunities
for immigrants consequently were limited, for the "conversion of arable
land to pasture entails a brutal reduction of optimum population levels."[22]
Although immigrants could be found to some degree within all social
classes (particularly the bourgeoisie), the region witnessed relatively few
arrivals during the Ancien Régime.[23]

Emigration from the pays d'Auge was equally modest—a finding that
might seem surprising, since transition to an economy based on animal
husbandry "does not go forward without a retreat of men."[24] Part of the
explanation lies in the timing of the shift, which began in the early
sixteenth century and was virtually complete by the mid-seventeenth. Also
important was the simultaneous drop in the Augeron birthrate, a decline
that marked the region as "a demographic case of hypermaturity."[25]
Augeron denatality, coupled with the low immigration rate, limited emigration from the region throughout the Ancien Régime.

In Upper Normandy, a similar tendency toward stabilization occurred
later, in the eighteenth century, as fertility began to decline and proto-
industrialization created manufacturing jobs throughout the countryside.[26]
Migrations into and out of the major cities slowed apace, and this slowing,
together with the reorientation of the Canada trade, explains the relative
cessation of Cauchois emigration to Canada in the eighteenth century.[27]
That the economic explanation alone does not suffice is shown by the
failure of emigration to increase substantially in the 1730s, when the efforts
of the merchant house of Dugard returned an important share of the
Canada trade to Rouen.[28]

To the extent that emigration, whether sparse or abundant, occurred as
a by-product of immigration, it is worth comparing Upper Norman
immigrants with emigrants to Canada or the Islands.[29] While the geographical origins of these immigrants are less well known than Brittany's
(the demographic basin of Rouen, for example, remains to be mapped),[30]
their social origins are somewhat better understood. In Rouen, as in the
pays d'Auge, "immigrants were present at all levels of society"—more
so among the elites. The rural immigrants were an ambitious lot, for,
according to Jean-Pierre Bardet, "it was the most educated, the most
literate, the most gifted, and the best endowed who took the road to

[Rouen]."[31] The city, in order to maintain itself, skimmed away the most upwardly mobile residents of the countryside. The selection noted among emigrants to Canada (a group more elite and more skilled than the norm) was thus characteristic of other migrants as well. In Upper Normandy, "movements of immigration selected the best-trained children of the hinterland."[32]

IN LOWER MORMANDY, patterns of migration were very different, for reasons that were demographic as well as economic. Emigration to Canada increased in the eighteenth century not only in rhythm with the economic activity of Granville but as demographic pressure built up aross the Cotentin and *bocage*.[33] Even areas without sustained connections to Granville (such as the northern Cotentin) exhibited a similar pattern of late emigration.

Geographically, the heaviest emigration occurred in a region with a long-standing tradition of codfishing migrations, the Avranchin.[34] Whereas in the seventeenth century fishermen were usually content to pay seasonal visits to Newfoundland, the Gaspé Peninsula, or Cape Breton, seasonal and permanent emigration shaded into each other in the eighteenth. Seasonal mobility did not disappear, as shown by the testimonial of freedom at marriage of the emigrant Barthélémy Alis. A native of the village of Marcey, Alis embarked for "la pêche de Gaspé" in 1755, at the age of twenty-three, and decided to settle in Canada. When asked to present witnesses to the legitimacy of his forthcoming marriage, he could state only that "in the same ship, there had come a man named François Obu from the same parish . . . [and that] others from his same parish had come the same year in different ships [but] are no longer in this province."[35]

At times, permanent settlement followed upon a number of seasonal campaigns; such was the case with François Hamel of Avranches and François Frigot, who both claimed to have "made several campaigns by sea as well as by land" before establishing themselves in Québec.[36] A fourth emigrant, Louis Alexandre of the village of Ronthon, continued the tradition of seasonal labor, while basing himself in Canada instead of Normandy. After leaving home in 1751, at the age of twelve, Alexandre spent the summer in Gaspé, then wintered upriver at La Rivière-Ouelle.

He still resided on the Côte-du-Sud at the time of his marriage fifteen years later, "going each summer to fish in Gaspé."[37]

Outside of the Avranchin, emigration to Canada tapered off, in part because traditional migration streams linking Lower Normandy to inland areas hindered the exploration of Atlantic migratory options. These traditional streams, organized around specific commercial or para-industrial activities, originated in clusters of contiguous parishes. Time-honored itineraries carried the migrants to a wide array of familiar destinations, some of them as far away as the Low Countries and northern Germany.

To the north of Granville, in the Coutançais, traditional migrations originated in both coastal and inland areas. Along the coast, emigrants from a dozen or so parishes in the vicinity of Agon specialized in the peddling of printed material, which took them to French-speaking cities across northern Europe.[38] Inland, where the migratory zone covered about fifty parishes in the orbit of Villedieu-les-Poêles and Percy,[39] emigrants specialized in selling objects of local fabrication: copper pots and sieves made from *rapatelle* (coarse linen and horsehair). Their territories were far-flung, extending to Nijmegen, Hamburg, and even Schleswig-Holstein, but their most common destination was Brittany, particularly in the seventeenth century.

The Coutançais was, of course, represented on the map of Canadian departures nonetheless. A spillover phenomenon—already evident in the pattern of internal migration, where not every destination was sanctioned by tradition—extended to Canada as well.[40] Thus, Julien Lorence of La Lande-d'Airou, which fell within the migratory sphere of Villedieu and Percy, departed not for Brittany but for Gaspé; André Laforge of Muneville-le-Bingard, near Agon, traveled not in northern France but in Québec. Perhaps it was easiest to buck tradition in families that did not participate in the economic activity fueling the dominant migration. Lorence, a fisherman, was the son of a *laboureur*, and Laforge, a soldier and fisherman, came from a family of artisans not associated with the printing trade. His father, to whom he was briefly apprenticed, was a carpenter, and the uncle with whom he lived after his father's death owned a flour and fulling mill.[41]

As might be predicted, migratory spillover into Canada assumed greater proportions close to the Atlantic than farther inland. Both the Coutançais and the *bocage* proper possessed strong traditions of internal migration, but the proximity of the first region to Granville increased the likelihood of Atlantic migratory deviations.[42] The sparsest emigration, however, came not from the *bocage*, but from the northern Cotentin, a coastal region of "secular isolation" up to the eighteenth century.[43] It seems that extant traditions of out-migration could impede the development of a new Atlantic current, while also guaranteeing a higher level of residual emigration than could be expected from areas without such traditions in the first place.

THE IMPACT of both Upper and Lower Norman demography on emigration to Canada is further apparent when patterns of prior mobility are examined. Prior mobility could be established for 57 Norman emigrants, 6 of them women. The regional origins of these previous migrants were no more wide-ranging than the rather weak rates of urban immigration in Upper Normandy would seem to suggest. Forty persons, including all of the women, were Norman by birth, and a further 5 came from elsewhere in the Northwest. The only other provinces that were represented were Ile-de-France, Picardy, Saintonge, and Guyenne.[44]

The urban-rural distributions were also characteristic. Prior movements between towns and cities were about as frequent as in Brittany, and deurbanization was equally rare. But relatively speaking, urbanization was more tepid. While twice as many colonists embarked from a town as were born in one, rural areas had continued to welcome migrants on a significant scale. As an indication of proto-industrialization or, more generally, a better integration of the countryside into broader economic circuits, this higher level of rural immigration went hand in hand with modernity. At the same time, however, it explains why this modernity would ultimately prove stillborn. In the nineteenth century, the slow growth of cities meant economic marginalization. Paradoxically, the precocious development of eastern Normandy set the stage for its future backwardness.

In Lower Normandy, in keeping with the less developed economy, the pattern of prior immigration was almost entirely local. The Avranchin, as Michel Le Pesant has noted, skimmed off a part of the surplus from the region of Percy, in this case Lorbehaie, Le Mesnil-Thibaut, and Saint-Denis-le-Gast.[45] For the Percynois, emigration to Canada could thus be an extension of, as well as a deviation from, tradition; it could be accomplished in two stepwise moves, each of which remained within familiar circuits.[46]

Thus, demographic analysis is able to clarify the geography and chronology of Norman emigration and to confirm the analysis of its social composition. The pays d'Auge produced fewer emigrants than the pays de Caux in my sample because the local immigration and birth rates slowed in, respectively, the seventeenth and eighteenth centuries. In Lower Normandy, by contrast, the eighteenth century was a time of over-population and, hence, higher emigration. The appeal of Canada was nonetheless uneven there, varying partly as a function of traditional itineraries. Fewer colonists arrived from the Coutançais than the Avranchin, not only because it was a little more remote, but because the inhabitants of Percy or Agon already had a full repertory of migratory possibilities that did not involve, at least initially, the Atlantic. Even so, their familiarity with long-distance migration made for a certain amount of spillover and guaranteed their presence in the Canadian migration stream.

Likewise, the social origins of Norman emigrants to Canada make sense in demographic terms. The broader class base and more equal sex ratio of emigration from eastern Normandy, while characteristic of a more modern region, were also related to migration. In eastern Normandy, Atlantic emigration, whether to the Islands or to Canada, was a partial spin-off of the region's immigration. Both migration streams drew from a fairly narrow regional base but a relatively broad social and sexual spectrum. In western Normandy, also, the patterns exhibited by internal and external migrations were similar; whether temporary or permanent, the area's major migration streams consisted of working-aged males from the popular classes of the countryside. Thus, diverse migratory traditions, in tandem with social and economic structures, defined Norman emigration to Canada.

Perche

At first glance, the migration history of Perche, at least as reported by contemporary observers, provides few clues to the successful transplantation of a Percheron community to North America. The intendant of Alençon, describing the "nature of the people," reported that "they seem sluggish, attached from father to son to the same work . . . do not like in the least to leave their country although unhappy, if not for a few who go help with the harvests in Beauce, which yields them some profits."[47]

Traditions of seasonal migration were, in fact, important in the province, yet the intendant was probably correct in treating them offhandedly. The harvest migrations he mentioned, no matter how numerous, could not truly disrupt a pattern of fundamental sedentariness. They involved relatively short distances (neighboring Beauce) and even shorter times ("the great July rendezvous").[48] Until the mechanization of agricultural labor in the nineteenth century, the mobility of Percheron harvesters rarely deviated from a rigorous periodicity.

Within their province, however, Percherons were by no means immobile. The bourg of Tourouvre, for instance, had always witnessed "relatively important migratory currents," which originated in and returned to the environs. Certain categories of Percherons, like the wire drawers *(tréfiliers)* and millers of Tourouvre, seemed particularly inclined toward micro-mobility.[49]

Yet if high levels of micro-mobility marked Perche as a province familiar with speculation, local exchanges of land and population hardly constitute a prolegomenon to Atlantic migration. Since the seasonal migrations, by their very regularity or marginality, merely accentuated parochialism, one must look elsewhere for the demographic origins of Percheron emigration to Canada.

As befits a movement as unspontaneous as Percheron colonization, these origins lie not in the mass mobility of the population, be it seasonal or local, but in the mobility of the elite that engineered the departures. Percheron notables were no strangers to micro-mobility themselves. The merchant father of the two most eminent recruiters for Canada, Jean and Noël Juchereau, involved himself "in all sorts of transactions, changing residence frequently, by turns in Marchainville, Saint-Denis-sur-Huisne, Feings, La Lande-sur-Eure, Tourouvre, La Lande again, Euchaumesnil (Normandy), Tourouvre, and finally La Ventrouze."[50] But such intense *"brassage"* did not totalize the migratory options of the elite; as early as the sixteenth century, a minority of wellborn Percherons were growing accustomed to seeking their fortune in long-distance migration. Their original outlet of choice was England: "Around 1553, one, then several young people from the region's notable families were noted [in the notarial archives] to be living in London in the capacity of crossbowmen for the king of England; they were four or five from the Thory, Gignon, and Roussin families. The first would return; others would remain in London."[51]

The tradition of emigration to England does not appear to have been perpetuated into the seventeenth century; however, viewed within this context, the previous long-distance migrations of Canada's promoters no longer seem anomalous. Noël Juchereau had spent time in Paris as a student of law, and Robert Giffard had done a temporary stint in Canada as a naval surgeon and fur trader for Guillaume de Caën.[52] Of course, this propensity toward temporary or permanent departure on the part of the elite fails to explain the success of Canadian recruitment among the Percheron rank and file. A closer look at the emigrants themselves, however, suggests that virtually none of them figured among the unfortunates who supplemented their poor living with seasonal voyages to the Beauce.

Historians writing in the nineteenth century already knew that the Percheron colonists made up a group "of a certain quality":[53] "Many were farmers, others tradesmen, masons, carpenters, blacksmiths; all had . . . tools, a small capital, some movables."[54]

More recent excavation of the local notarial records has yielded an even more surprising conclusion: "Now, all of these emigrants owned real estate."[55] Even those who indentured themselves as day laborers stemmed from families with a certain *avoir;* witness the Tourouvrain Antoine Méry, whose relative Master Jehan not only practiced his trade of apothecary, but also engaged in the large-scale commerce of wood for the fabrication of charcoal.[56] And day laborers could themselves possess considerable property in their own right, as is seen from the sale by Jehan Martheau the younger, "manoeuvrier," and Jehanne Le Court, his wife, to Jehan Gaignon, the father of an emigrant, of "each and every farmhouse and other high dwelling as well as the common barnyards, hemp patches, meadows, pastures, and other arable and nonarable lands generally, which belong to the said seller either on account of the division of the property of his said wife or from his exchanges and acquisitions."[57]

The case of Juchereau *père,* ironmaster, "buying and selling land according to his opportunities or needs"[58] was probably exceptional, but the notarial archives demonstrate conclusively that the Percheron emigrants were not "sorry wretches . . . Furthermore, a dozen of these Percherons were veritable merchants."[59]

Apparently, the willingness of notables to emigrate was not confined to men, nor even to men and their wives. One Percheronne, Marie-Geneviève de Manovely de Réville, arrived in Canada alone in 1662, at the age of nineteen. An orphan, she nonetheless belonged to what must have been one of the region's more considered families. Her father, the son of a Parisian banker, had settled in Perche, where thanks to the "savonette à vilains," (a venal office conveying noble status) he had presided as *écuyer* and *sieur* of Réville over the *maîtrise particulière des eaux et forêts*.[60] Her mother, Françoise de Blavette, had boasted a pedigree of impeccable Percheron nobility.

Except for Jean Juchereau, whose son Nicolas obtained letters of nobility in 1692, Marie-Geneviève de Manovely seems to have been the only emigrant from the seventeenth century with a connection or claim to the second estate.[61] Nonetheless, the Percheron nobility was not impervious to the lure of Canada, as illustrated by the bizarre biography of an eighteenth-century emigrant, Count Joseph de La Puisaye.

La Puisaye was born in Mortagne in 1755, long after the major flow of Percheron emigration had stopped. His career until the Revolution was unexceptional: studies in Paris at the Seminary of Saint-Sulpice followed by service in a regiment. In 1789, however, La Puisaye took a seat in the Estates General, and in 1791, he commanded the National Guard of Evreux. By 1793 he had taken up arms for the Federalists, and after stints in Brittany and London, he became the leader of the ill-fated expedition of Quiberon. Back in London, he took refuge from his failures by writing a "Political and Financial Sketch for a Settlement of French Emigrants."[62] Destined to become the short-lived émigré colony of Windham, Ontario, this project met with no more success than any of La Puisaye's previous ventures. He died in London in 1827, a picturesque footnote to the Percheron elite's penchants for Britain and North America.

Apart from Juchereau, Giffard, La Puisaye, and one emigrant from the mid-eighteenth century,[63] it does not appear that any of the Percherons had accomplished long-distance migrations prior to embarking for Canada. At least 18 men and 6 women who departed directly from Perche had already moved at least once, but few of them had traveled far. Eighteen (including Giffard and Juchereau) had been born in Perche, and all the others came from adjoining provinces: Maine (3), Beauce (2), and Normandy (1). Most of the prior migrants came from the countryside, and few had left it, even for the local center of Mortagne. Micro-mobility rather than urbanization was the predominant pattern of prior mobility.

Percheron emigrants for Canada thus belonged to a fairly active rural bourgeoisie, which was largely free from the parochialism attributed to the masses by the intendant. Although in the normal course of things they rarely moved beyond the region of their birth, they engaged freely in micro-mobility. And most of all, they were close to and susceptible to suggestion from a wider ranging and sometimes positively adventurous elite.

Maine and Anjou

Canada-bound emigrants from Maine and Anjou, like those from the other northwestern provinces, were no strangers to migratory tradition. As in Perche, the annual harvest migrants rarely engaged in other forms of mobility,[64] and as in the Norman *bocage,* the long-distance practitioners of artisanal and commercial activities plugged themselves only incidentally into Atlantic circuits.[65] But two types of prior mobility were reflected clearly in the pattern of emigration to Canada: micro-displacement, as in Perche, and the Tour de France, as in Brittany. The primary sources for my discussion of these movements are the contracts of indentured servitude drawn up in La Flèche in 1653 at the instigation of Jérôme Le Royer de La Dauversière, the *procureur* of the Société Notre-Dame pour la conversion des sauvages en Nouvelle-France mentioned in Chapter 2.

The *engagés* of La Flèche came primarily from localities in the immediate vicinity of the town; 106, or 87.6% of the 121 emigrants, described themselves as Manceaux or Angevins.[66] The nearby provinces of Normandy, Orléanais, Perche, and Touraine produced an additional 5 emigrants, or 4.1% of the sample. These figures suggest that the normal catchment area of La Flèche was narrow, a feature it apparently shared with Anjou's principal cities.[67] Of course, these 111 persons were not necessarily immigrants to La Flèche; they may simply have journeyed into town for the signing of their contracts. The language of the documents nonetheless suggests that a significant minority of these would-be emigrants had previously moved within the immediate region: the notary clearly distinguished between "natives of" and "residents in" particular parishes, and nearly a quarter of the local contractees found themselves in the second category.

Interestingly, the contribution of long-distance mobility was much more important than that from the surrounding provinces. Ten emigrants, or 8.3%, came from Ile-de-France (4), Champagne (2), Burgundy (2), Picardy (1), and Nivernais (1); their professions included carpenter (3), joiner (2), shoemaker, brewer, surgeon, *laboureur*, and *défricheur*. In an exception to the customary inattention to juridical status, all of the carpenters and joiners were specifically designated as *compagnons*.

All in all, 10 *compagnons* contracted to emigrate from La Flèche: 5 natives of Maine and Touraine, 2 Parisians, and 1 each from Dijon, Châtillon-sur-Seine, and Nevers. These formal affiliates of the Tour de France made up about a quarter of the artisans recruited in La Flèche, including 8 of the 18 from the building and woodworking trades, 1 of the 6 from the garment trades, and 1 of the 7 metalworkers. The further presence of a shoemaker from Senlis (Oise) and a brewer from Clermont-en-Bassigny (Haute-Marne) confirms that "without being affiliated officially, certain trades were on the limits of *compagnonnage:* thus the *garçons cordonniers*." It was not uncommon for such workers occasionally to practice the Tour de France; to shoemakers and brewers could be added bakers, blacksmiths, caulkers, and nail makers.[68]

The Tour de France was thus a central institution in Anjou, not only in Angers and Saumur, but also in smaller centers like La Flèche. The strength of this itinerant tradition probably created a more cosmopolitan climate than otherwise would have existed in a province whose sleepy capital failed to take advantage of its opportunities in the form of "a numerous population, a river network of the first order, and a hinterland rich in varied raw materials."[69]

The three long-distance emigrants who did not belong to the artisan class consisted of a master surgeon born in Paris but living in Epernay (Marne), a *laboureur* from Forges-en-Brie (Seine-et-Marne), and a *défri-

cheur living in Paris. They serve to demonstrate that even in a small town like La Flèche, long-distance travelers could straggle in through mechanisms other than *compagnonnage*.

Looking beyond the emigrants of 1653, one finds several other examples of prior migration among the Angevins and Manceaux who departed for Canada. Local mobility continued, as did artisanal mobility in the form of *compagnonnage*. In the eighteenth century, three designated journeymen, Pierre Rozé of Angers, François Cherrier of Le Mans, and Pierre Hulleaux of Château-du-Loir, interrupted their Tour de France in La Rochelle in order to try their luck in Canada. One middle-range migrant, René Ménard of La Gouhannière (Manche), arrived in Anjou involuntarily when he was arrested for salt smuggling and jailed in Château-Gontier. He was deported to Canada in 1740 at the age of twenty-six.

It is useful to compare Canadian emigrants with those to other colonies, for Anjou and Maine witnessed a more or less continuous stream of departures for the Islands in the seventeenth and eighteenth centuries. Recruitment was especially intense after 1664, during the able and activist term of Ogeron, an Angevin nobleman, as governor of La Tortue and Saint-Domingue.

The West Indian emigrants of the seventeenth century included linen manufacturers from Laval and Le Mans, surgeons, ordinary *engagés*, and, apparently, between 1680 and 1690, "poor people transported by force."[70] In the late eighteenth century, future "Américains" were still a mix of elite and popular types, and most were between nineteen and thirty years of age. They frequently came from towns, and, except for Laval, Upper Maine was better represented than Lower. Recruitment affected two rural areas in particular: the environs of La Flèche and the border with adjacent Perche.[71]

This geography, interestingly, coincides with the geography of emigration to Canada, although that movement had peaked more than a century earlier. It was defined, as argued above, by economic considerations distorted by the vagaries of recruitment; but once launched, these distortions perpetuated themselves in a tradition of expatriation. The Islands probably replaced Canada fairly early on as the destination of choice because of their reputation for easy wealth. The recruiting efforts of Ogeron may also have been instrumental in redirecting the migration stream that the decisions of previous recruiters had helped to shape.

Summary

Considered as a whole, the provinces of the Northwest contributed to the peopling of Canada in a way that accorded with their demographic as well their economic histories. Areas of high population mobility figured prominently in the cartography, whether the primary direction of that mobility was immigration or emigration. Heavy immigration gave rise not only to settlement but to the phenomenon of flow-through; ironically, more immigration also made for more emigration.

Traditions of migration were not always amenable to bending in an Atlantic direction. Seasonal harvest migrations appeared as the adjuncts of an otherwise stable population; they rarely signaled any predisposition for making adventurous moves. The temporary migrations associated with artisanal or commercial activities were more likely to feed into colonial migration streams. While many retained a seasonal component, which maximized ties with the region of origin, they also produced a residue of emigrants willing to absent themselves for long periods or even permanently. In addition, they rarely monopolized all the migratory options available to a given population, thereby leaving some people free to enlarge the tradition by traveling elsewhere. Migrants who lived close to the Atlantic and engaged in activities that fell outside the migratory mainstream were especially likely to explore Canadian possibilities.

In keeping with the phenomenon of flow-through, many new residents of cities eventually found themselves on a boat to Canada. Traditional forms of elite mobility also had colonial repercussions, as did movements associated with the army, navy, and merchant marine. Among artisans, the Tour de France was flexible enough the redirect a number of its affiliates overseas. Even micro-mobility created a reservoir of migrants, which Canadian recruiters tapped successfully on at least two occasions, in Perche and in Maine and Anjou.[72]

Thus, tradition, along with modernity, played a part in the creation of the migration stream between northwestern France and North America. But what, exactly, is meant by tradition? For this was tradition predicated not upon static routines and frozen customs, but upon mobility; this was tradition that revealed the too often overlooked vitality and dynamism of the Ancien Régime.

9

A Traditional Movement: Emigration Outside the Northwest

Outside as well as inside the Northwest, emigration to Canada reflected migratory tradition. Region by region, emigrants to Canada resembled emigrants to the other Atlantic colonies; they were also no strangers to dominant patterns of urban immigration. In areas of heavy urbanization, such as the Atlantic coast and the Paris Basin, the same currents fed both urban and Canadian growth. Migrants hailed from the surrounding countryside, nearby *villes-relais*, provincial capitals far and wide, and the proverbially impoverished mountain ranges in the Center and South.

The migrations of *montagnards*, which were insignificant in the Northwest, were extremely complex, although the best known were occupationally specific and temporary. In the Center-west, these streams fed all the more easily into emigration to Canada in that they failed to leave a durable imprint on the population of the great ports; in the Southwest, where the tendency to settle was greater, their spillover into Canada was more socially selective. Paris, like La Rochelle or Rochefort, threw off *montagnards* from the most visible migration streams: practitioners of the *petits métiers* unlikely to foresee their urban sojourns as permanent.

A study of central and southern migrations at their point of departure highlights both their complexity and their uneven contribution to the peopling of Canada. As was noted in Part One, some emigrants from these areas were not *montagnards* at all, but inhabited regions of passage in contact with the mountain ranges: river valleys, coastline, and major towns. Meanwhile, the actual *montagnards* who came to Canada represented certain characteristic currents but not others; less familiar streams were also crucial to this emigrant flow, despite their more diffuse and erratic nature.

Central-western Emigration to Canada

The Center-west had a mobile population as well as an active economy in the seventeenth and eighteenth centuries. The movement toward Canada was but one of the many migration streams that converged on or originated in the area. In the long run, urban immigration was predominant, but emigration was still significant. Indeed, as Louis Pérouas has written, "the two phenomena were linked, . . . even tributary of one another; it must have been a fraction of the immigrants who left."[1]

The relationship between urban immigration and colonial emigration can be explored more fully in the Center-west than the Northwest, owing to historians' better understanding of the immigrant flow. The attraction of central-western cities was complex; regional and interurban currents converged on La Rochelle and Rochefort as on Nantes and Rouen, but so too did a number of highly localized long-distance migration streams. These last contributed more to colonial emigration than to urban population growth because of the more evanescent nature of the arrivals, the greater volatility of the migrant flow.

As in the Northwest, the pattern of central-western emigration to Canada matched that of colonial emigration overall, most of which was directed toward the Antilles. Regardless of destination, transatlantic movements involved the same catchment areas and the same types of people. Central-western emigrants were somewhat distinct religiously, and in their substantial familial connections; their social background, in relation to their counterparts from Brittany, Maine, or Anjou, was unexceptional.

In the Center-west, as elsewhere in the vicinity of Atlantic ports, urban immigration was the primary form of mobility during the Ancien Régime. The two great cities of the region, La Rochelle and Rochefort, experienced "a veritable population transfusion" in the seventeenth century. La Rochelle rebounded from a postsiege low of 5,400 in 1628 to a healthy 18,000 less than a decade later. By 1675 the city had reached an all-time high of 25,000.[2] The development of Rochefort was even more spectacular: its population climbed from under 600 to 12,000 in the first five years of the arsenal's existence, 1666–1670.[3] Both cities seem to have approached the upper limit for urban growth through immigration.

Immigration into La Rochelle is well understood thanks to Jean-Pierre Poussou's study of the marriage and hospital registers.[4] Among immigrants at marriage, a demographic basin consisting of Aunis, Saintonge, and Lower Poitou predominated, while, at greater distances, the contributions of the Northwest and Southwest were fairly balanced. For the immigrants who were hospitalized, the area of heaviest attraction did not extend beyond Charente-Maritime, but the largest difference occurred outside the demographic basin. A strong extraregional current linked La Rochelle with the Northwest, primarily the pays de la Loire, but secondarily Sarthe, the Cotentin, and Brittany. A further migration stream flowed in from Limousin and Marche. Except for Bordelais, the area south of the Charente produced few immigrants, and this limited contribution dwindled away completely beyond the Rhône.

These two different sources appear to have captured two different kinds of mobility. Marriage, with its implications of intended settlement, affected people throughout a diffuse geographic zone of attraction, but the hospital catered to immigrants who belonged to specific, often temporary, migration streams. The presence in the city of Bretons or Limousins was work related and subject to interruption. Some of them eventually settled, as shown by the acts of marriage, but the residue of permanent immigrants gave little indication of the breadth of the overall movements. Northwestern sailors or building workers from the Massif central comprised a kind of floating population whose stability resided in their continued ties to their regions of origin. Their massive but ephemeral presence in the city was an important feature of early modern demography.[5]

The regional origins of the emigrants who embarked in La Rochelle for the Islands recall those of immigrants into La Rochelle. The closest resemblance, however, lay not with the immigrants at marriage but with those signaled in the hospital registers. The heaviest emigration, of course, originated in the Center-west proper; more than half of the 4,000 indentured servants studied by Gabriel Debien were natives of Aunis, Saintonge, Poitou, or Angoumois.[6] But outside of the immediate region, La Rochelle's attraction for Atlantic emigrants tilted sharply toward the north. The Loire Valley and the northwestern provinces accounted for more than a fifth of the departures, and, together with Ile-de-France, they made up a quarter. By contrast, the entire Southwest could muster only 222 emigrants (5.6%), a number surpassed by Brittany and Paris and nearly equaled by Normandy. The only other current of note involved the Massif central, with 4.6% of the emigrants. While fewer in number than southwesterners, Limousins, Marchois, and Auvergnats easily edged out natives of the Midi, Alps, East, and North.

The migration stream connecting La Rochelle with the Antilles thus served to prolong currents, both local and extralocal, that funneled immigrants into the city. It did so all the more easily in that some of these currents made a remarkably unstable demographic contribution to the port. Long-distance migration streams originating in the Northwest or Massif central included a minority of immigrants intent on settling in La Rochelle. Many no doubt regained their regions of origin, but others, accustomed to seeking temporary work at what could be great distances, accepted the propositions of recruiters and signed on for the Antilles. Clearly, there was a coincidence between the geography of emigration for the Islands and that of a certain kind of immigration into La Rochelle.

Emigration to Canada exhibited a similar pattern, although the colony's attraction for long-distance immigrants was not as strong. Instead of half, four-fifths of the Canadian *engagés* who passed through La Rochelle were central-westerners.[7] Perhaps emigration to Canada remained something of a family affair, a tradition that seized the imagination of natives of the region most strongly. Nonetheless, the long-distance component of the movement resembled the currents of temporary urban immigration more than those of immigration at marriage. The Northwest came first with 10.9%, followed by Ile-de-France (2%) and the Loire (1.5%). The Massif central at a modest 1.2% still outstripped the Southwest (.9%) and Midi (.2%). Canada, like the Antilles, attracted the poorly fixed masculine population of La Rochelle to a greater degree than the city's other long-distance immigrants.

In the Center-west, emigrants to the West Indies were the model for emigrants to Canada in other ways as well. Their social origins were mixed, their religious origins diverse, and their familial ties strong enough to distinguish them from the colonial emigrants of other Atlantic regions.

Emigrants who embarked in La Rochelle for the Caribbean came from a wide variety of social conditions. Indentured servants tended to be humble folk: artisans, peasants, or textile workers, but paying passengers were often highly advantaged. "Here there was a sort of 'Atlantic' life or society," which caused the appeal of the Islands to percolate from one end of the social spectrum to the other. Young men predominated in this as in other colonial migration streams, but, as Jean-Pierre Poussou and Lucile Bourrachot have pointed out, in the Center-west, "familial departures or departures for familial reasons were not rare."[8] Bourgeois emigrants, in particular, seem to have had sustained familial connections to the Caribbean.[9]

The cross-class nature of central-western emigration to Canada and its substantial familial component were consistent with this profile of the flow to the Caribbean. Jacques Mathieu has remarked upon both the social diversity of emigrants from La Rochelle and the surprisingly high number who accompanied or followed a family member to Canada. Furthermore, familial situations such as imprisonment, abandonment of religious community, decease or remarriage of a parent, or too many siblings also influenced emigration in particular circumstances.[10]

It is unclear to what extent religion, or the desire to escape persecution, was a factor in central-western emigration to the Caribbean. From a strictly chronological standpoint, the influence was certain, for the departures were never more numerous than around the time of the revocation of the Edict of Nantes.[11] In the case of Canada, as has been seen, a Huguenot element was discernible in the 80 central-westerners who made up more than three-fifths of the identified Protestants or ex-Protestants of New France.

The incidence of prior migration among central-western emigrants to Canada is, unfortunately, impossible to determine. A bare minimum consists of the 215 persons who resided in a central-western community that they were not native to at the time of their emigration. This figure, which includes 68 women, leaves out *compagnons*, whose stays in La Rochelle before embarking may have been very brief.

Three-quarters of these central-western immigrants came from elsewhere in the Center-west (an indication of slightly greater openness than in the Northwest, where the corresponding figure was four-fifths); the

Northwest then followed with 7.2%, but the Southwest came in third
(4.3%), before the Loire Valley (2.4%), Ile-de-France (1.9%), and the
Massif central (1.0%). While the numbers involved are small, this pattern
comes closest to that of the eighteenth-century immigrants at marriage.
The less pronounced nature of the temporary migration streams probably
stems from the fact that the least stable individuals were excluded from
this sample. All of these immigrants had taken up more or less long-term
residence in the Center-west before making the decision to leave.[12]

Central-western immigrants tended to be more rural than their long-
distance counterparts, 59.5% as opposed to 38.6%. Interurban movements
were important, but the most important phenomenon was the rural exodus.
Nearly half of the immigrants were country folk who had taken up
residence in a city. The most popular destination, irrespective of an
immigrant's origin, was La Rochelle.[13]

A minority of immigrants, 29 out of 215, had moved more than once
before embarking for Canada. Most of these multiple moves involved
short or medium distances, and some of them concerned *villes-relais*.
Suzanne Dionnet, a servant who emigrated from Rochefort in 1751, had
been born in rural Saintonge, but spent eight years in Tonnay-Charente
before moving to the larger city, and thence to Canada.[14] When immigrants
had moved more than twice, as several had, urban destinations tended to
predominate. The most complex recorded itinerary was that of Esther
Brandeau, the adventurous young Jew whose antics so shocked the Canadian authorities. Others would probably rival it if they were known in
detail. Pierre Verpillon, for example, described himself in 1762 as a "native
of besançon, forty years old, in Canada for ten years, away from his
country for about seventeen, lived for a year in Accadia [*sic*], had formerly
Traveled through France selling small wares from town to town for several
years, then embarked at la rochelle."[15]

Central-western emigration to Canada, like northwestern emigration,
was marked by the contribution of *compagnonnage*. About a fifth of the
designated *compagnons* in my sample came from the Center-west, not
only from major centers like La Rochelle and Poitiers, but also from
rural communities in the environs. The practice of *compagnonnage* by
natives of La Chapelle-Palluau (Vendée), Véniers (Vienne), or Lagord
(Charente-Maritime) is a good indication of prior urban immigration.
La Rochelle, as a principal staging point of the Tour de France, also

funneled *compagnons* from other regions into the Canadian migration stream. Parisians, Burgundians, Bretons, Angevins, Toulousains, and Berrichons all figured among the *compagnons* who embarked in La Rochelle for Canada.

Thus, both the general profile of central-western emigration to Canada and the specific migration histories of those emigrants whose prior movements could be retraced combine to portray the movement as one aspect of a much broader phenomenon. La Rochelle, Rochefort, and, by extension, the entire Center-west opened demographically onto both inland France and the Atlantic. The population flows into and out of the region, which sometimes attained massive proportions, were an integral part of its history, a part related to but not subsumed by economic development.

Southwestern Emigration to Canada

Southwestern emigration to Canada also fits neatly into the larger migratory picture. Its geography, as described in Part One, corresponds to that of both urban immigration and emigration to the Antilles. In the Pays basque, for example, immigration to Bordeaux involved a clear preponderance of Bayonnais: over a third of the total.[16] This urban character was even more pronounced in emigration to the Islands. "Cities and coastal towns regrouped eighty-five percent of the emigrants," with Bayonne alone intervening with nearly two-thirds.[17] Among emigrants for Canada, Bayonne stood at 39.5% and urban parishes at 55.3%, while the importance of rural bourgs was such that actual villagers made up only 8.8%. Some of these villagers, moreover, came from the coast or the immediate vicinity of towns.

In the Southwest, as in Brittany, the rural hinterlands of the great ports produced emigrants for the colonies insofar as they also contributed to the urban population. Thus, small groups of parishes that stood out for their demographic ties to Bordeaux—for example, Duras, Auriac, Monteton, and Allemans-du-Dropt, all on the banks of the Dropt—were prominent on the map of emigration to Canada as well.[18] Owing to the autonomy of migratory movements, within this region there were villages that sent immigrants to Bordeaux and others where immigration was insignificant.[19] These differences were clearly reflected in the geography of colonial departures.

The age, sex, and social distributions of emigrants to Canada could also be predicted by reference to general patterns. Long-distance migrants, whether for Bordeaux, the Antilles, or Canada, tended to be male, young, and anxious to work. In the southwestern countryside, the optimum age for immigration to Bordeaux was young adulthood.[20] Likewise, about four-fifths of the emigrants who booked passage in Bordeaux for the Islands were between fifteen and thirty-five, a highly characteristic, if narrow, distribution.

Women moved as well as men, but their moves were less far-reaching. The proportion of women among immigrants to Bordeaux declined exponentially with distance from the city: three-fifths for areas within 40 kilometers, one-fourth for areas between 40 and 150 kilometers, and one-fifth for areas beyond that.[21] Women did not figure prominently in the migration streams connecting the Southwest with the colonies, either.

Virtually all occupations were represented in both immigration and emigration, but artisans, and *compagnons* in particular, displayed a disproportionate inclination to move. In the Middle Garonne, tailors, shoemakers, coopers, carpenters, and rope makers figured prominently among immigrants and emigrants, to the extent that Bourrachot and Poussou could write of the essential importance for migration of the artisanal milieu, which "furnished the largest contingent."[22] At the same time, the underrepresentation of both agriculture and the petty trades was evident. Migration was largely a product of the middling and upper strata of the population, with Bordeaux, the Islands, and Canada serving as an outlet for a certain elite.

The strikingly similar profiles of migration toward Bordeaux and the colonies suggest once more that they were part of a single movement. Emigration to Canada may have frequently occurred as an additional step in a migratory process already under way, as a further extension of progressive urbanization. In any case, urbanization and colonization alike involved the same types of people: youths of working age and, more often than not, artisanal status.

The number of southwesterners for whom a dossier of prior migration could be established is not extraordinary—95 in all—but thanks to the testimonials of freedom at marriage, historical knowledge of their moves is exceptionally detailed. Southwesterners, like Bretons and Normans, were well represented in the testimonials because the documents were drawn up at a time when Bordeaux, the Pays basque, Saint-Malo, and Granville were all active in the Canada trade.

The regional origins of these prior migrants demonstrate the greater openness and attractive power of the Southwest relative to the rest of Atlantic France. Fewer than two-thirds of the migrants (62) came from within the region, in spite of its broadly defined boundaries. The adjacent Center-west came in a distant second (11 migrants), followed by the Massif central (6), the Midi (4), Ile-de-France (4), the Northwest (1), and the North (1). Five Italians and 1 Irishman brought the foreign contribution to the level of that from the Massif central.

Just over a third of the migrants arrived at their penultimate destination from the countryside, a share that rose to 45.8% for natives of the Southwest and declined to 14.3% for those who had covered longer distances. Of course, this destination was nearly always urban, and grandly so: the main receiving communities were Bordeaux and Toulouse. The greater importance of interurban movements relative to the rural exodus stems, in part, from the higher percentage of long-distance migrants; however, the two phenomena appear much more balanced when multiple prior migrations are taken into account. Of the 20 persons who made more than one move before embarking for Canada, 8 had abandoned the countryside for a small town in the Southwest before forging on to a more important center such as Albi, Toulouse, or Bordeaux.

The sample of prior migrants illustrates virtually all of the migratory paradigms that were important in the Southwest. Short- and middle-distance movements, interurban itineraries including but not restricted to the Tour de France, and migratory currents originating in the Pyrénées, the Massif central, and foreign countries all fed, upon occasion, into the migration stream linking the Southwest to Canada. As with emigration to the Islands, it is impossible to determine how often prior migration played a part in colonial departure; but the exemplary nature of the biographies preserved by historical accident suggests that previous movements must have occurred frequently indeed.

The first migration stream that overflowed into the movement toward Canada was the influx into Bordeaux from the rural hinterland. It has already been noted that the same parishes furnished both immigrants for Bordeaux and emigrants for Canada, and that immigration and emigration involved the same types of people. Examining the prior migrants shows that this coincidence was the result of a sequential process, at least in individual cases. As Poussou has shown, the countryside of Aquitaine was for Bordeaux "the great region of recruitment for traditional artisans."[23] Tailors and cobblers were especially numerous, but certain subregions could boast additional specialties. For whatever reason, bakers and pastry cooks came in disproportionate numbers from Périgord, Quercy, and Comminges.[24]

Not only were many prior immigrants from Aquitaine artisans, but even the specific professional currents asserted themselves: hence the pastry cooks Raymond Vert and Jean Pierre of Périgord and the bakers Pierre Bonnet and Pierre La Chaume of Comminges, all of whom had done apprenticeships in Bordeaux before embarking for Canada.[25] In contrast, some new arrivals did not remain long in the city before trying their luck elsewhere. Pierre Roy, a nurse at the Hôtel-Dieu of Québec, left his village in Agenais for Bordeaux at the age of eighteen; a mere four months later he was en route for Canada.[26]

Among interurban movements, *compagnonnage* made a significant contribution to southwestern emigration to Canada, as evidenced by the southwestern origins of nearly a quarter of the designated *compagnons*.[27] The testimonials of freedom at marriage make it possible to identify, in addition, a number of *compagnons* from other regions who embarked as they were passing through the Southwest on their Tour de France. Antoine Boudin, who arrived in Canada in 1757 with reinforcements for the Regiment of Berry, described his own odyssey while testifying for a friend:

> appeared before us antoine Boudin *dit* St-Germain, native to Paris, St Sulpice parish, about twenty-six years old, in the troops for two and a half years and in Canada for seven months in the Regt of berry, who . . . assured us that pierre d'arnonville whom he calls Bourninville is not married in france, and this for having known him since childhood, having lived with his father for five years to learn the trade of mason, after which having done his Tour de France for close to three years, he indentured himself in Bordeaux, from whence he returned to Paris to say farewell to his father, and from there came to Brest, where he embarked for Canada, where he found the said Bourninville.[28]

Boudin's story is typical in a number of ways. First and foremost, it reveals the interdependence of theoretically distinct migratory options:

the Tour de France, military service, and emigration to the colonies. In the eighteenth century, *compagnons'* itineraries were at best loosely defined, and, as such, served easily as springboards from which to tap into other migratory networks. The most common alternative network was that provided by the army, a veritable school of mobility widely attended by young men of the popular classes. Other points worthy of mention are Boudin's confusion about his friend's name, and the seeming unlikelihood of their coincidental reunion in Canada.

Compagnons and soldiers referred to one another commonly by surnames alone, to the point that baptismal and family names were often unknown to them. Boudin's mistake was in no way exceptional; he knew his friend not by his family name, Darnonville, but by his nickname, Bellehumeur.

When imprecision gave way to ignorance—as, for example, when Jean Louis Maillet presented as witnesses "two men whose names he does not know and one of whom is, he says, from marseille, and the other from perigord, with whom he has lived for three [years]"—the authorities grew concerned.[29] They responded by attempting to monitor, or even control, the use of surnames by these floating elements of the population.

André Corvisier has interpreted the progressive systematization of the nom de guerre in the military documents of the eighteenth century as an indication of military particularism. A soldier's surname, if have one he must, would henceforth be official and distinct from any nickname he might choose himself. Yet it is also possible to view the officialization of military surnames in a broader context: that of the elite offensive on popular culture. "The usage of surnames was frequent in the period," and it provided the elites, whether, civil, military, or ecclesiastical, with a concrete representation of the impenetrability of popular culture.[30] The attempt to control surnames was not, therefore, limited to the army, and it began well before the middle of the eighteenth century. In Canada, from the earliest years of the colony, civil and religious authorities alike paid close attention to the multiple appellations of their charges.[31]

As for the apparent coincidence of two childhood friends turning up independently of each other in as remote an outpost as Canada, actually, such things occurred all the time, not only among emigrants to Canada, but along the long and tortuous routes of the Tour de France. In spite of the sometimes vast distances involved, the social world of the *compagnon*, soldier, or *compagnon*-turned-soldier was restricted; it was defined by far-flung but tightly knit networks of social relations. The inns and other gathering places frequented by the *compagnons* gave them access to a store of information about migratory and employment activities; the written word, as well as conversation, played an important part in circulating the range of options. Ménétra's account of his Tour de France conveys the importance of letters in determining his movements, and, though similar evidence for emigrants to Canada is lacking, their high rate of literacy suggests that letters must have affected their decisions as well. It thus seems appropriate to take such "chance" encounters as those of the Parisians Darnonville *dit* Bellehumeur and Boudin *dit* Saint-Germain in stride.

Most *compagnons* resembled Boudin in eschewing a detailed description of their Tour; in fact, too careful a narrative could backfire by generating suspicion of an overly mobile individual.[32] Certain cities nonetheless recur in the fragmentary accounts that remain: Paris, Rouen, Angers, Nantes, La Rochelle, Angoulême, Bordeaux, Toulouse—in other words, the full western leg of the organized Tour.

Compagnonnage by no means monopolized the interurban patterns of mobility exhibited by future emigrants to Canada. Some of the emigrants from Bordeaux had arrived in the city as *chambrelans,* like the Parisian goldsmith Alexandre Picart.[33] Others, like the baker François Uzero of La Réole, came as simple apprentices and departed for Canada before ever initiating a Tour de France.[34] While most forms of interurban mobility involved artisans at some stage of their training, laborers could be represented as well. One of the witnesses of Sébastien René Aubert *dit* Aubert, a journeyman bookbinder from Paris, was a day laborer who told his story in the following testimony:

> appeared before us Jean Courti *dit* vadeboncoeur, native of angouleme, soldier of the Company of beaujeu, thirty-five years old, in Canada for four years, without a trade, who . . . assured us that the said aubert was not married in France, and this for having known him for fifteen years, saying that he had gone to paris as the lackey of a lord from his region . . . who, having been put in prison, he left him, and remained in Paris only about three years, during which time he became acquainted with the said aubert in the place Ste Genevieve, and then in angouleme, and from there in Bordeaux, and they came together to this country.[35]

There was also spillover from the migration streams connecting the Southwest to pockets of surplus population, especially in the mountainous border areas to the south and east. Where immigration was concerned, natives of the Pyrénées and Massif central could be found throughout the less elevated portions of the Southwest. Their gamut of specialties was wide, but representatives of the petty trades were the most highly visible: beggars, distillers, bear leaders, peddlers, ragpickers, carters, and charcoal burners among the Pyrénéens; masons among the Limousins; sawyers and tinkers among the Auvergnats.[36] To these mountain folk could be added Bretons and Normans (mariners, peddlers), and foreigners such as Savoyards (floor polishers, chimney sweeps, vagabonds), Italians (mariners, chair and table makers), and Irish (Catholics in flight from the Glorious Revolution). In Bordeaux, the Irish included merchants, tailors, mariners, and single women from a variety of economic backgrounds.[37]

Natives of these areas did reach Canada via southwestern cities, but there was a clear underrepresentation of the most picturesque migrants—in other words, the poorest. Where the colonies were concerned, "poor emigration from the Pyrénées was . . . less well developed than its opposite." Agricultural or para-agricultural activities were of slight importance, and the petty trades (porter, day laborer, etc.) made up only a fifth of the total.[38]

Emigrants from Auvergne came likewise from a bourgeois or petty-noble milieu; in my sample, several Auvergnat priests and an army officer from Cantal had stopped off in the Southwest before setting sail for Canada. These emigrants obviously had little in common with the porters or sweepers who comprised more than a third of the Auvergnat immigrants captured in Bordeaux's hospital registers; the resemblance was somewhat greater with the smaller number of Auvergnats who appeared in the city's marriage registers, nearly half of whom were artisans. Clearly, immigration from the Massif central was complex, in outcome if not intention. It encompassed both a seasonal or temporary current composed largely of unskilled laborers, and a current of more skilled or better-off migrants who sometimes saw an advantage in accomplishing the unexpected: settling in Bordeaux or continuing on across the Atlantic. As in La Rochelle, the general impermanence of *montagnard* migrations facilitated their diversion to the colonies; however, the spirit of adventure was strongest among the Limousins or Auvergnats who had climbed beyond the bottom rung of the economic ladder.

Foreigners, like *montagnards*, could also use the Southwest as a stepping-stone on the way to Canada. Philippe Lequezi, a migrant Italian plasterer working in Toulouse, belonged to a migration stream in every way comparable to that of the Limousins. More unusual was the case of Jean-Baptiste O'Donohue of Mitchelstown in Munster province, a member of Bordeaux's small Irish community. In 1759, after five years in Bordeaux, O'Donohue embarked for Canada armed with a letter from the city's Séminaire de Saint-Anne-la-Royale des Irlandais identifying him as an orphan "gone with the consent of his family to settle wherever divine providence might lead him." Had it not been for the intransigence of the urban authorities, O'Donohue, a mariner, would not have needed to have recourse to divine providence.

There were about 175 Irish in Bordeaux in 1756, when the city expelled them—ironically, as a security measure in the war against England. O'Donohue lived with his brother Timothy, a master tailor from Cork, who had come to Bordeaux in 1749 and was prospering at the time of the deportation order. While Timothy received a personal exemption as the husband of a native Bordelaise, he could do nothing for Jean-Baptiste, who after his expulsion remained permanently in Québec, marrying there in 1769.[39]

Southwestern emigrants to Canada thus give every evidence of familiarity with traditional patterns of mobility, which the voyage to Canada merely extended or transformed. Viewed in a demographic context, the decision to emigrate appears perfectly ordinary, at least for young men of artisanal or quasi-artisanal backgrounds. The only significant interior currents that did not leave their mark on the Canadian migration stream were the short-distance immigration of young women and the long-distance immigration of impoverished—as opposed to skilled—seasonal or temporary workers to Bordeaux.

Emigration to Canada from the Paris Region, Loire, North, and East

In the *pays de grande culture* of northern and eastern France, the migratory system oriented toward Atlantic ports and overseas colonies gave way to a pattern dominated by a different demographic phenomenon: the growth of Paris. Yet the lure of the capital, while sufficient to engender a net surplus of 5,000 to 7,000 immigrants annually in the mid-eighteenth century, was never absolute.[40] Like the Atlantic ports, Paris always witnessed a certain degree of flow-through.[41] Parisian emigration was unique in its multi-directionality, but Canada was one of the many destinations that managed to profit from the constant stream of footloose Parisians.

The expansion of Paris, while difficult to quantify accurately, proceeded rapidly in the seventeenth and eighteenth centuries. The population increase was probably on the order of 300 percent, boosting the number of inhabitants from 250,000 in 1600 to 450,000 in 1650, 500,000 in 1700, and perhaps 750,000 on the eve of the Revolution.[42] Up to 14,000 immigrants arrived each year, and three-fifths of the population at any one time consisted of nonnatives.[43]

The attraction of Paris extended to every province in France, and even to foreign countries. Nonetheless, immigration conformed to the familiar pattern, originating primarily in zones close to the capital. "In general," as Jeffry Kaplow has put it, "migrants arrived in the city from areas relatively nearby and of easy access . . . Normandy, the north and the east, together with the Parisian region itself, account for a majority of the individuals concerned. Large contingents also came from the center (Auvergne, Haute-Vienne, Creuse, la Marche, Vienne) and Savoie, areas of high birth-rates and limited agricultural resources."[44]

The social origins of Parisian immigrants were typical as well. On the one hand, "the whole world of work and the whole society were won over by migration." On the other, the movement into the city is yet another example of a "current where artisanal labor predominated."[45] Professional specialization according to geographic origin existed, but was by no means absolute. In the building industry, for example, "there was first of all a strong nucleus of Parisians—a good third—and the provincials arrived from everywhere; three regions, however, predominated: Ile-de-France (8%), Limousin (17%), Normandy." Domestics came primarily from the zone of attraction and particularly from the demographic basin; female servants, especially, tended to depart from the immediate countryside. Water carriers were Auvergnats, and chimney sweeps Savoyards. "In the textile and clothing trades," according to Daniel Roche, "one notes a large percentage of northerners, Lorrainers, and Champenois."[46]

Paris succeeded less well in fixing its population, whether native or immigrant, than in assembling it in the first place. Auvergnats, Limousins, Savoyards, and Lower Normans were often seasonal and temporary workers, and "it is difficult to know how many remained there definitively, how many cast down roots there and reached the rank of master."[47] Still, the volume of emigration exceeded that of the floating population that viewed life in the capital as a temporary arrangement. As the seat of government, Paris naturally provided administrative cadres for both provincial France and the colonies, and its population bore a disproportionate burden in the execution of royal projects such as military and colonial recruitment. Beyond that, "the proximity of this central power, the possibility of information and support, . . . [and] the superior means of transport enjoyed by the capital offered facilities and temptations to departure that were unknown elsewhere."[48] Sometimes residence in the capital conveyed with it privileges that made emigration particularly attractive. In the case of artisans, the *maîtrise de Paris* not only exempted its possessors from militia duty, it enabled them to practice their trades at the level of master anywhere in France without regard for local guild regulations.[49]

Once again, the pattern of regional emigration to Canada fits in well with this general picture. The geography of the movement, which radiated out from Paris to the provincial capitals and *villes-relais*, and which often followed the means of communication, faithfully transcribes the geography of mobility. The broad social spectrum represented among the emigrants reflects the resonance of mobility among the entire population; however, the high percentage of artisans also speaks to the particular affinity for movement exhibited by this group. Here as elsewhere the *compagnons du Tour de France* appear to have spearheaded artisanal mobility. The *pays de grande culture* of the North and East accounted for roughly the same number of designated *compagnons* as the Southwest.

Proof of prior migration exists, as usual, for a minority of individuals: 254 for Ile-de-France, the North, the East, and the Loire combined. Yet once again, the shape of these movements was far from random. On the contrary, the previous moves of the emigrants to Canada replicate in microcosm the migratory history of their extended region. The most active receiving area was Ile-de-France, whose communities absorbed 143 of the 254 migrants; Paris alone accounted for 136—113 men and 23 women. After Ile-de-France, the provinces within the Parisian zone of attraction cut the most robust figure: 83 arrivals for Picardy, Champagne, Burgundy, Lorraine, the Loire Valley, Flanders, and Artois. The remaining 28 were distributed between Lyonnais, Franche-Comté, and Alsace.

A comparison of the sending and receiving communities reveals the importance of large cities, which expanded at the expense of both the countryside and small towns. The place of rural sending communities, however, was somewhat greater than it appears owing to multistage migrations. Of the 22 migrants who had accomplished more than one previous move, 8 had left the country for the city prior to engaging in interurban migration.

The prior migrations to Ile-de-France all ended in Paris (136) or Versailles (6), with the exception of 1 short-distance rural move in the vicinity and direction of Paris (from Saint-Cloud to Passy). The regional origins of the immigrants were available in all but one case. Fourteen persons (9.9%) came from Ile-de-France itself, 9 from the countryside and 5 from towns, and a further 77 (54.2%) from the Parisian zone of attraction: Normandy (37), Champagne (11), Picardy (9), Orléanais (7), Lorraine (7), Burgundy (4), Flanders (1), and Artois (1). At distances greater than 300 kilometers, immigrants dribbled in from all over France, as well as from Italy and Switzerland. The only important concentrations in this zone, however, involved the Massif central, with 12 persons, and Brittany with 16.

This pattern diverges from the general pattern of immigration in several respects, but all of the divergences can be readily explained. The most important concerns Ile-de-France, which supplied a bare tenth of the province's future emigrants to Canada, in contrast with a quarter of Parisian immigrants at marriage and 15 percent of Parisian immigrants from the 1790s. Other issues to consider include the emphasis on Normandy within the city's zone of attraction and the surprisingly strong showing by normally peripheral Brittany. The origins of future Canadians within the Parisian population were clearly more northwestern than those of the Parisian population as a whole.

Upon close examination, the underrepresentation of Ile-de-France appears to stem from the underrecording of one particular category of immigrants: women. Women comprised less than a fifth of my sample's prior migrants into Paris, in spite of their importance to both Parisian immigration generally and Parisian emigration to Canada. Furthermore, female immigrants came disproportionately from the same villages and *villes-relais* in Ile-de-France that cut a paltry figure among prior migrants but made an important contribution to the "direct" cartography of female emigration to Canada. One may therefore suppose that the women who emigrated from rural Ile-de-France did not, in fact, do so directly, but rather through the intermediary of the capital.

This hypothesis appears all the more plausible when one considers that a third to a half of the 900 *filles du roi* who arrived in Canada between 1663 and 1673 did so by way of the Hôpital général of Paris.[50] The Hôpital général, whose role in recruitment is considered at greater length in the following chapter, was established in 1656 as a work of the Compagnie du Saint-Sacrement.[51] Its female annex, the Salpêtrière, gave shelter in 1680 to around 3,000 women and girls, among them the ill, the insane, the poor, and the merely less rich. *Hobereaux* employed the institution as a cheap alternative to a convent for their daughters, and administrators were happy to receive these "bijoux"(jewels), who raised the social tone of the establishment in spite of their straitened circumstances.[52] The only category of women not admitted to the Salpêtrière consisted of those whose loose morals disqualified them from assistance. The Refuge provided for *filles de famille* whose "debauchery" induced their families to lock them up, and common prostitutes were banished from the city when convicted until the creation of the infamous prison of La Force in 1684.[53]

The Salpêtrière provided emigrants for Canada in at least six different years: 1665, 1668, 1669, 1670, 1671, and 1673. Unfortunately, the earliest registers of the institution did not survive the combined ravages of Revolution and Commune, so it is impossible to identify these women and examine their regional origins; however, general information about recruitment for the hospital reinforces the sense that the female emigrants from the *proche* and *grande banlieue* were probably from the Salpêtrière.

Some of the inmates of the Salpêtrière were *enfants trouvés,* or abandoned children, whose regional origins have been studied. According to Claude Delasselle, the largest number came from the Diocese of Paris, followed by Picardy, Champagne, Burgundy, Normandy, and the North.[54] The Salpêtrière could thus have provided girls for Canada from the entire region under consideration, beginning with Ile-de-France, provided that some of its *enfants trouvés* survived to maturity.

Even if they did not, other immigrants arrived later in life from the same regions to take their place. Lists have survived of the 174 girls who left the Salpêtrière for Martinique in 1680 and 1682, armed each with a small chest, a coif, a handkerchief, a belt, shoelaces, 100 needles in a case, a thimble, a comb, white and gray thread, one pair each of stockings, shoes, gloves, and scissors, 1,000 pins, a bonnet, and laces. Most of them were native Parisians (149), but there were also 6 from the demographic basin (Crouy, Villeneuve, Nanterre, Dourdan, Nogent, Meulan), 6 from Normandy, 5 from Picardy, 2 from Champagne, 2 from Auvergne, and 1 each from Burgundy, Blois, and Lyon. Clearly, the Parisian hospital could serve as an intermediary between the city's zone of attraction and the colonies.[55]

A final piece of evidence for prior migration actually relates to a small number of Canadian *filles du roi*. The only organized convoy of hospital inmates that can be identified with certainty consists of 20 "bijoux" who filed a complaint against their chaperone while awaiting embarkment in Dieppe in 1667. Of these 20, 13 married in Canada, and, in so doing, left a record of their community of origin. Only 6 were native Parisians: 2 from Saint-Nicolas-des-Champs and 1 each from Saint-Gervais, Saint-Germain-l'Auxerrois, Saint-Séverin, and Saint-André-des-Arts. Two others came from the *banlieue* (Conflans and Brie-Comte-Robert), the rest from villages or towns in Picardy, Champagne, Lorraine, Berry, and Nivernais.[56]

The high concentration of Norman and Breton origins among Parisian emigrants for Canada also stands out from the norm. Normans tended to be well represented among Parisian immigrants generally, but at the same time, they rarely outnumbered Picards or Champenois.[57] That they did so where future Canadians were concerned perhaps indicates that as Normans they possessed a familiarity with the Atlantic that inclined them in that direction, even though their initial migration had carried them eastward. They were split about evenly between Upper and Lower Normandy, but only Rouen (8) produced more than 1 or 2 migrants.

The Breton contingent is more puzzling, since Brittany did not fall within the Parisian zone of attraction, except perhaps for the area around

Saint-Pol-de-Léon.[58] The solution lies in the identity of the migrants, nearly all of whom were priests. Paris siphoned off some of the many Breton vocations, for periods of study if not permanently. Perhaps priests of Breton origin were particularly amenable to the Canadian enterprise for the same reasons I have hypothesized for Normans: they felt unfazed by the prospect of overseas adventure.

Except for the underrepresentation of Ile-de-France and the overrepresentation of Brittany and Normandy, the pattern of Parisian immigration exhibited by future Canadians was highly characteristic. In social as well as geographical terms, these migrants were typical members of the various migration streams that converged on the capital. Natives of the Massif central included Pierre Rivet, an Auvergnat water carrier, and André Lecomte *dit* Vadeboncoeur, a mason from Marche. Rivet, the son of a "day laborer and proprietor" from a village near Le Puy, arrived in Paris at the age of seventeen, worked there for ten years before returning home for a two-week visit, then spent another five years in the capital. He arrived in Canada with the *troupes de la Marine*, working successively as a soldier, hired hand, and tinker (another Auvergnat speciality), before marrying in Québec at the age of forty-eight.[59] Lecompte, a native of Azérable (Creuse), came to Paris as a mason's helper at the age of fifteen, and lived for ten years in the rue de la Mortellerie, convenient to the hiring market of La Grève, before enlisting in the Regiment of Langue-doc. He settled in Canada shortly after his arrival.[60]

Both Rivet and Lecomte called as witnesses two representatives of yet another type of Parisian immigration. Jacques Joseph Le Geay *dit* Printemps, "native to Noyon in Picardy and living in Paris," and Emmanuel Bergeron, born in Saint-Germain-en-Laye and working as a journeyman baker in the rue de la Draperie, exemplify the importance of *villes-relais* in renewing the population of the city.[61] Like Rivet and Lecomte, Le Geay and Bergeron arrived in Canada with the troops, perhaps the primary means of emigration from the city.[62] Le Geay, who was forty years old and had a Parisian wife, probably conceived of his stay as temporary, either a remedy for unemployment or a vehicle for amassing a small savings.

The villages of the hinterland produced Parisian emigrants for Canada as well. Some were domestics, like the cook Alexandre Picard from the village of Le Mesnil-Saint-Georges in Picardy or the maid Jeanne Godin from Aunay near Vire in Normandy. Others were artisans like Ambroise Leguay *dit* La Grenade, "native to Coubron four leagues away from Paris, gold and silver plater." Leguay enlisted in the Canadian troops at the age of sixteen, after two years as an apprentice "in the shop of pierre desjardins, Rue d'argenteuil, parish of St Roch."[63] Both Picard and Godin embarked for the colony in the service of their respective employers, namely, the chevalier de Bourlamaque, an officer, and Médard Chouart, a merchant.[64] Chouart was himself a native of Champagne.

Finally, provincial capitals made an important contribution to the group of Parisians who went on to emigrate to Canada. The 8 Rouennais have already been mentioned, but there was also a Rennais, an Amiénois, a Bordelais, and a Lyonnais. They ranged in social status from Etienne Mouillé *dit* Saint-Etienne, a silk worker from Lyon who had worked and wandered as far afield as Turin before trying his luck in Paris, to Louis Artus de Sailly, a *négociant* whose grandfather was already a well established wool merchant in the northern town of Amiens.[65] The Rennais, Gilles Lenoir, arrived in Canada from the Hôpital général of Paris, undoubtedly after some contretemps in the exercise of his trade of executioner. Parisian emigrants to Canada did indeed reflect immigration into the capital in all its remarkable diversity.[66]

Emigration to Canada from the Massif central

The provinces of the Massif central, particularly Limousin, Auvergne, and Marche, were the largest reservoir of emigration in France under the Ancien Régime. Alone or in groups, the region's migrants scattered to all six corners of France and beyond. As the traveler P.-J.-B. Legrand d'Aussy wrote of the Auvergnats in 1792, "there is no department in France, no town at all considerable, where one does not find Auvergnats. One sees them in Holland, Switzerland, Germany, Flanders, Italy, England, Portugal. Among emigrants from Upper Auvergne, there were many who, before the present war, went to Spain. They were absent for several years, and they were distinguished from the others by the name of Espagnols. Some even, for a while, crossed the seas, and driven by the lure of gain, they went all the way to our American colonies."[67]

Yet the various migration streams emanating from the Massif central were reflected unevenly in the composite movement toward Canada. Some of the temporary occupational currents spilled over into Canadian destinations, but others did not. Those that did generally appeared in diluted form, accompanied by equally traditional but more diffuse currents of migration. As in Lower Normandy, regions of highly organized migrations found themselves in an ambiguous position vis-à-vis Canada. On the one hand, their populations were accustomed to long distances and long absences, but on the other, the established "lines of reception and support networks" worked to the advantage of old destinations at the expense of new opportunities.[68]

The province of Marche, which provided seasonal and temporary emigrants for the building industry from at least the sixteenth century, is a case in point.[69] Emigration from Marche to Canada was partly, but not entirely, a movement of masons. In Lower Marche, whose masons traditionally descended on La Rochelle, Rochefort, and Bordeaux, the sending communities did indeed belong to the mason-producing belt.[70] But in Upper Marche, whose primary demographic ties were with Paris, the link between sending communities and the zones of *émigration maçonnante* were weaker.[71] The regions of Aubusson and La Courtine did produce a few emigrants, but so did Guéret, whose inhabitants rarely worked the building sites; and though, in the northeast, a traditionally sedentary zone sent no one to Canada, neither did the most important source of the region's migrant masons in the northwest.[72]

An examination of the emigrants' occupations confirms the mixed nature of emigration from Marche. The army predominated with 11 men, a contingent that included an officer, a wig maker, a joiner, and a mason. Masonry per se was in second place with 5 masons or stonecutters; beyond that, emigrants belonged to the usual wide variety of trades: a priest, a nun, a surgeon, a shoemaker, a clog maker. The example of Canada thus points to the existence of movements not subsumed by the predominant migration stream. As Marie-Anne Moulin discovered of the region of Aubusson, demography reveals the coexistence, from at least the eighteenth century, of two types of emigration: the seasonal or temporary movement of masons to Lyon or Paris; and the ample but less structured departures of other men and women, "these last less spectacular, less well known."[73]

Emigration to Canada from Limousin and Auvergne likewise conformed only partly to the dominant pattern, although this pattern was itself more complex. Upper Limousin, like neighboring Marche, produced masons and stonecutters for all the great cities of the kingdom, starting with Paris. But in Lower Limousin, although masons were not unknown, most of the emigrants fell into two different categories. Unskilled laborers, domestics, and representatives of the petty trades predominated in the migration streams leading to Paris and the Atlantic coast.[74] Emigrants for Spain, on the other hand, usually had trades, and were more likely to be literate than the average inhabitant. The *gagne-deniers* came from the several towns of the region (Brives, Tulle, Ussel) or their environs. The "Spaniards" came from farther east, specifically, "the middle plateaus on each side of the Dordogne."[75]

Emigration to Spain continued from the Auvergnat part of the Dordogne, the present-day arrondissements of Mauriac and Aurillac. These emigrants set out with the intent of amassing a fortune in commerce, and, by and large, they appear to have done so.[76] But emigration to Spain was only one facet of a far more diverse movement affecting Upper Auvergne. Poor and middling emigrants (porters, ragpickers, sawyers, shoe repairers, tinkers, and other artisans) stemmed from the entire northern part of the Cantal, and further concentrations of sawyers set out from the border region of Livradois and Velay. Their most common destinations were Paris and the Southwest.[77]

Emigration from Lower Auvergne, the Limagnes, was equally complex. Masons for Lyon, cutlers for Spain, artisans, bourgeois, and nobles for Bordeaux, and soldiers for any number of destinations all originated in this region of passage sandwiched between mountain ranges. Currents of temporary migration, except those of the masons and cutlers, were probably less important from the outset than definitive migrations; the inverse situation prevailed in Upper Auvergne, where seasonal and temporary movements set the stage for a minority of permanent departures.[78]

As for emigration to Canada, in Limousin, its geography coincided generally with that of emigration; however, Limoges, the provincial capital, was more important for Canadians than emigrants as a whole, and areas of popular emigration were better represented than the zone of emigration to Spain. The army dominated the contingent occupationally with 43 emigrants, among them 2 officers, a surgeon, a domestic, a cooper, a shoemaker, a blacksmith, and 2 masons. As in Marche, the building industry came in second with 10 masons and stonecutters, but many other professions were represented by 1 or several emigrants. Limousin emigrants to Canada included not only soldiers or masons, but priests, merchants, textile workers, joiners, bakers, sawyers, and "hommes de service." Emigration spanned a broad part of the social spectrum, and the military rivaled cities as a focal point for departures.

Emigration from Auvergne to Canada originated primarily in the Limagnes and, within the Limagnes, the cities of Clermont and Riom. The unstructured cross-class movements from the Auvergnat plain into the army or great cities such as Bordeaux were easily translated into departures for Canada. At the same time, mountainous regions with important migratory traditions did not go unnoticed. The second-most-important sending zone, the border area of Livradois and Velay, sent 23 emigrants, one more than the city of Clermont, and the region of Aurillac/Mauriac witnessed the birth of 13 future Canadians. Fifty emigrants arrived with the army, 8 of whom were officers; there were also 5 priests, 4 merchants, 2 tinkers, 2 *laboureurs*, a *fille à marier*, a boatman, and others. Since only the merchants and tinkers were deviating from established temporary currents, it must be emphasized that these currents never succeeded in monopolizing all of the emigration from a given area. The region of Aurillac produced not just merchants and tinkers, but other artisans and *gagne-deniers*. Livradois and Velay witnessed both the departure of sawyers and the slow, unorganized, secular descent of its population into cities, the army, or Canada.[79] The more visible and dramatic movements of the organized emigrants, a few of whom also occasionally fell away from the pack, should not blind one to the existence of minority currents of less structured emigration.

As could be predicted, the prior migrations of emigrants to Canada rarely carried them into the Massif central; the region was simply not conducive to immigration. Of the 7 migrants who did arrive in an Auvergnat, Limousin, or Marchois community, 6 were already natives of the Massif. Four moved from local villages into Clermont or Tulle; one of these villages, Saint-Jean-d'Aubrigoux in Velay, habitually supplied Orléanais with teams of sawyers. Two migrants moved between towns, and 1, the only person to arrive from outside of the region, came to Limoges and Fromental by way of Picardy and Franche-Comté. A man-servant, this exceptional migrant arrived as the domestic of a curé who had been sent to Limousin.

The more substantial prior migrations involving the Massif central are already familiar: the departures of *montagnards* for the Center-west, Southwest, and greater Paris. Thus, in 1721, when officials recruited 9 building workers in Paris for the fortifications of Louisbourg, only 2 were Parisian. Two others came from Champagne and Lorraine and 5—François Bonnet of Limousin, François Granjan of Chanpoinsor (Châteauponsac) in Limousin, Jean Roche of Olance (Aulon) in Upper Marche, Jean Buistre of Bussière (Haute-Vienne), and François Lamarche of Limousin—were from the Massif central.[80] All in all, 26 denizens of the Massif central made their way into the regions that have already been discussed. To them must be added the Limousin and 3 Auvergnats who reached Canada from the Midi or the Alps. The Massif central was not a major recruiting ground for Canada either directly or indirectly; but the presence in Canada of one- and two-stage emigrants from all social classes and all geographical areas of the Massif testifies to the complexity of the region's migrations and belies the notion that structured temporary movements always succeeded in postponing the rural exodus.[81]

Emigration to Canada from the Midi and the Alps

The final regions to consider, the South and the Alps, help to confirm the patterns observed thus far. Mountainous areas, which were overpopulated relative to their limited resources, sent out steady streams of emigrants on a temporary or permanent, organized or individual basis. Low-lying areas received them, but in turn cast off smaller streams of emigrants of their own. Both these types of mobility were represented, if unevenly, among emigrants to Canada.

In the South, emigration to Canada was sparse but reflected the shape of general mobility. The geography emphasized coastal regions and towns, but the scatter of sending communities in the surrounding mountains demonstrates the tendency of Alpins and Ardèchois to descend.[82] The previous migrations of emigrants from the Midi were not numerous, largely because emigrants themselves were not. Over half of the prior migrants came from within the region, but others dribbled in from the Massif central, the Northwest, Dauphiné, Italy, and elsewhere. Twice as many people lived in cities after as before migration, with emigrants arriving typically from the rural hinterland. Departures from the distant mountains were more likely to be urban, like that of Antoine Vuidal, a journeyman shoemaker who arrived in Nîmes from Aurillac.[83]

Alpine emigration to Canada, likewise, focused on regions of passage, in this case, the Rhône Valley and Grenoble.[84] But the structured movements down from the high mountains also appeared on the cartography of Canadian migration, albeit in attenuated form. Oisans and Briançonnais were touched in precisely the areas that were famous for their peddlers; Bourg-d'Oisans and the adjacent parish of Abris produced 3 emigrants for Canada, Briançon and La Salle 4.[85] In Savoy, however, about two-thirds of the emigrants came from the lower part of the province, in spite of the vigorous migratory traditions of Faucigny and the Giffre Valley to the north.[86] The absence of Faucigny probably has to do with the overwhelmingly Germanic orientation of the movements, but the failure of the Giffre to produce a mason or two is more surprising.

In the south, Tarentaise and Maurienne produced a smattering of emigrants, at least one of whom, the pharmacist Joseph Dauquin, defies the stereotype of an emigration composed entirely of *petites gens*. The only chimney sweep in my sample, Pierre Pechereau of Saint-Clair in the Massif de Thônes, indentured himself in La Rochelle with a colleague from Saint-Denis, whom he had perhaps met in Paris.[87] Yet there were also others, as I discuss in the next chapter, which focuses on official policies of recruitment.

Prior migrations into the Alps were rare among emigrants to Canada and nearly always profited Grenoble or towns of Lower Dauphiné such as Vienne or Valence. Half of the migrants arrived from communities in Dauphiné, usually mountain villages; the others consisted of a Genevan, 2 Foréziens, an Auvergnat, a Périgourdin, and 3 Parisians. As in the Massif central, the previous out-migrations of Alpine natives proved more interesting. Among the Rochelais who settled in Canada were 2 Dauphinois: a tinker born in upper Durance and a merchant, François Viennay-Pachot, who reached La Rochelle from Bourg-d'Oisans. Viennay-Pachot was not a peddler but a genuine merchant, at least after his fortuitous marriage, at the age of twenty, to the widow of a local ironmonger *(marchand quincailler)*. Another merchant from La Rochelle, Pierre Allemand, was himself a native of the city, but his father had arrived there from Saint-Chef in the region of La Tour. One last case worth mentioning, that of Joseph Rivet, involves yet another occupational specialty of Alpine emigrants. A native of Aime in Tarentaise, Rivet arrived in Canada from the prison of Fort-l'Evêque in Paris, where he had been detained for smuggling.

Summary

The migration history of early modern France, viewed as a whole, is both a mosaic of different patterns and one from which certain common threads emerge. The general phenomena, visible nearly everywhere, include urbanization, interurban mobility, migration from highlands to lowlands, and structured seasonal and temporary movements. The various regional patterns that one can detect were generally permutations of these ubiquitous elements.

The respective importance of immigration and emigration depended on geography, with immigration predominant near great cities and emigration in mountainous or otherwise backward areas. Yet one never excluded the other. Seasonal and temporary migrations occurred north as well as south of the Loire, and no part of the country was immune to a degree of permanent rural exodus. Even in regions of highly organized seasonal movements, such as Lower Normandy, the Alps, and the Massif central, some emigrants always fell away from the pack and remained in their adopted communities.

No matter how dominant a particular migration stream, it never succeeded in preempting the movements of everyone who had a different trade or a different idea of where to go. Throughout the seventeenth and eighteenth centuries, the military served as a vehicle for just such an alternative migration. In recruiting soldiers, the state siphoned off a portion of the migrant or potentially migrant population and removed it from the normal channels of mobility in favor of destinations of its own choosing.

Emigration to Canada, and indeed colonial emigration generally, drew upon each and every one of these migratory traditions, in varying degrees. In some cases it probably functioned as an alternative; a native of Bordeaux could move as easily in an Atlantic direction as toward Paris. In other cases it transpired as a deviation or afterthought; an adventurous *compagnon* could decide to short-cut his Tour de France for excitement or a high colonial salary, and a disgruntled rural resident of a large city could throw in the towel in hopes of obtaining cheap and abundant land overseas. In still other cases, emigration to the colonies occurred as the involuntary consequence of a previous military enlistment; some soldiers, however, chose military duty as a means of further emigration.

It is unclear how many emigrants were already mobile when they made their decision to embark for the colonies. The sources are too scarce to warrant a firm conclusion, although when they do speak, they provide eloquent testimony to the close interweaving of internal and external movements. Migrants to Canada, like French migrants generally, came from every segment of French society, with an emphasis on males, the young, and artisans. And, like migrants generally, their commitments to the colony were of varying strengths. Canada, no less than a great metropolitan city, was a *terrain de passage*.

Thus, tradition, along with modernity, helped to shape the migration stream between France and Canada; emigration was closely tied to the secular demographic processes of the Ancien Régime. Taking tradition into account helps to illuminate aspects of the movement that are left unexplained by social and economic analysis: sexual specificity, for example, and also, perhaps, poor staying power. In France, the prominent role played by structured temporary movements meant that many of the emigrants who reached Canada never viewed their transatlantic voyage as irreversible. Currents composed of temporary emigrants could not only send, but also recall, people from Canada. In contrast, the much lower return rate of British emigrants for North America may be seen, in part, as a consequence of differing migratory traditions. According the Peter Clark and David Souden, Britain had few organized temporary migrants comparable to French mountain folk or *compagnons,* at least prior to the mid-eighteenth century.[88]

The notion of tradition is thus crucial, yet because of its dynamic nature, it still fails to explain why Frenchmen, once in Canada, became peasants. To understand that paradox fully, one must look beyond the French background of the emigrants entirely and examine instead the evolution of French Canadian society. That is my task in the conclusion, but before abandoning migratory history, I must consider the related question of emigrant recruitment.

CHAPTER | # 10

The Canadian System of Recruitment

Emigration to Canada may have occurred as a by-product of other, more perennial migrations, but this new migratory option still had to be created in the first place. Traditional forms of mobility needed to be channeled into the new migration stream through a process of recruitment.

For promoters of emigration to Canada, the problem of recruitment was particularly acute. All nations involved in colonization had to encourage emigration and settlement in the initial stages, when demographic ties between metropolis and colony were tenuous. In the case of Canada, however, encouragement had to continue for the entire French Regime, since the movement never became truly self-sustaining: "a tradition of emigration—like that which we see toward the Antilles—was not established toward New France, which did not pass for a country of rapid fortunes."[1]

The terms *myth, dream,* and *mirage* help to explain the snowballing attraction of urban, Spanish, and West Indian destinations for French migrants in the seventeenth and eighteenth centuries. But Canada never captured the French imagination to the same degree, and early enthusiasm was less a prelude to greater things than a false start. On the eve of departure for New France in 1665, Jean Talon, the colony's first intendant, wrote excitedly that the ships were full to capacity and that prospective emigrants continued to arrive: "Many people are presenting themselves for New France who mark their inclination by their eagerness and who, received in this manner, save the king the expense of the levy and the advance that the [West India] Company made to those whom it is transporting."[2] Little more than a year later, Talon's tone was already one of disillusionment. "I will no longer have the honor," he wrote peevishly to Louis XIV, "to speak to you of the great establishment that I formerly indicated could be created in Canada . . . , since you know that there are not enough supernumeraries and useless subjects in old France to people the new one."[3]

Military emigration disappointed official expectations nearly as bitterly. In 1665 Talon wrote of the companies of the Regiment of Carignan, the first regular troops to be stationed in Canada: "I have been assured that more than half of them have supernumeraries. They all testify that they are going with joy to Canada, which makes me very hopeful about the usefulness of their service."[4] The adjustment of these troops to Canadian life was indeed extraordinary—nearly half of them opted to remain—but it was also unique. Recruiters of the *troupes de la Marine,* which served in the colony from the 1680s until the end of the French Regime, found their job to be much more difficult. In 1687 the official in charge of recruitment in Le Havre informed the naval minister: "We are currently working on the levy of the 100 soldiers whom you ordered me to raise . . . I am going to raise them as we do for the navy, without indicating that they are to be sent to Canada, for we would have difficulty getting them on that footing."[5]

The situation improved somewhat, at least in terms of military emigration, in the final decade of the French Regime. Perhaps the mutation would have been lasting, for, whether internal or external, French migrations were intensifying at about the same time. Be that as it may, the British conquest did intervene and closed the book on emigration to Canada before it could truly surmount the objection "that it is a waste of time to work on New France, an intemperate country on account of the glacial sea that surrounds it, where the French can subsist only on what is brought from France."[6] From beginning to end, Canada suffered from a dubious reputation that inhibited emigration and made recruitment an urgent concern of all who desired the survival of the colony.

Attempts at recruitment crystallized in a system of Canadian colonization that underwent important modifications in the course of the French Regime. In this chapter I consider both the structure and the functioning of this system from the earliest years of the colony up until the British conquest. As I indicate, the changing apportionment of responsibilities for recruitment and the disparate identities and choices of the recruiters were the result of an uneasy partnership of private and public interests, a partnership called into being by the commercial marginality of the colony.

Responsibilities for Recruitment

In France as in England, the early structure of colonization emerged from a series of failed attempts, as would-be colonizers discovered by trial and error which features to discard and which to retain. By the beginning of the seventeenth century, a viable organization had developed, which prevailed until Louis XIV chose to increase the level of state intervention in this, as in so many other, spheres of French life. Before 1663 emigration took place within a framework of proprietorship and private entrepreneurship, although proprietors ultimately bore some responsibility to the crown. After 1663 the crown intervened directly in both administration and recruitment. Proprietors did not disappear until 1674, and chartered companies persisted until the conquest; the crown, however, succeeded in reducing them to mere partners in an essentially royal enterprise.

The first systematic attempts to colonize, rather than explore, America occurred in the mid-sixteenth century under the successive auspices of François I, Henri II, and Catherine de Médicis. The resulting settlements differed in both location and intent. In Canada, the courtier Roberval agreed to work for "the augmentation and increase of our holy Christian faith and holy mother Catholic church,"[7] while in Brazil and Florida, lieutenants of the Protestant Coligny tried to establish New World refuges for their coreligionists. The state adopted a similar attitude toward each of these efforts regardless of religion. Although it provided subsidies to the initial expeditions, it expected the established colonies to support themselves. The founders and their associates, as seigneurs and traders, took full responsibility for future defense, administration, and recruitment.

Roberval's settlement succumbed to the Canadian climate, the two Protestant outposts to Portuguese and Spanish incursions. French colonization as a whole then fell victim to the Wars of Religion, remaining at a virtual standstill until the end of the century. When it resumed during the reign of Henri IV, the age of royal subsidies and Protestant refuges was over. Henri distributed property rights and commercial monopolies in lieu of direct funding, and he made formulaic profession of Catholic evangelism. A new framework for French colonization was now in place. Proprietors would finance colonization from the proceeds of commercial monopolies; they, and not the crown, would bear responsibility for recruitment. Although Protestants would not be excluded, and indeed would figure among the proprietors, the official religion of the colonies and the metropolis would henceforth be the same.

The first decade of the seventeenth century witnessed the foundation of two French colonies in Canada: Port-Royal in 1604 and Québec in 1608. The initiative for both came from Pierre Du Gua de Monts, a Protestant officer who was then the exclusive proprietor of New France. The charter he received from Henri IV granted him seigneurial rights and a commercial monopoly over eastern North America from Philadelphia to Newfoundland; in return for these privileges, he agreed to transport 60 settlers across the Atlantic.

Port-Royal (today Annapolis Royal in Nova Scotia) lasted only until 1607; however, French Acadia survived owing to the first sub-infeudation practiced within a proprietary colony. Settlement resumed after a three-year hiatus under the direction of Jean Biencourt de Poutrincourt, a Catholic nobleman who had accompanied the first expedition to Port-Royal. A former participant in the Wars of Religion, he "had resolved to create an independent position in America and to have his family transported there, hoping to find more tranquillity than in Europe."[8]

With Poutrincourt, colonial recruitment entered a new phase. From the responsibility of a single overlord in possession of a commercial monopoly, it became a shared responsibility of the overlord and his seigneurs. The return on the latter's investments would come not from trade but from seigneurial revenues; the success of the enterprise would depend on agricultural settlement. Unfortunately for the colony, Poutrincourt died a pauper in 1615, bequeathing his seigneurie to his equally impoverished son Biencourt. At Biencourt's death in 1623, Port-Royal remained a trading post with no more than 20 year-round residents, none of them women.[9]

Meanwhile, the Canadian monopoly passed from de Monts, who lost it owing to merchant complaints, to a succession of members of the royal family. All but one of the new proprietors worked in tandem with a company of merchants, and all agreed to transport emigrants to the colony of Québec as a condition of their exclusive privilege. The obligation to recruit was never onerous; the prince de Condé and his associates agreed to send six families within eleven years, the duc de Montmorency the same number within fifteen.[10] But despite the leniency of these quotas, proprietors were reluctant to fulfill them. In 1627, when Richelieu revoked the most recent charter, Québec had a total population of 84 or 85; no more than two dozen were true habitants.

Richelieu decided to restructure New France in 1627 and create the organizational framework for an important settlement colony. The resulting Compagnie des Cent-Associés differed from earlier companies in scope rather than in structure. While it remained a private venture that possessed New France "en fief et seigneurie," it brought together moneyed interests from a broad geographical and social spectrum.[11] Participation in the company did not entail *dérogeance* (loss of noble status); on the contrary, Richelieu promised to ennoble twelve of the nonnoble associates. The company received a perpetual monopoly on the fur trade and a fifteen-year monopoly on all other trade except the fisheries. During the fifteen years, it agreed to transport 4,000 indentured servants of both sexes to New France. Prospective immigrants had to be both French and Catholic, but foreigners and Protestants were not prohibited from residing in the colony on a temporary basis.

The domain of the Cent-Associés extended northward from Florida to the Arctic Circle and westward from Newfoundland to the Great Lakes. In practice, however, their jurisdiction was confined to Canada, and they exploited the monopoly directly only in Québec. In Acadia the company had recourse, from the beginning, to *sous-seigneurs*, who themselves formed companies to subcontract a portion of the monopoly. The indentured servants recruited by these seigneurs counted against the total of 4,000 required of the company. The new seigneurs of Acadia belonged, with one exception, to the Cent-Associés, and the parent company looked favorably on their enterprises. The colonization of Acadia proceeded slowly nonetheless; jurisdictional disputes paralyzed the seigneurs, and in 1654 the British occupied all of the colony except for Miscou and the adjoining coast. The French population at the time of the occupation, though it now included women, did not exceed 300 souls.[12]

In Québec, the Cent-Associés subsidized recruitment directly, but their early efforts came to naught when the British seized the colony in 1629. Although the British occupation ended after negotiations in 1632, the company's capital had dwindled dangerously, and subcontracting remained the only option in the Saint Lawrence, as in Acadia. The system of subcontracting adopted in Québec differed from that practiced in Acadia in one major respect: seigneurs did not receive a portion of the monopoly. Instead, a single subsidiary, composed primarily of merchants from Rouen, agreed to manage the monopoly and assume the company's responsibilities for a period of six years. The *compagnie particulière*, which arranged for the transport of 200 immigrants in 1633, did not bear the full burden of recruitment, but shared it with the colony's seigneurs, who invested in their properties in anticipation of seigneurial revenues.[13] Laurentian seigneurs included individuals, with or without the backing of companies, and collectivities such as the Jesuits and the Société Notre-Dame de Montréal.

The Compagnie des Cent-Associés never recovered its initial vigor, although in 1642, the year of Richelieu's death, it resumed direct exploitation of the monopoly for lack of a willing subcontractor. In 1645 it had recourse to a new expedient: reconcession of the monopoly, not to a company, but to the inhabitants themselves in the form of a Communauté des Habitants. The Community, defined as all males permanently domiciled in the colony, took upon itself the annual recruitment of 20 persons complete with "provisions and conveniences."[14] But the Community derived no more profit from the monopoly than had its predecessors, and it successively tested a number of survival strategies, including subcontracting exportation (1652), leasing trading posts (1653), and reconceding the monopoly to yet another subcontractor (1660). Recruitment thus depended on individual seigneurs and on the Community or the latter's commercial associates from 1645 until the reorganization of the colony in 1663. The only innovation in recruitment policy during this period consisted of a 1647 decree of the Conseil de Québec mandating French shipowners to transport 1 immigrant per ten tons of cargo on all ships bound for Québec.[15]

The Compagnie des Cent-Associés did not long survive the personal reign of Louis XIV. Seconded by Colbert, the young king revoked the company's charter in 1663 and brought the colony directly under the royal administration. The company, he claimed, had failed to fulfill essential obligations, among them defending the colony, transporting immigrants, and converting the Indians. While "the company was able to prove before the Parlement of Paris, based on the Admiralty registers, that 5,000 people had been transported to New France under its authority," the failure of definitive settlement was palpable.[16] New France in 1663 had barely 3,500 inhabitants, several hundred of whom were Acadians under British occupation. By comparison, the combined population of British and Dutch North America was 90,000 in the same year, and New Englanders alone numbered 40,000.[17]

In reorganizing New France, Louis did not immediately reject the formula of the proprietary colony, but he modified it significantly. In 1664 he reconceded New France, together with the Antilles, to the newly created Compagnie des Indes occidentales "in full seigneurie, property, and justice."[18] The company received a long-term commercial monopoly, in return for which it contributed to colonial expenses, but it no longer controlled administration, defense, or immigration. Convinced that the proprietary framework was insufficiently dynamic, the king reserved initiative in these domains for himself. The company's sole responsiblity for recruitment consisted of supplying the colony with a sufficient number of priests. For the first time in a century, the crown returned to a policy of subsidizing emigration directly. Within months of the dissolution of the Cent-Associés, two ships of the royal navy set out from La Rochelle with about 300 passengers for Québec, and in the following two years, company ships transported over 700 emigrants at the expense of the king.

The system inaugurated by Louis XIV prevailed, with modifications, until the end of the French Regime.[19] Direct state intervention became a permanent factor of recruitment policy, although the extent of support varied according to the place of Canada within the royal priorities. In the first ten years of royal control, the colony received about 4,000 new settlers at the king's expense: 2,000 indentured servants, 1,000 soldiers, and 1,000 *filles à marier*.[20] In the eighteenth century, the bulk of royal emigrants were soldiers from the *troupes de la Marine* or the *troupes de terre*, to whom must be added perhaps 1,000 prisoners.[21] The state no longer subsidized the passage of *filles à marier*, and it rarely arranged for the transport of more than a handful of indentured servants.[22] It did, however, fund the deportation to Québec and Acadia of vagabonds, *fils de famille*, deserters, smugglers, and other petty criminals.

The participation of merchants in recruitment continued pursuant to the decree of the council, although they often complied with it grudgingly or not at all.[23] The king found himself obliged to renew its terms twice:

in 1714 and 1716 ordinances required merchant ships to transport indentured servants to Québec or troop reinforcements in their place.[24] In 1721,
in response to complaints, the king allowed shipowners to pay 60 livres
or transport a prisoner for each missing *engagé;* a circular of 1722 extended
these conditions from Québec to Ile Royale, which had previously been
exempt.[25] Passive resistance continued, and in 1724, an exasperated king
imposed a fine of 200 livres upon merchants who failed to embark the
requisite number of emigrants. Even this draconian measure failed to alter
the behavior of shippers for Ile Royale, whom a final ordinance recalled
to their duties in 1729. The obligation to recruit as a condition of trading
had moved from the center to the periphery of French recruitment efforts.
In the final century of the French Regime, it was simply an ancillary
feature of a recruitment system that relied far more heavily on direct state
intervention.[26]

Like state agents and merchants, Canadian seigneurs also continued to
bear responsibility for recruitment. Organized recruitment by the habitants, however, ended with the dissolution of the Community in 1666.
Seigneurs were especially active agents of colonization in Acadia, where
the loss of the mainland made the development of Ile Saint-Jean and Ile
Royale an urgent concern.[27] Responsibilities for recruitment thus came to
be shared among a broader spectrum of institutions and individuals in
the course of the French Regime. In the earliest years of the colony,
trader-proprietors and seigneurs consented to recruit in return for colonial revenues; under Richelieu, a proprietary company, commercial and
seigneurial subcontractors, and simple seigneurs took their place. During
the personal reign of Louis XIV, recruitment became an actual affair of
state, albeit with continued seigneurial and mercantile participation. The
Canadian commercial monopoly entailed few obligations to recruit after
1663, but beginning in 1647, merchants grudgingly guaranteed a small but
steady stream of embarkations.

The Process of Recruitment

The dispersal of responsibilities for recruitment created a numerous and
varied personnel of recruiters, especially after the liquidation of the
Compagnie des Cent-Associés. The recruiters, whether simple habitants,
seigneurs, merchants, or functionaries at various levels of the government

bureaucracy, made decisions about where to go, whom to address, and what arguments to employ. In interaction with the social, economic, and demographic structures I have discussed, their choices determined the shape of the emigrant population.

Two types of sources make it possible to study the individual recruiters and their choices: the notarial archives of the major ports and the administrative correspondence of the naval minister, whose jurisdiction extended to the colonies. The notarial archives of La Rochelle, which contain a series of Canadian indentures dating from 1619 to 1758, show private recruiters at work throughout the French Regime. The actions of state recruiters, although more dispersed, can be reconstructed thanks to the detailed instructions of the naval minister. Together, the notarial archives of La Rochelle and the ministerial correspondence provide a comprehensive view of France's hybrid system of recruitment, with its simultaneous reliance on private and public enterprise.

The Role of Merchants

The mercantile contribution to recruitment remained consistent in kind, although not in volume, throughout the French Regime. As traders moved from the forefront to the background of recruitment efforts, they continued to target roughly the same geographical areas and social groups. The vicissitudes of mercantile recruitment were reflected in the identity of the recruiters, the number of emigrants they indentured, and the more or less speculative nature of their enterprises. The evolving servant trade of La Rochelle in the seventeenth and eighteenth centuries was characteristic of the changing nature of mercantile recruitment.

Companies and individuals involved in the Canada trade concentrated their recruiting on a single geographic arena: La Rochelle itself. The idea seems to have been to recruit as close to home as possible, in order to keep the costs down. Indentured servants were thus natives, residents, or visitors to the port, which explains why both the city and the economic and migratory circuits connecting it to the outside were so evident in my sample.

The social parameters of mercantile recruitment were as broad, in theory at least, as the geographical profile was narrow. Although the state established guidelines for the selection of indentured servants, it permitted considerable freedom of choice. The statutes of the Cent-Associés mandated only that emigrants be male and female, French and Catholic. Subsequent rulings dropped the explicit reference to nationality and religion, while adding new provisions on age and height. Throughout the royal regime, merchants had to recruit emigrants who were between eighteen and forty years old, and who were no less than four feet tall.[28] The obligation to recruit women disappeared after 1663, when merchants became responsible for embarking "workmen" in proportion to tonnage; in the eighteenth century, royal edicts referred to "engagés" with no further gender specification.[29] With regard to social class and profession, merchants always had complete discretion. The edicts did, however, permit the double-counting of certain artisans against merchant quotas after 1714.

In La Rochelle mercantile recruitment produced a youthful and heavily male emigrant population in which artisans outnumbered peasants. Yet it is difficult to attribute this outcome to social selectivity on the part of the recruiters. While artisans may have seemed more desirable after 1714, they were no less prominent among seventeenth-century emigrants, nor were they solely targeted in mercantile propaganda. Instead, merchants framed their arguments to appeal to a broad spectrum of potential indentured servants, urban and rural, male and female.[30] The high proportion of male artisans among La Rochelle's indentured servants thus resulted less from merchant demand than from the pressures of supply. Women, who lacked traditions of long-distance migration, were less ready for a voyage into the unknown, and peasants appeared in small numbers because of the resolutely urban focus of recruitment.[31]

Mercantile recruitment did not merely exhibit continuities, however; in the course of the French Regime, it underwent structural transformations affecting both the identity of the recruiters and the scope and nature of their efforts. These changes proceeded in part, but in part only, from the state-mandated lessening of the mercantile responsibility to provide colonists. The continuous reassessment by the merchants themselves of the opportunities presented by the servant trade played a determining role as well, with the result that the evolution of mercantile recruitment depended on the complex interaction of private interest and public policy.

In La Rochelle, the vicissitudes of mercantile recruitment for Canada began with the decline of collective recruiters and their gradual replacement with individual merchants. The latter entered the market with a bang, retrenched somewhat, withdrew altogether in favor of sea captains, then made a cautious comeback just before the British conquest. The speculative accomplishments of traders thus rose, fell, and rose again, only to succumb in the end to military defeat.

Commercial recruiters for Canada arrived somewhat tardily in La Rochelle, as a result of both commercial rivalry and outright exclusion. The earliest titularies of the monopoly preferred to deal with Normans and Bretons, and Richelieu, while broadening the geographical base of the Canada trade, failed to extend it to La Rochelle. The absence of Rochelais merchants from the Compagnie des Cent-Associés was not accidental; Louis XIII ratified its charter of incorporation while preparing to lay siege to the Protestant port. Even after the capitulation, La Rochelle's perceived disloyalty prevented recruiting from moving southward in the early years of Richelieu's new regime.

Recruiters did reach La Rochelle between 1642 and 1645, when the Cent-Associés were again handling the Canada trade directly. The losses sustained by the Normans during the years of subcontracting made them amenable to Rochelais participation, and the objections of Richelieu disappeared with his death in 1642. Three mercantile recruiters worked out of La Rochelle in these years: a director and two employees of the company.[32] The director, who had previously operated in Normandy, now enlisted some 75 indentured servants in La Rochelle, and his clerks signed up another dozen.[33] Most of these servants became direct dependents of the company, but a few agreed to work for specific Canadian seigneurs.

In 1645 the Communauté des Habitants took over from the company, and its representatives replaced the latter's as recruiters. Until 1652, when the Community itself turned to expedients to maintain the Canada trade, its appointees made irregular levies of labor in La Rochelle. As recorded in the notarial archives, their activities were on a smaller scale than those of the Cent-Associés, but they resembled them in kind.[34] Most emigrants indentured themselves to the habitants collectively, while a few signed on by procuration with individual habitants.

The ruling on indentured servants passed by the Conseil de Québec in 1647 did not affect recruitment in La Rochelle, at least in the several years after its passage. Although it held shippers responsible for the embarkment of a minimum number of *engagés*, the efforts of the Community apparently sufficed to meet the quota. The first instance of recruitment by a

Rochelais merchant did occur in 1648, but, at the time, the merchant in question had a financial interest only in shipping to the West Indies. His decision to send an indentured servant to Canada was thus an isolated attempt to test the Canadian labor market rather than a response to governmental imperative.

In the final decades of the Cent-Associés, the struggling Communauté des Habitants ceased to recruit servants in La Rochelle, turning instead to the city's merchants for the fulfillment of its multiple obligations. Of the 10 merchants who responded to the call, 6 were Catholic and 4 Protestant. The Protestants, in keeping with their greater economic weight in the merchant community, operated on a larger and more speculative scale than the Catholics.[35]

In 1655 the Protestant François Péron inaugurated the new phase of merchant recruitment by embarking the annual quota of 20 servants required of the Community. The real innovation, however, occurred the following year, when Péron and his Protestant colleague Jacques Pépin recruited 50-odd emigrants on their own initiative and for their own benefit. Péron, who entrusted the disposal of his servants to a clerk, found the results sufficiently gratifying to renew the operation in subsequent years. By 1659 he had recruited some 70 emigrants for Canada, only 3 of them at the behest of specific colonists.

Catholic merchants soon followed the example of their religious and commercial rivals and became involved in speculative recruitment. As early as 1657, a partnership composed of Antoine Grignon, Pierre Gaigneur, and Jacques Massé embarked 33 indentured servants on their own account. But apparently success eluded them, for the endeavor was not repeated. At midcentury, Catholics commanded risk capital with greater difficulty than Protestants, and most of them preferred the safer course of responding to specific demands for labor.

Between 1663 and 1713, collective recruiters reappeared in the form of the Compagnie des Indes occidentales, the Compagnie du Nord, and the Compagnie d'Acadie. Individual merchants, however, continued to enlist the bulk of the servants, since Louis XIV had released the companies from most of their obligations to recruit. The royal regime thus failed to stem the atrophy of collective mercantile recruitment, which remained anemic in comparison to its highpoint under the Cent-Associés.[36]

The merchants, by now mostly Catholics, destined fully three-fifths of their recruits for unknown bidders.[37] This belated speculative success of the Catholics probably stemmed less from the elimination of their Protestant competitors than from the latters' withdrawal from a market judged insufficiently lucrative.[38] A few shippers began, in this period, to delegate their recruiting responsibilities, minimal as they were, to the sea captains they employed; all was not well with the Rochelais servant trade.[39]

Between 1714 and 1730, the role of captains increased as that of merchants waned. About half of the servants signed on with captains, an indication that the burden of complying with the servant legislation of these years was being transferred to them. Fifteen captains served as recruiters, as opposed to only 6 merchants, and all embarked the servants on their own account. Profits as well as losses accrued to them, but trade remained on a modest scale, with fewer than half a dozen servants embarking per voyage. Several captains, however, recruited quite consistently, obviously viewing recruitment as a profitable sideline.

From 1731 until the end of the War of the Austrian Succession, the captains carried on the servant trade virtually alone. Only 4 merchants went before the notary with indentures, and although 16 of the city's shippers were trading with Canada during the war years alone, just 1 felt compelled to involve himself in recruitment.[40] Neither the merchants nor the 27 captains enlisted servants with specific Canadians in mind.

This situation changed only in the final decade of the French Regime, when the Canada trade again appealed to a larger spectrum of La Rochelle's merchants. Not all of these merchants took a direct interest in recruiting servants, but their involvement increased to the point that they dominated the Acadian market and shared that of Québec more or less equally with captains. Overall, about twice as many servants embarked in this as in the previous decade.

Mercantile recruitment thus moved from the realm of collective to that of individual enterprise in the course of the French Regime, a development ratified rather than initiated by governmental policy. Individual merchants recruited more or less heavily, and more or less speculatively, in accordance with their own economic preferences. When they perceived the servant trade as lucrative, they recruited large numbers of emigrants on their own account, but when they did not, they restricted their efforts to filling colonial commissions or delegated observance of the servant legislation to their captains. In spite of these transformations, mercantile recruitment remained consistent in its approach to prospective colonists. Recruiters, whether agents of companies, independent shippers, or sea captains, sought servants in their home ports, and found them among young, urban males in modest economic circumstances.

The Role of Seigneurs

Seigneurial recruitment, with its emphasis on agricultural settlement, played a more important role in the pioneering stages of colonization than afterward. Its geographical focus therefore shifted from Québec and peninsular Acadia in the seventeenth century to Ile Saint-Jean in the eighteenth. Canadian seigneurs, as I have indicated, were either collectivities or individuals, simple rentiers or seigneurs-traders. The seigneurial traders were largely confined to Acadia and the individual or collective rentiers to Québec.

The servants recruited by seigneurs of all types exhibited a broader range of geographical and social origins than those recruited through mercantile interest or obligation. While not disdaining the great ports, the seigneurs or their agents cast their nets more widely when seeking emigrants; their native localities, in particular, furnished a considerable number of recruits. Socially, they made an effort to indenture families and peasants as well as single, young townsmen, so their efforts abetted the transplantation to Canada of a more representative cross-section of the French population.

The Atlantic ports, or La Rochelle at any rate, held a significant, if not preponderant, place in seigneurial recruitment. In the seventeenth century, seigneurs like Claude de Razilly of Acadia and seigneurial representatives like Jérôme Le Royer de La Dauversière of the Société Notre-Dame de Montréal appeared personally in La Rochelle to seek out colonists for their respective establishments.[41] Razilly indentured 2 servants there in 1636, and La Dauversière, "residing ordinarily in La Flesche," recruited 21 while lodging with the Rochelais merchant Jacques Mousnier in 1644.[42]

These same recruiters also looked to La Rochelle when they could not do the recruiting themselves. Razilly's cousin Charles de Menou d'Aulnay secured him a servant there in 1634, and in 1652 Mousnier enlisted emigrants for La Dauversière by proxy.[43] After the Treaty of Utrecht, the seigneur of Ile Saint-Jean, the comte de Saint-Pierre, formed a society with the merchants of La Rochelle for the peopling and exploitation of his seigneurie. At least 150 servants embarked there for Ile Saint-Jean in the early 1720s, perhaps the largest group of colonists to leave the port in the employ of a single seigneur.

Seigneurial recruitment did not, however, begin and end with La Rochelle. Unlike merchants, seigneurs sought some of their colonists in areas remote from the Atlantic and its commerce but familiar to them personally. Perhaps their behavior represents a conscious, if sporadic, attempt to bypass the anonymity of port recruitment, for seigneurs knew indentured servants not as negotiable commodities but as their own future *censitaires*.

The best-known case of local seigneurial recruitment has already been alluded to; it concerns Robert Giffard, the Percheron seigneur of Beauport. The scion of a quasi-seigneurial family from the environs of Mortagne (Orne), Giffard visited Canada as a ship's surgeon in the 1620s, then returned to Mortagne to ply his trade as a master apothecary. Perhaps he found the living too humble or the competition from the town's four other pharmacists too stiff. In any case, he chose to abandon the business in favor of settling in Québec, and he petitioned the Cent-Associés for a seigneurie in 1634.[44]

Giffard's main associates were the brothers Jean and Noël Juchereau, sons of a local merchant and proto-industrialist who had made a fortune in wine, wood, iron, land, and anything else that he could sell. Their involvement with Canada brought them not only monetary benefits but enhanced social prestige; Jean's son Nicolas acceded to the nobility in 1692, a century before his cousins in the French branch of the family.[45]

As was indicated in Part One, the three recruiters managed to generate a wave of colonial departures that was quite unprecedented in the region. It continued, in fits and starts, for over thirty years, its end coinciding roughly with the deaths of Giffard and Jean Juchereau in 1668 and 1672, respectively. Yet, although Giffard du Moncel, Juchereau du Maure, and Juchereau des Châtelets all held title to estates in the Perche, these estates did not, for the most part, provide their colonists. Recruitment was local and direct, but it did not depend on a preexisting relationship between *censitaire* and seigneur.

The Percheron example was not unique in the annals of seigneurial recruitment, of course. Neither of the aforementioned seigneurial recruiters in Aunis, Claude de Razilly or Jérôme Le Royer de La Dauversière, confined his activities to La Rochelle; both, in fact, recruited far more vigorously in their areas of origin. In 1636 Razilly, who owned estates in Touraine, enlisted 40 servants in Bourgueil and Chinon (Indre-et-Loire), and in 1653 La Dauversière recruited 121 around his home in La Flèche. Like the recruits of Giffard, these emigrants came primarily from country towns, not parishes under the seigneurial jurisdiction of the recruiters. Verron, Crosmières, and Malicorne (Sarthe), where the Le Royer family was ensconced, sent far fewer servants than La Flèche, while Beaumont-en-Véron (Indre-et-Loire) produced not a single permanent colonist for Razilly.

Only one bona fide case of recruitment on seigneurial estates has been established to date. It involves Razilly's cousin and successor, Charles de Menou d'Aulnay, whose family lands in Poitou helped to people his Acadian seigneurie. An examination of parish registers revealed that "more than half of the acts passed in the parish of La Chaussée [Vienne] between 1626 and 1650 concern about twenty family names that we find, in 1671, in the first census of Acadia; and three precise acts, passed in 1627, 1645, and 1646, pertain directly to families (Brault, Brun and Chebrat) recorded in the Acadian census . . . It thus appears that the seigneurie of Aulnay, possessed by the mother of Charles de Menou, could have been the cradle of about twenty of the oldest families who settled in Acadia."[46]

Menou's efforts, while startlingly successful, appear exceptional in every way. Seigneurial recruiters often sought out emigrants in their region of origin, and they probably used their social influence to persuade their interlocutors. This influence was not, however, the authority of the traditional seigneur, but rather the notability of any prosperous and respectable member of the community.

Seigneurs did not merely expand the geographical horizons of recruitment, but its social horizons as well. Because of their interest in agricultural settlement, they made a greater effort than merchants to include peasants among their recruits, and for the same reason, they sometimes looked beyond single young people to constituted families.

Seigneurial writings stressed the importance of peasant emigration to the creation of a successful Canadian colony. As early as 1636, the *Jesuit Relations* carried the following "Advice to those who desire to cross over into New France": "There are so many strong and robust peasants in

France who have no bread to put in their mouths; is it possible that they are so afraid of losing sight of the village steeple, as they say, that they would rather languish in their misery and poverty than place themselves someday at their ease among the inhabitants of New France?"[47]

The seigneurial appeal to peasants, unlike that of merchants, did not remain on the level of semantics. Razilly's recruits from 1636 consisted of 2 salt producers and 40 "peasants from Anjou," and, except for a gunsmith and a carpenter, those of his cousin Menou d'Aulnay were all *laboureurs* from Poitou.[48] Peasants also outnumbered artisans among the servants indentured by La Dauversière in 1653, and among those enlisted in Tourouvre-au-Perche by Jean and Noël Juchereau.[49]

The recruitment of families sometimes accompanied that of peasants, for seigneurs viewed family farms as the essential building blocks of a stable colonial society. As the Jesuit Le Jeune wrote in 1635: "It all lies in employing many men to cut down and clear the woods, in order to distribute the land to the families whom we are and shall be transporting."[50] The "peasants from Anjou" recruited by Razilly in the following year included 6 families of 3 to 5 persons each, and, on a larger scale, many of the Percherons arrived in Canada in family units.[51] Families did not, however, predominate in seigneurial recruitment because of the preference implied by Le Jeune for adult males during the initial stages of settlement.

Seigneurial recruitment thus produced a more diverse group of emigrants in terms of regional origin, social background, sex, and age than did mercantile recruitment. While it remained in the minority throughout most of the French Regime, its importance far exceeds its admittedly limited numerical scope. Emigrants located through the personal prestige of a recruiter were, on the whole, better candidates for permanent settlement than those raked together on the fly; ultimately, the provinces where seigneurial recruitment prevailed, such as Perche, Anjou, and Maine, made a disproportionate contribution to the agriculture and population of French Canada.

The Role of the State

The state's role in recruitment, by contrast, was complex and hierarchical. At the top of the pyramid of recruiters stood the naval minister; in consultation with the king, he determined how many emigrants the state could and should recruit.[52] Although he delegated the actual task of recruiting, he involved himself in the minutiae of policy making, providing his subalterns with specifications about whom and where to recruit.

Beginning in 1666, the minister relayed his will preferentially to upper functionaries within the naval bureaucracy. The administrators of Rochefort assumed the role of coordinating recruitment, partly because the port now became by fiat the principal base of the Atlantic fleet, and partly because Colbert could rely on its *intendant de la Marine*, his cousin Colbert de Terron. The domination of the Rochefortais remained absolute until the 1680s, when colleagues from Bordeaux and Le Havre became involved in recruitment, and visible thereafter. Even the participation of administrators from Bayonne, Nantes, and Saint-Malo in the eighteenth century did not pose a serious challenge to Rochefort's supremacy.

The naval officials, consisting of the intendants and their various subalterns—*commissionnaires, commissaires généraux, commissaires ordonnateurs, commissaires ordinaires,* and *inspecteurs*—took responsibility for both military recruitment and civilian recruitment in the form of skilled male labor. Although the state, as I discuss below, subsidized other categories of civilian emigrants such as indentured servants, *filles à marier,* and prisoners, it did so under the auspices of recruiters from outside the naval establishment. The naval bureaucrats approached their military and civilian responsibilities in different ways. Civilian recruitment was often direct, but military recruitment involved further delegation of the commissions received from the minister, in accordance with the established practices of the metropolitan army.

Thanks to André Corvisier, historians can sketch a clear picture of domestic military recruitment in the seventeenth and eighteenth centuries. Colonels, majors, and captains received an official mandate to recruit, in order to maintain troop strength at the stipulated levels. Sometimes they enlisted soldiers themselves, but, more often, they referred the task to subordinates: lieutenants, sergeants, corporals, or even simple soldiers. These "natural auxiliaries" usually sufficed, but since the market for recruits, like a labor market, responded to supply and demand, they sometimes had to look elsewhere to meet their quota.[53] In times of scarce manpower, they had recourse to intermediaries of all stripes, who brought in recruits in return for a per capita sum. Former soldiers, innkeepers, merchants, petty judicial officers, members of the mounted constabulary, and relatives of the official recruiters might occasionally supplement their incomes by finding takers for the *pain du roi*.

Soldiers made their way into the Canadian troops in much the same way. The men the *commissaires* relied upon included a colonel, 2 majors, 7 captains, 4 lieutenants, and a sergeant.[54] Those below the rank of captain acted in the name of their superior officers, enlisting soldiers for the entire company or regiment. There is little direct evidence of civilian meddling in recruitment, but accounts of periodic fiascoes point to the participation of disreputable "rabatteurs" in the recruitment process.[55] In 1750, for example, the governor of Québec complained to the minister of the military recruiters in the following terms:

> I cannot dispense . . . with representing to you that those who took care of raising these recruits have served the king very badly, and have abused your confidence; here is the proof. You will be surprised that they accepted people disabled from birth, men between sixty and seventy years old, sailors from the royal navy, married men who brought with them wives and children, people of all nations, including a great many Spaniards who neither speak nor understand French; lastly, among the rest, there are a number of knaves and scoundrels, certain of them repeat offenders who deserved to be on the galleys rather than to serve the king.[56]

Geographically, as I pointed out was the case with regard to Paris, military recruiters for Canada did not exactly replicate the movements of recruiters of the domestic troops. These last combined local recruitment during the dead season (among people known to the recruiting captain and his family) with *racolage* per se—the anonymous collective recruitment by way of poster and public drum beating in major cities.[57] Canada's military recruiters relied primarily on the second, or impersonal, approach. Direct, local recruitment was limited to a few specific instances; officers of the Swiss troops, which served on Ile Royale from the 1720s, "seem to have recruited in the vicinity of their family," and during the Seven Years' War, those of the Royal Roussillon moved outward from a home base in Roussillon and Catalonia.[58] Most of the time, however, recruiters simply had recourse to public announcements in urban squares, as stipulated by their superiors.

As with domestic *racolage*, the officer in charge of colonial recruitment "received from the king a 'route' that indicated the itinerary to follow."[59] More often than not, he centered his operations on a major port city such as Le Havre, Nantes, or Bordeaux, then radiated out, if necessary, into the towns of the hinterlands. The orders of one Pannetié, an officer working out of Le Havre in 1687, permitted him to send recruiters from the port "into all the cities of this province."[60]

Paris provided far fewer recruits than did Atlantic France, for reasons that appear more financial than geographic. In 1717, when the recruiter La Galissonière requested an itinerary for Paris, the council balked; it informed him flatly that "it has esteemed necessary to have them raised in the Department of Rochefort, where they will cost infinitely less than in Paris."[61] This higher price may have been justified, for, when troops did arrive from Paris in 1734, the governor and the intendant of Ile Royale wrote of them that "those who were enlisted in Paris . . . are the best who have come here to date, for age as well as for . . . the other dispositions necessary for the service; those who were raised in Rochefort are very different . . . by their infirmities and other defects."[62]

Recruiters of the domestic troops, wherever they were sent, addressed themselves indiscriminately to a broad segment of the male population. By law, they could not accept recruits under the age of sixteen and they could not enlist anyone against his will; beyond these broad guidelines, anything was acceptable. In practice, even these minimal constraints did not always obtain. Underage boys enrolled, with or without a dispensation,[63] and prisoners entered the service for life regardless of their personal preferences. Nor were wayward sons, vagabonds, smugglers, and deserters the only victims of forced recruitment. Unscrupulous *racoleurs* chose to meet their quotas through impressment, which became almost an institution in areas of heavy recruitment. Several taverns in Paris, for example, "acted as 'ovens,' that is to say, places where unfortunates who had been lured in or kidnapped were shut up until they signed an enlistment."[64]

The same criteria applied to Canadian as to domestic recruitment, and a cavalier attitude toward them appeared to be equally prevalent. With regard to age, the ministry routinely set standards, which the recruiters just as routinely violated. In 1725, for example, Lieutenant Paschot learned that his recruits "had to be between eighteen and thirty years of age," but within a week he had received "a young man named Villars who is only fourteen years old" but "who absolutely wanted to enlist."[65]

When recruitment proved difficult, as it often did during wartime, any lingering concern with age evaporated. The Canadians sometimes complained, as in 1712, when the governor of Québec wrote of the year's recruits that "all of these soldiers are mere children, and it will take at least three or four years before they will be able to be in a position to render service."[66] Even Canadians, however, could be complacent; in 1696 Governor Frontenac described the new soldiers as "strong, pretty, and alert," adding that "they are in truth very young, but in our experience, young people adjust better to the country than the others."[67]

The policy toward prisoners changed for the worse during the French Regime. In the seventeenth century, recruiters could not enlist them, no matter how desperate they were for manpower; but by 1702 the authorities had reversed themselves completely, permitting the family of one Henri-Claude Bernard to deport him from Nantes to Newfoundland, "where he will serve as a soldier pending further orders."[68] During the Regency, recruiters began to enlist vagabonds as well; in 1717 La Galissonière received permission to embark 28 of them, provided they were healthy and that "in the meantime, you keep the thing secret."[69] Sundry prisoners arrived with the Canadian troops up until the British conquest.

The correspondence does not abound in examples of impressment, which was, after all, a distasteful subject, but it indicates that even in peacetime some abuses occurred. Isolated victims could obtain justice in the form of a discharge, if not of a return to France; in 1702 a "young man from the region of Maine who was put by force into the reinforcements lately arrived in Canada" received his freedom.[70] Perhaps the most curious case involved a kidnapped priest who spent two years in the Canadian army while awaiting the outcome of his appeal. After an investigation, the minister informed the governor of Québec that "Monsieur Pierre Chauveau, who was sent to Canada among the new recruits of 1733, told you the truth when he stated to you that he was a priest. The Bishop of Orléans has sent me a certificate of his ordination."[71]

Unfortunately, when impressment took place on a larger scale, there was little that anyone could do. The infamous recruits of 1750 were not only crippled, aged, Spanish, naked, and criminal: "Furthermore, most of these soldiers had no enlistment, and they have complained stoutly, some that they had been taken by force, others by surprise, and practically all that they had not been paid what had been promised for their enlistment."[72]

Their morbidity and mortality rates were elevated, even for the time, and those who found the strength to rebel were put down by force.[73] Such callous and irresponsible recruitment was an aberration, as the very vehemence of the documents describing these soldiers shows, yet it stands as a reminder that at its involuntary worst, emigration could prey upon the most vulnerable members of society.

Attention to age and freedom of contract, no matter how imperfect, does not completely define the social selectivity of Canadian military recruitment. Especially in the eighteenth century, Canadian recruiters sometimes received a more specific mandate: the colony needed not just soldiers, but soldier-workers.

In the Maritimes, where an exposed position made fortifications a prerequisite of effective settlement, the recruitment of soldier-workers seemed the ideal solution. The average soldier served for six to eight years in France, and for even longer in the colonies. His advantage over an indentured servant, or *trente-six mois,* was therefore palpable, without even considering the pressing issue of defense.

Recruiters began to target workers in a major way at the turn of the century, in order to fortify French Newfoundland. In 1700 the minister arranged for the arrival there of "a levy entirely composed of masons, stonecutters, and carpenters."[74] The following year, while deploring that "it is difficult, especially in the present situation where soldiers are being raised everywhere," he nonetheless managed to include "a few masons, stonecutters, carpenters, and other workers" among the 71 new reinforcements.[75]

In 1714 the settlement of Ile Royale called forth another wave of artisanal recruiting. Indeed, the minister described the artisanal competence of the island's soldiers as a matter "of utmost consequence."[76] As in Newfoundland, the building trades topped the list of desirable skills, but the range was somewhat wider, as befitting the scope of the establishment. "The trades that are the most necessary," wrote the members of the naval council, "are those of mason, stonecutter, carpenter, joiner, blacksmith, and locksmith. Those of cooper, cobbler, and tailor would also be necessary, but in small quantity."[77]

In Québec the matter seemed less urgent, owing to both the larger population and the vaunted artisanal capacities of the habitant. Shortages of skilled labor did exist, however, for, in the words of the last intendant, "the Canadian is naturally a jack-of-all-trades but only for his own use."[78] Levies of workers for the Québec troops occurred more sporadically and tended to be more specialized than those for Ile Royale. The recruits ranged from tilers and potters (in 1717), to cordwainers (1732), to bakers and surgeons (1741). If conditions were favorable, heavier and more general labor recruiting could take place. After the Treaty of Aix-La-Chapelle, for example, the chief recruiting officer announced to the minister his success in enlisting "several masons, roofers, carpenters, blacksmiths, sawyers, a paver, a stonecutter, a cooper, and several bakers."[79]

Military recruiters for Canada thus exercised more discretion than their domestic confrères, at least upon occasion. The direct supervision they experienced from the naval ministry did not prevent them from yielding to familiar temptations such as cheating on age, nor did it completely eradicate impressment. It did, however, require them to fulfill specific commissions regarding skilled labor, which provided Canada with an important, if temporary, reservoir of artisans.

IN ADDITION to coordinating military recruitment, naval functionaries also filled specific requests for civilian emigrants. The minister turned to the navy for artisans as well as soldiers, and many *ouvriers du roi* arrived in the colonies by way of the great naval bases. The involvement of *commissaires,* Rochefort's in particular, in supplying skilled labor for the colonies grew out of their domestic role of guaranteeing a workforce in the royal arsenals. The Rochefort Arsenal employed 4,000 or 5,000 workers in wartime, who preoccupied administrators "in terms of both their recruitment in sufficient numbers and their professional competency."[80]

In recruiting civilians for the colonies, naval functionaries delegated their authority less readily than in recruiting soldiers. The correspondence refers to them consistently as *engageurs* in their own right; only François de Beauharnais, who as intendant of La Rochelle and Rochefort enjoyed a singularly elevated position, routinely passed recruitment orders along to his subalterns.[81] The *commissaires* accomplished the bulk of the work themselves, aided by the "assistance and facilities" of provincial governors and intendants.[82] The sergeants, corporals, and other humble *racoleurs* who helped to enlist the *troupes de la Marine* played little part in the naval recruitment of skilled civilians.

Administrators frequently sought out workers in the ports within their jurisdiction, but they also made efforts to locate them in zones associated with specific kinds of occupational competence.[83] The best ironworkers, they assumed, came from Burgundy and Franche-Comté, the best chimney sweeps from Savoy, and the best building workers from Limousin and Auvergne.[84] They obtained royal orders accordingly, such as that for a levy of masons, stonecutters, and carpenters "in the provinces of Le Puy-en-Velay, Auvergne, Bourbonnais, Limousin, and Poitou" in 1720.[85] Traditional migration streams did not always spill over accidentally into the movement toward Canada; when considered useful, they were voluntarily diverted.

Recruiters of such professionals worked at a disadvantage in that regions like Savoy or Velay had no obvious connection to Atlantic commerce. On the other hand, as seen earlier, these provinces had long-standing traditions of labor migration, and although migrants usually followed established routes, they still had considerable flexibility. Recruiters needed only make a somewhat better offer than the workers knew they could obtain in their customary destination and some of the more adventurous would willingly sign on for a stint in Canada.[86]

ALTHOUGH NAVAL FUNCTIONARIES and their deputies recruited the bulk of Canada's state-subsidized emigrants, the minister also commissioned recruiters without ties to the naval bureaucracy. The Compagnie des Indes occidentales, hospital administrators, churchmen, prison officials, and the Ferme générale provided the balance of the king's civilian recruits in the form of indentured servants, *filles du roi,* and prisoners.

The Compagnie des Indes occidentales recruited indentured servants at the behest (and expense) of the crown, which relied upon merchants to effect the large-scale levies characteristic of the early years of Canada's royal regime.[87] In 1665 Jean Talon described the company's efforts in La Rochelle to the minister: "The West India Company, being obliged . . . to transport 400 workmen to Canada, has ordered the directors who are here to raise 150 on its behalf through the levy that I am having carried out today on the deck of the ship. There are more than that number."[88]

Two years later, the company contracted for another levy of 400 men and appointed the merchant Pierre Gaigneur to supervise recruitment. This time the results were unfelicitous, and Talon wrote to Colbert that "it is with much displeasure that I feel obliged to tell you that instead of 400 good men with whom you wanted to fortify this country . . . I have received only 127 [who are] very weak, young, and of little service; I want to believe that the raising of men in France for the war has removed the means of better succeeding from those who were employed in the choice . . . of these passengers."[89]

The levy apparently prompted complaints from Bishop Laval as well, for at the time of the next shipment, in 1669, Colbert assured him that all abuses had been corrected: "I have taken all possible precautions this year to receive only those men suited for work to be transported to New France. To this end, I have asked Monsieur Colbert de Terron (my cousin) to take care of [raising] the 200 people who will be carried on the vessel of Monsieur Le Gagneur [Gaigneur]."[90]

The state thus responded to the company's failure to recruit emigrants of quality by imposing a recruiter of its own choice; that this recruiter happened to be Colbert de Terron, the marine intendant, reflects its growing preference for naval supervision. Individually and in companies, merchants continued to enlist emigrants under the auspices of the crown; however, after 1669, they played a minor role in comparison to the naval functionaries, whose direct dependence on the minister afforded better control of the proceedings.

THE RECRUITMENT of marriageable women also concerned the state in the mid-seventeenth century, for sexual imbalance discouraged male settlement and impeded population expansion. Private recruiters, whether French or Canadian, had limited success in embarking single women, who did not respond as readily to the arguments that persuaded men. In 1666, three years after the departure of the first *filles du roi*, women still comprised little more than one-third of the Canadian population.[91]

Many of the *filles du roi* of the 1660s and 1670s came, as mentioned earlier, from the Hôpital général of Paris, whose chief administrator, Christophe du Plessis de Montbard, had a long-standing interest in things Canadian.[92] Talon, who paid a visit to the institution upon his return to Paris in 1673, described the selection process for the *filles du roi* as follows: "I have seen two of the directors who must give me . . . a list of the girls who are disposed to go to Canada, and who are appropriate for the king's design."⁹³ The directors thus made a preliminary recommendation based on the inclinations and aptitudes of their wards and submitted it to the colonial authorities for ratification.

When institutions proved insufficient, state recruitment of women expanded to include the parishes of churchmen with an interest in colonization. In 1670, for example, Colbert asked the archbishop of Rouen, whose jurisdiction extended to Québec prior to the erection of a North American diocese in 1674, to "use the credit and the authority that you have over the vicars of thirty or forty of the said parishes [in the environs of Rouen] to see if they could voluntarily find in each, one or two girls to go to the said country [Canada]."⁹⁴ The Sulpicians, whose Canadian ministry dated from 1657, also cooperated in recruiting women, for, in 1673, Talon mentioned that a Sulpician abbot, Monsieur de Bretonvilliers, and the pastor of Saint-Sulpice "ordinarily find well qualified ones in their parish."⁹⁵

A willingness to emigrate did not in itself qualify a woman to become a *fille du roi*, as Talon's reference to the "king's design" suggests. What was at stake was her suitability, in terms that were phrased most explicitly by the minister in the following decade: "The king transports no women of ill repute to the American colonies, but gladly young ladies raised in hospitals who are healthy and have not been debauched."⁹⁶

Recruiters thus concerned themselves first and foremost with the morality of their prospective charges, yet social background did not prove an idle consideration. The baron de La Hontan, although not an eyewitness, insisted on the importance of class in the Canadian distribution of the *filles à marier:*

> The circumstances of their arrival were recounted to me, and I like to entertain you too much not to share them with you. This chaste herd was led to the conjugal pasture by old and prudish shepherdesses . . . As soon as they reached the habitation, the wrinkled commandants inspected their troops, and having separated them into three classes, each band entered a different room. As they pressed each other quite closely on account of the smallness of the place, it made for a pleasant enough decoration. These were not three shops where love made up the showcases and displays; these were three fully stocked warehouses.⁹⁷

For all its sarcasm, La Hontan's account accords with the more sententious comments preserved in the administrative correspondence. Recruiters began to seek out upper-class women in 1667, in order to bind seigneurs and officers to the colony. As Colbert informed Talon, "And in case there were gentlemen or officers of the troops residing in the country who were not married or who found no one to marry owing to the disproportion between their quality and that of the people, I would try to have some well-nourished and well-brought-up damsels sent from here to unite them."[98]

Apparently he kept his word, for six months later, Talon acknowledged the arrival of 15 or 20 women "of some birth . . . , several of them true damsels and fairly well brought up."[99] Another 15 followed in 1671, although Talon had asked for only 3 or 4.[100] It is unclear why "surplus women" embarked the second time. Colbert may have hoped to lure more gentlemen into marriage, or the administrators of the Hôpital général may have wished to rid themselves of expense. Or perhaps the women themselves took the initiative, preferring the prospect of hasty marriage in a distant colony to continuing institutional or familial dependency.

IN THE EIGHTEENTH CENTURY, the state ceased its large-scale shipments of indentured servants and *filles à marier,* but it compensated with the deportation of prisoners. Prison administrators dispatched poachers, wife beaters, and other common criminals to Canada in the 1720s, together with a few *fils de famille.*[101] The Ferme générale, under the authority of Comptroller General Orry, took over from the prison wardens in the following decade, shipping out hundreds of smugglers between 1730 and 1746.

Forced emigration was never as important in Canada as in Louisiana or Saint-Domingue. The first deportations, which took place in 1723 and 1724,[102] were discontinued on the instances of the bishop of Québec, who feared for the moral fiber of the nation in the presence of "unruly, alexic persons, guilty of almost every crime. . . . I beseech you," the bishop wrote the minister, "no longer to send such people who are without faith and religion and capable of the most awful crimes and vices, the continuation of these shipments being able to make those who compose it [the colony] lose the faith and become similar to the English and even the infidels."[103]

Between 1725 and 1728, French authorities limited their deportation orders to "young people of family locked up for correction in the hospitals," generally by lettre de cachet.[104] But in 1728 they recruited among the prisoners of the Hôpital général of Paris, and in 1730 they began to tap the resources of the Ferme générale, whose enforcement of the customs law always guaranteed a substantial pool of "faux-sauniers et contrebandiers" (smugglers of salt and other contraband).

Fewer than 70 *fils de famille* arrived in Canada between 1723 and 1734, when this type of deportation ceased. Not only did the Canadians prefer the salt smugglers, whose labor was more valuable, but authorities on both sides of the ocean seemed uncomfortable with the practice of allowing families to deport their wayward sons by lettre de cachet. Governor Beauharnais and Intendant Hocquart wrote repeatedly to Paris describing the straitened circumstances of the *fils de famille* and requesting familial pensions for them.[105] The naval minister, for his part, when solicited by a noble for an order to dispatch a young relative to Canada "to remove him from the unhappy results of a bad marriage to which he has committed himself with a girl older and cleverer than he," replied: "These sorts of misfortunes happen only too commonly to youth, but I do not know, once they have happened, how one can separate in conscience a husband and wife . . . I cannot for my part contribute to this separation."[106]

Common prisoners, in contrast, were recruited by prison wardens or farmers-general. Strictly speaking, these officials practiced selection rather than recruitment, since their recruits were given no choice in the matter. The criteria for selection, as expressed to the Canadians, consisted of physical condition, occupation, age, and marital status; the preference went to healthy, young bachelors trained in useful trades.[107] Most of these men were probably not professional criminals, but rather workers who had found themselves in need of supplemental income. In 1743 the minister wrote of the 25 smugglers destined for Québec that "they have in general occupations that ought to render them useful," a statement he echoed on several other occasions.[108]

The minister claimed repeatedly that the majority of prisoners were unmarried, but this statement seems dubious in the light of continued supplications by the Canadians "no longer to send here any but bachelors."[109] Married men, they complained, were too often haunted by the *esprit de retour*.[110] The deportees whose cases received the most attention tended to be married men seeking to rejoin their families. Pierre Odio from the bourg of Cossé (Mayenne) requested, after a three-year stint of service, that the minister "have sent to this country four children that he left in the said place, and of whom he has heard no more." The conveyors of his petition, Beauharnais and Hocquart, added that "this man who is about thirty-five years old will become a good habitant."[111] Several years later, they sponsored a similar request on the part of Etienne Gochereau "to have come to this country his wife and three children," domiciled in Saint-Barthélémy-d'Etay near Châtillon-sur-Seine. Gochereau, a master charcoal burner, was employed at his profession at the Forges Saint-Maurice in Trois-Rivières, and his superiors were pleased with his performance.[112]

In 1742 Beauharnais and Hocquart protested that there were 9 married men with children among the 21 newly arrived smugglers.[113] Perhaps the officials of the Ferme générale had simply failed to interview the candidates for deportation with care, or perhaps they had chosen to ignore the admonitions of the Canadians. But it is also possible that many of the prisoners were husbands who smuggled to maintain a threatened family economy and were willing to lie for the chance to establish it elsewhere on a healthier footing.

The attitude of both metropolitan and Canadian administrators toward the deportees was somewhat inconsistent, but it was not unenlightened, and rarely partook of the hysteria evinced by the ecclesiastical establishment. In 1728, for example, the minister commented on the "list of individuals drawn from the Hôpital général of Paris and destined by order of the king to go to Canada to remain there during their lifetime": "Though there are some in this number who are not very honest folk, they are nonetheless not partakers in big crimes; most of them are workers [ouvriers] and will be able to be useful to the colony . . . Antoine Mastec is a market porter who had been locked up for having cruelly maltreated his wife and who has asked to go to the colonies . . . There are also in this number three poachers."[114]

Nearly ten years later, the governor and the intendant of Ile Royale could still characterize deportees as potentially productive citizens down on their luck. Asking that the minister continue to send as many smugglers as possible annually, they noted that "there are sometimes found among them good subjects who eventually will be able to settle in the colony."[115]

This willingness on the part of the authorities to view exile to Canada as opportunity rather than punishment, whether or not it was shared by those who participated as subjects in the experiment, provides grounds for thinking somewhat subtly about the Grand Renfermement, or Great Confinement. None can contest that the poor were actually locked up during this period; the deportees considered here were, after all, recruited from prisons. Nonetheless, it is interesting to note that, except for the bishop of Québec, no one in authority seemed to view their continued imprisonment as a moral necessity. One could thus make a case, from the Canadian example, for the existence of a third approach to the problem of the poor in the eighteenth century: acquisition of economic independence in the colonies, as opposed to either traditional charity or punitive discipline.[116]

The participation of the state in recruitment thus ensured the emigration of a large and varied group of people in the final century of the French Regime. Like the contribution of the merchants, it emphasized single young people at the expense of families, and artisans at the expense of peasants, but like the seigneurial contribution, it exhibited a more even sex ratio and a geographical distribution extending well beyond the Atlantic ports. In terms of permanent settlement, recruitment by the state probably fell midway between mercantile and seigneurial recruitment for its efficacity. The *filles du roi* and some of the soldiers proved to be excellent colonists, and the prisoners were required to remain whether they liked it or not. At the same time, however, many state recruited soldiers and workers undoubtedly viewed their stint in Canada as temporary. For them, colonial emigration was analogous to a stay in the city or a foray into petty smuggling. It was simply one economic strategy among others, albeit a more unusual and adventurous one.

Summary

The combined recruiting efforts of merchants, seigneurs, and the state served to harness existing migratory traditions in the interests of Canadian development. They did not, however, manage to create a truly autonomous migratory movement centered on Canada. Canadian emigration, while called into being by the expansion of the Atlantic economy in the seventeenth century, remained a derivative of other, more secular migrations throughout the French Regime. Recruiters needed to tap into traditional migratory networks, whether of artisans, laborers, or young women, in order to maintain what was often a sputtering migratory stream.

This situation speaks to both the attraction of capitalism for the French and the marginality of Canada within the Atlantic world economy. The economic promises that tempted entrepreneurs from the days of Jacques Cartier never quite materialized, owing to the difficulties of exploiting Canada's varied resource base. And emigrants who found themselves stranded in a backwater had two choices: they could either seek greener pastures elsewhere, as many surely intended from the start, or they could accept their gradual, if incomplete, transformation from Frenchmen into peasants.

Conclusion: Frenchmen into Peasants

France's two-century involvement with Canada resulted in the departures of at least 30,000 temporary emigrants for Québec, and possibly even twice that many. Perhaps 7,000 others embarked for the Maritimes, and many thousands more did stints as seasonal fishermen or seafarers in Canadian waters. At the time of the British conquest, Québec had a population of 75,000, and the two Acadian islands, 15,000. The French residents of peninsular Acadia, under British jurisdiction since 1713, had already been deported in anticipation of the Seven Years' War. Another 5,000 Francophones lived in what is now the United States and, depending on their location, passed to either the British or the Spanish. From Louisiana to the Gulf of Saint Lawrence, New France in its entirety could boast about the same number of inhabitants as Nantes or Bordeaux, and fewer than Marseille or Lyon. As for the capital, there were 6 or 7 Parisians for each French person in North America.

The slenderness of this achievement becomes even more apparent when considered in relation to British North America. In an identical time span, the British colonies absorbed some 700,000 immigrants of various European and African nationalities, and their population at the Treaty of Paris stood at almost 2 million.[1] Viewed in the context of demography, the British conquest of New France appears less as the strategic victory of Wolfe over Montcalm than as the unstoppable progress of a human steamroller.

Historians of British extraction have traditionally attributed the numerical inferiority of French North America to lack of initiative on the part of ordinary Frenchmen, a condition these scholars say is also responsible

CONCLUSION |

for economic underdevelopment. Only the laissez-faire policies of the British, so the argument runs, could create optimum conditions for colonization. The authoritative voice here is, of course, that of Francis Parkman, who viewed the French and British contest for North America as a struggle between past and future: on the one hand, a feudal society dedicated to authority, hierarchy, and visions of aristocratic prowess; on the other, a modern metropolis fueled by commercial savvy and individual initiative. For Parkman, the outcome could never be in doubt. New France's resistance to British conquest was the hopeless, if heroic, last stand of an order condemned by history.[2]

French-Canadian historians have basically espoused this same interpretation, while giving it a different twist. Writers such as Abbé Ferland and Abbé Faillon, contemporaries of Parkman, could not, of course, deny that the British won the struggle for empire, but instead of dwelling on the defeat, they chose to emphasize what they called *la survivance*.[3] French Canadians, from "a traditional semi-feudal, ignorant, priest-ridden, and backward people, impervious to change and sealed to the outside world," became "a devout, obedient, pastoral, and god-fearing people, entrenched behind parish and family life, endowed with the noble mission of permeating materialistic Anglo-Saxon America with spiritual values."[4] For these historians no less than for Parkman, there was an attempt to reclaim Canada's first habitants for *la France profonde*.

The image of an Ancien Régime transporting itself overseas is, however, highly problematic. Although the state did intervene in recruitment, it did so not because the French were reluctant to emigrate, but because Canada was an unpopular destination. The majority of emigrants, as I have indicated, came from modern and mobile backgrounds and were no strangers to individual initiative.

Similarly, the society they created bore little resemblance to the Gemeinschaft of historiographical fantasy. Communitarian visions were prevalent in New France, as in New England, in the early years, but they faded as quickly, indeed more quickly, from the French scene as from the English.[5] In 1643 Abbé Jean-Jacques Olier (who never visited Canada) described the newly arrived residents of Ville-Marie as "living for the most part in common, as in a sort of inn, some from their private revenues, but all living in Jesus Christ . . . representing, in a way, the form of the early Church."[6] By midcentury, however, Ville-Marie had become Mon-

tréal, a rough-and-ready marketplace for Indian furs and illegal whiskey.[7]
The only vestige of earlier arrangements consisted of the communal
cultivation of fields belonging to victims of the Iroquois, an expression,
perhaps, of "the fraternity of soldiers on the battlefield."[8]

The settlement pattern, meanwhile, consisted of isolated farmsteads
along both banks of the Saint Lawrence, hardly a demonstration of
community. Louis XIV attempted to remedy this situation in the interests
of royal absolutism, and in 1663 he decreed that the New French population should henceforth live in agglomerated villages. He entrusted execution of the scheme to the newly appointed intendant, Jean Talon, who
set to work immediately upon his arrival. In 1667 three such villages were
created, and three more were set up later, all in the neighborhood of
Québec. But that was all. As the historian Emile Salone wrote in 1905,
"Even today, in this province of two million inhabitants, we would not
know what a village is . . . , if it were not for what remains of the work
of Jean Talon."[9]

Throughout the seventeenth and eighteenth centuries, administrators
charged with representing the French state in New France complained of
the recalcitrance of the Canadian population or urged that domestic
policies be adapted to colonial realities. An official of the latter persuasion,
Intendant Duchesneau, warned the minister in 1681 that "we should not
consider the cultivation of land and the raising of livestock . . . as solid
means to establish this country, since it is only commerce that will make
them pay, and the number of inhabitants, who will never be drawn here
except by profit, gentle government, and the hope of living more comfortably than in France."[10] Six years in Canada had transformed this
instrument of absolutism into an advocate of free enterprise and cheap
government!

Others were less complimentary in their assessment of the Canadian
environment and its effect on their countrymen. Jacques Raudot, who
served as intendant at the beginning of the eighteenth century, wrote that
"the French have never been . . . suitable for settlements, they want to
sow and reap at the same time . . . , they want besides to . . . get rich in
a short time; that is the conduct and the spirit of the greatest part, there
are even some who are so bad that they do not hesitate to sacrifice a whole
country provided they can get rich."[11]

Even the agricultural settlers themselves came in for criticism, with

Intendant Bigot writing in 1748 that the habitant was "avid for gain."[12] The very term "habitant" reflects a changed reality, having been coined by prosperous farmers to distinguish themselves from peasants. As early as 1684, La Hontan could observe that "the peasants here are very comfortable, and I would wish such a good cuisine on our whole petty nobility of France. What am I saying: peasants! my excuses to these good sirs. The word, taken in its ordinary sense, would put our Canadians in the fields. A Spaniard, if one called him a villager, would not frown more deeply, or bristle his mustache more proudly. These people are not wrong after all; they do not pay the salt tax or the taille; they hunt and fish freely; in a word, they are rich. Would you want to compare them with our raggedy peasants?"[13] Thus, the label "habitant," that direst of insults for the twentieth-century Quebecer, had a thoroughly opposite connotation during the French Regime.

The problem of French Canada's marginalization, if unsolved by simplistic oppositions between liberty and tyranny, modernity and traditionalism, nonetheless remains entire. It would not make sense to argue that the state was altogether blameless. On the contrary, its paranoia about Protestant disloyalty and sporadically mercantilist policy combined with an unstable military situation and unfavorable climatic conditions to inhibit immigration and development. These factors alone, however, do not suffice to explain the subsequent backwardness of French-Canadian society. One must also consider the short- and long-term results of the British conquest, which were at least as important as the legacy of the French Regime.

The policy of religious intolerance, while grounded in a legitimate fear of Protestant fraternization, was arguably the most serious mistake of the French Regime. By closing Canada to the flow of Huguenot refugees for northern Europe and colonies such as New England and South Africa, the French destroyed their only hope for mass emigration. Canada, as has been seen, never possessed the drawing power of the exotic and sugar-rich West Indies. The continual wars with the Iroquois and the climate, with its harsh winter, mosquito-laden summer, and radically shortened growing season, did little to boost its popularity. Perhaps only the prospect of constructing a "city on a hill" where none had existed and of worshiping openly after decades of persecution could have offset the relative unattractiveness of Canada as a destination.

Moreover, the French state, like the other colonial powers, including Great Britain, viewed its North American possessions in mercantilist terms. In practice, it was torn between desire for a healthy, expanding colony and fear of colonial competition; however, the fear won out often enough to compromise seriously Canada's ability to capitalize on economic opportunity. In 1704, for example, the governor and intendant earned a stinging rebuke from the king for their proposal to establish a factory with immigrant hemp weavers:

> His Majesty is most pleased to learn that the cultivation of hemp in this place is everything that one could have hoped for, but he must explain to them that his intention was never for them to make canvases in Canada so as to be able to do without those of France. Thus he will not send any weavers. He only intended the settlers to send this hemp to France . . . in order to do without that of foreigners by this means; and, in general, they must be mindful that anything that could compete with the manufactures of the kingdom must never be made in the colonies, which, on the contrary, cannot be overused to furnish materials needed for the manufactures of the kingdom . . . They must think about the utility of the countries that form them and never in the intention of doing without these countries.[14]

The resistance to Canadian exports was especially crucial in the domain of agriculture.[15] The privileged farmers of La Hontan witnessed yield ratios that exceeded those of the *pays de grande culture* and equaled those of Holland and Flanders. The wheat harvest produced "in the eights, elevens, fifteens and even, on new lands, still more."[16] Without reliable markets, Canadians risked a crisis of overproduction.

Such a crisis did occur in the second half of the seventeenth century, causing curés to refuse the product of their tithe as unsalable and administrators to rejoice over heavy November rains that could stem the price decline. In 1710, when the French experienced the last large-scale famine in their history, Canadians suffered also—from a persistent glut of the market that dated from 1702![17]

Under these circumstances, Canada's habitants began slowly to transform themselves from Frenchmen into peasants. As Louise Dechêne has remarked, "It looks as though the colonists, from the first decade of the eighteenth century, had given up producing above their needs and the urban demand that they could immediately count on."[18] There thus emerged what Gilles Paquet and Jean-Pierre Wallot have called a "dual socio-economy,"[19] composed of "two worlds, two different universes dominated, respectively, by the colonial elite linked to Atlantic commerce and culture, and the habitant himself, living in much more intimate relation to the territory. Between the two no clear break, but contrasts."[20]

One should not, however, exaggerate the extent of this development. Louise Dechêne has cautioned that there is no reason to view the "agriculture of the seventeenth and eighteenth centuries as a curiosity, a unique case in the West of cultural backwardness."[21] Peasants or not, Canada's habitants continued to speculate in land, to practice a highly individualistic agriculture, and to resist the exactions of a relatively benign seigneurial system.

Land speculation, that favorite activity of American colonists, turns out to have appealed to Canadian emigrants as well.[22] In seventeenth-century Beaumont, a rural community on the south bank of the Saint Lawrence, agriculture was not lucrative, but few of the best lands escaped a twenty-year wave of speculative exchange. Rather than farm, "the habitant preferred to sell his land and realize substantial profits." According to Céline Cyr, the acquisition of land constituted "a profitable short-term placement," the motives for which remained "economic and speculative" until the eighteenth century.[23]

When habitants did farm, they did so individually. There was no collective decision making about field use, as there would have been in a traditional two- or three-field system, and, along the Côte-du-Sud, there were not even common pastures as there were in New England.[24] Since, in addition, the tax burden was low and the parish fabric loose, the rural community was relatively unimportant. As John Dickinson has shown, habitants preferred to settle land disputes not by appealing to the "collective memory," as was the rule in France, but by relying on the written record and the services of experts.[25]

New France did, to be sure, have a seigneurial system, which Marxist historians have seized upon as evidence that the colony was mired in a "feudal mode of production."[26] Yet seigneurialism, particularly in the seventeenth century, was far less oppressive in the Saint Lawrence than in France, "although the landlord is never popular and the habitants emulated their French cousins in forgetting and disputing payments and obligations."[27] Because agricultural rents were scanty, seigneurs favored "the town and the fur trade over the development of their seigneurie," leaving the habitants largely to their own devices.[28] As Paquet and Wallot have written, "the prefabricated society, which had been envisioned as an organization where each would have his place, appeared more and more as a shattered society [*société éclatée*] that escaped regulatory control and deviated from original plans."[29]

The peasantizing of Canadian farmers in the seventeenth century was therefore incomplete, a fact that helps to explain the ease with which the process was reversed in the eighteenth century. When a more liberal commercial policy, combined with colonial development elsewhere, made market involvement feasible for a growing number of habitants, their latent commercial mentality came to the fore. Certainly, Québec did not undergo an agricultural revolution in the eighteenth century, any more than did France, but a growing quantity of produce was destined for export and limited improvements did occur. Meanwhile, the rural merchant was becoming a fixture in the Laurentian countryside, and a new and different kind of village was beginning to sprout up, particularly in the vicinity of Montréal.

As Jacques Mathieu has demonstrated, French trade policy in the first half of the eighteenth century was marked by sincere, if sometimes heavy-handed, efforts at liberalization.[30] Nor was this new sanctioning of intercolonial trade unimportant, for the growth of an important town on Ile Royale and, especially, a plantation economy in the West Indies meant the creation of large markets for Canadian wheat and other foodstuffs. The result was a significant rise in Canadian entrepreneurship, in the countryside as well as the towns.

Jacques Saint-Pierre has noted that at the beginning of the eighteenth century, the habitants of La Durantaye, a seigneurie on the south bank of the Saint Lawrence, "produced only with a view to satisfying their alimentary and vestmental needs." Yet as commercial outlets opened for their cereals, they acted with remarkable rapidity to increase their production; the average wheat yield per family grew from 61 *minots* in 1727 to 93 in 1730.[31] A jump of this magnitude may have been unusual, but Jacques Mathieu has estimated that agricultural production in the Saint Lawrence grew nearly 450% between 1706 and 1740, more than outstripping the 250% rise in population. When the harvest was good, which it was, on average, every other year in the first half of the eighteenth century, 12% to 25% of the grain harvest was exported as milled flour to Louisbourg and the Antilles.[32] When Louisbourg surrendered to the English, for the first time, in 1745, the price of grain on the Québec marketplace fell immediately by half.[33]

As commercial agriculture grew in importance, it gave rise to a number of agricultural improvements. Along the Côte-du-Sud, where access to Québec's consumer and export markets was a major incentive, habitants began to construct more outbuildings and better fences for their livestock. The changes were particularly noticeable on seigneuries whose poor soil, in the absence of innovation, would prevent full exploitation of the new marketing possibilities. Thus, in Beaumont and La Durantaye, which had the worst soils of the region, habitants were practicing crop rotation by the second quarter of the eighteenth century.[34]

This same period witnessed the rise of a new intermediary between the rural population and the urban commercial community: the country merchant who sold provisions at retail, marketed the agricultural surplus, and provided banking services. Especially in remote areas, the arrival of a country merchant could be a real stimulus to development. In Cap Saint-Ignace, for example, it set off a new wave of land clearances between 1737 and 1739.[35] Of course, the habitants were not the only ones to profit from this arrangement. Country merchants rarely began with much, but their success could be quite extraordinary. François-Augustin Bailly de Messein, the son of a petty officer who set up shop around Varennes in the early 1730s, saw his originally modest fortune expand by a factor of more than seven between 1741 and 1751, only to triple again in the years before the conquest.[36]

The emergence of a community of rural merchants went hand in hand with an important transformation of the Québec countryside: the growth of agglomerated villages. As Serge Courville has shown, "we already find the first stages of a real network of villages as early as the second half of the eighteenth century, especially in the Montréal region, which accounted for two-thirds of the nuclei in the St. Lawrence Valley in 1760–1762."[37] These villages, which were founded through the initiative of habitants or, occasionally, seigneurs, were not "statist creations in the manner of those founded by Intendant Talon in the second half of the seventeenth century." Instead, they were "entirely new structures of settlement that confirmed both the state of development attained by the local community and its clear choice of insertion into the market economy."[38] "Villages," in other words, "were really small towns with genuinely urban functions of commerce, administration, and industry."[39]

Thus, the habitants of New France in the seventeenth and eighteenth centuries were happy to forsake subsistence agriculture whenever the opportunity to do so presented itself. To the extent that they had become peasants, they had done so in the absence of alternatives. "What they lacked," according to Jean-Pierre Wallot, "was not dynamism or an open mentality, but the propitious circumstances that could have stimulated them."[40]

"The worst that can be said of habitant farming in the first half of the eighteenth century," Dale Miquelon has noted, "is that it did not measure up to the standards of intensive land use and care in the most advanced parts of Europe," such as the Netherlands.[41] Yet as R. Cole Harris has pointed out, even Dutch farmers, with their hypermodern roots, followed a trajectory very similar to that of the habitants after they left Holland and established themselves in South Africa. "Before 1685 the colony was an importer of food," but "by 1700 there were regular problems of overproduction," which persisted for much of the eighteenth century. Hence, "town and countryside became strikingly different social worlds," and the settler family "acquired a striking autonomy and independence." While the Great Trek "permitted the survival of the *trekboer* way of life into the twentieth century," at the Cape, "where there was a market for wheat, wine, and meat, . . . rural society had long been dominated by a few wealthy families. This society had not been created by a different class of immigrants, but by conditions that had made wealth possible for a few."[42] The Boers, like the habitants of the Saint Lawrence, had undergone a partial process of reverse development.

THE SITUATION of French settlers in the Maritimes was quite different, for whether in mainland Acadia or on the islands, these Frenchmen remained Frenchmen for the duration of the French Regime. Not only were Ile Royale and Ile Saint-Jean much more than a military fortress and its agricultural hinterland, but the Fundy marshlands too hosted a way of life that was untraditional in many ways.

Prior to the Grand Dérangement of 1755, mainland Acadians found it easier than French Quebecers to maintain an essentially modern outlook.

The weakness of metropolitan control, French or English, allowed them to flourish economically, in agriculture and trade, and to develop political stances consistent with their individualism. Yet to both the frustrated administrators who dealt with them and the philosophes, poets, or clerical nationalists who came after them, they were a simple peasant people, far removed from the economic and intellectual upheavals of the seventeenth and eighteenth centuries.[43] As I discuss below, this vision was erroneous— a product of the very success with which Acadians pursued their own interests, to the detriment of government plans for the colony.

Political authority in early Acadia was nothing if not mutable. From the founding of Port-Royal in 1604 to the formal cession of the colony to Great Britain in 1713, the Acadians experienced British occupation several times, once for well over a decade.[44] Metropolitan supervision, as a result, was very weak. In particular, mercantilist policies were virtually impossible to implement when what was legal trade one year was smuggling the next, and vice versa.

The Acadians took advantage of this situation to develop a prosperous economy based on sea-dependent agriculture, fishing, and trading.[45] Marshland farming, although it required a good amount of coordination, was basically individualistic.[46] Acadians lived on isolated homesteads, "very distant from each other,"[47] and, unlike Quebecers, they had individual rather than communal bake ovens.[48] Seigneurialism, meanwhile, was virtually meaningless in the colony; "even though seigneuries existed on paper, they had practically no influence on the daily lives of the settlers."[49] What little there was of the system, moreover, was destroyed by extended British occupation.[50]

French census records portray "an agriculture that provided a good standard of nutrition for the settlers." Indeed, it must have done much more, for "trade made the Acadians the very reverse of an isolated peasantry."[51] Statistics are lacking owing to the smuggling problem, but it is clear that surplus grains, cattle, sheep, poultry, pigs, and furs made their way from Acadian farms to both Boston and Louisbourg, and even to the Caribbean. In 1740 the illegal trade with Louisbourg alone occupied sixteen ships.[52]

The commercial nature of Acadian farming is further confirmed by the abundance of manufactured goods and specie that were received in trade. In the 1980s archaeological excavations at Belle-Isle and Port-Royal unearthed, for the period before 1710, kitchenware from New England, France, Germany, Spain, England (Staffordshire), the western Mediterranean, and China. No local pottery was found, despite the availability of clay. Other culinary items included a large number of knives and forks, the latter at a time when the Sun King himself refused to eat with such a newfangled instrument. Furniture was fairly sophisticated, and tailor-made clothing and shoes were common, as shown by the many brass buttons and shoe buckles.[53] That savings were significant is suggested by the fact that during the deportation, Acadians sent to Maryland and South Carolina possessed enough specie to purchase the ships that conveyed them.[54]

Modern economically, the Acadians were also sophisticated ideologically. In 1679 Governor Frontenac of New France complained that they were reluctant to obey orders, either from lack of habit, "or the divisions among them, or else a certain English and Parliamentary Inclination, which is inspired by the frequent contact and Commerce they have with those from Baston [sic]."[55] This independence continued after the transfer to British rule, culminating in an official form of self-government and a deliberate policy of neutrality in Franco-British imperial struggles.

By 1721 British authorities recognized the right of the Acadian communities to elect representatives annually. These representatives became the spokesmen for a policy of neutrality that had first been established by the inhabitants of Port-Royal in 1717, only to gain broad acceptance in subsequent years.[56] Far from an example of apolitical ignorance, neutrality was a conscious strategy, rooted in a view of the British as "nos amis les ennemis" and articulated in the language of the Enlightenment. Indeed, it was taken so seriously that after the deportation, Acadians who had taken refuge on Saint Pierre and Miquelon preferred to move on rather than take the oath of loyalty to France that would have allowed them to remain in French North America.[57]

How then could contemporary observers of the Acadians who viewed them as lazy, ignorant peasants have been so wrong? Perhaps because the Acadians made sure that these representatives of the state or church did not share in their prosperity. Acadian houses were indeed small, despite the abundance of timber, and aversion to conspicuous consumption seems to have been especially marked at tax time.[58] Neither the French nor the British had much luck in tapping the Acadian economic surplus; in fact, the British succeeded in collecting only thirty pounds sterling from the colony in 1732 and fifteen in 1745.[59] Acadians were less subsistence farmers, it appears, than world-class tax dodgers![60]

IN ILE ROYALE and Ile Saint-Jean as well, French settlers had little in common with traditional peasants. Although Ile Saint-Jean was intended from the first as the breadbasket of the great fortress at Louisbourg, it did not succeed in attracting a stable agrarian population, despite fertile soils. Acadians, whom the French were counting on as colonists, preferred British rule on their prosperous farms to pioneer agriculture in heavily forested territory. Those immigrants who did arrive, whether from Acadia or France, often preferred fishing and trading to the more arduous work of land clearance. The island's sole seigneur, the comte de Saint-Pierre, went bankrupt in 1726, and inland areas remained unsettled to the end of the French Regime.[61]

The situation on Ile Royale was even more clear-cut. Not only were there no peasants, there was no seigneurial system, and virtually no agriculture. Settlement was largely restricted to a small number of coastal communities, the most important of which by far was Louisbourg. Although originally intended as a garrison town, and never bereft of a huge military presence, Louisbourg rapidly became a major base for the North Atlantic fishery, and a busy entrepôt in the triangular trade between Europe, North America, and the West Indies.[62]

The fishing industry, which made Ile Royale the largest per capita exporter of any North American colony except British Newfoundland, was highly efficient and progressive in its reliance on resident fleets, local capital, and regional supply. The latter, of course, included not only Canadian wheat, but New England ships, building materials, and livestock, which were exchanged for sugar and rum.[63] So important was this trade, and so successful the lobbying efforts of Louisbourg's merchants, that "legislation hardly interfered with the incentives of the market."[64] As Christopher Moore has pointed out, "the essence of Ile Royale's foreign trade fell within the regulations, and it was supervised by local officials who supplied regular statistical reports about it to the ministry in France."[65] Far from being peasants, the inhabitants of Ile Royale were fishermen and traders who proved that "capital accumulation and en-

trepreneurial enterprise could thrive within the legal and political structures of New France, given the right economic conditions."[66]

THUS, IN THE MID-EIGHTEENTH CENTURY, the people of French Canada, taken as a whole, were still more Frenchmen than peasants. When
and how did this situation change? A logical assumption might be that
the insularity imposed by the British conquest was crucial in cutting
off French Canadians from their modern roots, and to the degree that
direct contact with France was indeed prohibited, this is no doubt true.
Nonetheless, the impact of the conquest was undeniably stronger in the
Maritimes, where entire communities were liquidated, than in the Saint
Lawrence, where the most drastic social change took place later, toward
the middle of the nineteenth century.

After the second siege of Louisbourg in 1758, the French repatriated
the nearly 15,000 military and civilian residents of Ile Royale and Ile
Saint-Jean, which were given over to British settlement or, in the case of
Louisbourg, abandonment. The communities of the Acadian mainland had
already been destroyed by the British beginning in 1755, and their former
inhabitants were scattered throughout France, Québec, Nova Scotia, Massachusetts, England, Maryland, New Brunswick, Connecticut, Pennsylvania, Louisiana, South Carolina, New York, Georgia, Maine, Saint-Domingue, and the Channel Islands.[67] While the refugees from the two islands
blended fairly easily back into the French population from which many
of them had come, the Acadian exiles found reinsertion to be much more
difficult. Their North American identity and political savvy led them to
demand collective redress, but the various settlement projects in places as
diverse as French Guyana, the Falkland Islands, Belle-Ile-en-Mer (Morbihan), and Archigny (Vienne) were not a success. In France, the Acadians
complained bitterly about the infertile land, monotonous diet, tithes, and
feudal restrictions; many of them reembarked for North America as soon
as it became feasible to do so. By 1769 more than 1,000 Acadians had
established themselves in Spanish Louisiana, and numerous others were
returning to the Maritimes. Since the abundant farms of the Annapolis
Valley had passed into the hands of British "planters," new Acadian
settlements in the Maritimes hugged the barren coastlines of New Brunswick, western Nova Scotia, the Cape Breton Highlands, and Ile Madame;

the north shore of Prince Edward Island; and the remote upper Saint John Valley.[68]

As Naomi Griffiths has pointed out, the postdeportation Acadians of the Maritimes were in a very different situation, politically and economically, from their earlier selves. Economically, they "were primarily dependent on subsistence farming, fishing, and the lumber trade," while, politically, they were "often excluded from the norms . . . of a broader polity of which they formed part, and their legal rights to establish themselves in certain areas were often successfully challenged."[69] Given these constraints, it is not surprising that they turned inward, nurturing the close-knit and eventually archaic culture that is captured so beautifully in the fiction of Antonine Maillet.

The Acadians of Louisana, for their part, fared quite differently. Though the Cajuns of today's backcountry bayous may not have a reputation for economic dynamism, some of their ancestors did very well for themselves indeed. Certainly, they had no intentions of living at the margins of Louisiana life; in 1768 hundreds of them participated in an insurrection against the Spanish governor "who had insisted on Acadian settlement at the dangerously isolated upriver post of San Luís de Natchez."[70] The governor expelled, Acadians were free to explore the opportunities afforded by an expanding frontier exchange economy. Their slaveholding proceeded apace in the 1760s and 1770s, and they quickly became important cattle traders in the Atakapas and Opelousas districts of Bayou Teche. According to Daniel Usner, the latter process was facilitated by an agreement between a group of Acadian immigrants and one Antoine-Bernard d'Auterive, a retired officer who owned at least 6,000 head of cattle:

> On April 4, 1765, he agreed to furnish "five cows with calves and one bull to each of the Acadian families during each of six consecutive years." The Acadians could sell a few cows or bulls, provided they kept a record of all transactions. "At the end of six years, they will each return the same number of cows and calves, of the same age and kind, that they received initially; the remaining cattle and their increase . . . will be divided equally between said Acadians and Mr. Dauterive."[71]

By the 1780s, most Acadians in the region still owned fewer than 50 head of cattle apiece, but some of them had become major dealers—for example, Martin Duralde, with 1,000 head, or Joseph Cormier, with nearly

700.[72] Clearly, the social trajectory of Acadians in the New World depended less on who they were than on the economic situation in which they found themselves.[73]

FOR THE FRENCHMEN of the Saint Lawrence, the impact of the British conquest was more ambiguous. It was certainly a major blow to Canadian merchants, large and small, who found themselves cut off from French sources of supply and credit. Yet the effect on habitants may have been less detrimental, at least after the initial shock, since British merchants moved rapidly to fill the commercial vacuum. Indeed, new research on the Québec countryside suggests that far from declining in the late eighteenth and early nineteenth centuries, it actually underwent a fairly widespread conversion to commercial capitalism. Meanwhile, liberal ideology penetrated rural areas in these years, culminating in the ill-fated Rebellions of 1837 and 1838, and the Catholic Church was losing ground. It was only in the second half of the nineteenth century, as growth proceeded unchecked and the failure of the rebellions gave rise to ideological realignments, that French Canadians were increasingly frozen out of economic development. Habitants who opened up the marginal lands to the north of the Saint Lawrence Valley were not immune to market forces, but they used them to bolster a traditional way of life in which family and land took precedence over individual advancement and profit. It should not be forgotten, however, that side by side with farmers who chose to try their luck in the Saguenay or Abitibi were those (sometimes the same people) who preferred to become workers rather than peasants and joined the rising tide of departures for Montréal or the factory towns of New England.

There is no question that Canadian merchants fared badly as a result of the conquest. While it may not have impoverished them, it certainly harmed their business, whether they were primarily involved in import-export or in retail operations in the countryside. Marie-Anne Barbel, the widow Fornel, one of the more adventurous traders of the time, was forced to liquidate her fishing and fur-trading enterprises on the Labrador coast after 1759, taking refuge in her investments in rural and urban real estate. Her family, wealthy at midcentury, came through the French defeat with only the relics of a fortune, "relics that were nonetheless significant," according to Liliane Plamondon.[74] Likewise, the aforementioned country merchant François-Augustin Bailly de Messein, whose fortune grew exponentially in the last decades of the French Regime, went into semiretirement in 1760, shutting down his store and curtailing his financial dealings. Here again, thanks to extensive investments in real estate, he was able to safeguard his assets, which actually appreciated 17 percent between the conquest and his death in 1771.[75]

Habitants, on the whole, probably suffered less than merchants, since British traders were not slow to scent opportunity in the countryside. In the Lower Richelieu, where six French merchants plied their trade before the conquest, a seventh was at work by 1761: Samuel Jacobs, a German Jew who had arrived in the colony two years earlier as a private supplier to General Wolfe's army. By 1763 an Englishman named John Grant had joined him, and several of the French merchants had managed to remain active.[76] Not only was there no interruption in the demand for habitant surpluses, but competition in the grain trade was brisker than ever.

With the market healthy, rural Québec continued to develop along commercial lines throughout the late eighteenth and early nineteenth centuries.[77] Habitants increased their production, shunning neither new techniques nor new crops, and they continued to avail themselves of credit. Village growth, which had begun toward the end of the French Regime, continued to accelerate after the conquest, only to reach a kind of takeoff point in the early nineteenth century. Habitants along with merchants profited from this further integration of Québec into the sphere of Atlantic capitalism; however, social differences in the countryside became more sharply defined. There were also regional variations from one part of the province to another, with the hinterlands of Québec and Montréal together with the Richelieu Valley being the most advanced.

Like their predecessors under the French Regime, habitants in the years after the conquest did not reject the idea of capital improvements. Propaganda in favor of the lighter English plow bore fruit in the vicinity of Québec, while the habitants of the Lower Richelieu replaced not only their plows, but their harrows.[78] The progress of new cash crops was notable, among them corn, oats, barley, and potatoes. By 1830, wheat, the traditional staple, made up only one-fifth of the agricultural output of the province, down from over two-thirds in the eighteenth century; by 1844 the figure was a mere 4 percent. Conversely, between 1833 and 1838 alone, the production of oats more than doubled, and that of barley tripled. The amount of livestock quadrupled in the early nineteenth century, growing from 100,000 to 400,000 head.[79] The regions of Montréal and Québec, in particular, became increasingly specialized, the former in commercial cereals, the latter in animal husbandry.[80]

To make these investments, as well as to purchase land and enhance consumption, habitants had recourse to an increasingly extensive credit network. This rural indebtedness was traditionally seen as a mark of the fragility of habitant society, but more recent studies have emphasized instead the link between rural credit and habitant capital accumulation. According to J. I. Little, the Eastern Townships of Québec resembled the potato country of northern Maine in that, in both places, "the elaborate system of credit and exchange that revolved around local merchants provided the economic basis for the development of agriculture."[81]

The phenomenon of village growth, launched in earnest under the French Regime, was not disrupted by the conquest either. Quite the contrary, for the number of new-style villages increased from some 20 in 1760 to around 30 in 1800, to over 200 by 1831![82] The township of Saint-Malachie-d'Ormstown, in the Châteauguay Valley, south of Montréal, was typical; its two villages, in addition to providing business services, inns, and artisans' shops, housed several mills and workshops, notably a carriage manufacturer and a maker of agricultural implements.[83]

Perhaps the most interesting midcentury village was L'Industrie (now Joliette), on the Assumption River north of Montréal. It was founded in 1824 by Barthélemy Joliette, a notary whose marriage into a seigneurial family transformed him, through his role as estate manager, into a French-Canadian entrepreneur. His original plans focused on the forest industry, from the cutting of timber to the sale of cut lumber, but the village "soon became the center of an important industrial and commercial development: saw mills, flour mills, carding mills sprang up along the Assumption River." By the time of Joliette's death in 1850, the village boasted a population of 1,000 souls, and a twenty-kilometer railroad linked it to nearby Lanoraie.[84] As Serge Courville has pointed out, "what we have here is a major phenomenon which has not previously been recognized. We may even ask if the growth of villages in Québec does not parallel the growth of towns in Upper Canada [Ontario], the latter development often cited to explain the future differences in the economic situations of the two provinces."[85]

In this expanding rural economy, profit was unequally distributed, but habitants as a group fared well. Gilles Paquet and Jean-Pierre Wallot have calculated that they actually doubled the real worth of their assets between 1792 and 1812.[86] At the same time, class differences among the habitants became more pronounced. While the least successful abandoned farming for the rapidly multiplying villages, a veritable "gentry" emerged that owed its position to land acquisition, lending, and even speculation. After incidents in 1809 and 1810 in which speculators cornered the market on meat and other farm products, a government investigation revealed many of the culprits to have been habitants from the farms around Québec.[87] Such trends, of course, were stronger around Québec and Montréal, where farming was competitive business, than in remoter or more recently colonized regions. According to Normand Séguin and Françoise-Eugénie Petit, "Québec agriculture, *taken as a whole,* took a half century (1840–1890) to accomplish the passage from subsistence dominated production to production dominated by commerce" (their emphasis).[88] By the mid-nineteenth century, however, the heart of the countryside had already been transformed by commercial capitalism.

Concurrent with these economic changes were new ideas. Once again, the point of departure was the final decades of the French Regime, but liberal views became more open and more widespread in the years after the conquest. Partisans of independence within the framework of an American-style democracy grew in number, and, as Louis Dechêne has pointed out, they were most vocal in areas where economic modernization was well under way by the turn of the century.[89]

Perhaps the first indication of the penetration of liberal ideology into Québec comes in the form of Freemasonry, which began to garner adherents at the time of the Seven Years' War. Roger Le Moine has concluded that "one lodge at least existed in Québec or Montréal" under the French Regime, with members as diverse as Jean Grelleau *fils,* a Protestant engineer and merchant from Montauban, and the Canadian-born officer Marin de la Malgue.[90] De la Malgue earned a place in the annals of Masonry in 1756 by rescuing an enemy general, Israel Putnam, from death upon recognition of certain Masonic signs.

In 1771 Father Montgolfier, the grand vicar of Québec, wrote to his absentee bishop: "We have a great number of Freemasons in this town. There were some, but few in number and hidden, under the French government. Several of our merchants, having gone to France at the time of the Revolution [the conquest] to straighten out their affairs, allowed themselves to be seduced there."[91]

This testimony seems accurate, for at the time of the conquest, a number of Canadian officers joined a francophone offshoot of the grand lodge of London called La parfaite Union in upstate New York, and in Québec, Saint Peter's Lodge no. 4 included officers, administrators, and bourgeois of the French Regime among its first members.[92]

It was not long before liberal ideas started to gain currency in less elite social milieux. According to Wallot, by 1774 (the year of the Québec Act) a petty bourgeoisie of "notaries, lawyers, doctors, surveyors, journalists, small merchants, and more prosperous farmers" had begun "to assert its influence upon the people," and by 1791 (the year of Québec's first constitution) its leadership had become dominant.[93] At the heart of its ideology was a new French-Canadian nationalism and "a social project centered on the development of Québec."[94]

The impact of liberalism in the countryside was already apparent in 1775, when "rural insurrection broke out during the American occupation of Canada."[95] By the 1790s, seigneurs had experienced "a total loss of their prestige and authority," to the point that habitants "simply refused to pay their tithes and dues, under the pretext that their ecclesiastical seigneurs (for example the Sulpicians) did not exist in law."[96] Anti-seigneurialism thus segued into anticlericalism, which was also rampant among petty bourgeois alienated by the church's stance on loans at interest. At the same time, rural religious practice left much to be desired. In the Lower Richelieu, for example, the Jewishness of merchant Samuel Jacobs was no obstacle to his full integration into the French-Canadian community. While he refused to marry in the church for religious reasons, he cohabited with two French-Canadian women in succession and begot them seven children. Two of his daughters went to convent school, and one of his sons received a Protestant education. Among this group of habitants, at least, tolerance rather than orthodoxy was the watchword.[97]

Discontent with the existing system culminated in the Rebellions of 1837 and 1838, which were particularly intense in the countryside around

Montréal. In 1838 the radical Patriotes Cyrille (Agricola) Côté, a young country doctor from the village of Napierville, and Robert Nelson of Montréal issued a "Declaration of Independence" calling for republican government, bilingualism, universal male suffrage, freedom of the press, separation of church and state, expropriation of church lands, abolition without compensation of seigneurial tenure, and the closing of confessional schools.[98] Their failure (martial law had already been proclaimed in 1837) led them to form a secret society along Masonic lines, the Frères chasseurs, devoted to armed insurrection, and it quickly acquired a mass following among habitants.[99]

As liberalism caught on in Québec, so too did one of its classic components: the ideology of separate gendered spheres. Patriotes in the Lower Canadian parliament disenfranchised women in 1834 (the Constitutional Act of 1791 had not prevented propertied women from voting), and when the rebellions broke out, Queen Victoria became, for more than one radical, a "damned whore with her legs in the air."[100] This gendered desacralization of the crown never became truly pornographic, but it nonetheless recalls the more vicious and imaginative campaign launched by French revolutionaries against Marie Antoinette.[101] According to the Patriotes, women's public role in the rebellions was to be modeled on that of "liberty's daughters" in the America Revolution: organizing spinning bees to replace British textiles with homespun.[102] Interestingly, support for the rebels among habitant women seems to have been weaker in 1837 than in 1775.

THE LIQUIDATION of the rebellions ushered in a new era for habitant society, precipitating, at last, its marginalization. In a series of ideological realignments with far-reaching consequences, the church abandoned seigneurialism (with full compensation), the bourgeoisie anticlericalism, and the British authorities anti-Catholicism. The granting of permission for new Catholic orders to enter Québec was particularly significant, since it coincided with a missionary offensive by a French church steeped in militant counterrevolutionism. What Wallot has called the "clericalization" of French-Canadian society began in earnest in the 1840s and 1850s, only to make its full impact on habitant behavior in the last quarter of the nineteenth century.[103]

The Catholic Church, which had endured the hostility of every British administration since the conquest, emerged from the rebellions remarkably strengthened. Clerics accustomed to decades of harassment could scarcely believe their good fortune, but they had been conspicuous in opposing the unrest and now reaped the rewards of loyalism. In what Lord Wellington sweepingly described as a "total departure . . . from the principle of the Reformation,"[104] the British government entered into tacit alliance with a fellow bulwark of the social order. Limitations on clerical recruitment were removed, and Québec received 25 new female orders (9 of them French) and 12 new male orders (all of them French) in the second half of the nineteenth century. Despite rapid population growth, the ratio of priests to congregants more than doubled during the same period.[105] The Sulpician superior of Montréal, with a grandiosity equal to Wellington's, praised the new arrangement as "the most Catholic and Papist law that it [Britain] had sanctioned in over three hundred years."[106]

There was, however, a quid pro quo. In return for greater political influence, the church would have to renounce what the British considered its antiquated privilege—namely, its seigneurial role. On the whole, this transition from seigneurialism to freehold tenure proceeded smoothly. Negotiations were protracted but amicable, and, in the end, the commutation took place on terms advantageous for the clergy. Nor did they squander their advantage. To take the example of the Sulpicians, between 1840 and 1870, they transformed themselves from "the symbol of seigneurialism" in Montréal into "an important accessory to the process of urbanization and industrialization," with an investment portfolio that included stock in the Grand Trunk Railway and bonds of the City and Port of Montréal.[107]

The church's new position in Québec society was further bolstered by changed attitudes on the part of much of the French-Canadian bourgeoisie. In the 1840s and 1850s, former Patriotes such as George-Etienne Cartier, a merchant's son turned lawyer, abandoned their youthful ideals to create a French-Canadian version of middle-class Toryism: responsible government, capitalist expansion, and social control. Although the Rouges made an attempt to keep alive the principles of the rebellions, their support dwindled steadily through the middle decades of the century.[108] By the 1870s, they too felt compelled to make peace with the church. In a highly publicized speech from 1877, the Liberal leader and future prime minister Wilfrid Laurier bowed to expediency and distinguished between political and religious liberals—the former British and respectable, the latter French and dangerously radical.[109]

Liberal retrenchment was all the more significant in that the francophone church, unlike the Church of England, was no friend of the modern world. Though it accommodated itself, in practice, to economic change, its ideology, born of reaction against the French Revolution, remained militantly medieval. Monseigneur Ignace Bourget, the bishop of Montréal, made clear his opinion of liberty when he admonished his followers, "Let us each say in his heart, 'I hear my curé, my curé hears the bishop, the bishop hears the Pope, and the Pope hears Our Lord Jesus Christ.'"[110]

Since Bourget's ultramontane message was trumpeted throughout the province by an expanding and aggressive clergy, it is not surprising that habitant mores began to change in the second half of the nineteenth century. Particularly on the agricultural frontier, where lack of an alternative infrastructure conveyed enormous authority to the curé, the practices of confession, communion, fasting, and abstinence were approximating prescribed norms by around 1875.[111] This was a far cry from the situation in the 1830s, when as many as two-thirds of parishioners could not have been bothered to perform their paschal duties.[112] Ironically, the conservative Catholicism that prevailed among French Canadians until the 1960s was more a product of France's postrevolutionary quarrels, imported into Canada, than of the Ancien Régime.

Meanwhile, economic change, for the first time, was passing the habitants by. "Up until the 1850s," according to Serge Courville, "Québec seems to have behaved like the other developed countries of the North Atlantic world economy"; however, with the advent of industrial capitalism, French Canadians began to face difficulties owing to their inability "to acquire and control large-scale capital."[113] Although they participated in the first wave of industrialization, particularly in and around Montréal, by the 1890s increasing concentration led to "the disappearance, or at least the marginalization, of the class of French-Canadian entrepreneurs."[114] In the countryside, although the family farms of the Laurentian lowlands remained viable by switching from grains to dairy products, they could not absorb the rapidly growing population. Migration away from the agricultural heartland was in full swing by the middle of the nineteenth century.

The career of George-Etienne Cartier (1814–1873), corporate lawyer and conservative politician, illustrates the increasingly precarious position of the French-Canadian bourgeoisie in the second half of the nineteenth century. Cartier's primary concern was commercial expansion, which made him a "tireless promoter" of improved communications, whether in politics or the private sector. His fortune, consisting of urban and rural real estate together with railroad, banking, and mining stocks, was substantial; however, he derived less than half as much income from his portfolio as from his rents.[115] By the late 1860s, Cartier, "largely mercantile in orientation, was being eclipsed by the rise of a national and industrial bourgeoisie." While he suffered humiliating electoral loss in his Montréal riding in 1872, finance capitalists such as the anglophone Hugh Allan were in the ascendant.[116] Basically, French-Canadian bourgeois were unable to make the transition from "a colonial entrepreneurial class" to "a new industrial bourgeoisie replete with tough professional managers and sources of capital."[117]

The situation of French-Canadian farmers was changing as well. Agricultural development continued in the Saint Lawrence after the middle of the nineteenth century, causing farm size to increase and rural society to grow more stratified. Some habitants benefited from these conditions, to be sure, but an ever larger group began to experience social and economic marginalization for the first time.

In the Laurentian lowlands, as in nearby Vermont, agricultural modernization took the form of conversion to dairy farming, which doubled in importance in the second half of the nineteenth century.[118] Concurrent with this shift was a trend toward farm consolidation, which increased the size of the average farm from roughly 84 arpents in 1851 to nearly 100 ten years later.[119] While substantial farmers profited from these developments, the smaller units were ceasing to be viable. The result was a "proletarianization of large strata" of the rural population. A significant population of landless day laborers was created, and the remaining smallholders found it increasingly difficult to ensure their subsistence.[120]

To make matters worse, the demand for hired labor on farms and in country villages was growing more slowly than the rural population. On average, habitant couples produced 7 or 8 children in the course of their life cycle, and rarely fewer than 5. Quebecers of French-Canadian descent were doubling in number every twenty-five to thirty years, with the result that the postconquest population of 75,000 had become 750,000 by 1865.[121]

Under these circumstances, outmigration appeared to be the only solution. The rural exodus was under way in the Saint Lawrence by the 1860s, and agricultural colonization onto the less fertile soils of the Appalachians and Canadian Shield was attracting a swelling stream of smallholders and day laborers.[122] As Gérard Bouchard has shown, this process of colonization was "accompanied by a sort of regression." Agricultural techniques, social relations, and cultural practices all assumed more primary forms, and farm products were "very feebly commercialized."[123] The primitive peasant existence immortalized in Louis Hémon's *Maria Chapdelaine* (1914), a portrait of Québec frontier life by a fascinated and somewhat horrified Frenchman, had at last come into being.

Of course, these "peripheral societies largely shaped by clerical hegemony" were not the only destination of rural emigrants in the late nineteenth century.[124] It has been estimated, in fact, that for every departure for the frontier, there were ten for industrial cities.[125] The mill towns of New England were the most popular choice, with Montréal coming in second.[126] Some of the emigrants who chose industrial work, moreover, did so after initial sojourns in the regions of colonization. Maria Chapdelaine's suitor Lorenzo, who abandoned his love for the more seductive lure of Lowell, Massachusetts, had his real-life counterparts throughout New England.[127]

Summary

An examination of New French society reveals that the small number of settlers in New France as compared with New England cannot be attributed to the more traditional nature of French immigrants. French-Canadian backwardness, to the degree that it existed, was the outcome of a complex and gradual historical process, one that was scarcely under way during the French Regime. As I have indicated, the French settlements in Québec and the Maritimes were more modern than otherwise before 1763.

The British conquest of Québec was something of a blow to the French-Canadian bourgeoisie, but it was also one from which they largely recovered in subsequent decades. Likewise, the first half of the nineteenth century was a time of relative prosperity for habitants, whose farming continued to develop along commercial lines regardless of the change in political authority. The second half of the century produced a more profound mutation, as the bourgeoisie found itself excluded from the capitalist vanguard and habitants became divided into a class of substantial yeomen, on the one hand, and an even larger class of struggling small-holders and day laborers, on the other. While this situation caused hundreds of thousands of marginalized country dwellers to take up residence in the industrial city, it also inspired a significant number to re-create a traditional peasant society on the agrarian frontier. The irony of Frenchmen becoming peasants is thus compounded by yet another irony: the archaic traditional society whose epitaph Parkman wrote and whose survival beyond the grave Ferland and Faillon celebrated was not really archaic at all, but a recent historical development—one that had literally taken place within those historians' lifetimes.

THE PEOPLING of French Canada in the seventeenth and eighteenth centuries was a process that involved both modernity and tradition, in different ways. In economic and social terms, it was primarily a modern movement; the regional, social, and religious origins of the emigrants set them clearly apart from *la France profonde*. In demographic terms, however, the movement was more traditional, for it built upon established patterns of population mobility. Although emigrants to Canada were embarking for new destinations in the seventeenth century, they were doing so through eminently familiar channels such as the rural exodus, military enlistment, or interurban labor migration.

The regional origins of the first French Canadians defined what I have called a geography of modernity. Cities and towns made a contribution far out of proportion with their weight in the population, and rural areas contributed to the degree that they were integrated into the Atlantic economy. Cosmopolitan origins, although especially important in the case of women, were also conspicuous for men.

Emigration to Canada was unrepresentative in other ways as well. While exact numbers are impossible to ascertain, it is clear that urban social classes and occupations outnumbered rural ones. Religious nonconformity proved more important than might have been expected in an officially Catholic colony, and Catholic piety was less pronounced. A spirit of independence and adventure could be discerned in the words and deeds of individual emigrants, most of whom were young, single adults. Their departures, which spanned periods of bust and boom in French agrarian history, took place in a context of Atlantic expansion and opportunity, which was probably the one that mattered most to this outwardly turned and ambitious group. To borrow the terminology of Eugen Weber, Canada's hardy pioneers set sail from Europe as Frenchmen, not as peasants.

Yet Ancien Régime tradition also played an important part in French emigration to Canada—migratory tradition, to be exact. Time-honored currents of internal mobility such as urbanization, interurban exchange, migration from highlands to lowlands, and structured seasonal and temporary movement all contributed, in varying degrees, to the transatlantic migrant stream. Emigration could occur as a deviation from, an extension of, or an alternative to established patterns. It was always, however, at the confluence of familiar migratory flows.

Canada was not, for all that, a popular destination. From the beginning, most emigrants in search of new horizons embarked instead for the West Indies, and those who did choose Canada rarely viewed their stay as permanent. Although public and private recruitment efforts compensated for this situation in part, Canada was not thickly settled by the eighteenth century, particularly in comparison with the thirteen colonies.

Nonetheless, French Canadians succeeded in establishing reasonably prosperous colonial societies in both Québec and the Maritimes. The simple, pious habitants of historical myth scarcely existed in New France, which is not surprising given the urban and commercial roots of so many of the settlers. Their transition from Frenchmen into peasants, which was neither rapid nor linear, was more a product of the nineteenth century than of the French Regime.

SINCE THE SEVENTEENTH CENTURY, French and British North America have been viewed largely in terms of their rivalry with each other, with the emphasis on what has distinguished them. There were indeed differences of note, such as the size and diversity of the respective populations, which it would be foolish to ignore. But there were also important parallels that deserve attention. Whether one considers the initial transatlantic migration or the subsequent history of settlement, the French and British experiences may even have been more alike than different.[128]

Emigration to the thirteen colonies has been much studied in recent years, and the picture it presents is not unfamiliar. Prior to the late eighteenth century, English emigrants came disproportionately from towns and their agricultural hinterlands.[129] Men outnumbered women; single youths, families; and artisans and laborers, farmers. With the notable exception of the New Englanders, "there is little evidence that the pioneers were inordinately religious."[130] Yet along with modernity came tradition. English emigration too "must be viewed within the context of general levels of physical mobility in the English economy."[131] For Great Britain as for France, the peopling of North America "was an extension outward and an expansion in scale of domestic mobility in the lands of the immigrants' origins, and the transatlantic flow must be understood within the context of these domestic mobility patterns."[132]

As for settlement, although the British colonies exhibited far greater ethnic and religious diversity than French Canada, there were still some striking similarities. The rough-and-tumble fishwife of Louisbourg had her counterpart in British colonial ports from Marblehead to Newfoundland; and who could resemble the Laurentian habitant more than the comfortable New England farmer, his horizons bounded by "belief in the virtues of a competence and the importance of kinship ties?"[133] Moreover, for every nineteenth-century habitant family that chose the hardscrabble peasant life of the northern frontier, there were ten that followed the lure of city lights or the American dream; between 1850 and 1900, over 1 million French Canadians poured into New England, for a net immigration of at least 340,000.[134] Jack Greene's description of "the single most important element in the emerging American mind—the ideal of the pursuit of happiness by independent people in a setting that provided significant opportunities for success," could be said to characterize the French-Canadian mind as well.[135]

What distinguished French and British North America more than anything else, in the eighteenth century, was numbers—a distinction that stemmed from policy as well as geography and had momentous political consequences. But patterns of mobility, economic life, family reproduction, social structures, and even culture had much in common, and are perhaps best understood as part of a shared, if highly variegated, Atlantic colonial experience.

Notes

Abbreviations

AC	Archives des Colonies (France)
AD	Archives départementales (France)
AM	Archives de la Marine (France)
AN	Archives nationales (France)
ANQ	Archives nationales du Québec
ASQ	Archives du Séminaire de Québec
CNRS	Centre national de la recherche scientifique
INED	Institut national d'études démographiques
PRDH	Programme de recherches en démographie historique (Université de Montréal)
PUF	Presses universitaires de France
PUM	Presses de l'Université de Montréal

Introduction

1. Yvette Daubèze and Jean-Claude Perrot, "Un programme d'étude démographique sur ordinateur," *Annales: économies, sociétés, civilisations,* 27 (1972): 1051.

2. Letter of Pontchartrain to the comptroller general, 19 October 1714, AN: G7, vol. 535. All translations mine unless otherwise noted.

3. The term "Canada" is used in its present-day sense throughout this study. During the Ancien Régime, the French more often referred to "New France," which was in turn composed of Canada and Acadia. Roughly speaking, Canada meant today's province of Québec, Acadia the provinces of Nova Scotia and New Brunswick. The French settlements on Newfoundland were evacuated when they were lost to the English in 1713.

4. Hubert Charbonneau, *Vie et mort de nos ancêtres: étude démographique* (Montréal: PUM, 1975), p. 19.

5. André Corvisier, *L'Armée française de la fin du XVIIe siècle au ministère de Choiseul: le soldat* (Paris: PUF, 1964), 1: 415–418.

6. Acadia constitutes a sad exception to this situation of abundant documentation. Because of the more traumatic nature of the British conquest in the Maritimes, much of the early archival material has been destroyed. In addition to scattered parish registers, the extant documents consist of several censuses, some judicial records, and various lists of Acadian refugees. See Centre d'études acadiennes, Université de Moncton, *Inventaire général des sources documentaires sur les Acadiens,* 3 vols. (Moncton, N.B.: Editions d'Acadie, 1975–1977).

7. More than 250,000 acts for the period of the French Regime.

8. Of course, to the extent that accidental deaths (usually by drowning or freezing) were common in the early years of colonization, the acts of burial also contain records of would-be temporary emigrants.

9. "Témoignages de liberté au mariage," *Rapport de l'archiviste de la province de Québec,* 32–33 (1951–1953): 65.

10. Agricol Perdiguier, *Mémoires d'un compagnon* (1854; Paris: Librairie du compagnonnage, 1964), pp. 13, 16, 48.

11. "Témoignages de liberté," pp. 95, 122; M. Dumas de Rauly, "Extraits d'un livre de raison de la famille Dumas de Nègrepelisse, dite de Lacaze," *Bulletin archéologique et historique de la Société archéologique de Tarn-et-Garonne,* 11 (1883): 109–110.

12. Georges Frêche, *Toulouse et la région Midi-Pyrénées au siècle des lumières vers 1670–1789* (Paris: Cujas, 1974), p. 796.

13. For Québec the extant censuses date from 1666, 1667, 1681, and 1713. That of 1759, which tallied a population of 75,000, has been lost. Peninsular Acadian censuses, most of which are only partial, exist for 1671, 1679, 1683, 1686, 1689, 1693, 1698, 1701, 1703, 1707, and 1714. Censuses of Ile Saint-Jean (Prince Edward Island) and Ile Royale (Cape Breton Island) were taken in 1724, 1726, 1728, 1734, and 1735. There is also a partial census of Ile Royale, exclusive of Louisbourg, dating from 1752. Exceptionally thorough, it is the only Canadian census to concern itself with both the regional origins and social status of the observed population.

14. Hubert Charbonneau and Yolande Lavoie, "Introduction à la reconstitution de la population du Canada au XVIIe siècle: étude critique des sources de la période 1665–1668," *Revue d'histoire de l'Amérique française,* 24 (1970–1971): 485.

15. The designations of cleric, functionary, and farmer do not, however, figure in the census. Results are further skewed by the failure to record the 1,200 soldiers of the Regiment of Carignan, many of whom had exercised artisanal trades in France. Talon probably chose not to include them because prior to demobilization, it was impossible to estimate who would and would not choose to remain in Canada. For a detailed discussion of this census, see Jean Hamelin, *Economie et société en Nouvelle-France,* Cahiers de l'Institut d'histoire, no. 3 (Québec: Presses de l'Université Laval, 1960), and Hubert Charbonneau, Yolande Lavoie,

and Jacques Légaré, "Recensements et registres paroissiaux du Canada durant la période 1665–1668: étude critique," *Population*, 25 (1970): 97–124.

16. Again, this remark applies only to Québec, Acadian notarial records having disappeared almost in their entirety.

17. Marcel Trudel has suggested that the signature of a marriage contract provided an excuse for a social occasion, always welcome in this sparsely settled society of isolated farms; see Marcel Trudel, *Histoire de la Nouvelle-France* (Montréal: Fides, 1963–1983), 3, pt. 2: 517–525.

18. Because it is very difficult to determine the directionality of these migrations, I have somewhat arbitrarily opted for the anteriority of the places mentioned in the acts of marriage, under the assumption that the priests were probably more concerned with places of baptism and hence more specific in their questions than the notaries.

19. Trial of Guillaume Regnault, Baillage of Louisbourg (1736), AC: G2, vol. 196, dossier 93; trial of René Antoine Lemoine *dit* Saint-Amant, Conseil supérieur of Louisbourg (1740), AC: G2, vol. 186, p. 323. Unfortunately, the court records of Québec do not provide comparable information about the French origins of indicted emigrants.

20. On the Ancien Régime church, in particular, as a modernizing force, see Jean Quéniart, *L'Homme, l'Eglise, et Dieu dans la France du XVIIIe siècle* (Paris: Hachette, 1978).

21. Gabriel Debien, "Engagés pour le Canada au XVIIe siècle vus de La Rochelle," *Notes d'histoire coloniale*, 21 (1952): 178. This statement does not apply to women, who made up about an eighth of all emigrants.

22. Much ink has been spilled about the origins of the indenture system, with early accounts of its barbarous novelty gradually giving way to comparisons with other sorts of contracts. Gabriel Debien has made a case for the maritime origins of indenture, arguing that "it was at the beginning only a particular form of maritime enrollment." He has also pointed out, however, that in La Rochelle, the acts of indenture were indistinguishable in the inventories from "those that young people signed with employers of La Rochelle to become apprentices on the spot." A third source of indentured servitude has been suggested by David Galenson, for whom it was, in England at least, a geographical extension of the institution of service in husbandry. French emigrants tended, on the whole, to be more maritime and urban than their English counterparts, so this hypothesis must be treated with circumspection across the Channel. Still, it is perhaps relevant that in the one region of France where emigrants agreed to indenture themselves for five rather than three years (the current department of Sarthe), a system of *métivage* prevailed in agriculture. *Métivage* was a service contract of up to nine years between a farmer and an agricultural servant, male or female. The servant generally received 100 livres per year, an amount comparable to that earned by an indentured emigrant. See André Bouton, *Le Maine: histoire économique et sociale, XVIIe et XVIIIe siècles* (Le Mans: n.p.,

1973), p. 485; Debien, "Engagés pour le Canada," pp. 184, 196; and David Galenson, *White Servitude in Colonial America: An Economic Analysis* (Cambridge: Cambridge University Press, 1981), pp. 6–7.

23. The admiralties were administrative and judicial bodies with jurisdiction over maritime commerce, fishing, and crimes and misdemeanors committed in ports or on the seacoast; see Marcel Marion, *Dictionnaire des institutions de la France aux XVIIe et XVIIIe siècles* (Paris: Picard, 1968). For an idea of the type of material preserved in the Archives de l'Amirauté, see Henri-François Buffet, *Répertoire numérique de la sous-série 9B, Amirauté de Saint-Malo* (Rennes: Imprimeries réunies, 1962).

24. Archange Godbout, "Le Rôle du Saint-Jehan et les origines acadiennes," *Mémoires de la Société généalogique canadienne-française*, 1 (1944): 21.

25. The most significant improvement concerns the second half of the eighteenth century, because beginning in 1749 French port officials began to deposit copies of the crew lists required by the admiralties with the naval minister in Paris. This collection, which subsequently became part of the Archives des Colonies, provides information on colonial departures from twenty-five different ports.

26. In fact, in an ideal scenario, the Archives de l'Amirauté would duplicate this information. In addition to collecting the passenger lists, officials of the admiralty were supposed to conduct on-site inspections of the *engagés* before their departure. The minutes of these inspections were then to be deposited with the clerk of the admiralty. Such inspections, however, were conducted with less than religious regularity.

27. Debien, "Engagés pour le Canada," p. 185.

28. There is a lacuna for the years 1784–1787, but copies of the missing documents are located in AC: F5B. In any case, this gap is of no concern to the Canadian historian, since the colony was lost in 1763.

29. More than 33,000 paying passengers boarded ships in Bordeaux for foreign (but not necessarily colonial) destinations during the seventy-five years covered in the passport registers. Relatively few of these passengers, however, were en route to Canada.

30. Passenger lists, Bayonne, AC: F5B, vol. 38.

31. Passenger lists, Saint-Jean-de-Luz, ibid., vol. 58.

32. There are some military rolls among the passenger lists, but most of them (those originating in Brest, Lorient, Port-Louis, and Rochefort, for example) are purely nominative and provide no information other than military rank. Bordeaux's passenger rolls alone identify Canadian soldiers by age and birthplace as well; see passenger lists, Bordeaux, ibid., vol. 39.

33. Claude de Bonnault, "Le Canada militaire: état provisoire des officiers de milice de 1641 à 1760," *Rapport de l'archiviste de la province de Québec*, 30–31 (1949–1951): 263.

34. W. J. Eccles, "The Social, Economic, and Political Significance of the Military Establishment in New France," *Canadian Historical Review*, 52 (1971): 5.

35. Outgoing correspondence, AC: B; incoming correspondence, AC: CᴵᴵA–CᴵᴵD, CᴵᴵG.

36. One therefore learns how many officers, ecclesiastics, domestics, soldiers, and artisans embarked for a given Canadian destination in a given year at the expense of the king, but further identification of these emigrants is impossible. Sometimes the officers were mentioned by name, as, for example, in the list of "passages granted for Canada" in 1720. Here the reason for doing so appears to have been simple politeness; in any case, nothing else is revealed about them. See AC: B, vol. 42, p. 190. (In my citations to the general correspondence, the page number always refers to the beginning of the document, even if it is several pages long.)

37. The largest annual convoy of *fils de famille*, that of 1729, comprised 15 persons. Overall, about 68 of them arrived in Canada between 1723 and 1734, when this type of deportation ceased.

38. See Jacques Légaré, André La Rose, and Raymond Roy, "Reconstitution of the Seventeenth-Century Canadian Population: An Overview of a Research Program," *Historical Methods Newsletter,* 9 (1975): 1–8, and Jacques Légaré, "Le PRDH de l'Université de Montréal: fondements, méthodes, moyens, et résultats," *Etudes canadiennes,* 10 (1981): 149–182. In spite of its primarily Canadian focus, the PRDH synthesis does not neglect French sources. Contracts of indentured servitude and passenger lists also make up part of the database, to the extent that they are readily available.

39. It should be noted that the project of the PRDH concerns Québec only, because the poor state of preservation of Acadia's parish registers prohibits a complete reconstruction of its population beginning with the first generation. To date, the best resource for the study of emigration to Acadia is Bona Arsenault's *Histoire et généalogie des Acadiens,* 6 vols. (Ottawa: Leméac, 1978).

40. *Répertoire des actes de baptême, mariage, sépulture, et de recensements du Québec ancien,* 47 vols. (Montréal: PUM, 1980–1990). In addition, a second edition of the first seven volumes, covering the seventeenth century, appeared in 1991.

41. Mario Boleda, "Trente mille Français à la conquête du Saint-Laurent," *Histoire sociale/Social History,* 23 (1990): 153–177; Hubert Charbonneau, Bertrand Desjardins, André Guillemette, Yves Landry, Jacques Légaré, and François Nault with Réal Bates and Mario Boleda, *Naissance d'une population: les Français établis au Canada au XVIIᵉ siècle* (Paris: INED; Montréal: PUM, 1987). An English version of the latter work has been published under the title *The First French Canadians: Pioneers in the St. Lawrence Valley,* trans. Paola Colozzo (Newark: University of Delaware Press, 1993). See also Mario Boleda, "Les Migrations au Canada sous le Régime français" (doctoral diss., Université de Montréal, 1983), and "Les Migrations au Canada sous le Régime français (1608–1760)," in PRDH, *Rapport de l'année 1982–1983* (Montréal, 1984).

42. Information from the following sources was included in the emigrant sample: Roland Auger, *La Grande Recrue de 1653* (Montréal: Société généalogique

canadienne-française, 1955); "Les Passagers du Taureau—1663," *Mémoires de la Société généalogique canadienne-française,* 24 (1974): 158–160; "Les Soldats de la Guerre de Sept Ans," ibid., 4 (1951): 240–247; 5 (1952): 42–58, 110–116; 6 (1954): 40–46; 7 (1956): 70–76; 8 (1957): 244–250; 9 (1958): 116–122; 10 (1959): 86–96; 11 (1960): 57–67, 171–178; 12 (1961): 21–26, 87–90, 230–232; 13 (1962): 157–159; 14 (1963): 16–19; 17 (1966): 100–106; 19 (1968): 50–57, 116–122; 20 (1969): 47–59; Paul Beauchet-Filleul, "Les Bas-Poitevins du Canada," *Revue du Bas-Poitou,* 32 (1919): 57–64, 208–216; Berneval [Archange Godbout], "Le Contingent de filles de 1639," *Bulletin des recherches historiques,* 45 (1939): 3–15; "Les Contingents de filles à marier de 1649–1653," ibid., pp. 257–270; "Les Filles venues au Canada de 1654 à 1657," ibid., 46 (1940): 338–350; "Les Filles venues au Canada de 1658 à 1661," ibid., 47 (1941): 96–115; Jean-Noël Biraben, "Les Périgourdins au Canada à l'époque du Régime français," *Bulletin de la Société historique du Périgord,* 94 (1967): 36–67; Russel Bouchard, *Les Armuriers de la Nouvelle-France* (Québec: Ministère des Affaires culturelles, 1987); Ivanhoé Caron, "Liste des prêtres séculiers et religieux qui ont exercé le saint ministère en Nouvelle-France, 1604–1699," *Bulletin des recherches historiques,* 47 (1941): 160–175, 193–201, 225–235, 257–268, 289–299; Emmanuel de Cathelineau, "Gens d'Auvergne en Canada: le sieur de Vernerolles et ses amis," *Nova Francia,* 3 (1927–1928): 150–161; census records of Ile Royale and Ile Saint-Jean, AC: G1, vol. 466; Bernard de Chaunac-Lanzac, "Les Limousins en Canada," *Bulletin de la Société scientifique, historique, et archéologique de la Corrèze,* 62 (1940): 41–45; E. Cheminade, "Deux Bourbonnais au Canada," *Nova Francia,* 1 (1925–1926): 131; "Emigrants au Canada venant du Nivernais," ibid., pp. 75–76; court records of Ile Royale and Ile Saint-Jean, AC: G2, vols. 178–215; Gabriel Debien, "Les Engagés pour le Canada au XVIIe siècle," *Revue d'histoire de l'Amérique française,* 6 (1952–1953): 221–233, 374–407; "Les Engagés pour le Canada partis de Nantes," ibid., 33 (1979–1980): 583–586; Canon Dechavassine, "L'Emigration savoyarde au Canada," *Revue savoisienne,* 99 (1959): 27–36; Denis De La Ronde, "Colons angoumois venus au Canada au XVIIe siècle," *Bulletin et mémoires de la Société archéologique et historique de la Charente-Maritime,* 27–28 (1937–1938): 51–55, 87–93; Emile Demaizière, "Les Colons et émigrants bourguignons au Canada," *Rapport de l'archiviste de la province de Québec* (1923–1924): 394–398; Raymond Douville, "L'Apport de l'Auvergne et du Massif central dans le peuplement de la Nouvelle-France," *Cahiers des Dix,* 33 (1968): 243–289; Françoise Dufresne, "Pierre Michaud et les engagements pour la Nouvelle-France, en 1656," *Mémoires de la Société généalogique canadienne-française,* 24 (1973): 42–49; Silvio Dumas, *Les Filles du roi en Nouvelle-France,* Cahiers d'histoire, no. 24 (Québec: Société historique de Québec, 1972); Marcel Fournier, *Dictionnaire biographique des Bretons en Nouvelle-France: 1600–1765,* Collection études et recherches archivistiques, no. 4 (Québec: Archives nationales du Québec, 1981); Marc Gaucher, "Carnet d'un Albertain: quelques notes sur l'émigration française au Canada au XVIIIe siècle," *Revue d'histoire de l'Amérique française,* 4 (1950–1951): 90–114; Marc Gaucher, Marcel Delafosse, and Gabriel Debien, "Les Engagés pour le Canada au XVIIIe siècle," ibid., 13 (1959–1960): 250–261, 406–418, 550–557; 14 (1960–1961): 87–108, 246–258, 430–440, 583–591; general correspondence between France and New France, AC: B, C11A–C11D, C11G; Raymond Gingras, "Ancêtres de Fontenay-le-Comte en Poitou venus en Nouvelle-France aux XVIIe et XVIIIe siècles: liste sommaire," *Mélanges généalogiques,* 7 (1977); "Liste sommaire de colons venus de l'Ile de Ré au XVIIe et XVIIIe siècle pour s'établir en Nouvelle-France," ibid., 6 (1977); Godbout, "Le Rôle du Saint-Jehan," pp. 19–30; "Angevins en Canada en avril 1636," *Nova Francia,* 2 (1926–1927): 284; "Les Emigrants de 1664," *Mémoires de la Société généalogique canadienne-française,* 4 (1951): 217–225; "Engagés pour le Canada en 1658," ibid., 9 (1958): 78–84; "Familles venues de La Rochelle en Canada," *Rapport de l'archiviste de la province de Québec,* 48 (1970): 115–367; "Nos ancêtres au XVIIe siècle," ibid., 32–33 (1951–1953): 449–544; 34–35 (1953–1955): 445–536; 36–37 (1955–1957): 377–490; 38–39 (1957–1959): 383–440; 40 (1959–1960): 275–354; "Notes additionnelles sur quelques engagés de 1658," *Mémoires de la Société généalogique canadienne-française,* 9 (1958): 239–241; *Origine des familles canadiennes-françaises: extrait de l'état civil français,* lst ser. (Lille: Desclée, 1925); *Les Passagers du Saint-André: la recrue de 1659* (Montréal: Société généalogique canadienne-française, 1964); "Les Pionniers de la région trifluvienne, I^e série, 1634 à 1647," *Pages trifluviennes,* ser. A, 14 (1934): 5–77; "Vieilles familles de France en Nouvelle-France," *Rapport des Archives nationales du Québec,* 53 (1975): 105–264; Godbout Collection, ANQ; Jean Houpert, *Les Lorrains en Amérique du Nord* (Sherbrooke, Qué.: Naaman, 1985); René Jetté, *Dictionnaire généalogique des familles du Québec des origines à 1730* (Montréal: PUM, 1983); Le Ber Papers, Bibliothèque municipale de Rouen; Rénald Lessard, "Faux-sauniers déportés au Canada (1730–1743)," ANQ: ms., 1987; "Médecins, chirurgiens, et apothicaires ayant pratiqué ou vécu dans la province de Québec entre 1760 et 1791," ANQ: ms., 1982; Gérard Malchelosse, "Les Fils de famille en Nouvelle-France, 1720–1750," *Cahiers des Dix,* 11 (1946): 268–310; Albertus Martin, "Les Emigrants bourguignons au Canada sous le Régime français," *Annales de Bourgogne,* 45 (1973): 5–44; Edouard-Zotique Massicotte, "Les Colons de Montréal de 1642 à 1667," *Bulletin des recherches historiques,* 33 (1927): 170–192, 224–239, 312–320, 379–384, 433–448, 467–482, 538–548, 613–625; "Une Recrue de colons pour Montréal, en 1659," *The Canadian Antiquarian and Numismatic Journal,* 10 (1913): 63–96; "La Recrue de 1653: liste des colons qui partirent de France pour Montréal," *Rapport de l'archiviste de la province de Québec* (1920–1921): 309–312; François Mérieux, "L'Emigration lyonnaise (1632–1760)," *Mémoires de la Société généalogique canadienne-française,* 9 (1958): 205–208; Maria Mondoux, "Les Hommes de Montréal," *Revue d'histoire de l'Amérique française,* 2 (1948–1949): 59–80; Françoise Montagne, "Léonarde Fouquet femme de Zacharie Maheux et sa famille, et la famille de Toussaint Giroux," *Mémoires de la Société généalogique canadienne-française,* 23 (1972):

163–169; *Le Perche des Canadiens*, special issue of *Cahiers percherons* (1974); Guy Oury, "Les Manceaux de Montréal d'après la correspondance de Marie de l'Incarnation (1639–1672)," *La Province du Maine*, 74 (1972): 243–250; passenger lists, AC: F5B, vols. 1–2, 10–11, 14–16, 20–21, 23, 26–30, 34, 38–60; Normand Robert, *Nos origines en France des débuts à 1825: Béarn et Gascogne* (Montréal: Société de recherche historique archiv-histo, 1984); Joseph-Edmond Roy, "Des Fils de famille envoyés au Canada: Claude Le Beau," *Mémoires de la Société royale du Canada, Section 1*, 2nd ser., 7 (1900–1901): 8–21; Régis Roy and Gérard Malchelosse, *Le Régiment de Carignan* (Montréal: Ducharme, 1925); "Tableau des contrats d'engagements pour le Canada passés en l'étude notariale de Tourouvre, 1641–1651," *Cahiers percherons*, 26 (1967): 45; "Tableau des Percherons émigrés au Canada au XVIIe siècle," ibid., 20 (1963): 40–52; Cyprien Tanguay, *Dictionnaire généalogique des familles canadiennes*, 7 vols. (Montréal, 1871–1890); "Témoignages de liberté au mariage," *Rapport de l'archiviste de la province de Québec*, 32–33 (1951–1953): 5–159; testimonials of freedom at marriage, ASQ: ms. 430; Philippe Tiersonnier, "Un Bourbonnais au Canada," *Nova Francia*, 1 (1925–1926): 178–179; "Deux Bourbonnais au Canada," *Nova Francia*, 2 (1926–1927), 39–45, 90–91, 139–140; J. Toussaint, "Prêtres coutançais chassés par la Révolution et émigrés au Canada," *Semaine religieuse de Coutances et Avranches*, 29–30 (1967): 429–454; Marcel Trudel, *Catalogue des immigrants, 1632–1662* (Montréal: Hurtubise HMH, 1983); *La Population du Canada en 1663* (Montréal: Fides, 1973); Emile Vaillancourt, *La Conquête du Canada par les Normands* (Paris: Dumont, 1933); vital records of Ile Royale and Ile Saint-Jean, AC: G1, vols. 408–409. The dictionaries of Tanguay and Jetté (unlike the other works listed) were not used exhaustively: Tanguay because of its many errors, and Jetté because it appeared after much of my data had been collected. I did, however, check all of my data entries against the corresponding entries in Jetté.

43. All of the Acadians in the sample, with the exception of those identified from the parish registers of Ile Saint-Jean by Gabriel Debien, were identified through French exit documents.

44. Fournier, *Dictionnaire biographique*, p. 10.

45. See Abel Châtelain, "Problèmes de méthodes: les migrations de population," *Revue économique*, 14 (1963): 2. Definitions of the second sort tend to appeal, understandably, to genealogists; see, for example, Archange Godbout, "Nos hérédités provinciales françaises," *Archives du folklore*, 1 (1946): 35.

46. Fournier, *Dictionnaire biographique*, p. 10. Fournier also compiled an appendix of 545 Bretons (as against 1,040) who failed to meet this criterion. Most of them were sailors and fishermen whose seasonal migrations left traces in Québec's hospital registers.

47. Trudel, *Catalogue des immigrants*, p. 9.

48. Robert, *Nos origines en France*, p. 9.

49. Abel Châtelain, *Les Migrants temporaires en France de 1800 à 1914: histoire économique et sociale des migrants temporaires des campagnes françaises au XIXe*

et au début du XXe siècle (Villeneuve-d'Ascq: Publications de l'Université de Lille, 1976), 1:54–55.

50. Châtelain, "Problèmes de méthodes," p. 3.

51. The Acadian genealogist Roger Comeau has noted that between 1632 and 1666 seasonal fishing contracts accounted for more indentures than any other type of contract registered in La Rochelle; see Roger Comeau, "Origine des Acadiens," *Mémoires de la Société généalogique canadienne-française,* 6 (1955): 253.

52. Studying the indentured servants of La Rochelle, Father Archange Godbout estimated that of the 147 who signed contracts between 1642 and 1644, "15 percent settled and 10 percent left descendants." Between 1655 and 1657, even fewer opted permanently for Canada; of 42 engagés, "12 percent settled and 8 percent left descendants." "In subsequent years," according to Godbout, "the acclimatization seemed better. Nevertheless, we would not be far from the truth in asserting that overall two-thirds and even three-quarters of the recruits made only a more or less extended stay in the colony" (Godbout, "Familles venues de La Rochelle," p. 125).

53. Corvisier, *L'Armée française,* 1:156.

54. André Corvisier, "Service militaire et mobilité géographique au XVIIIe siècle," *Annales de démographie historique* (1970): 198. See also André Sévigny, "'S'habituer dans le pays': facteurs d'établissement du soldat en Nouvelle-France à la fin du Grand Siècle," *Les Cahiers des Dix,* 46 (1991): 61–86.

55. On the generally good relations between Canadian habitants and French soldiers, see Eccles, "Military Establishment," p. 19.

56. As with the engagés, it is difficult to determine precisely what proportion of the soldiers returned to France. More than 500 of the 1,200 soldiers from the Regiment of Carignan availed themselves of the royal encouragements to settlement. For the Regiments of Montcalm, more than 4,000 strong, estimates vary between 500 and 2,000. About the *troupes de la Marine,* it is known only that at least one-fifth of the 3,000 to 3,500 soldiers dispatched to Canada between 1683 and 1715 married there, as did two-thirds of the Breton recruits identified by Fournier. See Fournier, *Dictionnaire biographique,* p. 28; Yves Landry, "La Population militaire au Canada pendant la Guerre de Sept Ans," *Annales de démographie historique* (1978): 351; Jean Leclerc, "Les Soldats mariés," *Mémoires de la Société généalogique canadienne-française,* 12 (1961): 42; and André Sévigny, "Le Soldat des troupes de la Marine (1683–1715)," *Les Cahiers des Dix,* 44 (1989): 55–56.

57. The frequently unstable political situation in Canada introduced further distortions into these already fluid migratory patterns. The population exchanges associated with the Grand Dérangement—which uprooted 10,000 Acadians and destroyed their communities—and with the conquests of Louisbourg and Québec made doubly sure that seasonal, temporary, and permanent currents would not be rigidly separate but, rather, flow into one another.

58. On Louis Hébert, see Jean Toussaint, "Coutançais, pionniers du Canada,"

Semaine religieuse de Coutances et Avranches, 19 (1967): 292, and Raymond Douville and Jacques-Donat Casanova, *La Vie quotidienne en Nouvelle-France: le Canada, de Champlain à Montcalm* (Montréal: Hachette, 1982), p. 16. Hébert's curiosity about Canada had no doubt been raised by his cousin Jean de Biencourt de Poutrincourt, the seigneur of Port-Royal.

59. The complex relationship, exemplified by Louis Hébert, between the different types of migration as classified by time provides added perspective on a debate that has preoccupied historians of French migrations. The chief proponent of employing this type of classification, Abel Châtelain, posited an essentially linear relationship between temporary (primarily seasonal) migrations, which he claimed were "characteristic of the precapitalist era," and definitive migrations, which he thought gradually supplanted them during the nineteenth century. Michel Vovelle disagreed, arguing that this chronological schema led Châtelain to "underestimate two elements of importance: on the one hand, loss of social position . . . in terms of individual failure or collectively experienced crisis; and, on the other hand, assimilation." Both of these factors, Vovelle asserted, were capable of disrupting the periodicity of seasonal migrations and, furthermore, did so frequently under the Ancien Régime. The pattern of French emigration to Canada lends support to Vovelle's position, since important streams of seasonal, plurinannual, and definitive migrants both coexisted and fed into one another. See Abel Châtelain and Michel Vovelle, "Tribune à propos d'un article de démographie historique: migrants temporaires et population flottante à Marseille sous la Révolution française," *Annales de démographie historique* (1970): 426–437.

60. Boleda, "Les Migrations (1608–1760)," in PRDH, *Rapport*, p. 115.

61. R. Cole Harris, ed., *Historical Atlas of Canada: From the Beginning to 1800* (Toronto: University of Toronto Press, 1987), pl. 45.

62. See Michel Fleury and Louis Henry, *Nouveau manuel de dépouillement et d'exploitation de l'état civil ancien* (Paris: INED, 1976).

63. Marcel Trudel, *Histoire de la Nouvelle-France,* 3, pt. 2: 71.

64. Both the lower and upper ranges proposed for the soldiers were probably uncharacteristic. The 30 percent return rate of the Breton *troupes de la Marine* derived exclusively from Canadian sources, which were more likely to record settlers than they were short-term migrants. As for the 85 percent of returnees in the Regiments of Montcalm, this figure was probably inflated by the political instability accompanying the loss of the Battle of the Plains of Abraham and the subsequent ceding of Québec to the British.

65. Louise Dechêne, *Habitants et marchands de Montréal au XVIIᵉ siècle* (Paris: Plon, 1974), pp. 75–76. It should be noted that the estimates of return rates are both better and more numerous for the seventeenth than for the eighteenth century—a paradoxical situation given that record keeping undoubtedly improved over the course of the French Regime. It seems that the relative scarcity of the earlier documents has led historians to examine them more completely.

66. It is, however, possible that the return rate decreased in the course of the French Regime, as the colony offered more amenities to its inhabitants.

67. Marcel Fournier has compiled a preliminary database of first-generation Acadian immigrants based on the genealogical research of Bona Arsenault and Father Archange Godbout. It contains information on 1,773 persons, 292 of them women. He notes, however, that "applying the same norms as for New France, it is estimated that some 7,000 French people came to Acadia during the French Regime," fewer than 600 of whom settled there permanently. See Marcel Fournier, *Les Européens au Canada des origines à 1765* (Montréal: Editions du fleuve, 1989), pp. 28–30.

68. The very low sex ratio of Acadia-bound emigrants, although it must be interpreted with caution owing to the deficiencies in the archives, appears consistent with the prevalence of temporary movements within the Acadian migratory stream. Many of these movements were so abbreviated as to resemble traditional seasonal migrations, a category that, in France, tended to include men only. French women did participate heavily in the various harvest migrations, but these were distinguished by their purely agricultural nature and essentially local itineraries. In contrast, seasonal migrations involving artisanal or commercial capacities, and conceivably ranging over long distances, were almost exclusively the province of men. See Châtelain, *Les Migrants temporaires*, 1: 58–61.

69. Father Archange Godbout and Louise Dechêne estimated return rates for indentured servants whose minimum term of service was three years, and Yves Landry's figures applied to soldiers whose time commitment was generally even longer. Marcel Trudel, while accepting chronological limitations, dealt with the immigrant population more comprehensively, but he defined immigrants as those who spent at least one winter in the colony. Given that French ships generally arrived in Canada during the summer and departed in the fall, this definition ensured that only pluriannual migrants would be counted; since the average crossing took about two months, spending the winter in Canada involved an absence from France of not less than a year and a half.

70. The sample did, however, include the crew members of the *Saint-André* of La Rochelle, which set sail for Canada in 1659, and the *Léopard*, which made the voyage from Normandy in 1756.

71. Boleda's initial estimate for observable migration was in the range of 20,000 to 25,000; however, he raised it to 30,000 to compensate for the years in which it was lower than his calculation of net migration.

72. Charbonneau et al., *The First French Canadians*, p. 51.

1. Regional Origins

1. The title of this chapter, as of this book, was inspired by Eugen Weber's well-known study *Peasants into Frenchmen: The Modernization of Rural France*,

1870–1914 (Stanford: Stanford University Press, 1976). Weber argued in that work that in the late nineteenth century, peasants from the most primitive and isolated parts of France gradually became acculturated and transformed into full-fledged citizens of the modern French state. Peasants, as defined by Weber, were country folk whose labors served primarily to assure their own subsistence. By modernization he meant "the passage from relative isolation and a relatively closed economy to union with the outside world" through communications and a money economy (p. xii). This process had implications not only for material conditions but for mentalities and political awareness as well.

2. Le marquis de Chennevières, "Perche et Canada," *Bulletin de la Société historique et archéologique de l'Orne*, 9 (1890): 429–431.

3. Ibid., pp. 435–437.

4. Louis Hamilton, *Ursprung der Französischen Bevölkerung Canadas: Ein Beitrag zur Siedlungsgeschichte Nord-Amerikas* (Berlin: Neufeld and Henius, 1920).

5. Ibid., pp. 5–6.

6. Ibid., p. 34.

7. Cyprien Tanguay, *Dictionnaire généalogique des familles canadiennes*, 7 vols. (Montréal, 1871–1890); Stanislas Lortie and Adjutor Rivard, "De l'origine des Canadiens-Français," in *L'Origine et le parler des Canadiens-Français: études sur l'émigration française au Canada de 1608 à 1700, sur l'état actuel du parler franco-canadien, son histoire et les causes de son évolution* (Paris: Champion, 1903), p. 11; Edouard-Zotique Massicotte, "D'où vinrent les colons au XVIII⁰ siècle?" *Bulletin des recherches historiques*, 43 (1937): 54–55; Archange Godbout, "Nos hérédités provinciales françaises," *Archives du folklore*, 1 (1946): 32–34.

8. Table 1.1 data are from R. Cole Harris, ed., *Historical Atlas of Canada: From the Beginning to 1800* (Toronto: University of Toronto Press, 1987), pl. 45.

9. A different pattern of recruitment is suggested by the only study to date of French emigration to Acadia, which lists provincial contributions in the following order: Brittany, 19.6%; Normandy, 15.9%; Gascony, 8.3%; Saintonge, 5.3%; Poitou, 4.8%; Guyenne, 4.3%; Ile-de-France, 4.1%; and so on. See Marcel Fournier, *Les Européens au Canada des origines à 1765* (Montréal: Editions du fleuve, 1989), pp. 28–29.

10. There is reason to believe that the emigrants of unknown origin were distributed more or less randomly among the various emigrant-producing regions because the majority of lacunae concern the Canadian documents. The only major exception to this rule consists of the passenger lists from Bordeaux, in which geographical information was not recorded and emigrants from the Southwest undoubtedly predominated. Together, these lists provided 662 names, or 4.2 percent of the emigrant sample.

11. These figures are roughly, but not exactly, comparable to those of the PRDH. Because emigration was tabulated for my study at the departmental as well as the provincial level, it was possible to distinguish between Upper Languedoc (Southwest) and Lower Languedoc (Midi). Had the regional distributions been

calculated on the basis of province alone, an additional 159 emigrants would have been obtained for the Southwest at the expense of the Midi.

12. This grouping excludes emigrants from Savoy, the Comtat, and Monaco, who were included with their French counterparts.

13. According to the PRDH, the founding immigrants of Québec included about 350 non-French settlers, not all of whom would have arrived from French ports of embarkation. Marcel Fournier estimates that about 1,200 non-French Europeans were present in Canada at some point during the French Regime. Of the three-quarters whose presence has left archival traces, 406 were from the British Isles, 281 from Germanic states, 121 from the Mediterranean, 100 from the Low Countries, Luxembourg, or Sweden, and 11 from Slavic areas. See Fournier, *Les Européens au Canada*, pp. 42, 73.

14. A comparison of my data with that of the PRDH also reveals that my sample underestimates founding immigration, although not unilaterally. An integral reading of the *Répertoire* would have provided a minimum of 401 additional emigrants from six provinces: Poitou (130), Ile-de-France (111), Saintonge (95), Angoumois (38), Marche (24), and Artois (3). Although these numbers may appear substantial, they actually have little effect on the overall distribution of emigration.

15. François Furet and Jacques Ozouf, *Lire et écrire: l'alphabétisation des Français de Calvin à Jules Ferry* (Paris: Editions de minuit, 1977), p. 37; Paul Hohenberg, "Migrations et fluctuations démographiques dans la France rurale, 1836–1901," *Annales: économies, sociétés, civilisations*, 29 (1974): 490. Others have proposed an alternative imaginary divider running between Belfort and Pau; see, for example, Olwen H. Hufton, *The Poor of Eighteenth-Century France, 1750–1789* (Oxford: Clarendon, 1974), pp. 70–71.

16. It should nonetheless be noted, in deference to proponents of the division between the North and the South, that with the albeit important exception of Charente-Maritime, the departments that contributed most heavily to Canada's immigrant population were all located to the north of the Loire.

17. Jean-Pierre Poussou, *Bordeaux et le Sud-Ouest au XVIIIᵉ siècle: croissance économique et attraction urbaine* (Paris: Touzot, 1983), p. 73.

18. "Saint-Michel, Diocese of Sens," for example, might refer to either a village or an urban parish within the diocese.

19. Categorizing the communities involved distinguishing between rural, semirural, and urban communities. The rural community, or village, as defined by the *Dictionnaire de l'Académie française* (1694), was a "number of rural houses for lodging peasants, which ordinarily are not enclosed by any common fence." The semirural bourg is usually described as a "large village that presents certain aspects of the town [*la ville*] *(Larousse)*. Urban communities are more difficult to classify because there was no clear-cut definition of a "ville" in the seventeenth and eighteenth centuries. Seventeenth-century authors viewed the town first and foremost as a legal entity, a privileged space set off from the surround-

ing countryside by its fortifications. In the eighteenth century, in response to urban growth, a new and more functional concept began to emerge. Trévoux observed in his *Dictionnaire* (1732) "that it is rather difficult to give a good definition of the word town [*ville*] because [common] usage has always retained the name of bourg or village for certain places that are nevertheles veritable towns: for example, The Hague in Holland, except for a surrounding wall, has everything that makes up a town" (cited in François de Dainville, "Un dénombrement inédit au XVIIIe siècle: l'enquête du contrôleur général Orry 1745," *Population*, 7 [1952]: 52). For the purpose of my study, I supplemented a list of "villes de juridiction" drawn from major eighteenth-century dictionaries with a list of bourgs having 500 or more hearths. (A population of 500 hearths corresponds roughly to the current threshold of 2,000 inhabitants used by the French government to define a "ville.") I also considered cities of more than 10,000 inhabitants separately, since they were the major agglomerations of the time.

20. A list drawn up at the instances of Calonne in 1787 to facilitate the election of the provincial estates contains the names of only 78 important towns, with a collective population of just under 2 million, excluding Paris, which had another .5 million residents. Since the eighteenth century was one of generalized, if not always spectacular, urban growth, even these modest numbers represent an upper bound in evaluating the importance of major cities during the period of French emigration to Canada.

21. Its population was a mere 600 in 1754, up from 273 in 1739.

22. On Acadian demography, see Gisa Hynes, "Some Aspects of the Demography of Port Royal, 1650–1755," *Acadiensis*, 3 (1973): 3–17.

23. Even the military recruits examined by André Corvisier, an atypical group in that they often enlisted in major cities, remained predominantly rural into the second half of the eighteenth century. Sixty to 70 percent of the recruits declared a rural place of origin, so taking into account previous migrations to urban areas, "the inhabitants of cities represented perhaps 40 percent of the total forces." See André Corvisier, *L'Armée française de la fin du XVIIe siècle au ministère de Choiseul: le soldat* (Paris: Presses universitaires de France, 1964) 1:392–393, and "Service militaire et mobilité géographique au XVIIIe siècle," *Annales de démographie historique* (1970): 200.

24. Studies of overseas departures from Bordeaux by Lucile Bourrachot, Charles Huetz de Lemps, and Jean-Pierre Poussou indicate that this pattern was not unique to Canada but, rather, characterized certain emigrants for the Antilles as well, notably those from the Charentes, Bordelais, the Pyrénées, Upper Languedoc, and the East.

25. Foreign emigrants also came from urban areas to an extraordinary degree, 95.5%. Of the 112 foreigners whose communal origins could be determined (out of 171), only 7 were from the countryside.

26. Poussou, *Bordeaux*, p. 92.

27. In keeping with this pattern, the level of dispersion among foreign emigrants was also very high, with the 7 rural and 105 urban emigrants stemming, respectively, from 7 villages or bourgs and 51 towns or cities.

28. Charles Huetz de Lemps, *Géographie du commerce de Bordeaux à la fin du règne de Louis XIV* (Paris: Mouton, 1975), p. 516.

29. The departments of Seine-et-Oise and Seine-et-Marne exhibited a similar pattern. City dwellers and country folk participated in the movement in roughly equal numbers, and the degree of dispersion remained quite high, resulting in an overall average of two emigrants per community. The inhabitants of the hinterland of Paris, like those from the environs of Bordeaux, clearly possessed a familiarity with urban migratory options greater than could be expected in rural areas less exclusively focused on production for expanding urban markets.

30. See, for example, Mohammed El Kordi, *Bayeux aux XVIIe et XVIIIe siècles: contribution à l'histoire urbaine de la France* (Paris: Mouton, 1970), and Michel Riou, "L'Immigration dans les villes du Vivarais au XIXe siècle," in *Vivarais et Languedoc, Actes du 44e Congrès de la Fédération historique du Languedoc méditerranéen et du Roussillon, Privas, 1971* (Montpellier, 1972).

31. A good case can be made for extending this argument into other domains as well. Charles Higounet, while including the region in his *Histoire de l'Aquitaine*, nonetheless described it as "a rural civilization of the Nordic type," adducing as evidence the "grouped habitat, definite boundaries, and banal forests and pastures." Likewise, Agricol Perdiguier noted, in the early nineteenth century, that upon visiting Rochefort and La Rochelle he culturally entered another France: "Once I had gone past Médoc and arrived in Saintonge, in the countryside as in the towns, I no longer heard patois but French." See Charles Higounet, ed., *Histoire de l'Aquitaine* (Toulouse: Privat, 1971), p. 309, and Agricol Perdiguier, *Mémoires d'un compagnon* (1854; Paris: Librarie du compagnonnage, 1964), p. 174.

32. Alsace cut a somewhat better figure than its immediate neighbors because of the government-sponsored emigration to Canada of Alsatian families in 1758. See letter of the minister to Bégon, 2 May 1758, AC: B, vol. 108, p. 72 [147], and passenger lists, Dunkerque, AC: F5B, vol. 44.

33. Thus, several generations of Lorraine-born middle-class daughters with poor dowry prospects made their way to Hungary, Poland, and Russia as schoolteachers and governesses. See Abel Châtelain, *Les Migrants temporaires en France de 1800 à 1914* (Villeneuve-d'Ascq: Publications de l'Université de Lille, 1976). 1: 58.

34. The regional sex ratios run as follows: Center-west, .30; Northwest, .12; Paris region, .80; East, .14; Loire, .30; North, .25; Southwest, .02; South, .03; Massif central, .01; Alps, .02; and foreign countries, .10. The figure for the Northwest is somewhat low because of the inclusion of male seasonal emigrants from Brittany. Those for the Center-west and Southwest would have declined also had I been able to include such emigrants more consistently. The low ratio in

the East stems in part from the prevailing directions of migration streams. Women and many men tended to move farther east, while a number of men found themselves in the West as a result of the vagaries of military service.

35. In his study of Bordeaux and the Southwest, Jean-Pierre Poussou also noted the weakness of women's demographic response to increased economic opportunity. According to his calculations, immigration to Bordeaux between 1740 and 1780 favored men over women by seven to one. Poussou's observations nonetheless suggest that while traditional gender roles created a time lag between the possibility and the fact of female mobility, they were unable to obstruct it completely. Indeed, female immigration to Bordeaux increased proportionally faster than did male immigration during the period, enabling Poussou to write of a "very slight feminization of immigration" (Poussou, *Bordeaux*, p. 110).

36. Châtelain, *Les Migrants temporaires*, 2: map 11.

37. In the Northwest also, the presence of traditions of temporary migration affected the sex ratio among emigrants to Canada. Mayenne and Manche, where such movements were customary, accounted for a higher proportion of male than of female emigrants. Similarly, Brittany sent a disproportionate number of men owing to its role as the first maritime province of France.

38. The following departments did not count any women among their emigrants to Canada: Ain, Allier, Ardèche, Ariège, Aude, Cantal, Corrèze, Creuse, Dordogne, Gard, Hautes-Alpes, Haute-Garonne, Haute-Loire, Hautes-Pyrénées, Haute-Savoie, Haute-Saône, Indre, Landes, Loire, Lozère, Meuse, Tarn, Tarn-et-Garonne, and Vaucluse.

39. The proportion of unmarried women within Ancien Régime cities could reach 50 percent.

2. A Geography of Modernity: The Northwest

1. On this diversity as it relates broadly to family history, see Gérard Bouchard, "La Reproduction familiale en terroirs neufs: comparaison sur des données québécoises et françaises," *Annales: économies, sociétés, civilisations,* 48 (1993): 421–451.

2. For my maps, see Leslie Choquette, "French Emigration to Canada in the Seventeenth and Eighteenth Centuries" (Ph.D. diss., Harvard University, 1988).

3. A specific community of origin could be attributed to 333 of the 346 emigrants from Loire-Atlantique. Throughout this chapter and the next, departmental totals include only those emigrants whose precise community of origin was known.

4. Emile Gabory, "La Marine et le commerce de Nantes au XVIIᵉ siècle et au commencement du XVIIIᵉ (1661–1715)," *Annales de Bretagne,* 17 (1901): 276. See also minister to Luzançay, 9 January 1709, AC: B, vol. 30, p. 239.

5. Hocquart to Ricouart, 17 October 1740, AC: C11A, vol. 73, p. 162.

6. Jean Bérenger and Jean Meyer, *La Bretagne de la fin du XVIIe siècle: d'après le mémoire de Béchameil de Nointel,* Institut armoricain de recherches économiques et humaines, Textes et documents, no. 1 (Paris: Klincksieck, 1976), p. 133.

7. Jean Delumeau, ed., *Histoire de la Bretagne* (Toulouse: Privat, 1969), p. 256; Bérenger and Meyer, *Bretagne de la fin du XVIIe siècle,* p. 48.

8. Bérenger and Meyer, *Bretagne de la fin du XVIIe siècle,* pp. 147–153.

9. Ibid., p. 140.

10. Delumeau, *Histoire de la Bretagne,* pp. 289–290.

11. Rouen, another a major locus of Atlantic capitalism, maintained important ties with Canada during the seventeenth and eighteenth centuries. In the 1650s and 1660s, some of the colony's commercial affairs, including labor recruitment, were transacted through Rouen's merchants. After 1664 these traders relinquished the better part of their Canadian interests to the Compagnie des Indes occidentales, but they continued to engage in two activities in which their competence was recognized: cod fishing and the servant trade. Rouen's relations with Canada persisted at a fairly low level through the early years of the eighteenth century, only to revive for both commerce and recruitment around 1730. Between 1730 and 1740, the Rouennais Dugard was single-handedly responsible for 10 to 20 percent of Canada's annual import trade, and in 1759, another Rouennais, Lemoine, was the principal purveyor of the king's storehouses in Canada. See Paul Butel, *Les Négociants bordelais: l'Europe et les Iles au XVIIIe siècle* (Paris: Aubier-Montaigne, 1974), p. 250; Pierre Dardel, *Navires et marchandises dans les ports de Rouen et du Havre au XVIIIe siècle* (Paris: SEVPEN, 1963); Lionel Laberge, *Rouen et le commerce du Canada de 1650 à 1670* (L'Ange-Gardien: Bois-Lotinville, 1972); and Dale Miquelon, *Dugard of Rouen: French Trade to Canada and the West Indies, 1729–1770* (Montréal: McGill–Queen's University Press, 1978).

12. Furthermore, the mapping of emigration from the pays d'Auge is incomplete because of the substantial number of emigrants (48 to be exact) who gave their origin only as the Diocese of Lisieux.

13. Faubourgs are included in the Le Havre and Dieppe totals.

14. Jean-Pierre Bardet, *Rouen aux XVIIe et XVIIIe siècles: les mutations d'un espace social* (Paris: SEDES, 1983), 1:139.

15. J. Levainville, *Rouen: étude d'une agglomération urbaine* (Paris: Armand Colin, 1913), p. 332.

16. Jean-Pierre Bardet has defined four major zones within the city, primarily in order to take population as well as economic differences into account. I have simplified these divisions into three.

17. Marie-Claude Gricourt, "Etude d'histoire démographique, sociale, et religieuse de cinq paroisses de l'archidiaconé du Petit-Caux: Douderville, Canville, Bac-

queville, Brachy, et Luneray du milieu du XVIIe siècle à la fin de l'Ancien Régime," in *A travers la Normandie des XVIIe et XVIIIe siècles*, Cahier des Annales de Normandie, no. 3 (Caen, 1963).

18. Bardet, *Rouen*, 1: 106–107.

19. Some historians have pointed to inheritance patterns to explain Cauchois emigration because the pays de Caux, alone among France's regions of customary law, possessed a system of impartible inheritance. Yet this legal arrangement appears less significant as a factor of emigration than a commercialized rural economy with Atlantic outlets for its produce, for many regions of partible inheritance, including the nearby pays d'Auge, also sent many emigrants to the colonies. See Patrice Higonnet, "French," in *Harvard Encyclopedia of American Ethnic Groups*, ed. Stephan Thernstrom (Cambridge: Harvard University Press, Belknap Press, 1980), p. 381.

20. As early as the sixteenth century, the pays d'Auge had begun to cater to large urban markets—an orientation that grew increasingly dominant in the following two centuries. See Michel Bouvet, "Troarn: étude de démographie historique (XVIIe–XVIIIe siècles)," in *A travers la Normandie des XVIIe et XVIIIe siècles*, Cahier des Annales de Normandie, no. 6 (Caen, 1968), p. 34.

21. The *négociants* of Honfleur, while they maintained regular ties with Canada, did so more as agents of the Rouennais than as shippers in their own right; see Dardel, *Navires et marchandises*, p. 304.

22. The principal road through the pays d'Auge ran east-west from Caen to Pont-Audemer and thence to Rouen, yet between the Dives and the Touques, emigration touched coastal parishes only and left the north-south orientation of the movement unaltered.

23. Michel Le Pesant, "Un centre d'émigration en Normandie sous l'Ancien Régime: le cas de Percy," *Bibliothèque de l'Ecole des chartes*, 130 (1972): 171.

24. The tax lists provide an eloquent, if indirect, commentary on the extent of commercialized agriculture in the pays d'Auge and around Bernay. In 1688 the Election of Lisieux, with 34,832 taxpayers, paid 128,500 livres in tailles, the highest per capita rate in the Generality of Alençon. The Election of Bernay paid the lowest rate by a factor of more than ten, 12,000 livres from 35,779 taxpayers. See Pommereuil, "Extrait du mémoire de la généralité d'Alençon" (1698), BN: Nouvelles acquisitions françaises, vol. 2031, p. 19.

25. In the second half of the seventeenth century, an intendant wrote of the Vexin: "This region surpasses the Caux by the fertility of the countryside; the acre of good land commonly rents for sixteen to eighteen livres per year, and in the Caux, it scarcely passes ten livres" (Edmond Esmonin, ed., *Voysin de la Noiraye: Mémoire sur la généralité de Rouen* [*1665*], *analyse et extraits, avec notes et appendices* [Paris: Hachette, 1913], p. 2).

26. Richard Cobb, *Paris and Its Provinces, 1792–1802* (London: Oxford University Press, 1975), p. 94.

27. La Bourdonnaye, "Extrait du mémoire de la généralité de Rouen" (1697), BN: Nouvelles acquisitions françaises, vol. 2035, p. 352.

28. Charles de la Morandière, *Histoire de Granville* (Bayeux: Colas, 1947).

29. Since, at the turn of the eighteenth century, Granville had about 4,000 inhabitants versus Saint-Malo's 20,000, the per capita contribution of the two ports was comparable if seasonal migrants are excluded; see ibid., p. 96, and Jean Delumeau, "Démographie d'un port français sous l'Ancien Régime: Saint-Malo (1651–1750)," *Le XVIIe siècle: revue*, 86 (1970): 19.

30. This primacy of geography over administration was not always so pronounced. The Upper Norman coastline varied little geographically, but east of Dieppe, emigration declined in proportion to proximity with the border of Picardy. Given the history of Breton particularism, it is curious that the Normandy-Picardy line proved a greater barrier to emigration than that between Normandy and Brittany. The key distinction here is again economic; whereas Granville and Saint-Malo participated in the same commercial circuits, the channel ports of Picardy exhibited a northern-European orientation that contrasted with the colonial focus of Dieppe.

31. Foucault, "Extrait du mémoire de la généralité de Caen" (1698), BN: Nouvelles acquisitions françaises, vol. 2032.

32. Ibid., pp. 157, 160.

33. Le Pesant, "Un centre d'émigration en Normandie," pp. 200, 210.

34. The populations of the individual cities were Rouen, 60,000; Dieppe, 20,000; Honfleur, 5,000; Le Havre, 17,000; Saint-Malo, 20,000; Granville, 4,000.

35. Jean-Pierre Poussou, *Bordeaux et le Sud-Ouest au XVIIIe siècle: croissance économique et attraction urbaine* (Paris: Touzot, 1983), p. 364.

36. Georges Friedmann, ed., *Villes et campagnes: civilisation urbaine et civilisation rurale en France* (Paris: Armand Colin, 1953), p. 24.

37. On Percheron industry, see François Dornic, "L'Industrie dans le Perche: textile et fer," *Cahiers percherons*, 18 (1963): 3–34. On horse raising, see Georges Chabot, *Géographie régionale de la France* (Paris: Masson, 1966), pp. 335–336. This agricultural specialization did not come into its own until the second half of the eighteenth century, when emigration to Canada had ceased, but it was preceded by a long period of active trading in land which did involve prospective (and actual) emigrants to Canada.

38. Léon Gérin, "Les Emigrants du Perche," *Bulletin des recherches historiques*, 5 (1926), 294.

39. Pommereuil, "Extrait du mémoire," pp. 27, 31, 41.

40. Hubert Charbonneau, *Tourouvre-au-Perche aux XVIIe et XVIIIe siècles: étude de démographie historique*, Institut national d'études démographiques, Travaux et documents, no. 55 (Paris: PUF, 1970), p. 6.

41. Cited in Louis Duval, *Etat de la généralité d'Alençon sous Louis XIV* (Alençon, 1890), pp. 217–218.

42. Françoise Montagne, "Du nouveau sur Robert Giffard, promoteur de l'émigration percheronne," *Cahiers percherons*, 25 (1967): 29.

43. Archange Godbout, "Nos hérédités provinciales français," *Archives du folklore*, 1 (1946): 36.

44. Robert Giffard was the sieur of Le Moncel, a village in the parish of Autheuil, and his cousin Jean Viron was the temporal seigneur of the parish of Normandel. Giffard's main associates, the brothers Juchereau, were the sieurs of Le Maure and of Le Châtelet (parish of L'Hôme). See Montagne, "Robert Giffard," p. 27.

45. François Lebrun, *Les Hommes et la mort en Anjou aux XVIIe et XVIIIe siècles* (Paris: Flammarion, 1975), p. 19.

46. Like the adjacent parts of Lower and Upper Poitou, southwestern Anjou came under the jurisdiction of the Diocese of La Rochelle from the time of its founding in 1648.

47. Lebrun, *Anjou*, pp. 21–23.

48. On the economy of the Mauges, see ibid., pp. 17–19, 79, and Louis Pérouas, *Le Diocèse de La Rochelle de 1648 à 1724: sociologie et pastorale* (Paris: SEVPEN, 1964), pp. 122–125.

49. Seventeen emigrants out of 281 from Anjou.

50. On the Loire Valley, see Lebrun, *Anjou*, pp. 27–34, 106, and Abbé Expilly, *Dictionnaire géographique, historique, et politique des Gaules et de la France* (Paris, 1762), 2:683.

51. Lebrun, *Anjou*, p. 26.

52. Migration and misery are equated in much of the writing on early modern France, whether general or specific; see, for example, Olwen H. Hufton, *The Poor of Eighteenth-Century France, 1750–1789* (Oxford: Clarendon, 1974), pp. 69–106. Historians are now beginning to challenge this widely accepted interpretation, however, using arguments based on a solid knowledge of regional economic history; see, most notably, Poussou, *Bordeaux*.

53. Lebrun, *Anjou*, pp. 24–25.

54. Marie-Claire Daveluy, *La Société Notre-Dame de Montréal, 1639–1663: son histoire, ses membres, son manifeste* (Montréal: Fides, 1965).

55. Mondoux, "Les Hommes de Montréal," p. 76.

56. Paul Bois, *Paysans de l'Ouest* (Paris: Flammarion, 1971), p. 269.

57. André Bouton, *Le Maine: histoire économique et sociale, XVIIe et XVIIIe siècles* (Le Mans: n.p., 1973), p. 358.

58. Bois, *Paysans*, pp. 152 (quoted), 187–188, 198–199, 229; Bouton, *Maine*, pp. 476–480.

59. Bois, *Paysans*, pp. 148, 224, 270.

60. Ibid., pp. 259, 270.

61. Ibid., p. 259.

62. Albert Soboul, *Problèmes paysannes de la Révolution (1789–1848): études d'histoire révolutionnaire* (Paris: Maspero, 1976), p. 20.

3. *A Geography of Modernity: Non-Northwesterners and Women*

1. Louis Papy, *L'Homme et la mer sur la côte Atlantique de la Loire à la Gironde: étude de géographie humaine* (Bordeaux: Delmas, 1941), p. 309.

2. Jean-Pierre Poussou, *Bordeaux et le Sud-Ouest au XVIIIe siècle: croissance économique et attraction urbaine* (Paris: Touzot, 1983), p. 338.

3. Louis Pérouas, *Le Diocèse de La Rochelle de 1648 à 1724: sociologie et pastorale* (Paris: SEVPEN, 1964), p. 178.

4. Georges Musset, ed., "Michel Bégon, mémoire sur la généralité de La Rochelle, 1699," *Archives historiques de la Saintonge et de l'Aunis*, 2 (1875): 28.

5. John Clark, *La Rochelle and the Atlantic Economy during the Eighteenth Century* (Baltimore: Johns Hopkins University Press, 1981), p. 41.

6. Marc Delafosse, "La Rochelle et le Canada au XVIIe siècle," *Revue d'histoire de l'Amérique française*, 4 (1950–1951): 140.

7. Clark, *La Rochelle*, p. 5.

8. For a more detailed description of La Rochelle's social geography, see Pérouas, *Diocèse de La Rochelle*, pp. 91–95.

9. As in Rouen, however, residents of La Rochelle's *robin* neighborhood were the least likely to emigrate. In the city center, the commercial quarter outproduced the *robin* parish 65 to 50.

10. Pérouas, *Diocèse de La Rochelle*, p. 207.

11. Jean-Pierre Poussou, "Les Relations villes-campagnes en Aquitaine dans la deuxième moitié du XVIIIe siècle: quelques réflexions méthodologiques sur les attractions urbaines et les échanges migratoires," in *Démographie urbaine: XVe aux XXe siècles*, Centre d'histoire économique et sociale de la région lyonnaise, no. 8 (Lyon, 1977), p. 203.

12. Pérouas, *Diocèse de La Rochelle*, p. 81.

13. Arcère, *Histoire de la ville de La Rochelle et du pays d'Aulnis, composée d'après les auteurs et les titres originaux et enrichis de divers plans* (La Rochelle, 1756), p. 462.

14. Pérouas, *Diocèse de La Rochelle*, p. 104.

15. The economy of the *banlieue* was considered exemplary by local physiocrats, one of whom wrote: "I hear it said that the vineyards occupy too much land, which means that in years of full harvest, abundance is almost as ruinous as scarcity, the low sale price not exceeding the price of cultivation and the purchase of barrels . . . We are presented here with an economic problem to resolve: is it expedient to diminish the area planted in vines? It is important to the state that the land be cultivated, but the choice of crop applicable to this land must be left to the proprietor. It is not possible for him to err in his choice; interest is his rule. We must let him follow his inclination, test, hazard, venture. What is his goal when he plants, sows, or clears the land? It is to subsist, to gain . . . [I]nterest orders, he obeys." Arcère, *Histoire*, pp. 461–462.

16. There were 26 emigrants in all, or 2.4% of the Aunisian total.

17. Pérouas, *Diocèse de La Rochelle*, p. 103.

18. Edmond-René Labande, ed., *Histoire du Poitou, du Limousin, et des pays char-entais (Vendée, Aunis, Saintonge, Angoumois)* (Toulouse: Privat, 1976), p. 250.

19. Pérouas, *Diocèse de La Rochelle*, p. 109.

20. J[oseph] Dehergne, *Le Bas Poitou à la veille de la Révolution*, Commission d'histoire économique et sociale de la Révolution française, Mémoires et documents, no. 16 (Paris, 1963), pp. 37–38.

21. This figure includes 16 heads of families who had established themselves in La Rochelle before leaving for Canada.

22. Papy, *L'Homme et la mer*, p. 108.

23. Poussou, *Bordeaux*, p. 234.

24. Pérouas, *Diocèse de La Rochelle*, p. 220.

25. Poussou's study of persons deceased in the Hospital of Rochefort at the end of the eighteenth century revealed that only twenty of the current departments failed to send someone (and he systematically excluded the soldiers from consideration); see Poussou, *Bordeaux*, p. 361.

26. They averaged 150 to 200 inhabitants per square kilometer, which exceeded those of the *banlieue* of La Rochelle by a factor of four; see Pérouas, *Diocèse de La Rochelle*, pp. 104–106.

27. Musset, "Michel Bégon," p. 54.

28. I use the plural here to indicate that this discussion refers not only to the *bocage* proper, but also to the *gâtine*, the even poorer hedge region to the east.

29. In 1679, for example, a merchant from La Châtaigneraie signed a contract in La Rochelle with two Canadian merchants for the marketing of his fabrics in Québec. See Delafosse, "La Rochelle," p. 482.

30. Dehergne, *Bas Poitou*, p. 60.

31. Paul Raveau, *L'Agriculture et les classes paysannes dans le Haut-Poitou au XVIe siècle* (Paris: Rivière, 1926), p. 302.

32. Dehergne, *Bas Poitou*, p. 44.

33. See, for example, Pérouas, *Diocèse de La Rochelle*, p. 119, and Louis Merle, *La Métairie et l'évolution agraire de la gâtine poitevine de la fin du Moyen Age à la Révolution* (Paris: SEVPEN, 1958), pp. 91–92.

34. Dehergne, *Bas Poitou*, p. 41.

35. In 1744, for example, the *subdélégué* (intendant's subordinate) of the Election of Niort wrote that after a hiatus, the royal navy was once again purchasing flours processed in La Mothe-Saint-Héray for the West Indies; see Léo De-saivre, "L'Election de Niort au XVIIIe siècle: notes et documents," *Mémoires de la Société de statistique, sciences, lettres, et arts du département des Deux-Sèvres*, 3d ser., 3 (1886): 303.

36. Ties between Niort and Canada were particularly close, since the city counted the processing of Canadian furs among its industrial specialties.

37. Since the election was disproportionately long in an east-west direction, only the fifty-four parishes located within twenty-five kilometers of the city were

considered. Together they contained 6,873 households, of which 1,406, or 21%, were households of *métayers*. It is interesting that in the eighteen sending communities from this area, this proportion declined to 17%, while in the remaining thirty-six parishes it rose to 23%. Although a corresponding figure for the zone of Fontenay was not available, it appears from Cassini's map (which depicts individual *métairies*) that *métayers* were somewhat commoner in the Niortais; see César-François Cassini de Thury, *Carte générale de la France*, 2 vols. (Paris, 1744–1787).

38. Desaivre, "l'Election de Niort," p. 86.

39. In 1777 a physician of La Rochelle wrote of the farmers of the region: "Even the peasant, who is in proximity to the towns, also strays from the frugal life" (cited in Poussou, *Bordeaux*, p. 338).

40. Pérouas, *Diocèse de La Rochelle*, pp. 99–100, 114. The two parishes of Fontenay that were dominated by weaving, Saint-Nicolas and Saint-Jean, like their analogues in Rouen, did not produce emigrants for Canada. Most of the departures involved the Parish of Notre-Dame, where merchants, magistrates, and nobles set a more elegant social tone.

41. Ibid., p. 114.

42. Labande, *Histoire du Poitou*, pp. 292–293; Gabriel Debien, *En Haut-Poitou: défricheurs au travail, XVe aux XVIIIe siècles* (Paris: Armand Colin, 1952), p. 46.

43. Of 69 emigrants from Poitiers whose parish origins could be determined, 17 (24.6%) came from wealthy, central parishes characterized by commercial or administrative activity; 38 (55.1%) from largely artisanal parishes intermediate between wealth and poverty; and 14 (20.3%) from poor, peripheral parishes. See Natalie Rogues, "Emigration poitevine et charentaise au Canada aux XVIIe et XVIIIe siècles" (mémoire de DEA, Université de Paris IV [Sorbonne], 1991), pp. 75–76, and Robert Favreau, *Histoire de Poitiers* (Toulouse: Privat, 1985), pp. 191–193.

44. On Angles, Châtellerault, Chauvigny, and Civray, respectively, see Abbé Expilly, *Dictionnaire géographique, historique, et politique des Gaules et de la France*, 1:185; 2: 286, 307, 354.

45. Poussou, *Bordeaux*, pp. 20, 29.

46. Christian Huetz de Lemps, "Les Engagés du Bazadais au XVIIIe siècle," *Cahiers du Bazadais*, 10 (1966): 29. See also Christian Huetz de Lemps, "Indentured Servants Bound for the French Antilles in the Seventeenth and Eighteenth Centuries," in *"To Make America": European Emigration in the Early Modern Period*, ed. Ida Altman and James Horn (Berkeley: University of California Press, 1991).

47. Poussou, *Bordeaux*, pp. 245–246.

48. Bordeaux's commercial ties with Canada were slow to develop. Completely episodic in the late seventeenth century, they began to constitute a secondary but regular aspect of the city's commercial network during the Regency. The takeoff occurred in the 1740s, when Bordeaux's most important shipper, Abra-

ham Gradis, received the contract "to supply the king's warehouses in Québec with victuals, munitions, and diverse commodities." This contract, which eventually interested three more of the city's great shippers (Desclaux, O'Quin, and Jaure) made Bordeaux into Canada's foremost trading partner. Between 1753 and 1755, ninety ships set sail from Bordeaux for Québec, as opposed to only nineteen from La Rochelle. See Charles Huetz de Lemps, *Géographie du commerce de Bordeaux à la fin du règne de Louis XIV* (Paris: Mouton, 1975); François-Georges Pariset, ed., *Bordeaux au XVIIIe siècle* (Bordeaux: Fédération historique du Sud-Ouest, 1968); and Paul Butel, *Les Négociants bordelais: L'Europe et les Iles au XIIIe siècle* (Paris: Aubier-Montaigne, 1974), p. 36 (quoted above).

49. It is easy to make too much of these geographical distinctions, for aside from the small numbers involved, Bordeaux's neighborhoods were not yet, in the eighteenth century, "perfectly homogeneous ensembles, exempt from social and professional contrasts" (Robert Boutruche, ed., *Bordeaux de 1453 à 1715* [Bordeaux: Fédération historique du Sud-Ouest, 1966]: 511). The waterfront housed merchants and naval officers as well as maritime artisans and common sailors, while residents of the center-city could be artisans, shopkeepers, or the truly wealthy. Saint-Seurin and Sainte-Eulalie were more homogenous; as *sauvetés* exempted from guild regulations, they regrouped many of the city's secondary activities, the building trades in particular. Journeymen tended to congregate there, so it is possible that the faubourgs played a greater role in emigration than the documents show. On the social geography of Bordeaux, see Poussou, *Bordeaux*, p. 33, and Jean Cavignac, "Le Compagnonnage dans les luttes ouvrières au XVIIIe siècle: l'exemple de Bordeaux," *Bibliothèque de l'Ecole des chartes*, 126 (1968): 381, 387.

50. Poussou, *Bordeaux*, p. 245.

51. On the economy of Bazadais, see Jean-Pierre Poussou, "La Population du Bazadais au XVIIIe siècle," *Cahiers du Bazadais*, 8–9 (1965): 23.

52. Charles Higounet, ed., *Histoire de l'Aquitaine* (Toulouse: Privat, 1971), pp. 307–310; Boutruche, *Bordeaux de 1453 à 1715*, p. 104.

53. Pierre Deffontaines, *Les Hommes et leurs travaux dans les pays de la Moyenne Garonne (Agenais, Bas-Quercy)* (Lille: SILIC, 1932), pp. 129, 295, 305, 413–414.

54. Georges Frêche, *Toulouse et la région Midi-Pyrénées au siècle des lumières vers 1670–1789* (Paris: Cujas, 1974), p. 779.

55. Deffontaines, *Hommes et leurs travaux*, pp. 278–280.

56. On Rouergue, see Roger Beteille, *Les Aveyronnais: essai géographique sur l'espace humain* (Poitiers: L'Union, 1974), pp. 17, 26, 31.

57. Higounet, *Histoire de l'Aquitaine*, pp. 302–304; Jean-Pierre Poussou, "Les Migrations dans la Haute-Lande aux XVIIIe et XIXe siècles," in *La Grande Lande: histoire naturelle, et géographie historique, Actes du Colloque de Sabres, 1981*, ed. A. Klingebiel and J.-B. Marquette (Paris: Editions du CNRS, Parc naturel régional des Landes de Gascogne, 1985).

58. Like Saint-Malo, Bayonne owed its initial prosperity to its codfishing fleet, but its shippers later diversified into the colonial trade per se. Bayonne always retained privileged relations with Canada's maritime regions, owing to the predominance of Basques in the fishing industry. In the 1730s the city's merchants expanded their operations into Québec, and up until the conquest Bayonne's ships regularly shuttled between the home port and the Saint Lawrence Valley. In the three years prior to the outbreak of war, when Bordeaux dispatched ninety ships to Québec versus La Rochelle's nineteen, Bayonne managed a distant but respectable third place with nine.

59. Bayonne's population in the eighteenth century held steady at about 20,000, with a further 6,000 for Saint-Esprit. Bordeaux's had already reached 60,000 by 1747.

60. Poussou, *Bordeaux*, p. 263.

61. Ibid., p. 228.

62. Spanish historians have coined the term *comprador* to describe an economy in which a dynamic coastline is juxtaposed with a stagnant and isolated interior.

63. André Corvisier, *L'Armée française de la fin du XVIIe siècle au ministère de Choiseul: le soldat* (Paris: PUF, 1964), 1: 415–418.

64. Fernand Braudel and Ernest Labrousse, eds., *Histoire économique et sociale de la France* (Paris: PUF, 1970–1982), 2: 141–142.

65. Georges Lefebvre, *Les Paysans du Nord pendant la Révolution française* (Bari: Laterza, 1959), pp. 34–35.

66. Braudel and Labrousse, *Histoire économique et sociale*, 2:107.

67. An additional 50 emigrants, while of unknown parish origin, came from very distinct places in the city—namely, the Hôpital général (28), Fort-l'Evêque (13), the Grand-Châtelet (4), Saint-Martin Prison (3), and the Bastille (2).

68. Daniel Roche, *Le Peuple de Paris: essai sur la culture populaire au XVIIIe siècle* (Paris: Aubier-Montaigne, 1981), p. 35.

69. Daniel Roche has written of parishes such as Saint-Germain-l'Auxerrois and Saint-Jacques-de-la-Boucherie that "the city dwellers—shopkeepers, artisans, merchants, bourgeois, indeed, people of higher levels . . . rubbed shoulders there with misery, indigence, violence: more than 20% of the inhabitants would receive aid in these old parishes at the end of the 1780s; the map of places where violence erupted in the third quarter of the century coincides with a zone stretching from the Louvre to Saint-Gervais" (Jacques-Louis Ménétra, *Journal de ma vie: Jacques-Louis Ménétra, compagnon vitrier au 18e siècle*, ed. Daniel Roche [Paris: Montalba, 1982], pp. 356–357).

70. Cited in Roche, *Peuple de Paris*, p. 16.

71. Ibid., p. 35.

72. Louis-Sébastien Mercier, *Le Tableau de Paris*, ed. Jeffry Kaplow (Paris: Maspero, 1979), p. 75.

73. Cited in Jeffry Kaplow, *The Names of Kings: The Parisian Laboring Poor in the Eighteenth Century* (New York: Basic Books, 1972), p. 10 (his translation).

74. M. G. Darboy, *Statistique religieuse du diocèse de Paris* (Paris, 1856), pp. 264–265.
75. In addition, some emigrants mentioned churches that had never been associated with parishes: Saint-Honoré, Sainte-Geneviève, Saint-Victor, and, of course, Notre-Dame.
76. Darboy, *Statistique religieuse du diocèse de Paris,* p. 264.
77. In this regard, it is significant that regimes concerned with political participation divided Paris into smaller units than those concerned with police power alone. The sixty districts and forty-eight sections succeeded the twenty *quartiers* of the Ancien Régime, only to give way in turn to the twelve arrondissements.
78. Six emigrants mentioned Saint-Honoré, but it is unclear whether they meant the faubourg or the street.
79. It is surprising that there were not more Alsatians among the emigrants, given the importance of the Alsatian exodus to the thirteen colonies in the eighteenth century. Religion was perhaps a significant factor, as undoubtedly was the region's proximity to the Rhine, which made Rotterdam far more accessible than French Atlantic ports. In an interesting letter written in 1740 Governor Beauharnais of Québec informed his French superiors of the arrival in Canada of two "Lorrainers . . . who told me that they had been to Rotterdam to seek to embark for Canada, and that instead of having been brought there as they had been promised, they had been led to New England (to Philadelphia). These two men say that they were among thirteen to fourteen families; they demand justice and to be brought back here because the difference in religion is thoroughly repugnant to them" (Beauharnais to the minister, 29 October 1740, AC: CIIA, vol. 74, p. 112). See also Jean-Pierre Kintz, "La Mobilité humaine en Alsace: essai de présentation statistique, XIVe–XVIIIe siècles," *Annales de démographie historique* (1970): 180.
80. Northern and eastern emigration forsook roads and rivers only in the mining and metallurgical districts of Burgundy, Champagne, and Franche-Comté. The presence of these otherwise remote areas in the sample was due as I discuss later to eighteenth-century recruiting for the iron foundry in Trois-Rivières.
81. Françoise Mournand, "Les Allobroges au Canada," *Revue des questions historiques,* 60 (1934): 105.
82. Expilly, *Dictionnaire,* 4:617.
83. Familial emigration and mechanisms of recruitment are examined further in subsequent chapters.
84. Oddly, these origins were better known for women than for all emigrants: 84% as opposed to 60%. Women's origins were also better known in La Rochelle.
85. Expilly, *Dictionnaire,* 5:216.
86. The provinces of Ile-de-France, Champagne, Picardy, and Orléanais together accounted for 34% of the women but only 14% of all emigrants.
87. In Rouen itself female emigration did not differ markedly from emigration as a whole. Women's origins were again better known (88% as opposed to 68%)

and again showed a slightly more popular emphasis. The poverty zone furnished 47% (up from 42%), while the commercial and aristocratic zones declined two and three points, respectively, to 42% and 11%.

4. An Urban Society

1. Mario Boleda, for example, restricted himself to estimating broad "categories" of emigrants, such as soldiers, women, and indentured servants; see Mario Boleda, "Les Migrations au Canada sous le régime français," doctoral diss., Université de Montréal, 1983, pp. 87–113.

2. See, for example, David Galenson, "Middling People or Common Sort? The Social Origins of Some Early Americans Reexamined, with a Rebuttal by Mildred Campbell," *William and Mary Quarterly*, 35 (1978): 499–540.

3. André Corvisier's description of military administrators could be applied to Ancien Régime bureaucrats in general: "Their conception of the social hierarchy took little account of institutional facts. The terms *sharecropper, journeyman, apprentice* . . . were practically absent. Those of *bourgeois, master artisan* . . . were no longer attached to the Ancien Régime status of people or work . . . [The administrators] had a singularly modern conception of eighteenth-century society . . . Rights of bourgeoisie, corporations were making way for notability and capacity. The idea of caste, of social orders was disappearing, that of class was being born" (André Corvisier, *L'Armée française de la fin du XVIIe siècle au ministère de Choiseul: le soldat* [Paris: PUF, 1964], 1:459).

4. See Fernand Braudel and Ernest Labrousse, eds., *Histoire économique et sociale de la France* (Paris: Presses universitaires de France, 1970–1982), 2: 114–115.

5. Ibid., p. 607.

6. Had I assumed, contrary to common sense, that all of the emigrants of unknown class and provenance were peasants, the figure still would not have reached 40%; in the highly unlikely event that all unclassifed emigrants, rural or urban, belonged to this category, it would account for just 61% of the men and women in the sample.

7. Braudel and Labrousse, *Histoire économique et sociale*, 2:607. Unlike the nobility, the bourgeoisie grew substantially in the course of the eighteenth century, perhaps doubling its proportional share of the French population between 1700 and the Revolution.

8. He did, however, hesitate to qualify all master artisans and shopkeepers as bourgeois. See ibid., pp. 606–607.

9. See François-Georges Pariset, ed., *Bordeaux au XVIIIe siècle* (Bordeaux: Fédération historique du Sud-Ouest, 1968), p. 360.

10. Braudel and Labrousse, *Histoire économique et sociale*, 2: 658–659.

11. Furthermore, by entertaining the possibility that artisans, like nobles and bourgeois, generally appear as such in the documents, and by classifying all of the urban or probable urban emigrants as laborers, I obtain a total of 6,346, or

40% of the emigrants. This extreme scenario is improbable, but the numerical superiority of artisans over laborers may be somewhat exaggerated in my table.

12. Pariset, *Bordeaux*, p. 360.

13. Paul Bois, "Structure socio-professionnelle du Mans à la fin du XVIIIᵉ siècle: problèmes de méthode et résultats," in *Actes du 87ᵉ Congrès national des sociétés savantes*, Poitiers, 1962, Section d'histoire moderne et contemporaine (Paris: CTHS, 1963), p. 705.

14. Michel Bouvet, "Troarn: étude de démographie historique (XVIIᵉ–XVIIIᵉ siècles), in *A travers la Normandie des XVIIᵉ et XVIIIᵉ siècles*, Cahier des Annales de Normandie, no. 6 (Caen, 1968), p. 46.

15. Pierre Goubert, *L'Ancien Régime: la société* (Paris: Armand Colin, 1969), p. 138.

16. Marcel Trudel, *Histoire de la Nouvelle-France* (Montréal: Fides, 1963–1983), 3, pt. 1: 132–135.

17. Distributing the 223 unknowns among peasants, laborers, and artisans, I obtain the following estimates for La Rochelle's emigrant population: nobles, 1.5%; bourgeois, 17.5%; peasants, 12.5%; laborers, 15.3%; and artisans, 53.2%.

18. The estimated figures for Paris are as follows: nobles, 8.6%; bourgeois, 20.1%; peasants, 4.3%; laborers, 8.6%; and artisans, 58.5%. These estimates may again exaggerate the proportion of artisans at the expense of laborers, but there is qualitative evidence to suggest that the Parisian laboring poor, or at least the males among them, did not willingly participate in the colonial enterprise. In 1720, 1750, and 1769, riots broke out in the city in response to police arrests of vagabonds and beggars for shipment to the colonies. The arrestees were mostly males between the ages of thirteen and twenty-five, either apprentices or unskilled workers. The rioters, "representative of all sections of the laboring poor," included apprentices, journeymen, street merchants, shoeshine boys, water carriers, coal heavers, militia men, and beggars. At least one of the deportees, Charles Durand, ended up in Canada, where he was executed for theft at the age of sixteen, three years after his arrival. Another Parisian emigrant of humble circumstances, René Antoine Lemoine of Saint-Jean-en-Grève, insisted during his theft trial that he had come to Canada of "of his own free will," but as the son of a footman, he had perhaps been exposed to wider than average horizons. See Arlette Farge and Jacques Revel, *Logiques de la foule: l'affaire des enlèvements d'enfants, Paris 1750* (Paris: Hachette, 1988); Jeffry Kaplow, *The Names of Kings: The Parisian Laboring Poor in the Eighteenth Century* (New York: Basic Books, 1972), pp. 24–26; trial of Charles Durand, Conseil supérieur of Louisbourg (1724), AC: G2, vol. 178, pp. 371–456; and trial of René Antoine Lemoine *dit* Saint-Amant, Conseil supérieur of Louisbourg (1740), ibid., vol. 186, pp. 323–331.

19. Michel Mollat, ed., *Histoire de Rouen* (Toulouse: Privat, 1979), p. 246.

20. This figure was unusually high owing to the familial emigration of the Le Gardeurs and Le Poutrels.

21. The figures from Rouen, La Rochelle, and Paris showed a smaller percentage

of noblewomen across the board, together with a larger percentage of bourgeoises, for a comparable share of elite emigrants overall.

22. The departure of a sexually mixed group of emigrants for Cayenne provoked
a riot in Le Havre in 1652, and a similar incident occurred outside of La
Rochelle seven years later. See Gabriel Debien, "Les Femmes des premiers
colons aux Antilles (1635–1680)," *Notes d'histoire coloniale*, 24 (1952): 9–10, and
François Dollier de Casson, *Histoire de Montréal*, ed. Marcel Trudel and Marie
Baboyant (Montréal: Hurtubise HMH, 1992), pp. 201–202.

23. The appearance of soldiers in the Canadian documents was clearly aleatory,
but there is no reason to suppose that it was also arbitrary. While stopping
short of an exact correlation between the documentation and definitive emigration, the likelihood of an appearance certainly increased with the length of a
soldier's stay and his degree of engagement in colonial life. The size of the
soldier sample, 25%, thus serves as a rough indicator of the rate of military
settlement (and such an indicator is sorely needed). Military emigration as a
means of peopling Canada may have been effective, but it was not necessarily
efficient.

24. Of the 68 *fils de famille* deported to Québec between 1722 and 1749, only 10
could not be identified. The gaps in the sample thus concern common prisoners
almost exclusively.

25. The remaining 13 women in this category could not be classified by marital
status.

26. It should be stressed that while nuclear families involved only one emigrant in
twelve, the choice was not simply between emigration within a family unit and
emigration as an isolated individual. Rather, a huge middle ground existed,
and "single" emigrants could be linked to one another through ties of kinship
or friendship. Family connections were particularly important among "founding immigrants," and may have played a crucial role in differentiating them
from the far more numerous birds of passage. See Yves Beauregard, Serge
Goudreau, Andrée Héroux, Michele Jean, Rénald Lessard, Johanne Noel, Lucie
Paquet, and Alain Laberge, "Famille, parenté, et colonisation en Nouvelle-
France," *Revue d'histoire de l'Amérique française*, 39 (1986): 391–405; André
Guillemette and Jacques Légaré, "The Influence of Kinship on Seventeenth-
Century Immigration to Canada," *Continuity and Change*, 4 (1989): 79–102;
Jacques Mathieu, "Mobilité et sédentarité: stratégies familiales en Nouvelle-
France," *Recherches sociographiques*, 28 (1987): 211–227; and Jacques Mathieu
and Lina Gouger, "Transferts de population," *Annales de Bretagne et des pays
de l'Ouest*, 95 (1988): 337–345.

27. Louis Pelletier with PRDH, *Le Clergé en Nouvelle-France: étude démographique
et répertoire biographique* (Montréal: PUM, 1993), p. 44. This estimate omits
Acadian religious but includes temporary migrants provided that they spent at
least one winter in Québec. Fully half of these clerics eventually returned to
France.

28. Two of these women were not counted as religious by the PRDH because they made their professions after emigrating to Canada.

29. "Témoignages de liberté au mariage," *Rapport de l'archiviste de la province de Québec*, 32–33 (1951–1953): 127.

30. Michel Sarrazin took such a degree in 1677, eight years before emigrating as a surgeon for the *troupes de la Marine*. The sample included 5 other emigrants who qualified themselves as "médecins."

31. On midwives, see Hélène Laforce, *Histoire de la sage-femme dans la région de Québec* (Québec: Institut québécois de recherche sur la culture, 1985).

32. Only 8 emigrants mentioned such by-occupations: 5 shoemakers, a clog maker, a tailor, and a weaver.

33. The social standing of indentured servants was surely varied as well, but it was nearly impossible to discern. The one-tenth with identifiable family backgrounds included 1 noble, 19 bourgeois, 19 peasants, 7 laborers, and 30 artisans, but little can be said of the other nine-tenths.

34. They included 6 surgeons, 4 merchants, 2 *écrivains* (public writers), 1 son of an artisan, and 1 son of a laborer.

35. It was possible to ascertain the social class of one soldier or *bas-officier* in six.

36. See the statistical appendixes in Corvisier, *L'Armée française*, vol. 2. Several of his more numerous categories have been conflated here, and the sons of professional soldiers have been omitted from the calculations.

37. Nine-tenths of military emigrants did not state an occupation.

38. Corvisier, *L'Armée française*, 1:471.

39. My findings are comparable to those of André Sévigny, who examined the occupations of 266 Canadian *troupes de la Marine* from the period 1683 to 1715. In his sample, the same sectors of activity produced the following percentages: textiles/clothing, 22.9%; medicine, 6.4%; building/woodworking, 19.5%; metal trades, 4.9%; agriculture, 5.6%; commerce, 2.3%; administration/law, 11.7%; food trades, 9.8%; transport/services, 11.3%; luxury artisans, 1.1%; maritime trades, 3.4%; diverse artisans, 1.1%. Likewise, a list of the most common tradesmen among soldiers in Louisbourg and Québec in the 1750s included cobblers, tailors, bakers, *laboureurs*, weavers, masons, and wig makers, leading Gilles Proulx to conclude that "housing, food, clothing, and health appear as the principal interests of the people of the time." See André Sévigny, "Le Soldat des troupes de la Marine (1683–1715)," *Les Cahiers des Dix*, 44 (1989): 69–71, and Gilles Proulx, "Soldat à Québec, 1748–1759," *Revue d'histoire de l'Amérique française*, 32 (1979): 556–557.

40. Gérard Malchelosse, "Les Fils de famille en Nouvelle-France, 1720–1750," *Les Cahiers des Dix*, 11 (1946): 310.

41. The manner of their recruitment, however, is described in the administrative correspondence between France and Canada, and is considered in Part Two.

42. The total number of masters in the maritime trades was 11. The rubric *compagnon* did not appear at all, but there were 6 *garçons* or *aides*.

43. René Mémain, *Le Matériel de la marine de guerre sous Louis XIV: Rochefort, arsenal modèle de Colbert (1666–1690)* (Paris: Hachette, 1936), p. 549. For a general discussion of conditions of work in the industry, see ibid., pp. 534–559.

44. "Témoignages de liberté," pp. 55–56, 84–85 (p. 84 quoted).

45. René Jetté, *Dictionnaire généalogique des familles du Québec des origines à 1730* (Montréal: PUM, 1983), p. 1046.

46. ANQ: Godbout Collection, vol. 3. Sevestre's shop was located in the courtyard of the Palais-Royal.

47. Marcel Trudel has shown that 56.8% of immigrants could sign their names in the mid-seventeenth century. The figure for men alone was 62.2%. See Trudel, *Histoire de la Nouvelle-France*, 3, pt. 2: 49.

48. Ibid., p. 499. Charles Sevestre did, however, entitle himself "marchand-libraire" while visiting Paris in 1650.

49. Furthermore, one migrant soldier, Jean-Louis Tenant from the village of Evauge in Bugey, described himself as a "maître laboureur."

50. Braudel and Labrousse, *Histoire économique et sociale*, 2:114. Journeymen gardeners still existed in the nineteenth century, as shown by this recollection of Agricol Perdiguier: "I had made the acquaintance, in the Gard, of a very distinguished young gardener from the department of Basses-Alpes. He was doing his Tour de France, insofar as the nature of his estate permitted him" (Agricol Perdiguier, *Mémoires d'un compagnon* [1854; Paris: Librairie du compagnonnage, 1964], p. 99).

51. Corvisier, *L'Armée française*, 1:442.

52. Separate consideration of Canada's *troupes de la Marine* and *troupes de terre* shows that the latter conformed more closely to the standard French pattern, with strong roots in the East, Southeast, and North of France. The *troupes de la Marine*, however, were strongly identified with the West, the Southwest, and Brittany. See Sévigny, "Le Soldat," pp. 51–54.

53. Corvisier, *L'Armée française*, 1: 186, 402, 406.

54. Corvisier has stressed the popularity of fairs and markets, labor and otherwise, among recruiters. If the role played by the Foire Saint-Germain in military recruitment for the colonies remains conjectural, its more sinister place in the annals of civilian recruitment is less obscure. The alleged vagabonds and "gens sans aveux" arrested in the spring of 1750 for deportation to Louisiana included one Nicolas-François Savoye, aged twelve, "apprentice to sieur Savoye, his father, café owner, rue de Bussy," seized by police at the Foire Saint-Germain. By paying blackmail, the Savoyes succeeded in retrieving their son. Cited in Commandant Hertaut, "Les Enlèvements d'enfants à Paris en 1720 et en 1750," *Revue historique*, 139 (1922): 214; see also Corvisier, *L'Armée française*, 1:186.

55. André Sévigny has noted that colonial recruiters often began their "manhunt" in and around Paris, since that is where they ordinarily received their commissions to recruit. Subsequently, some of them headed straight for Rochefort, via

Orléanais and Touraine, while others took a more circuitous route to Saintonge through Normandy, Maine, and Anjou. See Sévigny, "Le Soldat," p. 55.

56. Provincial origin was known for 329 deportees, or 56.8% of the total.

57. Olwen H. Hufton, *The Poor of Eighteenth-Century France, 1750–1789* (Oxford: Clarendon, 1974), pp. 285–296.

58. As I discuss in Part Two, the large number of women and children from Perche was the direct result of recruitment policies that favored familial emigration. The same is true of Alsace, where the government sponsored the emigration of families displaced by the Seven Years' War in 1758.

59. Owing to an accident of recruitment, Burgundy also produced single and married women emigrants. The Burgundian women who did not arrive as *filles à marier* tended to do so as companions of carefully recruited men such as the metalworkers of the iron foundry in Trois-Rivières.

60. Charles Huetz de Lemps, *Géographie du commerce de Bordeaux à la fin du règne de Louis XIV* (Paris: Mouton, 1975), p. 579, map 34.

61. "Témoignages de liberté," p. 49.

62. For a map of metallurgical production under the Ancien Régime, see Braudel and Labrousse, *Histoire économique et sociale*, 2:234.

63. Jean-Pierre Poussou, "Les Mouvements migratoires en France et à partir de la France de la fin du XVe siècle au début du XIXe siècle: approches pour une synthèse," *Annales de démographie historique* (1970): 15.

64. Emigration to Canada differed, in this regard, from emigration to the much more popular thirteen colonies. There was, however, at least one example of British colonization that relied heavily on military settlement: Northern Ireland, where soldiers from the Elizabethan army were recruited by officers to settle their Ulster estates. See Nicholas Canny, "Migration and Opportunity: Britain, Ireland, and the New World," *Irish Economic and Social History*, 12 (1985): 27–28.

5. Religious Diversity

1. See J. F. Bosher, *The Canada Merchants, 1713–1763* (Oxford: Oxford University Press, 1987), pp. 43, 119, 161; Bernard Cottret, *The Huguenots in England: Immigration and Settlement, c. 1550–1700* (Cambridge: Cambridge University Press, 1991), p. 265; and Patrice Higonnet, "French," in *Harvard Encyclopedia of American Ethnic Groups*, ed. Stephan Thernstrom (Cambridge: Harvard University Press, Belknap Press, 1980), p. 383–385.

2. Cited in Marcel Trudel, *Histoire de la Nouvelle-France* (Montréal: Fides, 1963–1983), 2:25.

3. Cited ibid., p. 51.

4. Cited in Marc-André Bédard, *Les Protestants en Nouvelle-France*, Cahiers d'histoire, no. 31 (Québec: Société historique de Québec, 1978), p. 20.

5. The Jesuit historian Lucien Campeau has provided an alternative reading of

the charter of the Compagnie des Cent Associés, based on the distinction between "the common and general law, which made the whole country under the authority of the king a Catholic country, and the exceptional law, which accorded liberty of conscience to the Huguenots on every territory under royal jurisdiction." According to this reading, "it is not true that New France was made off-limits to the Calvinists in 1627. It could not have been because they were free to live everywhere in French territory in conformity with their faith. When the charter of the Compagnie des Cent Associés, fundamental law of New France, prescribed the establishment of a colony of Catholics, it was simply conforming to the laws of the realm: every dependency of the French crown was by definition Catholic. Any exclusion of the Huguenots would have had to be explicit, for the Edict of Nantes would then have been abrogated on this point" (Lucien Campeau, *Monumenta Novae Franciae* [Québec: Presses de l'Université Laval, 1967–1994], 2: 100–102). Nonetheless, as Marcel Trudel has pointed out, de facto revocation is exactly what did take place, legal hairsplitting notwithstanding; see Marcel Trudel, "Le Protestantisme s'établit au Canada," *Revue de l'Université Laval,* 10 (1955): 3.

6. Cited in Campeau, *Monumenta*, 2:105.

7. The siege itself lasted from November 1627 until October 1628, but Louis XIII arrived outside the city in October 1627, and Richelieu several months before that; see Louis Canet, *L'Aunis et la Saintonge de Henri IV à la Révolution* (La Rochelle: Pijollet, 1934), pp. 24–32.

8. Campeau, *Monumenta*, 2:101.

9. Cited in Trudel, *Histoire de la Nouvelle-France,* 3, pt. 1: 318.

10. Cited in Bédard, *Protestants,* pp. 29–30.

11. Beauharnais and Hocquart to the minister, 18 September 1741, AC: C11A, vol. 75, p. 14; Dale Miquelon, *Dugard of Rouen: French Trade to Canada and the West Indies, 1729–1770* (Montréal: McGill–Queen's University Press, 1978), pp. 18, 70, 72, 142.

12. Louis Pérouas, *Le Diocèse de La Rochelle de 1648 à 1724: sociologie et pastorale* (Paris: SEVPEN, 1964), p. 136. Sailors and merchants were clearly temporary emigrants, but the status of *engagés* was more ambiguous. While technically recruited as colonists, they could not be termed habitants prior to the expiration of their contracts, "hence the possibility for Huguenot *engagés* to spend several successive winters without being incovenienced" (Trudel, *Histoire de la Nouvelle-France,* 3, pt. 2: 28–29).

13. Bédard, *Protestants,* pp. 32–35.

14. The 123 Protestants named by Bédard who were not studied here were mostly soldiers and merchants whose stays in Canada may or may not have been temporary.

15. An estimated 7% of the population of Lower Poitou was made up of Protestants in 1685; see François Baudry, *La Révocation de l'Edit de Nantes et le protestantisme en Bas-Poitou au XVIIIe siècle* (Trévoux: Jeannin, 1922), pp. 283–284.

16. Gabriel Debien, *Les Engagés protestants de Chef-Boutonne ou les difficultés de l'histoire sociale* (Poitiers: Oudin, 1956), pp. 8–9.

17. This figure includes 2 foreigners.

18. Or 78, according to Bédard, *Protestants*, p. 43.

19. Bédard's occupational sample is not directly comparable to mine, because it includes the British and Anglo-American element; however, our conclusions are not dissimilar. Among the most important categories in his table are the army, commerce, the maritime trades, and carpentry; see ibid., p. 61.

20. André Corvisier, *L'Armée française de la fin du XVIIe siècle au ministère de Choiseul: le soldat* (Paris: PUF, 1964), 1: 288–291 (p. 288 quoted).

21. Bédard cited only 16 *filles à marier* for the entire French Regime, whereas my sample included 41 women. The discrepancy is in part a matter of definition, since I counted as Protestant some women who may have converted before their departure. See Bédard, *Protestants*, pp. 54–55.

22. For example, of the roughly 300 abjurations that occurred in La Rochelle in the three years following the siege, fully 80% involved women. According to Pérouas, "the principal explanation of these conversions appears to be the jump in the birthrate, habitual in the aftermath of hecatombs, doubtless linked to the disappearance of numerous young Protestant men. Even supposing that the vital registers are not fully complete, we must admit that the movement toward conversion barely affected the Huguenot population as a whole" (Louis Pérouas, "Sur la démographie rochelaise," *Annales: économies, sociétés, civilisations,* 16 [1961]: 1133–1134). Similarly, among New England captives in New France, women were far more likely to convert to Catholicism than men; see John Demos, *The Unredeemed Captive: A Family Story from Early America* (New York: Knopf, 1994), p. 79.

23. Nelson Dawson, "Les Filles à marier envoyées en Nouvelle-France (1632–1685): une émigration protestante?" *Revue d'histoire de l'Eglise de France,* 72 (1986): 286–288. Dawson's hypothesis, while fascinating and plausible, nonetheless lacks conclusive proof.

24. Cited in Denis Vaugeois, *Les Juifs et la Nouvelle-France* (Trois-Rivières: Boréal Express, 1968), p. 52.

25. Vital records of Louisbourg, Baptisms (1752–1754), AC: G1, vols. 408–409.

26. Hocquart to the minister, 15 September 1738, AC: C11A, vol. 70, p. 129.

27. Hocquart to the minister, 27 September 1739, ibid., vol. 71, p. 134.

28. Corvisier, *L'Armée française,* 1:337. The Canadian archives contain one other case of transvestism as well, that of the Demoiselle André, whom the authorities wished to deport to France for bad conduct in 1734. Once embarked, "she found the means to escape disguised as a man"; however, "uncertain of what to do," she sought out the bishop, governor, and intendant the following day. They convinced her to return to Paris "to go join her family" (Beauharnais and Hocquart to the Minister, 28 October 1734, AC: C11A, vol. 61, p. 259). For a general study of transvestism in early modern Europe, see Rudoph Dekke and

Lotte van de Pol, *The Tradition of Female Transvestism in Early Modern Europe* (New York: St. Martin's Press, 1989).

29. AC: C11A, vol. 70, p. 129.

30. "Rapport des assemblées mensuelles, 1978–1979," *Mémoires de la Société généalogique canadienne-française*, 30 (1979): 145.

31. Benjamin Sack, *History of the Jews in Canada from the Earliest Beginnings to the Present Day* (Montréal: Canadian Jewish Congress, 1945), p. 21.

32. Testimonial of freedom at marriage, 2 June 1767, ASQ: ms. 430.

33. Raymond Douville and Jacques-Donat Casanova, *La Vie quotidienne en Nouvelle-France: le Canada, de Champlain à Montcalm* (Montréal: Hachette, 1982), p. 233.

34. Cited in Archange Godbout, "Les Emigrants de 1664," *Mémoires de la Société généalogique canadienne-francaise*, 4 (1951): 224.

35. In any case, he wrote to Laval forthwith that the king would desist from recruiting there. See René Le Tenneur, *Les Normands et les origines du Canada français* (Coutances: OCEP, 1973), p. 165.

36. Jacques Mathieu has speculated that up to a quarter of La Rochelle's emigrants may have been of Huguenot descent, but even this figure would leave a large majority of Catholics; see Jacques Mathieu, "Mobilité et sédentarité: stratégies familiales en Nouvelle-France," *Recherches sociographiques*, 28 (1987): 216.

37. Cited in Ed. de Lorière, "Quelques notes sur les émigrants manceaux et principalement fléchois au Canada pendant le XVIIe siècle," *Annales fléchoises*, 9 (1908): 24.

38. François de Nion, ed., *Un outre-mer au XVIIe siècle: voyages au Canada du baron de La Hontan* (Paris: Plon, 1900), pp. 102–103.

39. Ibid., p. 139.

40. Ibid., p. 42. This description was echoed a century later by another observer, who claimed that the traders did not leave the city "until they had expended all the money from their furs in debauchery" (cited in Robert-Lionel Séguin, *La Vie libertine en Nouvelle-France au XVIIe siècle* [Ottawa: Leméac, 1972], 1:68.

41. Nion, *Un outre-mer*, pp. 110–112; Séguin, *Vie libertine*, 1: 83, 90 (quoted).

42. Séguin, *Vie libertine*, 2: 503–505, 513, 515. The situation in Acadia was hardly more edifying. Before the deportation, the colonists built no stone churches, and there was not a single vocation for the religious life. See Naomi Griffiths, "The Golden Age: Acadian Life, 1713–1748," *Histoire sociale/Social History*, 17 (1984): 33, and Séguin, *La Vie libertine*, 1:43.

43. Réal Bates, "Les Conceptions prénuptiales dans la vallée du Saint-Laurent avant 1725," *Revue d'histoire de l'Amérique française*, 40 (1986): 253–272; Lyne Paquette and Réal Bates, "Les Naissances illégitimes sur les rives du Saint-Laurent avant 1730," ibid., 40 (1986): 239–252.

44. Her father was a merchant in the well-to-do parish of Saint-André. Her brother Jacques became a merchant in Montréal, where she joined him while still in her midteens. Both of them married there into a prominent merchant family from

Rouen. See René Jetté, *Dictionnaire généalogique des familles du Québec des origines à 1730* (Montréal: PUM, 1983), pp. 636, 1070.

45. Séguin, *Vie libertine*, 1: 79, 85, 116–139, 276–279.

46. Cited ibid., p. 138.

47. Since the performance occurred on February 15, it may have been a novel way to celebrate Mardi Gras. The pastor had, in any case, forbidden traditional celebrations with masks. See Nion, *Un outre-mer*, p. 103, and Séguin, *Vie libertine*, 1: 207–211.

48. Cited in Séguin, *Vie libertine*, 1: 209, 211.

49. Trudel, *Histoire de la Nouvelle-France*, 3, pt. 1: 308–316, 323–330.

50. W. J. Eccles, *France in America* (New York: Harper and Row, 1972), p. 71. The new royal government was also responsible for lowering the tithe from one-thirteenth to one twenty-sixth, an arrangement that persisted through the French Regime. Even this lower rate was optimistic, since there were too few priests to supervise the collection. See Cornelius Jaenen, *The Role of the Church in New France* (Toronto: McGraw-Hill Ryerson, 1976), pp. 84–89, and Louise Dechêne, *Habitants et marchands de Montréal au XVIIe siècle* (Paris: Plon, 1974), pp. 251–252.

51. Séguin, *Vie libertine*, 1:84.

52. Gustave Lanctôt, *A History of Canada from the Treaty of Utrecht to the Treaty of Paris, 1713–1763*, trans. Margaret Cameron (Cambridge: Harvard University Press, 1965), pp. 126–127.

53. There was no parish church in Louisbourg because inhabitants refused to pay the tithe. One result of this lack of religious infrastructure was an illegitimacy rate four times the Laurentian norm and a double rate of prenuptial conceptions. See A. J. B. Johnston, *Religion in Life at Louisbourg, 1713–1758* (Montréal: McGill-Queen's University Press, 1984), pp. 22, 134, 153.

54. Trial of Yacinthe Gabriel Lebon, Conseil supérieur of Louisbourg (1753–1754), AC: G2, vol. 189, pp. 148–269.

55. Reuben Gold Thwaites, ed., *The Jesuit Relations and Allied Documents: Travels and Explorations of the Jesuit Missionaries in New France, 1610–1791* (Cleveland, 1896–1901), 7:256.

56. "Les Véritables Motifs de messieurs et dames de la Société Notre-Dame de Montréal pour la conversion des sauvages de Nouvelle-France," *Mémoires de la Société historique de Montréal*, 9 (1880): 17. Although published anonymously in 1643, this tract was probably written by Abbé Jean-Jacques Olier, the founder of Saint-Sulpice.

57. Thwaites, *Jesuit Relations*, 7:260.

58. Women did not, it should be noted, increase their religious authority without cost to themselves. The years of the great *dévotes* were also those of frequent witch burnings and exorcisms. The famous *possédées* of Loudun (1631–1638) were the persecuted counterparts to the spiritual *pionnières* of Canada.

59. Thwaites, *Jesuit Relations*, 7:258.

60. Georges Goyau, *Les Origines religieuses du Canada: une épopée mystique* (Montréal: Fides, 1951), p. 140.

61. Eventually, he dropped the suit, having been inspired by the *Jesuit Relations* (and a lettre de cachet of the queen). Sister Saint-Augustin arrived in Canada in 1648. See Françoise Juchereau de Saint-Ignace, *Histoire de l'Hôtel-Dieu de Québec* (Montauban, 1751), p. 71.

62. François Dollier de Casson, *Histoire de Montréal,* ed. Marcel Trudel and Marie Baboyant (Montréal: Hurtubise HMH, 1992), pp. 201–202.

63. Thwaites, *Jesuit Relations,* 7:260.

64. Ibid., 15:282.

65. Ibid., 19:56; 20: 138, 140.

66. For a more detailed discussion of sexual politics among the missionaries of New France, see Leslie Choquette, "*Cès Amazones du Grand Dieu:* Women and Mission in Seventeenth-Century Canada," *French Historical Studies,* 17 (1992): 627–655.

6. The Age of Adventure in an Age of Expansion

1. According to André Corvisier, this term of service could be even longer in the colonies; see André Corvisier, *L'Armée française de la fin du XVIIe siècle au ministère de Choiseul: le soldat* (Paris: PUF, 1964), 2:605.

2. In 1778 Moheau described a normal French age distribution as follows: ages 1 through 10, 1/4 of the population; 11–29, 4/21; 21–30, 2/13; 31–40, 1/7; 41–50, 1/8; 51–60, 1/13; 61–70, 1/20; 71–80, 1/55; 81–90, 1/480; 91–100, 1/1600. See Moheau, *Recherches et considérations sur la population de la France* (1778; Paris: Paul Geuthner, 1912), p. 44.

3. Additional peaks did, however, appear at the ages of eighteen, twenty-two, and thirty-two.

4. Only in the province of Perche, where established families dominated emigration, did the age structure begin to approximate a normal pyramid. The ages of Percheron emigrants were distributed as follows: 0–14, 31.1%; 15–19, 10.8%; 20–24, 14.5%; 25–29, 15.4%; 30–34, 7.9%; 35–39, 5.4%; 40–44, 5.4%; 45–49, 5.0%; 50–54, 1.2%; 55–59, .8%; 60 and over, .4%.

5. Testimonials of freedom at marriage, 1766, 1767, 1770, ASQ: ms. 430.

6. The commercial sector nonetheless included a number of "clerks and interpreters" who were still in their teens. The difficulty of learning Indian languages may have induced merchants to employ unusually young assistants, in hopes that they would acquire fluency more quickly than adults.

7. David Galenson, "Middling People or Common Sort? The Social Origins of Some Early Americans Reexamined," *William and Mary Quarterly,* 35 (1978): 503–506.

8. One must be wary of drawing too many conclusions from this age differential, for it may, to some extent, reflect a bias intrinsic to the documentation. In a

colony where women were often in scarce supply, new female immigrants could be expected to marry sooner than their male counterparts. The time lag between arrival and appearance in the records could thus have been significantly smaller in the case of women. See Charbonneau et al., *Naissance d'une population* (see the introduction, n. 41, above), pp. 43–44.

9. The modal ages of artisanal and bourgeois women were, however, distinct at eighteen and twenty-one, respectively.

10. Trial of Claude Amiot, Conseil supérieur of Louisbourg (1739), AC: G2, vol. 185, pp. 425–457.

11. Robert Mandrou, "Les Français hors de France aux XVIᵉ et XVIIᵉ siècles," *Annales: économies, sociétés, civilisations*, 14 (1959): 671–672.

12. Louis Pérouas, "Sur la démographie rochelaise," *Annales: économies, sociétés, civilisations*, 16 (1961): 1139–1140.

13. The figures were, respectively, 7,358 exact dates (46.6%) and 8,431 approximate dates.

14. For the debate over the seventeenth-century crisis, see Fernand Braudel and Ernest Labrousse, eds., *Histoire économique et sociale de la France* (Paris: PUF, 1970–1982), 1, pt. 2: 903–999; 2: 325–366.

15. On the distinction between "founding" and "observed" immigration, see the introduction.

16. Mario Boleda, "Les Migrations au Canada sous le Régime français (1608–1760)," in PRDH, *Rapport de l'année 1982–1983* (Montréal, 1984), p. 128. The data from the first two periods listed in Table 6.7 were too incomplete to support demographic analysis.

17. For example, a comparison of the average rate of male immigration at marriage into Rouen over two fifty-year periods, one of "depression" (1670–1720) and one of "expansion" (1720–1770), yields the respective figures of 47% and 46.4%; the overall average for the period 1670–1789 was 47.1%. In Caen as well, the dominant characteristic of immigration seems to have been stability. See Jean-Pierre Bardet, *Rouen aux XVIIᵉ et XVIIIᵉ siècles: les mutations d'un espace social* (Paris: SEDES, 1983), 2:108, and Jean-Claude Perrot, *Genèse d'une ville moderne: Caen au XVIIIᵉ siècle* (Paris: Mouton, 1975), 1:165.

18. Braudel and Labrousse, *Histoire économique et sociale*, 1, pt. 1: 441–442.

19. Pierre Goubert, *L'Ancien Régime: la société* (Paris: Armand Colin, 1969), pp. 38–39.

20. Louise Tilly has made a persuasive case for the growing "nationalization" of grain prices during the Ancien Régime. See Louise Tilly, "The Food Riot as a Form of Political Conflict in France," *Journal of Interdisciplinary History*, 2 (1971): 23–57.

21. For graphs of the relevant *mercuriales* (market pricelists), see Micheline Baulant and Jean Meuvret, *Prix des céréales extraits de la mercuriale de Paris (1520–1698)*, 2 vols. (Paris: SEVPEN, 1960–1962), and Jacques Dupâquier, Marcel Lachiver,

and Jean Meuvret, *Mercuriales du pays de France et du Vexin français (1640–1792)* (Paris: SEVPEN, 1968).

22. Prévost to the minister, 14 October 1755, AC: C11B, vol. 35, p. 220.

23. Jean Meyer, *La Noblesse bretonne au XVIIIe siècle* (Paris: Flammarion, 1972), pp. 170–172, 365.

24. Braudel and Labrousse, *Histoire économique et sociale*, 2: 282, 295.

25. The date figured prominently on all the graphs of central-western emigration. In addition, a letter written by Talon from La Rochelle implied that the officers of the regiment were recruiting successfully around the city; see Talon to Colbert, 22 April 1665, AC: C11A, vol. 2, p. 124.

26. Dates associated with the persecution of central-western Protestants, such as the expulsion of Protestants from La Rochelle in 1661 or the revocation of the Edict of Nantes in 1685, did not stand out on the graphs with any more clarity than subsistence crises. While many Protestants fled at these times, it is not surprising that they chose more hospitable havens than Canada. I have encountered only one instance of a move to Canada impelled by religious persecution, and it was accompanied by a conversion to Catholicism. The emigrants in question were Isaac Bédard, a Protestant carpenter from La Rochelle; Marie Girard, his wife; and Jacques Bédard, his son and apprentice. Bédard was forty-five years old in 1661, when fellow Protestants were expelled from the city. Four hundred people converted, and 1,800 fled; Bédard and his family did both. He first appeared in the Canadian records on 27 June 1661, one week after the arrival of the first merchant ship from La Rochelle. On that date, he occupied a concession purchased for him by a straw man, perhaps a cautionary measure, since he settled in a seigneurie owned by the Jesuits. Jacques was confirmed as a Catholic on 5 January 1662, and that same year, his father was deemed sufficiently orthodox to receive a concession in his own right. See Pérouas, "Sur la démographie," pp. 1134–1137; Marcel Trudel, *Catalogue des immigrants, 1632–1662* (Montréal: Hurtubise HMH, 1983), p. 431; and René Jetté, *Dictionnaire généalogique des familles du Québec des origines à 1730* (Montréal: PUM, 1983), p. 72.

27. Archange Godbout, "Le Rôle du Saint-Jehan et les origines acadiennes," *Mémoires de la Société généalogique canadienne-française*, 1 (1944): 19–30.

28. Corvisier, *L'Armée française*, 1:442. With the exception of the Regiment of Carignan, however, earlier troops had belonged to the *troupes de la Marine*, which were recruited primarily in the West.

29. Virtually all the nuns, however, emigrated in the seventeenth century; see Louis Pelletier with PRDH, *Le Clergé en Nouvelle-France: étude démographique et répertoire biographique* (Montréal: PUM, 1993), p. 44.

30. Pierre Deyon, *Amiens, capitale provinciale: étude sur la société urbaine au XVIIe siècle* (Paris: Mouton, 1967), p. 494; Michel Vovelle, "Chartres et le pays chartrain: quelques aspects démographiques," in *Contributions à l'histoire*

démographique de la Révolution française, Mémoires et documents, no. 14 (Paris: Commission d'histoire économique et sociale de la Révolution française, 1962), p. 144.

31. La Dauversière did not indenture any women at La Flèche in 1653; however, 3 married women and 9 *filles à marier* embarked as passengers at Saint-Nazaire and made their way to Canada with the indentured servants. See Edouard-Zotique Massicotte, "La Recrue de 1653: liste des colons qui partirent de France pour Montréal," *Rapport de l'archiviste de la province de Québec* (1920–1921): 312.

32. The emigration of children followed the same pattern as that of married women, although it remained quite substantial until about 1670. The slower drop-off rate was probably due to the extreme youth of some of the soldiers and *filles à marier* who arrived in Canada in the 1660s.

33. Alain Cabantous, *Dix mille marins face à l'océan: les populations maritimes de Dunkerque au Havre aux XVIIe et XVIIIe siècles (vers 1660–1794), étude sociale* (Paris: Publisud, 1991), p. 108; Pierre Dardel, *Commerce, industrie, et navigation à Rouen et au Havre au XVIIIe siècle: rivalité croissante entre ces deux ports, la conjoncture* (Rouen: Société libre d'émulation de la Seine-Maritime, 1966), p. 35, and *Navires et marchandises dans les ports de Rouen et du Havre au XVIIIe siècle* (Paris: SEVPEN, 1963): 246; François-Georges Pariset, ed., *Bordeaux au XVIIIe siècle* (Bordeaux: Fédération historique du Sud-Ouest, 1968), pp. 305, 322.

34. Pierre Chaunu, "Le XVIIe siècle: problèmes de conjoncture, conjoncture globale, et conjonctures rurales françaises," in *Mélanges d'histoire économique et sociale en hommage au professeur Antony Babel* (Geneva: n.p., 1963); *Le Renversement de la tendance majeure des prix et des activités au XVIIe siècle: problèmes de fait et de méthodologie* (Milan: Guiffrè, 1962).

35. Trial of Julien André and Jean Galon, Conseil supérieur of Louisbourg (1737), AC: G2, vol. 184, pp. 407–429; lawsuit of Jean-Baptiste Lascarret vs. Michel Daccarette, Conseil supérieur of Louisbourg (1736), ibid., vol. 183, pp. 434–470.

36. A similar pattern prevailed in French emigration to Spain; see Guy Lemeunier and María Teresa Perez Picazo, "Les Français en Murcie sous l'Ancien Régime: des migrations populaires au grand commerce," in *Les Français en Espagne à l'époque moderne: XVIe–XVIIIe siècles* (Paris: Editions du CNRS, 1990), p. 129.

37. On the autonomy and particularity of demographic phenomena, see Philippe Ariès, *Histoire des populations françaises et de leurs attitudes devant la vie depuis le XVIIIe siècle* (Paris: Self, 1948), p. 548.

7. *Traditional Patterns of Mobility*

1. Jean-Pierre Poussou, "Réflexions sur l'apport démographique des études consacrées aux migrations anciennes," in *Migrations intérieures: méthodes d'observa-*

tion et d'analyse, Caen, 2–4 avril 1973, Actes du 4ᵉ Colloque national de démographie du CNRS (Paris, 1975), pp. 148–149. Poussou described, for example, how emigration "secreted" its own social structures in the case of Savoyards, Auvergnats, and Limousins.

2. Ibid., p. 150.

3. See *Annales de démographie historique* (1970) for examples drawn from different regions of France. By exogamous couples, I refer to situations in which at least one spouse was born outside the parish where the marriage took place.

4. Statistics cited in Jean-Pierre Poussou, "Les Mouvements migratoires en France et à partir de la France de la fin du XVᵉ siècle au début du XIXᵉ siècle: approches pour une synthèse," *Annales de démographie historique* (1970): 19.

5. Both of these patterns are described in Emmanuel Todd, "Mobilité géographique et cycle de vie en Artois et en Tuscane au XVIIIᵉ siècle," *Annales: économies, sociétés, civilisations*, 30 (1975): 730–742. Although Todd's example of sharecropper mobility is Italian rather than French, Louis Merle has attested to the same phenomenon in Poitou; see Louis Merle, *La Métairie et l'évolution agraire de la gâtine poitevine de la fin du Moyen-Age à la Révolution* (Paris: SEVPEN, 1958), pp. 91–92.

6. On harvest migrations, see Abel Châtelain, *Les Migrants temporaires en France de 1800 à 1914: histoire économique et sociale des migrants temporaires des campagnes françaises au XIXᵉ et au début du XXᵉ siècle* (Villeneuve-d'Ascq: Publications de l'Université de Lille, 1976), 1: 155–157.

7. Poussou, "Les Mouvements migratoires," pp. 19–21.

8. Châtelain, *Migrants temporaires*, 1:161.

9. Abel Poitrineau, *Remues d'hommes: essai sur les migrations montagnardes en France aux XVIIᵉ et XVIIIᵉ siècles* (Paris: Aubier Montaigne, 1983), pp. 116–118.

10. The regional migrations of families tended to be exceptional; in the seventeenth and eighteenth centuries, such moves resulted largely from the disruptive effects of warfare: hence the recolonization of Alsace and Franche-Comté by Savoyard and Swiss families after the Thirty Years' War, or the exodus of Alsatian families in the 1750s, around the outbreak of the Seven Years' War. Several of the Alsatian families were resettled in Canada. See Poussou, "Les Mouvements migratoires," p. 48; minister to Bégon, 2 May 1758, AC: B, vol. 108, p. 72 [147]; and passenger lists, Dunkerque, AC: F5B, vol. 44.

11. Louis Henry and Claude Lévy, "Quelques données sur la région de Paris au XVIIIᵉ siècle," *Population*, 17 (1962): 315.

12. The consequences of urban immigration were more disruptive in the nineteenth than in previous centuries, primarily because extramigratory factors altered the demographic balance in favor of the city. Birth control, by producing a "Malthusian" countryside, and modern sanitation, by producing a healthier city, altered the traditional relationship between rural overpopulation and urban demographic deficit more profoundly than did immigration itself.

13. Jean-Pierre Poussou, "Les Relations villes-campagnes en Aquitaine dans la deuxième moitié du XVIIIe siècle: quelques réflexions méthodologiques sur les attractions urbaines et les échanges migratoires," in *Démographie urbaine: XVe– XXe siècles*, Centre d'histoire économique et sociale de la région lyonnaise, no. 8 (Lyon, 1977): 190–192.

14. Louis Henry and Daniel Courgeau, "Deux analyses de l'immigration à Paris au XVIIIe siècle," *Population*, 26 (1971): 1091.

15. Poussou, "Réflexions," p. 146. Poussou has also identified a veritable "demographic basin," or zone of maximal attraction, within the city's regional sphere of influence. This basin, which, in Bordeaux, extends for roughly fifty kilometers around the city, is virtually immobile over time. Because of its size, the emigrants from this zone span the two categories of slippage and middle-distance migrants. On Bordeaux's demographic basin, see Jean-Pierre Poussou, *Bordeaux et le Sud-Ouest au XVIIIe siècle: croissance économique et attraction urbaine* (Paris: Touzot, 1983), pp. 63–101.

16. Abel Châtelain estimated that "the number of temporary migrants at the beginning of the nineteenth century was at least 200,000." The figure was probably somewhat lower in the period under consideration here, for the volume of these movements apparently increased in the second half of the eighteenth century. Of course, Châtelain's estimate applies to all temporary migrants, not simply those engaged in long-distance travel. See Châtelain, *Migrants temporaires*, 1:42, and Olwen H. Hufton, *The Poor of Eighteenth-Century France, 1750–1789* (Oxford: Clarendon, 1974), pp. 70–71.

17. Jean Meyer, *Etudes sur les villes en Europe occidentale (milieu du XVIIe siècle à la veille de la Révolution française): généralités, France* (Paris: SEDES, 1983), p. 63.

18. Louis-Sébastien Mercier, *Le Tableau de Paris*, ed. Jeffry Kaplow (Paris: Maspero, 1979) p. 144.

19. Balzac, for example, grumbled that the building boom had attracted more Limousins to Paris than remained in Limoges, while Voltaire, in a short poem cited by Mercier (ibid., p. 142), treated the Savoyard chimney sweeps more sympathetically: "Ces honnêtes enfants, / Qui de Savoie arrivent tous les ans, / Et dont la main légèrement essuie / Ces long canaux engorgés par la suie." (These honest children, / Who arrive from Savoy each year, / And whose hand lightly wipes / These long channels engorged with soot.)

20. Jean-Claude Perrot, *Genèse d'une ville moderne: Caen au XVIIIe siècle* (Paris: Mouton, 1975), 1:176.

21. Ibid., p. 522.

22. Ibid., p. 171.

23. Emile Coornaert, *Les Compagnonnages en France du Moyen Age à nos jours* (Paris: Editions ouvrières, 1966), p. 186.

24. On bachelor societies, see Natalie Zemon Davis, *Society and Culture in Early Modern France* (Stanford: Stanford University Press, 1975), pp. 97–123. Of the

many works dealing with the rites of *compagnons*, see Pierre Barret and Noël Gurgand, *Ils voyageaient la France: vie et traditions des compagnons du Tour de France au XIXe siècle* (Paris: Hachette, 1980); Abbé Douais, "Le Pseudo-baptème et les pseudo-serments des compagnons du devoir à Toulouse, en 1651," *Mémoires de l'Académie des sciences, inscriptions, et belles-lettres de Toulouse*, 9th ser., 5 (1893): 432–458; E. Martin de Saint-Léon, *Le Compagnonnage: son histoire, ses coûtumes, ses règlements et ses rites* (1901; Paris: Librairie du compagnonnage, 1977); M. J. Pradelle, "Réception des compagnons menuisiers et serruriers du devoir de liberté sous l'Ancien Régime à Toulouse," *Mémoires de l'Académie des sciences, inscriptions, et belles-lettres de Toulouse*, 13th ser., 3 (1941): 135–153; and Cynthia Truant, "Solidarity and Symbolism among Journeymen Artisans: The Case of Compagnonnage," *Comparative Studies in Society and History*, 21 (1979): 214–226.

25. Indeed, the artisan turned autobiographer Jacques-Louis Ménétra (Parisien le Bienvenu) referred to his fellow *compagnons* exclusively by their place of origin: "a Rennais," "a Lyonnais," "a Rochelais," etc.

26. Late-eighteenth-century registers drawn up to monitor the mobility of *compagnons* in Rouen show that among wig makers, "over a quarter (28.4 percent) of the measurable periods of employment were for less than a month." Among tailors, "over two-thirds of all the periods of employment lasted for no more than a month." See Michael Sonenscher, *Work and Wages: Natural Law, Politics, and the Eighteenth-Century French Trades* (Cambridge: Cambridge University Press, 1989), pp. 158, 165.

27. Of course, the self-styled "cast-off from all estates" did not take to the road with the goal of perfecting himself in a trade. Instead, he abandoned, as he put it, "my studies, my hopes, and the expectation of a nearly sure fortune, to begin the life of a true vagabond." Rousseau's adolescent voyages bore little resemblance to the structured itineraries followed by journeymen, but they did have familial precedents of a more traditional nature. His uncle, an engineer, had done military service in the Holy Roman Empire and in Hungary, while his father, a master watchmaker, had exercised his trade as far afield as Constantinople. See Jean-Jacques Rousseau, *Les Confessions* (Paris: Livre de Poche, 1972), 1: 7, 154, 184.

28. As an expression of labor militancy and popular culture, *compagnonnage* posed a threat to both lay and religious authorities, and it operated in clandestinity throughout much of its history; see Luc Benoist, *Le Compagnonnage et les métiers* (Paris: PUF, 1966), p. 9.

29. Ibid., p. 35.

30. Agricol Perdiguier, *Mémoires d'un compagnon* (1854; Paris: Librairie du compagnonnage, 1964), p. 311.

31. See note 16 above.

32. In any case, it was apparently common practice to forget these rivalries when labor relations were at stake.

33. When Rétif de la Bretonne condemned traditional forms of popular entertainment, which he did with all the fervor of his recent *embourgeoisement,* he reserved his sharpest criticism for the apprentices and journeymen who participated in them; see Nicolas Rétif de la Bretonne, *Les Nuits de Paris ou le spectateur nocturne,* ed. Jean Varloot and Michel Delon (Paris: Gallimard, 1986), pp. 111–114, 163–166.

34. Henri Hauser, *Les Compagnonnages d'arts et métiers à Dijon aux XVIIe et XVIIIe siècles* (1907; Marseille: Laffitte Reprints, 1979), pp. 12–13.

35. Jean-Pierre Bayard, *Le Compagnonnage en France* (Paris: Payot, 1977), p. 177.

36. Arras and Sedan were extensions of a Belgian circuit traveled by journeymen cloth shearers, and the cities of Lorraine lent their hospitality to Germany's errant *Zimmermänner.*

37. Bayard, *Compagnonnage en France,* pp. 177–178.

38. Coornaert, *Compagnonnages en France,* p. 142.

39. Ibid., pp. 47–48.

40. Jacques-Louis Ménétra, *Journal de ma vie: Jacques-Louis Ménétra, compagnon vitrier au XVIIIe siècle* (Paris: Montalba, 1982), pp. 46–108. Ménétra's account is all the more valuable in that it is the only surviving autobiography by an eighteenth-century *compagnon.*

41. Actually, Ménétra's travels had not quite come to an end, for the delights of Paris made him so forget his Nîmoise that his own father tried to obtain his deportation to the colonies as a "debaucher of girls." Deeming it prudent to make himself scarce, he returned to Nîmes, quarreled with the widow, and resumed his Tour de France in Lyonnais and Burgundy. His father forgave him upon his second return in 1764, and he remained in Paris until his death in the early nineteenth century.

42. Hauser, *Compagnonnages d'arts et métiers,* pp. 36–37.

43. Even in the nineteenth century, when the itineraries of *compagnons* were more clearly fixed, the prefect of Ain estimated that a third of the young men who set out on their Tour de France settled outside of their department of origin; see Jean Tulard, "L'Immigration provinciale à Paris sous le Premier Empire," *Cahiers d'histoire,* 16 (1971): 430.

44. The *milices royales* were not a militia in the English sense of the word, but were rather a selective service system based on a lottery of men aged sixteen to forty; see Pierre Goubert, *L'Ancien Régime: les pouvoirs* (Paris: Armand Colin, 1973), p. 117.

45. For example, Bordeaux's *compagnons passants,* Ménétra among them, successfully resisted the draft in 1759. Ménétra, *Journal de ma vie,* pp. 69–72.

46. Ménétra, for instance, referred to a Comtois who joined the Regiment of Lyonnais after being chased out of the society of *compagnons* "for knavery" (ibid., p. 128). By the nineteenth century, the stigma attached to military service was much greater. Agricol Perdiguier wrote of a childhood friend who enlisted in the service while working in Paris: "He had written me from Paris . . . a

letter full of desolation . . . Probably, if I had been able to go to him when he called, his enlistment would not have occurred; my reason, firmer than his, would have encouraged him . . . I arrived too late . . . Instead of a cook I found a soldier" (Perdiguier, *Mémoires d'un compagnon,* p. 225).

47. André Corvisier, *L'Armée française de la fin du XIIe siècle au ministère de Choiseul: le soldat* (Paris: PUF, 1964), 1: 97–98, 129.

48. Ménétra himself nearly chose to pursue a military career, although the episode antedated his Tour de France. He was enlisted by a relative, a recruiter for the Regiment of Auvergne, in a tavern on the quays after a row with his father: "I pack my bag. The *compagnon* says he wants to leave with me when my father arrives accompanied by his cousin, who says to me: Jacques, you have just done something crazy; your father promises never to strike you again, I to hold him to it. After long negotiations, I went to find the recruiter, [who] . . . returned my enlistment. So, for a bottle of wine and a three-sou meal in the name of cousinly friendship, my father got off for eighteen francs." Ménétra's traveling companions on his Tour de France included soldiers as well as *compagnons.* He left Béziers for Montpellier, for example, in the company of a sergeant from the Regiment of Béarn. Ménétra, *Journal de ma vie,* pp. 45–46.

49. The proportion was somewhat higher for colonial than for regular troops. Among recruits for the Compagnie des Indes, it ranged between 18% and 24%; see André Corvisier, "Service militaire et mobilité géographique au XVIIIe siècle," *Annales de démographie historique* (1970): 201.

50. Ibid., p. 185.

51. Ibid., pp. 193–194.

52. Moheau, *Recherches et considérations sur la population de la France* (1778; Paris: Paul Geuthner, 1912), p. 173. Moheau's final remark does not refer to homelessness per se, but rather to the lack of a fixed residence. As evidence, he pointed to the 4,000 Lyonnais who lived in lodging houses.

53. Henri Bunle, *Mouvements migratoires entre la France et l'étranger,* Etudes démographiques, no. 4 (Paris: Service national des statistiques, 1943), pp. 6–7.

54. Jean-Pierre Poussou, "Mobilité et migrations," in *Histoire de la population française,* ed. Jacques Dupâquier (Paris: PUF, 1988), 2:130.

55. Moheau claimed that there were up to 4,000 documented cases of desertion each year, and although not all deserters abandoned France, those who did fueled a significant migratory stream; see Moheau, *Recherches et considérations,* p. 174. On Martin Guerre, see Natalie Zemon Davis, *The Return of Martin Guerre* (Cambridge: Harvard University Press, 1983).

56. J. Nadal and E. Giralt, *La Population catalane de 1553 à 1717: l'immigration française et les autres facteurs de son développement* (Paris: SEVPEN, 1960), p. 125.

57. Poitrineau, *Remues d'hommes,* pp. 32–33.

58. Bunle, *Mouvements migratoires,* p. 13.

59. Moheau, *Recherches et considérations,* p. 175.

60. On Nantes and La Rochelle, see Paul Bois, ed., *Histoire de Nantes* (Toulouse:

Privat, 1977), p. 178; Gabriel Debien, "La Société coloniale au XVIIe et XVIIIe siècle: les engagés pour les Antilles (1634–1715)," *Revue de l'histoire des colonies,* 38 (1951): 141; and Jean Tanguy, "Les Premiers Engagés partis de Nantes pour les Antilles," *Actes du 97e Congrès national des sociétés savantes,* Section d'histoire moderne et contemporaine, Nantes, 1972 (Paris, 1977), pp. 53–81. The total figure for Dieppe is unknown, but Abbé Le Ber unearthed 2,000 contracts simply for the period 1654–1686; see Papers of Abbé Le Ber, Bibliothèque municipale de Rouen.

61. For example, the notarial archives of Le Havre yielded 3,600 *engagés* for the years 1627 to 1652, when colonization of the Antilles was just getting under way. A further 600 emigrants left the port of Honfleur for the Islands between 1637 and 1639. See A. Anthiaume, *Cartes marines, constructions navales, voyages de découverte chez les Normands, 1500–1650* (Paris: Dumont, 1916), 2: 137, apps., and Tanguy, "Les Premiers Engagés," pp. 53–54.

62. Christian Huetz de Lemps, "Indentured Servants Bound for the French Antilles in the Seventeenth and Eighteenth Centuries," in *"To Make America": European Emigration in the Early Modern Period,* ed. Ida Altman and James Horn (Berkeley: University of California Press, 1995), p. 186; Debien, "La Société coloniale," pp. 247–248.

63. Poussou, *Bordeaux,* pp. 245–246; Bois, *Histoire de Nantes,* p. 179. In Nantes, there were 5,000 passengers between 1694 and 1746 and 3,000 between 1763 and 1792. Statistics for the intervening years are unavailable.

64. Bunle, *Mouvements migratoires,* p. 15; Poussou, "Mobilité et migrations," p. 127; Daniel Usner, *Indians, Settlers, and Slaves in a Frontier Exchange Economy* (Chapel Hill: University of North Carolina Press, 1992), pp. 32–33. On departures for Louisiana, see also passenger lists for Lorient and La Rochelle, AC: F5B, vols. 49, 57.

65. Bunle, *Mouvements migratoires,* p. 14.

66. Marcel Trudel, *Histoire de la Nouvelle-France* (Montréal: Fides, 1963–1983), 3, pt. 2: 18.

67. Passenger lists, La Rochelle, AC: F5B, vol. 57.

68. Passenger lists, Bordeaux, ibid., vols. 39–40.

69. Bunle, *Mouvements migratoires,* p. 19.

70. Bernard Bailyn, *Voyagers to the West: A Passage in the Peopling of America on the Eve of the Revolution* (New York: Knopf, 1986), pp. 24–25. From the total of 700,000, one must subtract the 75,000 Germans, the 175,000 Africans, and the 150,000 Scotch-Irish.

71. The populations of England and France in 1700 were, respectively, 6 million and 20 million, yielding annual rates of colonial emigration of 3 in 10,000 and 1 in 10,000. The difference would be even greater if emigration to the British West Indies could be included in the English totals. That figure is elusive, although David Galenson has estimated a net migration of some 176,000 whites for the period 1650 to 1780, and Henry Gemery, some 220,000 for the period

1630 to 1700; see David Galenson, *White Servitude in Colonial America: An Economic Analysis* (Cambridge: Cambridge University Press, 1981), p. 219, Henry Gemery, "Emigration from the British Isles to the New World, 1630–1700: Inferences from Colonial Populations," *Research in Economic History,* 5 (1980): 204.

72. Bunle, *Mouvements migratoires,* p. 20.

73. Debien, "La Société coloniale," p. 246.

74. Gabriel Debien, "L'Emigration poitevine vers l'Amérique au XVIIe siècle: études des engagés poitevins de La Rochelle," *Bulletin de la Société des antiquaires de l'Ouest et des musées de Poitiers,* 4th trimester (1952): 293–295.

8. *Northwestern Emigration to Canada*

1. For the traditional view, see Abel Châtelain, *Les Migrants temporaires en France de 1800 à 1914: histoire économique et sociale des migrants temporaires des campagnes françaises au XIXe et au début du XXe siècle* (Villeneuve–d'Ascq: Publications de l'Université de Lille, 1976), 1: 433–434.

2. Jean Delumeau, ed., *Histoire de la Bretagne* (Toulouse: Privat, 1969), p. 261.

3. Northern Brittany as a whole suffered economic dislocation after 1690, and especially after 1715–1720, as a result of this shifting pattern of trade. Saint-Malo's population may have declined by as much as 25% between 1700 and 1750. See Jean Bérenger and Jean Meyer, *La Bretagne de la fin du XVIIe siècle: d'après le mémoire de Béchameil de Nointel,* Institut armoricain de recherches économiques et humaines, Textes et documents, no. 1 (Paris: Klincksieck, 1976), pp. 56–57, 64, and Jean Delumeau, "Démographie d'un port français sous l'Ancien Régime: Saint-Malo (1651–1750)," *Le XVIIe siècle: revue,* 86 (1970): 19.

4. See Chapter 6. In this regard, the cases of several Breton emigrants who appeared in the Louisbourg court records are suggestive of lost opportunities at home. Pierre Benoist, a merchant who died in the Louisbourg Hospital in 1732, had left behind a wife, child, and debts in Saint-Malo to come "with a small stock to trade in this town." Four years later, Guillaume Regnault, an accused thief from Dinan, described himself as the seventeen-year-old son of a tanner, who knew no trade himself but "went to class with the secular fathers at the College of Dinan." Of his emigration, he stated "that he came as a passenger on the vessel . . . called . . . *Le Henry* [and] that he embarked in Saint-Malo with the idea of finding a situation on this island." That same year, Louis Davory, a navigator from Saint-Grégoire, near Rennes, in Brittany was arrested for theft while trying to return to Saint-Malo after a four-year stint in Québec. He too claimed that he had left France "in the quality of passenger and that it cost him twenty crowns." As for his occupation in Québec, "he taught reading and writing there to children and several habitants." Finally, Yacinthe Gabriel Lebon, the thirty-three-year-old from Bazouges (Ille-

et-Vilaine) who survived a harrowing trial for sacrilege in the years 1753–1754, told a judge that he had embarked for Louisbourg "based on what people had told him in France, that he would be able to earn his living teaching reading and writing as well as arithmetic." All of these emigrants were educated, and all had difficulty adjusting to what turned out to be their downward social mobility. Whether they were guilty or innocent (two were eventually acquitted), their disappointed middle-class expectations combined with their dwindling capital to get them into trouble. They were quite possibly casualties of the commercial crisis that temporarily beset their region. See estate of Pierre Benoist, Conseil supérieur of Louisbourg, (1732), AC: G2, vol. 181, pp. 574–644; trial of Louis Davory, Conseil supérieur of Louisbourg (1736), ibid., vol. 186, pp. 228–322; trial of Yacinthe Gabriel Lebon, Conseil supérieur of Louisbourg (1753–1754), ibid., vol. 189, pp. 148–269; and trial of Guillaume Regnault, Baillage of Louisbourg (1736), ibid., vol. 196, dossier 93.

5. Census of Ile Royale (1734), AC: G1, vol. 466.

6. Likewise, a number of Bretons from the environs of Saint-Malo, Saint-Brieuc, and Dol settled in the Côte-du-Sud (Québec) between 1730 and 1770. In addition to the commerical woes of northern Brittany, structural shifts in the fishing industry helped to transform these fishermen from temporary into permanent emigrants. See Alain Laberge, "Communautés rurales et présence étrangère au Canada au XVIIIᵉ siècle: les Granvillais sur la Côte-du-Sud (1730–1770)," in *Famille, économie, et société rurale en contexte d'urbanisation (XVIIᵉ–XXᵉ siècle)*, ed. Gérard Bouchard and Joseph Goy (Chicoutimi: SOREP; Paris: EHESS, 1990), p. 360, and Christopher Moore, "Cape Breton and the North Atlantic World in the Eighteenth Century," in *The Island: New Perspectives on Cape Breton's History, 1713–1990*, ed. Kenneth Donovan (Fredericton, N.B.: Acadiensis, 1990), pp. 36–38.

7. See Chapter 2.

8. Jacques Depauw, "Immigration féminine, professions féminines, et structures urbaines à Nantes au XVIIIᵉ siècle," in Université de Nantes, Centre de recherches sur l'histoire de la France Atlantique, *Enquêtes et documents*, no. 2 (Nantes, 1972), pp. 45–47, 60.

9. Gabriel Debien, "Les Engagés pour le Canada partis de Nantes," *Revue d'histoire de l'Amérique française*, 33 (1979–1980): 583–586.

10. According to the hospital registers of the seventeenth century, a plurality of Nantes's immigrants (40.1%) came from the demographic basin as defined by the diocese, and a majority (58.4%) were Breton. More than half of the non-Bretons arrived from Poitou, Anjou, Maine, and Normandy, while the remainder (19.5%) drifted in from non-neighboring provinces and foreign countries. The exact figures are as follows: Diocese of Nantes, 2,215; rest of Brittany, 1,008; Normandy, Maine, Anjou, and Poitou, 1,223; elsewhere in France, 911; foreign countries, 163. See Alain Croix, *La Bretagne aux XVIᵉ et XVIIᵉ siècles: la vie, la mort, la foi* (Paris: Maloine, 1981), 1:209.

11. Passenger lists, Saint-Malo (1749–1763), AC: F5B, vol. 58; Delumeau, "Démographie," p. 11.

12. There were 102 of known regional origin in trades where *compagnonnage* was practiced.

13. They were Pierre Chereau, Similien Gendron, Antoine LeBeaux, Noël Legall, Jacques-Henri Picauron, and Pierre Rouault. It is difficult to generalize from the example of 6 people, when Brittany produced more than 2,000 emigrants, but the geographic and occupational origins of Breton emigrants suggest that these *compagnons* were not unique. Nantes and Rennes, the province's two major centers of *compagnonnage*, together sent 345 emigrants, and of those whose social class was known, one-third were artisans. Almost a fifth of the civilian Bretons whose occupations were recorded worked in the building, metal, or clothing trades.

14. Perhaps they immigrated to Nantes for their apprenticeship, or perhaps the two types of mobility were telescoped together. Agricol Perdiguier provides an example of the latter pattern; he learned the rudiments of his trade in his native bourg of Morières and moved to Aix only to begin his Tour de France.

15. Colonial recruitment of *compagnons* may have been facilitated by seasonal fluctuations of employment in these trades. Tailors, for instance, took on extra help "immediately after Easter and just before the Feast of All Saints," making the summer—the time of departures for Canada—a period of relative worker availability; see Michael Sonenscher, *Work and Wages: Natural Law, Politics, and the Eighteenth-Century French Trades* (Cambridge: Cambridge University Press, 1989), pp. 162–163.

16. There is some evidence that *compagnons* maintained an organized presence outside of Europe, beginning in the seventeenth century and continuing thereafter. According to Jean-Pierre Bayard, Protestant *compagnons* established themselves in the thirteen colonies, particularly in Philadelphia, at the time of the revocation of the Edict of Nantes, and "numerous *compagnons* settled in Argentina and Chile in the nineteenth century." Likewise, Agricol Perdiguier referred in his memoirs to Narbonne-L'Espérance, a fellow *compagnon du Tour de France*, "now domiciled in New York." *Compagnons* did not, however, perpetuate their organizations in Canada. Aside from the hostility of the Canadian authorities toward corporatism in the trades, the organization of work itself militated against the continuation of structured *compagnonnages*. As in New England, "in early Canada there was no large or stable class of journeymen," so there was little need for separate institutions to represent journeyman interests. The *compagnons* who embarked for Canada did so as individuals, without the benefit of collective support. Canada, perhaps to an even greater degree than Philadelphia or New York, remained outside the established channels of journeyman mobility. The departures of *compagnons* for the colony were not so much simple extensions of the French pattern than they were accidental deviations from it; they were comparable in nature to Ménétra's abortive

embarkment at Saint-Malo. See Jean-Pierre Bayard, *Le Compagnonnage en France* (Paris: Payot, 1977), pp. 172, 181; Agricol Perdiguier, *Mémoires d'un compagnon* (1854; Paris: Librairie du compagnonnage, 1964), p. 136; and Peter Moogk, "In the Darkness of a Basement: Craftsmen's Associations in Early French Canada," *Canadian Historical Review*, 57 (1976): 418–419.

17. Paul Bois, ed., *Histoire de Nantes* (Toulouse: Private, 1977), pp. 178–179. See also Jean Tanguy, "Les Premiers Engagés partis de Nantes pour les Antilles," *Actes du 97ᵉ Congrès national des sociétés savantes*, Section d'histoire moderne et contemporaine, Nantes, 1972 (Paris, 1977), pp. 60–66.

18. Louis Merle and Gabriel Debien, "Colons, marchands, et engagés à Nantes au XVIIᵉ siècle," *Notes d'histoire coloniale*, 29 (1954): 32.

19. Ibid., pp. 53–54.

20. Bois, *Histoire de Nantes*, p. 179.

21. The metaphor of the colander was coined by Jean-Pierre Bardet, that of the pump by Emmanuel Le Roy Ladurie. Breton historians have emphasized the importance of both emigration and immigration to Brittany's cities. See Jean-Pierre Bardet, *Rouen aux XVIIᵉ et XVIIIᵉ siècles: les mutations d'un espace social* (Paris: SEDES, 1983), 1:217, and Georges Duby, ed., *Histoire de la France urbaine* (Paris: Seuil, 1980–1985), 3:301. On Nantes and Saint-Malo, see Depauw, "Immigration féminine," p. 58, and Delumeau, "Démographie," p. 12.

22. Pierre Chaunu, "Malthusianisme démographique et malthusianisme écono-mique: réflexions sur l'échec industriel de la Normandie à l'époque du démar-rage," *Annales: économies, sociétés, civilisations*, 27 (1972): 17. By the turn of the nineteenth century, the percentage of immigrants among military recruits was lower in the pays d'Auge than anywhere else in the Department of Calvados: 31% compared with 70% in the plaine de Caen; see Gabriel Désert, "Listes de recrues et étude d'une société au début du XIXᵉ siècle," *Annales de Normandie*, 13 (1963): 119.

23. The most mobile groups in Augeron society were merchants, officers, and professionals, followed by artisans and laborers; see N. W. Mogenson, "Struc-tures et changements démographiques dans vingt paroisses normandes sous l'Ancien Régime," *Annales de démographie historique* (1975): 347–349.

24. Pierre Chaunu, *Le Renversement de la tendance majeure des prix et des ac-tivités au XVIIᵉ siècle: problèmes de fait et de méthodologie* (Milan: Guiffrè, 1962), p. 13.

25. Pierre Chaunu, *Réflexions sur le tournant des années 1630–1650* (Lyon: n.p., 1967), p. 113. The change came about, of course, through widespread practice of contraception.

26. Upper Normandy witnessed "a brutal reduction of natality in the eighteenth century," to the point that the figures for the Generality of Rouen were the lowest in all of France. See ibid., p. 14; Chaunu, *Renversement*, p. 20 (quoted); and Bardet, *Rouen*, 1:208. On proto-industrialization, see Marie-Claude Gri-court, "Etude d'histoire démographique, sociale, et religieuse de cinq paroisses

de l'archidiaconé du Petit-Caux: Douderville, Canville, Bacqueville, Brachy, et Luneray du milieu du XVIIᵉ siècle à la fin de l'Ancien Régime," in *A travers la Normandie des XVIIᵉ et XVIIIᵉ siècles*, Cahier des Annales de Normandie, no. 3 (Caen, 1963), p. 466; Bardet, *Rouen*, 1: 208–209; Michel Le Pesant, "Immigration sur le plateau de Neufbourg vers 1804," *Annales de Normandie*, 11 (1961): 172; and André Dubuc, "Immigrations ouvrières en Seine-Inférieure sous le Premier Empire," ibid., 1 (1951): 248.

27. Upper Norman cities displayed a unique combination of economic growth and demographic lethargy in the eighteenth century—lethargy derived from low levels of immigration, particularly immigration from the hinterland. See Jean Legoy, *Le Peuple du Havre et son histoire des origines à 1800* ([Le Havre]: n.p., 1980), p. 96; André Corvisier, ed., *Histoire du Havre* (Toulouse: Privat, 1983), pp. 113–114; Bardet, *Rouen*, 1: 50, 214; and Michel Mollat, ed., *Histoire de Rouen* (Toulouse: Privat, 1979), p. 224.

28. In this regard, it is perhaps no accident that the only emigrant to mention in court documents being transported by Dugard's company was Louis Davory, the navigator from Saint-Grégoire discussed in n. 4 above; see AC: G2, vol. 186, pp. 228–322.

29. Emigration from Upper Normandy to the Islands has been little studied, although it was important, at least in the seventeenth century. As in Brittany, there was probably a correspondence between the regional origins of emigrants for the Islands and urban immigrants, and an even closer resemblance between the regional origins of emigrants to the Islands and Canada. Taken collectively, Le Havre's emigrants for the Islands were two-thirds urban and one-third rural, with the most important towns being Le Havre, Honfleur, and Rouen. Among non-Normans, the proportion of city dwellers was higher still: 72%. The origins of women who emigrated from Dieppe were similar, though even more urban. Most of them came from Dieppe, Rouen, Paris, or bourgs in the vicinity of Dieppe. See A. Anthiaume, *Cartes marines, constructions navales, voyages de découverte chez les Normands, 1500–1650* (Paris: Dumont, 1916), 2: 137, apps.; Gabriel Debien, "Les Femmes des premiers colons aux Antilles (1635–1680)," *Notes d'histoire coloniale*, 24 (1952): 9, 22; H. Cahingt, "Les Registres du tabellionage de Dieppe et les Antilles," *Revue historique des Antilles*, 5 (1930): 4; and Bardet, *Rouen*, 2, pl. 85.

30. Mollat, *Histoire de Rouen*, p. 224.

31. Bardet, *Rouen*, 1:212. Bardet has gone so far as to argue a "palpable intellectual superiority of immigrants over natives" (243).

32. Immigration to the Lower Norman city of Caen was similarly selective. Immigrants ranged in age from twelve to fifty, but their numbers thinned substantially "after the age of occupational crystallization, around age thirty." As in Rouen, "the newcomers did not belong to the most intellectually deprived milieux of the countryside . . . Immigration issued from penury—of work or remuneration—but not from misery. It tossed into the city wellborn people

whose activity and aptitudes were perhaps greater than those of the city dwellers." Jean-Claude Perrot, *Genèse d'une ville moderne: Caen au XVIIIe siècle* (Paris: Mouton, 1975), 1: 157, 310.

33. Chaunu, *Réflexions*, p. 114; Philippe Wiel, "Tamerville: une grosse paroisse du Cotentin aux XVIIe et XVIIIe siècles; démographie, société, mentalité," *Annales de démographie historique* (1969): 169–170.

34. Like Brittany, the Avranchin has given rise to a stubborn myth of peasant immobility; see, for example, Emile Vivier, "La Condition du paysan de l'Avranchin aux XVIIe–XVIIIe siècles," *Revue de l'Avranchin: bulletin semestriel de la Société d'archéologie, de littérature, sciences, et arts des arrondissements d'Avranches et de Mortain*, 17 (1912): 166. The roots of this myth are identical for both provinces; Avranchins and Bretons were indeed absent from major movements of internal migration, particularly at the interprovincial level. They compensated, however, by moving across the Atlantic.

35. Testimonials of freedom at marriage (1771), ASQ: ms. 430.

36. "Témoignages de liberté au mariage," *Rapport de l'archiviste de la province de Québec*, 32–33 (1951–1953): 150–151.

37. Testimonial of freedom at marriage, 12 September 1766, ASQ: ms. 430.

38. Michel Le Pesant, "Un centre d'émigration en Normandie sous l'Ancien Régime: le cas de Percy," *Bibliothèque de l'Ecole des chartes*, 130 (1972): 212. While many of these emigrants plied their trade on a seasonal or temporary basis, others ended up settling in what was familiar, if distant, territory. A number even made the transition from peddling to large-scale commerce; in Paris, Lower Normans played a key role in the publishing industry into the nineteenth century.

39. Ibid., pp. 167, 210.

40. For example, although northern or Parisian destinations were prevalent among the "marchands d'estampes" (book peddlers), the prescription of an itinerary was never absolute. Some of them apparently bucked tradition so far as to travel in the opposite direction; in Agen, an eighteenth-century hotel register noted their presence. Likewise, in the inland zone, standard itineraries branched out, in the eighteenth century, to include other western provinces, central and southern France, and the North. The greater dispersion of receiving communities probably resulted from the reorientation of northern Breton commerce in the eighteenth century, but population growth in the Coutançais may also have conditioned the search for additional migratory outlets. See ibid., p. 212; Pierre Deffontaines, *Les Hommes et leurs travaux dans les pays de la Moyenne Garonne (Agenais, Bas-Quercy)* (Lille: SILIC, 1932), p. 405; and Marie-Hélène Jonan, "Les Originalités démographiques d'un bourg artisanal normand au XVIIIe siècle: Villedieu-les-Poêles (1711–1790)," *Annales de démographie historique* (1969): 92.

41. Testimonial of freedom at marriage, 19 June 1767, ASQ: ms. 430; "Témoignages de liberté," pp. 26–27, 54–55, 146. Even among internal migrants, not

everyone practiced the predominant trade. Around Percy, peasants and laborers sometimes joined the peddlers in temporary or permanent movements.

42. On traditional migrations from the Norman *bocage*, which included the Elections of Falaise, Vire, Domfront, and Mortain, see Michel Le Pesant, "Du bocage normand aux Ardennes," in *Mélanges d'histoire normande dédiés. . .à René Jouanne*, special issue of *Le Pays bas-normand* (1970), and André Dubuc, "Les Migrations temporaires d'ouvriers dans les départements normands," *Annales de Normandie*, 4 (1954): 168–173.

43. Wiel, "Tamerville," p. 139.

44. In addition, 1 emigrant, who came from an eminent Rouennais merchant house, was born in Rouen but arrived in Canada by way of Morocco, where he had apprenticed in the family business; see Georges Vanier, "Les Le Gendre: Thomas Le Gendre (le Jeune) 1638–1706," *Bulletin de la Société libre d'émulation, du commerce, et de l'industrie de la Seine-Inférieure: exercises, 1947–1948* (Dieppe, 1950): 69–94.

45. Le Pesant, "Un centre d'émigration," p. 212.

46. In the same way, a Percynois who moved to a traditional destination in Brittany could decide later to embark for Canada. Some of the Coutançais who reached the colony through Saint-Malo were conceivably prior immigrants into Brittany.

47. Pommereuil, "Extrait du mémoire de la généralité d'Alençon" (1698), BN: Nouvelles acquisitions françaises, vol. 2031, p. 26.

48. In the early 1800s, Eure-et-Loir received 2,300 immigrant harvest workers annually, most of them from Orne; see Abel Châtelain, *Les Migrants temporaires en France de 1800 à 1914: histoire économique et sociale des migrants temporaires des campagnes françaises au XIXe et au début du XXe siècle* (Villeneuve-d'Ascq: Pubications de l'Université de Lille, 1976), 1: 164–165.

49. Hubert Charbonneau, *Tourouvre-au-Perche aux XVIIe et XVIIIe siècles: étude de démographie historique*, Institut national d'études démographiques, Travaux et documents, no. 55 (Paris: PUF, 1970), pp. 35, 161.

50. Françoise Montagne, *Tourouvre et les Juchereau: un chapitre de l'émigration percheronne au Canada* (Québec: Société canadienne de généalogie, 1965), p. 9.

51. Françoise Montagne, "Essai sur les raisons de l'émigration tourouvraine au Canada," *Revue de l'Université Laval*, 19 (1964): 55.

52. Montagne, *Tourouvre*, pp. 2–4. De Caën, a Protestant merchant from Dieppe, at one time held title to the Canadian commercial monopoly.

53. Charbonneau, *Tourouvre-au-Perche*, p. 17.

54. Léon de la Sicotière, "L'Emigration percheronne au Canada pendant le XVIIe siècle," *Bulletin de la Société historique et archéologique de l'Orne*, 6 (1887): 357.

55. Montagne, "Essai," p. 54.

56. Françoise Montagne, "La Ventrouze et les Canadiens," *Mémoires de la Société généalogique canadienne-française*, 23 (1972): 32.

57. Cited ibid., pp. 28–29.

58. Montagne, *Tourouvre*, p. 9.

59. Charbonneau, *Tourouvre-au-Perche*, p. 17.

60. Françoise Montagne, "Marie-Geneviève de Manovely de Réville: une 'pionnière' canadienne du XVIIe siècle," *Cahiers percherons*, 40 (1973): 17–18.

61. Robert Giffard came from a seigneurial but nonnoble family.

62. See N.-E. Dionne, *Les Ecclésiastiques et les royalistes français réfugiés au Canada à l'époque de la Révolution—1791–1802* (Québec: n.p., 1905), p. 134.

63. Pierre Roger of La Ferté-Vidame, who embarked for Canada after seven years of military service in France.

64. In Anjou, the winegrowers of the Saumurois supplemented their earnings by bringing in the grapes of the Montreuillais and Loudunois, and the villagers of Upper Maine participated both in the wheat harvests of Beauce and the wine harvests of the Loire; see François Lebrun, *Les Hommes et la mort en Anjou aux XVIIe et XVIIIe siècles* (Paris: Flammarion, 1975), p. 28, and André Bouton, *Le Maine: histoire économique et sociale, XVIIe et XVIIIe siècles* (Le Mans: n.p., 1973), p. 467.

65. Thus, the region of Couptrain (Mayenne), which sent masons and roofers to Norman cities, and tinkers and peddlers to Paris, provided only 1 emigrant for Canada—from the village of Le Ham; see Bouton, *Maine*, pp. 467, 561.

66. Maria Mondoux, "Les Hommes de Montréal," *Revue d'histoire de l'Amérique française*, 2 (1948–1949): 59–80.

67. Angers and Saumur, the two largest cities in Anjou, received important contingents from the outlying communities only when harvest failures transformed them into *villes-refuges*. Despite these periodic, short-lived influxes, Anjou's main population centers stagnated or even shrank slightly in the seventeenth and eighteenth centuries. See Lebrun, *Anjou*, pp. 81, 98–102.

68. Jean Cavignac, "Le Compagnonnage dans les luttes ouvrières au XVIIIe siècle: l'exemple de Bordeaux," *Bibliothèque de l'Ecole des chartes*, 126 (1968): 403–404. Actually, no one pattern prevailed in the case of shoemakers. Some did maintain formal ties with the *compagnonnages*, while others practiced a semi-independent but ancillary form of mobility. The emigrants from La Flèche included examples of both types. Louis Chevallier of Caen and Pierre Anselin of Senlis indentured themselves as simple "*cordonniers et défricheurs*," but Gessé Des Sommes was a "journeyman cobbler from the town of La Ferté–Bernard."

69. Lebrun, *Anjou*, p. 39.

70. Bouton, *Maine*, pp. 447–449.

71. Gabriel Debien, "Les Départs de Manceaux pour Saint-Domingue, 1771–1791," *La Province du Maine*, 67 (1965): 246–249.

72. Along with harvest migrations, the only northwestern movements that failed to extend to Canada in a significant way were those of the Protestant exodus. To be sure, Normandy came in a distant second to Aunis in providing Canada with Protestants, but the total number of people involved was a paltry 15. Anjou and Maine produced no Canadian Protestants at all, although there were Protestant departures from the region, and Brittany sent only a few. For obvious

reasons, the Jesuit-dominated colony did not inspire confidence in persecuted Huguenots from northwestern France.

9. *Emigration Outside the Northwest*

1. Louis Pérouas, "Sur la démographie rochelaise," *Annales: économies, sociétés, civilisations,* 16 (1961): 1139.

2. Ibid., pp. 1139–1140; Louis Pérouas, *Le Diocèse de La Rochelle de 1648 à 1724: sociologie et pastorale* (Paris: SEVPEN, 1964): 92.

3. Louis Papy, *L'Homme et la mer sur la côte Atlantique de la Loire à la Gironde: étude de geographie humaine* (Bordeaux: Delmas, 1941), p. 34; Pérouas, *Diocèse de La Rochelle,* pp. 111, 220, 247.

4. Jean-Pierre Poussou, *Bordeaux et le Sud-Ouest aux XVIIIe siècle: croissance économique et attraction urbaine* (Paris: Touzot, 1983), pp. 361, 367.

5. Immigration into Rochefort consisted primarily of migration streams with an important temporary component. The city's population fluctuated wildly with state demand for the arsenal's production. In 1752, as the nation geared up for colonial war, 25,000 people crowded willy-nilly into Rochefort; only 10,000 remained in the aftermath of defeat in 1763. The city's demographic basin stretched to the south of La Rochelle's, focusing most heavily on the area between the Charente and Seudre, and flowing eastward with the two river valleys. The extralocal population "came from everywhere," with an emphasis on the Center-west, Southwest, and Massif central. The Paris Basin provided fewer immigrants for Rochefort than La Rochelle, but Brittany was an important region of origin. The strongest ties were with southern and eastern Brittany rather than Finistère, in spite of personnel exchanges affecting the two arsenals of Rochefort and Brest. See Poussou, *Bordeaux,* p. 359; "Questions et réponses," *Revue de la Saintonge et de l'Aunis,* 10 (1890): 158; René Mémain, *Le Matériel de la marine de guerre sous Louis XIV: Rochefort, arsenal modèle de Colbert (1666–1690)* (Paris: Hachette, 1936), pp. 164–165 (quoted).

6. Gabriel Debien, "La Société coloniale au XVIIe et XVIIIe siècle: les engagés pour les Antilles (1634–1715)," *Revue de l'histoire des colonies,* 38 (1951): 99.

7. Gabriel Debien, "Engagés pour le Canada au XVIIe siècle vus de La Rochelle," *Notes d'histoire coloniale,* 21 (1952): 207.

8. Lucile Bourrachot and Jean-Pierre Poussou, "Les Départs de passagers charentais pour les Antilles (1713–1787)," *Recueil de la Société d'archéologie et d'histoire de la Charente-Maritime et Section archéologique de Saintes,* 25 (1974): 177.

9. The biography of Jean Barré de Saint-Venant, a planter from Niort, was typical in this regard. Barré was born in 1737 to a *procureur du roi* in comfortable circumstances. His position as one of seven boys certainly limited his prospects in Niort, but at the same time, the geography of his extended family made emigration relatively easy. One of his uncles had established himself as a merchant in Rochefort, another as a planter in Saint-Domingue. The West

Indian uncle called for him in 1754, and he spent the next twenty-five years as the manager or owner of various plantations. A second brother became a planter as well, as did another uncle born in Niort but living in the plaine de Fontenay. Only three of his brothers remained in Poitou, two as *procureurs* in Niort and one as the curé of Aulnay (Vienne). The other two became, respectively, a surgeon in Rochefort and a lawyer in Paris, where Jean himself settled after a stint as a landowner in Beauce. He died in 1810 on the eve of departing for Naples to supervise the introduction of sugarcane cultivation into southern Italy. See Françoise Thésée and Gabriel Debien, *Un colon niortais à Saint-Domingue: Jean Barré de Saint-Venant* (Niort: Imbert-Nicolas, 1975).

10. Jacques Mathieu, "Mobilité et sédentarité: stratégies familiales en Nouvelle-France," *Recherches sociographiques*, 28 (1987): 215–216. See also Jacques Mathieu and Lina Gouger, "Transferts de population," *Annales de Bretagne et des pays de l'Ouest*, 95 (1988): 337–345; Jacques Mathieu, "De France à Nouvelle-France au XVIIᵉ siècle," in *Les Chemins de la migration en Belgique et au Québec du XVIIᵉ au XXᵉ siècle*, ed. Yves Landry, John Dickinson, Suzy Pasleau, and Claude Desama (Louvain-la-Neuve: Editions Académia, 1995), p. 198. It should be noted that Mathieu has studied only founding immigrants, who were more likely to have relatives in Canada than emigrants overall.

11. Analysis at the level of the individual community is, however, more ambiguous. In two heavily Protestant parishes near Niort, 40% of the indentured servants could not be traced through the parish records. The remaining emigrants were natives, 7 from Catholic and 5 from Protestant or mixed backgrounds. This example does not disprove the hypothesis of Protestant emigration, for one of the effects of persecution was precisely to increase internal mobility. Since the countryside around Niort witnessed the frenzied movements of people seeking a safe opportunity to emigrate, it is quite possible that a more substantial portion of colonial emigrants belonged to the Protestant diaspora than historians are able to prove. See François Baudry, *La Révocation de l'Edit de Nantes et le protestantisme en Bas-Poitou au XVIIIᵉ siècle* (Trévoux: Jeannin, 1922), pp. 231–239, and Gabriel Debien, *Les Engagés protestants de Chef-Boutonne ou les difficultés de l'histoire sociale* (Poitiers: Oudin, 1956), pp. 7–11.

12. The relatively prominent place of the Southwest may also reflect the social background of the immigrants. Nearly all of the native southwesterners were bourgeois, and the Rochelais merchant class received an influx of southwesterners in the mid-seventeenth century; see Marcel Delafosse, "Origine géographique et sociale des marchands rochelais au XVIIᵉ siècle," in *Actes du 87ᵉ Congrès national des sociétés savantes*, Poitiers, 1962, Section d'histoire moderne et contemporaine (Paris: CTHS, 1963), pp. 663–668.

13. Immigration to La Rochelle reflected the structure of the urban parishes to a remarkable degree. The partly suburban Notre-Dame received the largest number, followed by the maritime parishes and, lastly, the center-city. The

immigrants for the maritime parishes came from provinces with a maritime vocation, first and foremost those of the Center-west. In the center-city, more than half of the immigrants came from long distances, and the presence of Picards, Tourangeaux, Béarnais, and Lyonnais testified to the breadth of La Rochelle's commercial relations. Notre-Dame welcomed immigrants from the Northwest, Val de Loire, Paris, and Limousin, in addition to a core of central-westerners. The long-distance origins are a likely indication of *compagnonnage*.

14. "Témoignages de liberté au mariage," *Rapport de l'archiviste de la province de Québec*, 32–33 (1951–1953): 5.

15. Ibid., p. 127.

16. Jean-Pierre Poussou, "Recherches sur l'immigration bayonnaise et basque à Bordeaux au XVIIIe siècle," in *De l'Adour au Pays basque: Fédération historique du Sud-Ouest*, . . . *Actes du 21e Congrès d'études régionales . . . Bayonne, les 4 et 5 mai 1968* (Bayonne: Société des sciences, lettres, et arts de Bayonne, 1971), p. 77.

17. Lucile Bourrachot and Jean-Pierre Poussou, "Les Départs de passagers basques par les ports de Bordeaux et de Bayonne au XVIIIe siècle," in *De l'Adour au Pays basque*, pp. 89, 94.

18. Jean-Pierre Poussou, "Note sur l'immigration lot-et-garonnaise à Bordeaux au XVIIIe siècle," *Revue de l'Agenais*, 103 (1976): 408.

19. Jean-Pierre Poussou, "Les Chemins de la migration," in *Les Chemins de la migration* (see n. 10 above), pp. 9–20. See also Jean-Pierre Poussou, "Faut-il parler d'une autonomie des mouvements migratoires? L'exemple de Bordeaux à la fin du Premier Empire," in *Immigration et société urbaine en Europe occidentale, XVIe–XXe siècles*, ed. Etienne François (Paris: Editions recherche sur les civilisations, 1985), pp. 23–30.

20. Lucile Bourrachot and Jean-Pierre Poussou, "Bordeaux et l'émigration foyenne au XVIIIe siècle," in *Sainte-Foy-la-Grande et ses alentours: Actes du 19e Congrès d'études régionales tenuà Sainte-Foy-la-Grande les 7 et 8 mai 1966* (Bordeaux, Bière, 1968), p. 97; Christian Huetz de Lemps and Jean-Pierre Poussou, "Les Départs de passagers bazadais par Bordeaux au XVIIIe siècle (1717–1787)," *Cahiers du Bazadais*, 10 (1966): 46.

21. Poussou, *Bordeaux*, pp. 333–335.

22. Bourrachot and Poussou, "Bordeaux et l'émigration foyenne," p. 111. See also Poussou, "Note sur l'immigration," p. 407.

23. Poussou, *Bordeaux*, p. 135.

24. Charles Higounet, ed., *Histoire de l'Aquitaine* (Toulouse: Private, 1971), p. 345; François-Georges Pariset, ed., *Bordeaux au XVIIIe siècle* (Bordeaux: Fédération historique du Sud-Ouest, 1968), p. 338.

25. "Témoignages de liberté," pp. 20–21, 116–117, 121.

26. Testimonial of freedom at marriage, 22 August 1768, ASQ: ms. 430.

27. In 1764 the *subdélégué* of Agen wrote that "many peasants gave a trade to their children, and those made what is called the Tour de France." (cited in Pierre

Deffontaines, *Les Hommes et leurs travaux dans les pays de la Moyenne Garonne* [*Agenais, Bas-Quercy*] [Lille: SILIC, 1932], p. 133).

28. "Témoignages de liberté," p. 48.

29. Ibid., p. 86.

30. André Corvisier, *L'Armée française de la fin du XVIIe siècle au ministère de Choiseul: le soldat* (Paris: PUF, 1964), 2:851.

31. See Marcel Trudel, *Histoire de la Nouvelle-France* (Montréal: Fides, 1963–1983), 3, pt. 2: 34–36. Likewise, in Dijon, local administrators evinced a particular interest in the names, surnames, and birthplaces of *compagnons* as soon as the city became a rendezvous for organized itinerant labor; see Henri Hauser, *Les Compagnonnages d'arts et métiers à Dijon aux XVIIe et XVIIIe siècles* (1907; Marseille: Laffitte Reprints, 1979), p. 36.

32. Hence Nicolas Lelat—"sent away for false letters and for contradictions not written here," after a careful description of his year and a half long tour; "Témoignages de liberté," p. 48.

33. Ibid., p. 83. A *chambrelan* was a freelance artisan who practiced his trade at home, in his chamber. He had no connection to the corporative structures of either masters or *compagnons*.

34. Ibid., p. 116.

35. Ibid., p. 10.

36. E. Delage de Luget, "La Mobilité géographique de la population à Uzeste et dans le pays du Ciron au XVIIIe siècle," *Cahiers du Bazadais*, 22 (1972): 31; Deffontaines, *Hommes et leurs travaux*, pp. 405–406; Higounet, *Histoire de l'Aquitaine*, p. 338.

37. See Jean-Pierre Poussou, "Recherches sur l'immigration anglo-irlandaise à Bordeaux au XVIIIe siècle," in *Bordeaux et les Iles Britanniques du XIIIe au XXe siècle: Actes du Colloque franco-britannique, York, 1973* (Bordeaux, 1975), pp. 62, 68.

38. Jean-Pierre Poussou, "Aspects de l'immigration pyrénéenne (Béarn, Comminges, Ariège) à Bordeaux au milieu et à la fin du XVIIIe siècle," *Bulletin de la Société des sciences, lettres, et arts de Pau*, 4th ser., 1 (1967): 100, 106.

39. Testimonial of freedom at marriage, 24 June 1769, ASQ: ms. 430. See also Poussou, "Recherches sur l'immigration anglo-irlandaise," p. 77.

40. See Louis Henry and Daniel Courgeau, "Deux analyses de l'immigration à Paris au XVIIIe siècle," *Population*, 26 (1971): 1083–1084.

41. See Robert Dauvergne, "Paris, foyer d'émigration au cours des ages," *Bulletin de la Société d'études historiques, géographiques, et scientifiques de la région parisienne*, 112–113 (1961): 1.

42. This last estimate includes the city's substantial floating population; a more conservative estimate would be 650,000. See Leon Bernard, *The Emerging City: Paris in the Age of Louis XIV* (Durham, N.C.: Duke University Press, 1970), p. 285; Jean Meyer, *Etudes sur les villes en Europe occidentale (milieu du XVIIe*

siècle à la veille de la Révolution française): généralités, France (Paris: SEDES, 1983), p. 51; and Jeffry Kaplow, *The Names of Kings: The Parisian Laboring Poor in the Eighteenth Century* (New York: Basic Books, 1972), pp. 18–19.

43. Daniel Roche, "Nouveaux Parisiens au XVIIIe siècle," *Cahiers d'histoire,* 24 (1979): 8–9.

44. Kaplow, *Names of Kings,* p. 33.

45. Roche, "Nouveaux Parisiens," p. 15; Jean Tulard, "L'Immigration provinciale à Paris sous le Premier Empire," *Cahiers d'histoire,* 16 (1971): 425.

46. Roche, "Nouveaux Parisiens," pp. 15–16.

47. Ibid., p. 15.

48. Dauvergne, "Paris, foyer d'émigration," pp. 1–4 (pp. 3–4 quoted).

49. Thus, when Ménétra agreed to marry his widowed employer from Nîmes during his Tour de France, he informed her "that as for property I had none, that I had only my *maîtrise* which authorized me to settle anywhere. She was delighted." See Jacque-Louis Ménétra, *Journal de ma vie: Jacques-Louis Ménétra, compagnon vitrier au 18e siècle,* ed. Daniel Roche (Paris: Montalba, 1982). pp. 53, 88 (quoted).

50. Gustave Lanctôt has proposed the lower figure, Silvio Dumas the higher one. The *filles du roi* were young women of marriageable age who agreed to emigrate in return for a dowry. The state provided the necessary funds, and the church and state together found the women. See Gustave Lanctôt, *Filles de joie ou filles du roi: étude sur l'émigration féminine en Nouvelle-France* (Montréal: Chantecler, 1952), pp. 121–122; Silvio Dumas, *Les Filles du roi en Nouvelle-France,* Cahiers d'histoire, no. 24 (Québec: Société historique de Québec, 1972), pp. 47–48; and Yves Landry, *Les Filles du roi au XVIIe siècle: orphelines en France, pionnières au Canada* (Ottawa: Leméac, 1992), p. 57.

51. Gérard Malchelosse, "L'Immigration des filles de la Nouvelle-France au XVIIe siècle," *Cahiers des Dix,* 15 (1950): 63.

52. Jacques Petitjean Roget, "Les Femmes des colons à la Martinique au XVIe et XVIIe siècle," *Revue d'histoire de l'Amérique française,* 9 (1955): 207–208.

53. Ibid., p. 221. Perhaps these lines were more blurred in practice than in theory. Manon Lescaut, if fiction is an accurate guide, found herself a inmate of the Hôpital général, not the Refuge.

54. See Claude Delasselle, "Les Enfants abandonnés à Paris au XVIIIe siècle," *Annales: économies, sociétés, civilisations,* 30 (1975): 189–191.

55. Petitjean Roget, "Femmes des colons," pp. 208–209.

56. Petition of 20 *filles du roi,* 17 June 1667 (the original document is in the notarial archives of Dieppe, but a transcription exists among the papers of Abbé Le Ber in the Bibliothèque municipale de Rouen).

57. Messance, a political arithmetician, noted in 1766 that "the Generality of Rouen is within reach of Paris; this proximity makes a great number of young people leave, who go to the capital and spend part of their life in the state of

domesticity." See Messance, *Recherches sur la population du royaume avec des réflexions sur la valeur du bled tant en France qu'en Angleterre depuis 1674 jusqu'en 1764* (Paris, 1766), pp. 140–141.

58. The Diocese of Léon specialized in horse and cattle raising, which gave it an important commercial connection with Paris. This connection served, in turn, to orient emigration.

59. Testimonial of freedom at marriage, 12 September 1766, ASQ: ms. 430.

60. "Témoignages de liberté," pp. 43–44.

61. Ibid., p. 44; Testimonial of freedom at marriage, 12 September 1766, ASQ: ms. 430.

62. Jean Chagniot has shown that recruiters for the troops often concentrated their efforts on immigrants. Indeed, "a certain number of specialized lodgers and innkeepers, sometimes described as 'père' or 'mère' of the *compagnons* or *garçons* of such and such a trade, are expressly indicated in random notes [about recruitment]." See Jean Chagniot, *Paris et l'armée au XVIIIe siècle: étude politique et sociale* (Paris: Economica, 1985), p. 340.

63. "Témoignages de liberté," p. 67.

64. On Picard, see "Témoignages de liberté," p. 45. On Godin, see Berneval [Archange Godbout], "Les Filles venues au Canada de 1658 à 1661," *Bulletin des recherches historiques*, 47 (1941): 114.

65. The archives of the Cathedral Chapter of Amiens contain a "Lease by the chapter to Louis Artus and Nicolas Choquet, merchants in Amiens, Saint-Leu parish, of a mill appropriate for fulling serges belonging to the said gentlemen of the chapter, located in the rue des Poulies, on the river current," dated 16 October 1598. The grandson of Nicolas Choquet also emigrated to Canada, settling, like Artus, in Montréal. See AD (Somme): G, vol. 1423, and René Jetté, *Dictionnaire généalogique des familles du Québec des origines à 1730* (Montréal: PUM, 1983), pp. 23, 251.

66. A brief look at prior migration into the other provinces of the North and East confirms the picture presented by Ile-de-France, but on a more modest scale. Moves from country to city and from city to city predominated, the latter being of various kinds. Antoine Griseau embarked at Dunkerque at the end of a Tour de France, having left his native Châlon-sur-Saône "at the age of about fifteen for several towns of France, where he spent seven years in the capacity of journeyman confectioner." More unusual was the case of Philippe Guillemin *dit* Saint-Cyr of Issoudun, who joined the Canadian troops in Auxerre after a seasonal migration as a vineyard worker. Guillemin worked the vines for three months, "from All Saints until Candlemas," then joined one of the vintner's three sons and the journeyman baker across the street in embarking for Canada. Even seasonal migration then, that most stable, traditional, and rhythmic of movements, could bring migrants into contact, at least exceptionally, with migratory circuits of a far more expansive nature. See Testimonial of freedom at marriage, 1772, ASQ: ms. 430, and "Témoignages de liberté," p. 22.

67. Pierre-Jean-Baptiste Legrand d'Aussy, *Voyage fait en 1787–1788 dans la ci-devant Haute et Basse Auvergne* (1792; Roanne: Horvath, 1982), p. 259.

68. Abel Poitrineau, *Remues d'hommes: essai sur les migrations montagnardes en France aux XVIIe et XVIIIe siècles* (Paris: Aubier Montaigne, 1983), p. 224.

69. This tradition continued through the nineteenth century. See Marie-Antoinette Carron, "Prélude à l'exode rural en France: les migrations anciennes des travailleurs creusois," *Revue d'histoire économique et sociale*, 43 (1965): 313; *Entre faim et loup . . .: les problèmes de la vie et de l'émigration sur les hautes terres françaises au XVIIIe siècle, Actes de la Rencontre inter-universitaire . . .*, Publications de l'Institut d'études du Massif central, no. 16 [Clermont-Ferrand, 1976], p. 271, and Martin Nadaud, *Mémoires de Léonard: ancien garçon maçon*, ed. Maurice Agulhon (Paris: Hachette, 1976).

70. Alain Corbin, "Migrations temporaires et société rurale au XIXe siècle: le cas du Limousin," *Revue historique*, 500 (1971): 299; *Entre faim et loup*, p. 64.

71. Carron, "Prélude à l'exode rural," pp. 312–319.

72. *Entre faim et loup*, pp. 208–227. Pockets of minimal or nonexistent emigration often coincided with the geography of great estates, whether bourgeois, ecclesiastical, or noble. Peasant property was "one of the best, if not the best, correlated factor with emigration" (210).

73. Ibid., p. 271.

74. Jean-Pierre Poussou, "Aspects de l'émigration limousine vers Bordeaux au XVIIIe siècle," in *Le Bas-Limousin: histoire et économie, Actes du Congrès interfédéral des sociétés savantes du Centre, de Languedoc-Pyrénées-Gascogne et du Sud-Ouest, tenu à Tulle, les 8, 9, 10 mai 1964* (Tulle: Société des lettres, sciences, et arts de la Corrèze, 1966), pp. 178–179; *Entre Faim et Loup*, pp. 15, 64.

75. Jean Perrel, "L'Emigration bas-limousine en Espagne aux XVIIe et XVIIIe siècles," in *Actes du 88e Congrès national des sociétés savantes, Clermont-Ferrand, 1963* (Paris: CTHS, 1964), pp. 716–720; "Une région d'émigration vers l'Espagne aux XVIIe–XVIIIe siècles: le plateau de Roche-de-Vie (Corrèze)," in *Le Bas-Limousin*.

76. M. Trillat, "L'Emigration de la Haute-Auvergne en Espagne du XVIIe au XXe siècle," *Revue de la Haute-Auvergne*, 57 (1955): 279, 293.

77. M. Leymarie, "Emigration et structure sociale en Haute-Auvergne à la fin du XVIIIe siècle," ibid., 59 (1957): 323; Abel Poitrineau, *Les Espagnols de l'Auvergne et du Limousin du XVIIe au XIXe siècle* (Aurillac: Malroux-Mazel, 1985), p. 39; Poitrineau, *Remues d'hommes*, pp. 224–226; *Entre faim et loup*, p. 252.

78. Suzanne Delaspre, "L'Emigration temporaire en Basse-Auvergne au XVIIIe siècle jusqu'à la veille de la Révolution," *Revue d'Auvergne*, 68 (1954): 3–52.

79. The Auvergnats who were recruited into the army in Paris fit this pattern perfectly; see Chagniot, *Paris et l'armée*, p. 332.

80. Naval Council to Beauharnais, 5 June 1721, AC: B, vol. 44, p. 166.

81. The masons recruited for Louisbourg were not simply temporary workers. Of

the 5 mentioned, both François Granjan and Jean Roche settled in Louisbourg, the former by 1726 and the latter by 1724. The census records of Ile Royale list 27 masons and stonecutters among the permanent residents of the 1720s and 1730s, only 2 of them of unknown origin. Of the remaining 25, 11 came from the Massif central: 8 from Limousin and 1 each from Auvergne, Marche, and Bourbonnais. The others were from Ile-de-France (6), Brittany (3), Rochefort (2), Poitou (1), Switzerland (1), and Lorraine (1). See Census records of Ile Saint-Jean and Ile Royale (1724–1735), AC: G1, vol. 466, p. 36.

82. Michel Vovelle, *De la cave au grenier: un itinéraire en Provence au XVIIIe siècle, de l'histoire sociale à l'histoire des mentalités* (Québec: Serge Fleury, 1980), p. 63.

83. "Témoignages de liberté," p. 122. The passage of *compagnons* through the region made itself doubly felt owing to the "crossing of two axes of journeyman mobility: the north/south itinerary from Avignon to Marseille, one of the five great cities of the Tour de France, and the west/east itinerary . . . from Languedoc via Arles, another important relay, . . . [to] the Sainte-Baume"; see Michel Vovelle, *L'Irrésistible Ascension de Joseph Sec, bourgeois d'Aix* (Aix: Edisud, 1975), p. 62.

84. Lower Dauphiné and Grenoble received a steady stream of migrants from the mountains, only to send off another toward the region's commercial horizons: Lyon, Beaucaire, Bordeaux, the Antilles. This exodus expanded in the nineteenth century, and the destinations multiplied to include South and North America, Russia, Spain, Portugal, Egypt, and Turkey. Dauphinois emigration also profited the army, which could pose significant competition to other migratory options, as illustrated by the predominance of military occupations among the region's emigrants to Canada. See Pierre Léon, *Les Dolle et les Raby: marchands et spéculateurs dauphinois dans le monde antillais du XVIIIe siècle* (Paris: Les Belles Lettres, 1963), pp. 25–34, 41; André Allix, "Anciennes émigrations dauphinoises," *Revue de géographie alpine*, 20 (1932): 125–126; and Corvisier, *L'Armée française*, 1:441.

85. During the Ancien Régime, Oisans and Briançonnais spawned complex movements in which organized seasonal departures figured prominently. To a greater degree than in the Massif central, these migrations centered on commerce, peddling at its most basic level, and they took as their theater all of urban France south of the Loire. Important sending communities such as Bourg-d'Oisans and La Salle in Briançonnais also lost a portion of their populations permanently, as emigrants "sent for their families, thus marking their break with their native *pays*." See *Entre faim et loup*, pp. 24, 30 (quoted).

86. The region of Faucigny produced peddlers for Germany, some of whom went on to become successful domiciled merchants in Frankfurt, Munich, and Vienna. Farther south, Tarentaise, Maurienne, and the Massif de Thônes supplied Paris, Lyon, and other cities with emigrants from the petty trades: peddlers, porters, and, especially, chimney sweeps. It is unclear whether the chimney sweeps

predominated numerically or simply in the conscience of contemporaries. Sébastien Mercier wrote of them that "it is very cruel to see a poor, eight-year-old child, eyes blindfolded and head covered with a sack, climb with knees and back through a narrow chimney fifty-feet high; not to be able to breathe except at the perilous summit, to come back down as he went up, at the risk of breaking his neck, it taking so little for the decrepit plaster to give way under his frail holds; and mouth filled with soot, almost choking, eyelids heavy, ask you for five sous as the price of his danger and his pains. Thus are swept all the chimneys of Paris" (Louis-Sébastien Mercier, *Le Tableau de Paris*, ed. Jeffry Kaplow [Paris: Maspero, 1979], p. 143). See Paul Guichonnet, ed., *Histoire de la Savoie* (Toulouse: Privat, 1973), pp. 258–259.

87. Passenger lists, La Rochelle. AC, F5B, vol. 57.
88. Peter Clark and David Souden, eds., *Migration and Society in Early Modern England* (Totowa, N.J.: Barnes and Noble, 1988), pp. 33–34, 242. On the mobility of British artisans and its divergence from continental patterns, see E. J. Hobsbawm, *Labouring Men: Studies in the History of Labour* (New York: Basic Books, 1964), p. 36.

10. The Canadian System of Recruitment

1. Marc Gaucher, Marcel Delafosse, and Gabriel Debien, "Les Engagés pour le Canada au XVIIIᵉ siècle," *Revue d'histoire de l'Amérique française*, 14 (1960–1961): 594. Hence the importance of recruitment efforts in determining the chronology of emigration to Canada, as was noted in Chapter 6.
2. Talon to Colbert, 24 May 1665, AC: C11A, vol. 2, p. 140.
3. Talon to Louis XIV, 11 November 1666, ibid., p. 216.
4. Talon to Colbert, 22 April 1665, ibid., p. 124.
5. Pannetié to the naval minister, 23 January 1687, AM: B3, vol. 53, p. 48.
6. "Les Véritables Motifs de messieurs et dames de la Société Notre-Dame de Montréal pour la conversion des sauvages de Nouvelle-France," *Mémoires de la Société historique de Montréal*, 9 (1880): 66.
7. Cited in Marcel Trudel, *Histoire de la Nouvelle-France* (Montréal: Fides, 1963–1983), 1:131.
8. Lomier, "Les Picards au Canada," *Bulletin de la Société de géographie de Québec*, 19 (1925): 11.
9. Trudel, *Histoire de la Nouvelle-France*, 2: 423, 440.
10. Ibid., p. 276; Georges Goyau, *Les Origines religieuses du Canada: une épopée mystique* (Montréal: Fides, 1951), p. 84.
11. For a list of the original 100 associates and their successors, see Trudel, *Histoire de la Nouvelle-France*, 3, pt. 1: 415–437.
12. Marcel Trudel, *Initiation à la Nouvelle-France: histoire et institutions* (Montréal: Holt, Rinehart, and Winston, 1968), p. 54.
13. Trudel, *Histoire de la Nouvelle-France*, 3, pt. 1: 122.

14. Ibid., p. 171.

15. Hubert Charbonneau and Yves Landry, "La Politique démographique en Nouvelle-France," *Annales de démographie historique* (1979): 33. Founded in 1647, the Conseil de Québec brought together the governors of Québec and Montréal, the superior of the Jesuits, and, on a consultative basis only, elected representatives of Québec, Montréal, and Trois-Rivières.

16. Lucien Campeau, *Les Cent-Associés et le peuplement de la Nouvelle-France, 1633–1663*, Cahiers d'histoire des Jésuites, no. 2 (Montréal: Editions Bellarmin, 1974), p. 152.

17. Trudel, *Histoire de la Nouvelle-France*, 3, pt. 1: 399.

18. Gustave Lanctôt, *Histoire du Canada: du régime royal au traité d'Utrecht, 1663–1713* (Montréal: Beauchemin, 1963), p. 44.

19. The Compagnie des Indes was liquidated in 1674, bringing an end to the proprietary phase of the colony. All subsequent monopolies on the Canada trade were partial.

20. These efforts profited Québec almost exclusively. The British returned Acadia to France in 1667, but the French reoccupation did not begin until 1670. The king paid to send 55 indentured servants and 5 *filles à marier* to Acadia in 1672, the same year he announced the end of major subsidies for emigration. See Lanctôt, *Histoire du Canada*, pp. 255–264.

21. This figure, like that for the *filles à marier*, is an upper bound. For detailed estimates of the number of emigrants in both categories, see Rénald Lessard, "Faux-sauniers déportés au Canada (1730–1743)," ANQ: ms., 1987; Silvio Landry, *Les Filles du roi au XVIIe siècle: orphelines en France, pionnières au Canada* (Ottawa: Leméac, 1992), pp. 33–44.

22. There were exceptions to this rule. Colbert's son Seignelay, for example, provided passage for about 200 indentured servants in 1684 and 1685. See De Meulles to the minister, 1684, AC: C11A, vol. 6, p. 399, and minister to Arnoul, 8 March 1685, AC: B, vol. 11, p. 82.

23. In 1665 the Conseil souverain, which replaced the Conseil de Québec, renewed the provisions of the 1647 edict on indentured servants. The captain of a merchant ship not already carrying royal emigrants could acquire a permit for Québec only by embarking 1 workman per ten tons of cargo. See *Jugements et délibérations du conseil souverain de la Nouvelle-France* (Québec, 1885–1891), 1:269.

24. Royal ordinance of 20 March 1714, AC: C11G, vol. 8, p. 55; B, vol. 36, p. 336. See also minister to the comte de Toulouse, 20 March 1714, AC: B, vol. 36, p. 121; memorandum of the minister to Vaudreuil and Bégon, 19 March 1714, ibid., p. 338; naval council to Bégon, 16 June 1716, ibid., vol. 38, p. 204½; royal ordinance of 15 February 1724, AM: B3, vol. 368, p. 41.

25. Royal ordinances of 14 January, 20 May 1721, AC: B, vol. 44, pp. 56½, 161½; naval council to Gaudion, 13 June 1721, ibid., p. 56½; circular to the intendants

and commissars of the ports, 9 April 1722, ibid., vol. 45, p. 279$\frac{1}{2}$; naval council to Marin, 29 April 1722, ibid., p. 297$\frac{1}{2}$.

26. In this regard, the behavior of French shippers contrasts sharply with that of shippers in Rotterdam or the British Isles. Elsewhere in northern Europe, the transport of servants was big business; in France, it required compulsion. Perhaps the explanation lies in the different structures of colonial commerce. With the exception of New England, which attracted few servants after the Puritan exodus, British North America had an economy based on intensive commercial agriculture. The profitability of trade thus depended on maintaining an adequate labor supply. In Canada, as I discuss below, commercial agriculture failed to develop to the same degree, and the economy continued to revolve around the fur trade. For French shippers involved in the Canada trade, the obligation to transport servants must have seemed a distraction from the principal activity. In addition, the underdevelopment of the French colony with respect to the British warrants consideration. A tradition of mass emigration to British America already existed by the end of the seventeenth century, and entrepreneurs had only to take advantage of it. In France, the appeal of Canada remained limited and localized, while the bulk of French emigrants went elswhere. Neither in periods of monopoly nor those of free trade did French shippers make servants a major part of their Canadian commerce. On the servant trade outside of France, see Bernard Bailyn, *Voyagers to the West: A Passage in the Peopling of America on the Eve of the Revolution* (New York: Knopf, 1986); David Galenson, *White Servitude in Colonial America: An Economic Analysis* (Cambridge: Cambridge University Press, 1981); David Sacks, *Trade, Society, and Politics in Bristol, 1500–1640,* 2 vols. (New York: Garland, 1985); and Marianne Sophia Wokeck, "A Tide of Alien Rogues: The Flow and Ebb of German Immigration to Pennsylvania, 1683–1776" (Ph.D. diss., Temple University, 1983).

27. Peninsular Acadia returned temporarily to English control between 1690 and 1697 and definitively after 1710. Seigneurialism was used to colonize Ile Saint-Jean, which was intended to become the breadbasket of Ile Royale.

28. See royal orders in AC: B, vol. 36, p. 336; ibid., vol. 38, p. 204$\frac{1}{2}$; AM: B3, vol. 368, p. 41.

29. *Jugements et délibérations,* 1:269.

30. Although broadsheets from La Rochelle have not survived, posters sponsored by the merchant houses of Le Havre to promote emigration to the West Indies promised "the rank of master to artisans who indenture themselves; lumber, tools, and farm animals to cultivators; as much land as they can cultivate [to everyone]." Women were lured through the offer of a trade (cotton spinner) and marriage. See Jean Legoy, *Le Peuple du Havre et son histoire des origines à 1800* ([Le Havre]: n.p., 1980), p. 151.

31. Similarly, the relative youth of the indentured servants may have resulted as

much from the propensity of the young to migrate as from legislative imperative. Assuming that they were observed, however, the edicts must have excluded
willing men in their early forties, as well as adolescents below the age of
eighteen.

32. Four sources were used for nominative identification of the recruiters: Gabriel
Debien, "Les Engagés pour le Canada au XVIIe siècle," *Revue d'histoire de
l'Amérique française*, 6 (1952–1953): 221–233, 374–407; Gaucher, Delafosse, and
Debien, "Engagés pour le Canada au XVIIIe siècle," pp. 250–261, 406–418,
551–557 and 87–108, 246–258, 430–440, 583–591; Marc Delafosse, "La Rochelle
et le Canada au XVIIe siècle," *Revue d'histoire de l'Amérique française*, 4
(1950–1951): 469–511; list of Canadian recruiters in La Rochelle, ANQ: Godbout Collection, vol. 3.

33. The numbers cited throughout this discussion are only approximate. Lacunae
in both the preservation and examination of the documents make it impossible
to state exactly how many emigrants were recruited in a given time period.

34. Debien and Godbout uncovered fewer than 20 indentures for this period.

35. In the third quarter of the seventeenth century, Huguenots dominated La
Rochelle's overseas commerce; see Louis Pérouas, *Le Diocèse de La Rochelle de
1648 à 1724: sociologie et pastorale* (Paris: SEVPEN, 1964): 137.

36. The companies recruited only 55 servants, as compared with 128 for merchants
in the same time period.

37. The Catholics included Pierre Gaigneur, Arnaud Péré, Alexandre Petit, Jean
Péré, Jean Gitton, and Jean Grignon. Neither of the two Protestants, Daniel
Biaille and Louis Allaire, recruited on a large scale, although Allaire was one
of the city's most important merchants.

38. Religious persecution may have been a factor in the disappearance of Protestants as well.

39. In 1668 Heurtin became the first captain to dabble in the servant trade, and
Duret followed suit in 1684. The captains, some of whom were Canadian, never
embarked more than a handful of emigrants, but their trade was entirely
speculative despite its small size; unlike merchants, captains did not recruit by
proxy.

40. John Clark, *La Rochelle and the Atlantic Economy during the Eighteenth Century*
(Baltimore: Johns Hopkins University Press, 1981), pp. 117–118.

41. Claude de Razilly was the brother of Isaac de Razilly, the governor of Acadia
from 1632 to 1665. Together, they recruited some 120 permanent settlers for
the colony. See *Dictionary of Canadian Biography* (Toronto: Toronto University
Press, 1966–1990), 1: 567–569.

42. Debien, "Engagés pour le Canada au XVIIe siècle," pp. 221, 376 (quoted).

43. La Rochelle's seigneurial recruiters in this period included two women, Judith
Moreau, the mother superior of the Hospitalières of Montréal, and Jeanne
Mance, her lay administrator. Mance, in fact, was the most active recruiter of

the time, enlisting over 30 emigrants in 1659. Such recruiting efforts speak not only to the growing role of La Rochelle in the Canada trade but to the enhanced importance of its Catholic majority. A mere ten years earlier, the recruitment of colonists in La Rochelle by missionaries of the Catholic Reformation would have been unthinkable. See Debien, "Les Engagés du Canada au XVIIe siècle," p. 376, and list of Canadian recruiters, ANQ: Godbout Collection, vol. 3.

44. Joseph Besnard, "Les Diverses Professions de Robert Giffard," *Nova Francia*, 4 (1929): 325.

45. Françoise Montagne, *Tourouvre et les Juchereau: un chapitre de l'émigration percheronne au Canada* (Québec: Société canadienne de généalogie, 1965), p. 16.

46. Geneviève Massignon, "La Seigneurie de Charles de Menou d'Aulnay gouverneur de l'Acadie, 1635–1650," *Revue d'histoire de l'Amérique française*, 16 (1962–1963): 471.

47. Reuben Gold Thwaites, ed., *The Jesuit Relations and Allied Documents: Travels and Explorations of the Jesuit Missionaries in New France, 1610–1791* (Cleveland, 1896–1901), 9:187. The Jesuits also suggested sending artisans whose mobility would otherwise carry them beyond French territory, but peasants rather than artisans were the cornerstone of their conception of the colonial edifice.

48. Godbout, "Le Rôle du Saint-Jehan," pp. 22–23. Bourgueil and Chinon were actually on the Angevin border with Touraine.

49. Maria Mondoux, "Les Hommes de Montréal," *Revue d'histoire de l'Amérique française*, 2 (1948–1949): 59–80; "Tableau des contrats d'engagement pour le Canada passés en l'étude notariale de Tourouvre, 1641–1651," *Cahiers percherons*, 26 (1967): 45.

50. Thwaites, *Jesuit Relations*, 7:242.

51. Likewise, Jeanne Mance's Rochelais recruits from 1659 included 8 single men, 1 single woman, and 8 families with young children.

52. During the brief period of "polysynodie" (1715–1723), a Conseil de la Marine (naval council) replaced the minister.

53. André Corvisier, *L'Armée française de la fin du XVIIe siècle au ministère de Choiseul: le soldat* (Paris: PUF, 1964), 1: 147–148, 168.

54. Namely, Karrer, colonel of a Swiss regiment; Jacques de Pensens d'Espiet, major at Ile Royale; Daniel d'Auger de Subercase, captain and later major in the *troupes de la Marine;* the marquis de Vaudreuil, captain and later governor; Chacornacle, captain; François Amariton, captain; Jean-Charles de Sabrevois, captain; the comte d'Agrain, captain; Gourville, captain; the marquis d'Aloigny de la Groye, lieutenant; Paschot, lieutenant; De Gannes, lieutenant; Vallier, lieutenant; and Loppinot, sergeant.

55. The only explicit reference to the recruitment of soldiers by civilians occurred in 1694, when the minister announced an augmentation of 40 soldiers for the garrison of Plaisance in Newfoundland. The letter reads: "Some merchants from Bayonne have contracted, in return for two vessels which the king has

provided, to raise and transport the forty additional soldiers" (Minister to Du Brouillan, 10 March 1694, AC: B, vol. 17, p. 10).

56. La Jonquière to the minister, 1 November 1750, AC: C11A, vol. 93, p. 335.

57. Corvisier, *L'Armée française*, 1: 163–179.

58. Ibid., pp. 274, 410–411. The regional character of this regiment, however, weakened in the course of the eighteenth century, and the change was reflected in the composition of the Canadian troops. Of the 65 "Roussillonnais" who married in Canada in the 1750s and 1760s, 43 came from the South or Southwest, but there were also 12 easterners, 4 northerners, and 3 each from the Loire and the Center. See Yves Landry, "Quelques aspects du comportement démographique des troupes de terre envoyées au Canada pendant la Guerre de Sept Ans" (master's thesis, University of Montreal, 1977), p. 115.

59. Corvisier, *L'Armée française*, 1:159.

60. Minister to Pannetié, 4 February 1687, AM: B3, vol. 53, p. 59.

61. Naval council to La Galissonière, 29 June 1717, AC: B, vol. 39, p. 7.

62. Saint-Ovide and Le Normant to the minister, 24 October 1734, AC: C11B, vol. 15, p. 72.

63. Corvisier, *L'Armée française*, 1:275.

64. Ibid., p. 186.

65. Minister to Bégon, 8, 15 May 1725, AC: B, vol. 48, pp. 380, 387.

66. Vaudreuil to the minister, 6 November 1712, AC: C11A, vol. 33, p. 50.

67. Frontenac to the minister, 1696, ibid., vol. 14, p. 119.

68. Royal order, May 1702, AC: B, vol. 23, p. 90.

69. Naval council to La Galissonière, 21 July 1717, ibid., vol. 39, p. 77.

70. Minister to Ramesay, 6 May 1702, ibid., vol. 23, p. 73.

71. Minister to Beauharnais, 19 April 1735, ibid., vol. 63, p. 480½.

72. La Jonquière to the minister, 1 November 1750, AC: C11A, vol. 95, p. 335.

73. After mentioning the high incidence of disease and death, La Jonquière wrote that "Monsieur des Herbiers, Commander in Louisbourg, is in the same situation as myself . . . He must have had the honor of informing you of the rebellion of the soldiers detailed in Port Toulouse" (La Jonquière to the minister, 1 November 1750, ibid).

74. Minister to Durand, 1 April 1700, AC: B, vol. 22, p. 72.

75. Minister to Monic, 1701, ibid., p. 187; minister to Lhermite, 13 April 1701, ibid., p. 199.

76. Minister to Beauharnais, 9 April 1714, ibid., vol. 36, p. 56.

77. Naval council to La Galissonière, 22 April 1716, ibid., vol. 38, p. 106½.

78. Bigot to the minister, 16 October 1748, AC: C11A, vol. 92, p. 106.

79. Rousseau de Villejouin to the minister, 1 October 1750, ibid., p. 347.

80. René Mémain, *Le Matériel de la marine de guerre sous Louis XIV: Rochefort, arsenal modèle de Colbert (1666–1690)* (Paris: Hachette, 1936), pp. 32, 555.

81. Even Beauharnais sometimes took charge of recruiting himself, as when he engaged some 20 building workers for Ile Royale in 1714; see minister to

Beauharnais, 23 March 1714, AC: B, vol. 36, p. 143, and minister to Lhermite, 26 January 1714, ibid., p. 419. More often, he relied on his subordinates in the naval and civilian administrations: the *commissaires* and *subdélégués*.

82. Royal order to D'Agrain, 28 January 1720, AC: B, vol. 42, p. 466. Orders to recruit bore a formulaic appeal to governors and intendants on behalf of the recruiter. This one reads, in its entirety: "His Majesty informs all governors, intendants, and commissars . . . in the said generalities to give [him] . . . the assistance and facilities that he might need to carry out the said levy."

83. In 1750, for example, the minister commissioned the recruitment of 50 to 60 ship's carpenters in the ports of the kingdom. See minister to La Jonquière and Bigot, 15 April 1750, AC: B, vol. 91, p. 25; minister to Le Tourneur, 30 March 1750, ibid., vol. 92, p. 77½; and minister to du Ronsay, 30 March 1750, ibid., p. 79.

84. The ironworkers were needed for the opening of a foundry in Trois-Rivières, the Forges Saint-Maurice. On their recruitment, see minister to the comtesse de Grancey, 2 March 1737, AC: B, vol. 65, p. 24½; minister to De la Croix, 13 May 1737, ibid., p. 178½; minister to Beauharnais and Hocquart, 30 April 1737, ibid., p. 413½; minister to Olivier de Vezin, 14 March 1740, ibid., vol. 70, p. 35; minister to Tavannes, ibid., p. 52½; minister to Vezin, 2 May 1740, ibid., p. 54; and royal order, 2 January 1740, ibid., vol. 71, p. 1. The recruitment of Savoyard chimney sweeps was also discussed periodically in the correspondence; see Beauharnais and Hocquart to the minister, 9 November 1729, AC: C11A, vol. 51, p. 114; Hocquart to the minister, 25 October 1730, ibid., vol. 53, p. 205; minister to Hocquart, 17 April 1731, AC: B, vol. 55, p. 491; minister to Bigot, 4 May 1749, ibid., vol. 89, p. 25 [227].

85. Naval council to Beauharnais, 24 April 1720, AC: B, vol. 42, p. 175; royal order to D'Agrain, 28 January 1720, ibid., p. 466.

86. Beauharnais and Hocquart made use of this economic argument in their plea for Savoyard chimney sweeps: "They will be usefully occupied for the public and will be able to earn their living better than in any place in the kingdom. There are no days when they cannot not earn seven to eight livres" (Beauharnais and Hocquart to the minister, 9 November 1729, AC: C11A, vol. 51, p. 114).

87. As I have noted, the company also recruited small numbers of servants on its own account in La Rochelle.

88. Talon to Colbert, 22 April 1665, AC: C11A, vol. 2, p. 124.

89. Talon to Colbert, 27 October 1667, ibid., p. 306.

90. Colbert to Laval, 15 May 1669, AC: B, vol. 1, p. 144. Colbert's instructions to Colbert de Terron appear in AM: B2, vol. 9, p. 68.

91. Hubert Charbonneau, *Vie et mort de nos ancêtres: étude démographique* (Montréal: PUM, 1975), p. 41.

92. A member of the Compagnie du Saint-Sacrement, Montbard became an associate of the Société Notre-Dame de Montréal in 1642; see Marie-Claire Daveluy,

La Société Notre-Dame de Montréal, 1639–1663: son histoire, ses membres, son manifeste (Montréal: Fides, 1965), pp. 197–199.

93. Memorandum of Talon, 9 March 1673, AC: C11A, vol. 4, p. 28.

94. Minister to the archbishop of Rouen, 27 February 1670, AC: B, vol. 2, p. 15.

95. See n. 93 above.

96. Minister to Daguesseau, 24 May 1684, AM: B2, vol. 53, p. 112.

97. François de Nion, ed., *Un outre-mer au XVIIe siècle: voyages au Canada du baron de La Hontan* (Paris: Plon, 1900), pp. 17–18.

98. Colbert to Talon, 5 April 1667, AC: C11A, vol. 2, p. 290.

99. Talon to Colbert, 27 October 1667, ibid., p. 306.

100. Memorandum of Talon to Colbert, 10 November 1670, ibid., vol. 3, p. 77; Talon to Louis XIV, 2 November 1671, ibid., p. 159.

101. Minister to Beauharnais and Dupuy, 4 May 1726, AC: B, vol. 49, p. 645; minister to the bishop of Québec, 4 May 1726, ibid., p. 674.

102. An earlier attempt at deportation may have occurred in 1663, when the colony came directly under royal jurisdiction; in that year the Parlement of Paris, in response to bloody riots, prohibited kidnapping in the streets, "by stealth and violence, of girls and boys under the pretext of sending them to America" (cited in Jean Nicolas, "La Rumeur de Paris: rapts d'enfants en 1750," *L'Histoire,* 40 [1981]: 50).

103. Saint-Vallier to the minister, 4 October 1725, AC: C11A, vol. 47, p. 462.

104. Minister to Beauharnais and Dupuy, 4 May 1726, AC: B, vol. 49, p. 645; Minister to Saint-Vallier, 4 May 1726, ibid., p. 674.

105. See letters of Beauharnais and Hocquart to the minister, 15 October 1730, AC: C11A, vol. 52, p. 86, and 5 October 1735, ibid., vol. 62, p. 43.

106. Minister to Croisil, 28 June 1712, AC: B, vol. 34, p. 375.

107. Minister to Beauharnais and Hocquart, 25 April 1730, ibid., vol. 54, p. 472, and 8 May 1743, ibid., vol. 76, p. 70.

108. Minister to Beauharnais and Hocquart, 8 May 1743, ibid., vol. 76, p. 70. In this regard, French deportees resembled the much larger group of criminals deported from the British Isles to America in the eighteenth century; "lawbreaking was for them not so much a source of gain as a way to make do during harsh times" (A. Roger Ekirch, "Bound for America: A Profile of British Convicts Transported to the Colonies, 1718–1775," *William and Mary Quarterly,* 42 [1985]: 197).

109. Beauharnais and Hocquart to the minister, 28 October 1742, AC: C11A, vol. 77, p. 33.

110. Reading the administrative correspondence, one runs across frequent admonitions to ensure that the prisoners "cannot return to France." A couple of smugglers resorted to flamboyant tactics to put an end to their exile; Joseph Bertet received his discharge in 1734 "for having declared himself a hermaphrodite," although, back in France, "they judged that there exist in this individual none of the signs that have given rise to his return" (Minister to Beauharnais

and Hocquart, 2 May 1729, AC: B, vol. 53, p. 548½, and 19 April 1735, ibid., vol. 63, p. 475½). As for Pierre Revol, who "had made an honest fortune in the colony, had married there," needing "his liberty . . . to . . . follow the operations of maritime commerce in which he had an interest," he "embarked clandestinely on a ship. . . Upon the arrival of a detachment of troops come to arrest him, he provoked a mutiny" (minister to La Galissonière and Bigot, 4 May 1749, ibid., vol. 89, p. 71).

111. Beauharnais and Hocquart to the minister, 5 October 1736, AC: C11A, vol. 65, p. 55.

112. Hocquart to the minister, 29 October 1744, ibid., vol. 82, p. 85.

113. Beauharnais and Hocquart to the minister, 28 October 1742, ibid., vol. 77, p. 33.

114. Minister to Beauharnais and Dupuy, 19 May 1728, AC: B, vol. 52, p. 549.

115. Brouillan and Lenormant to the minister, 28 October 1737, AC: C11B, vol. 19, p. 33.

116. The correspondence of Orry, however, suggests yet another reality—namely, that Canada also served as a dumping ground for the undesirables of the Ferme générale. In the mid-1730s deportation orders were issued to such incorrigible *chefs de bande* as Phillipe Guerry *dit* le Dragon and Simon Monny *dit* la Mort, and in 1734 the smugglers were so unsavory that the ship's captain in La Rochelle refused to embark four of them, including one who was stricken with "inveterate mange." Of course, the Canadians soon caught on, but Orry exerted enough influence to maintain the convoys at a reduced level for another decade. His successor tried unsuccessfully to renew the deportations in 1750. Interestingly, British deportees also included "more than a handful" of criminals belonging to organized gangs. See Orry to the minister, 15 February 1734, AM: B3, vol. 373, p. 65; Orry to the minister, 31 January 1735, ibid., p. 69; minister to the comptroller general, 18 September 1750, AC: B, vol. 92, p. 217½; Ekirch, "Bound for America," p. 199.

Conclusion

1. Bernard Bailyn, *Voyagers to the West: A Passage in the Peopling of America on the Eve of the Revolution* (New York: Knopf, 1986), p. 25. See also Henry Gemery, "European Emigration to North America, 1700–1820: Numbers and Quasi Numbers," *Perspectives in American History,* new ser., 1 (1984): 320.

2. Francis Parkman, *France and England in North America,* 12 vols. (Boston, 1851–1892). Recent Anglo-Canadian historiography has strayed surprisingly little from Parkman's original formulations on this point; however, some authors do question his value judgments. Finlay and Sprague, for example, wrote in 1984 that "in attempting to weigh English libertarianism and French absolutism, those who prefer size-growth of an economy will be forever troubled by the comparatively unimpressive economic development of New France . . . Those who place human development above property rights, on

the other hand, will forever defend the statism of New France and denounce the New Englanders" (J. L. Finlay and D. N. Sprague, *The Structure of Canadian History*, 2d ed. [Scarborough, Ont.: Prentice-Hall, 1984], pp. 45–46).

3. Jean Baptiste Antoine Ferland, *Cours d'histoire du Canada*, 2 vols. (Québec, 1861–1865); Etienne Michel Faillon, *Histoire de la colonie française en Canada*, 3 vols. (Villemarie [Montréal], 1865–1866).

4. Jean-Pierre Wallot, "Religion and French-Canadian Mores in the Early Nineteenth Century," *Canadian Historical Review*, 52 (1971): 51. This traditional view has come under increasing attack in the years since the Quiet Revolution.

5. On the lingering communitarianism of colonial New England's "distinct society," see Jack Greene, *Pursuits of Happiness: The Social Development of Early Modern British Colonies and the Formation of American Culture* (Chapel Hill: University of North Carolina Press, 1988), pp. 30–52, and Patrice Higonnet, *Sister Republics: The Origins of French and American Republicanism* (Cambridge: Harvard University Press, 1988), pp. 11–47.

6. "Les Véritables Motifs de messieurs et dames de la Société Notre-Dame de Montréal pour la conversion des sauvages de Nouvelle-France," *Mémoires de la Société historique de Montréal*, 9 (1880): 20. Ironically, this utopian image was perpetuated in the eighteenth century by the *philosophes*—most notably, Abbé Raynal; see Naomi Griffiths, "Longfellow's *Evangeline:* The Birth and Acceptance of a Legend," *Acadiensis*, 11 (1982): 28–41.

7. The name change, it should be noted, came about because Montréal's inhabitants refused to call their town Ville-Marie. Louise Dechêne, in her classic study of seventeenth-century Montrealers, emphasized their difference from ordinary Frenchmen: "In a primarily peasant France, wrote Goubert, I tried to get to know the peasants . . . We would gladly write: in a primarily mercantile Canada, we must get to know the merchants" (Louise Dechêne, *Habitants et marchands de Montréal au XVIIᵉ siècle* [Paris: Plon, 1974], p. 125).

8. Emile Salone, *La Colonisation de la Nouvelle-France: étude sur les origines de la nation canadienne-française* (1905; Trois-Rivières: Boréal Express, 1970), p. 138. On the development of Montréal, see Phyllis Lambert and Alan Stewart, eds., *Opening the Gates of Eighteenth-Century Montréal* (Montréal: Centre canadien d'architecture, 1992).

9. Salone, *Colonisation*, pp. 191–192. For reasons that I discuss below, Salone did not consider the rural agglomerations of contemporary Québec to be villages in the traditional sense.

10. Duchesneau to the minister, 13 November 1681, AC: C11A, vol. 5, p. 316.

11. Memorandum of Raudot, 20 August 1708, ibid., vol. 6, p. 39½. Within two years, however, Raudot was sounding just like Duchesneau, only more so. He not only expressed enthusiasm about the growing trade with the Antilles but proposed that allowing free trade with the English would produce a good profit! See memorandum of Raudot, 27 February 1710, ibid., p. 72.

12. Bigot to the minister, 7 November 1748, AC: C11A, vol. 92, p. 189.

13. François de Nion, ed., *Un outre-mer au XVIIe siècle: voyages au Canada du baron de La Hontan* (Paris: Plon, 1900), p. 14.

14. Memorandum of the king to Vaudreuil and Beauharnais, 14 June 1704, AC: B, vol. 25, p. 107. This policy was, however, reversed in 1750; see minister to Bigot, 15 April 1750, AC: B, vol. 91, p. 19 [246].

15. The case of Canada's first agricultural settler, Louis Hébert, suggests that from the outset, colonizers viewed commerce, not subsistence, as the primary function of Canadian agriculture. In 1617 Hébert indentured himself for two years for an annual sum of 300 livres, and he contracted to continue marketing his produce through the trading company after the expiration of his indenture. See Marcel Trudel, *Histoire de la Nouvelle-France* (Montréal: Fides, 1963–1983), 2:244.

16. Salone, *Colonisation*, p. 374. See also Dale Miquelon, *New France, 1701–1744: A Supplement to Europe* (Toronto: McClelland and Stewart, 1987) pp. 199, 317–318.

17. Dechêne, *Habitants et marchands*, pp. 340–342. See also Christopher Moore, "Cape Breton and the North Atlantic World in the Eighteenth Century," in *The Island: New Perspectives on Cape Breton's History, 1713–1990*, ed. Kenneth Donovan (Fredericton, N.B.: Acadiensis, 1990), p. 43. Wheat prices in the Saint Lawrence went into a seventy-five-year decline beginning in the 1650s.

18. Dechêne, *Habitants et marchands*, p. 342.

19. Gilles Paquet and Jean-Pierre Wallot, "Sur quelques discontinuités dans l'expérience socio-économique du Québec: une hypothèse," *Revue d'histoire de l'Amérique française*, 35 (1982): 496.

20. Serge Courville, "Espace, territoire, et culture en Nouvelle-France: une vision géographique," ibid., 37 (1983): 421. See also Jacques Mathieu, "Les Relations ville-campagne: Québec et sa région au XVIIIe siècle," in *Société rurale dans la France de l'Ouest et au Québec, XVIIe–XXe siècles, Actes des Colloques de 1979 et 1980*, ed. Jean-Pierre Wallot (Montréal: PUM; Paris: EHESS, 1981).

21. Louise Dechêne, "Observations sur l'agriculture du Bas-Canada au début du XIXe siècle," in *Evolution et éclatement du monde rural: structures, fonctionnement et évolution différentielle des sociétés rurales françaises et québécoises, XVIIe–XXe siècles, Colloque franco-québécois d'histoire rurale comparée (1982: Rochefort France)*, ed. Joseph Goy and Jean-Pierre Wallot (Paris, EHESS; Montréal: PUM, 1986), p. 189.

22. On land speculation in British North America, see Bernard Bailyn, *The Peopling of British North America: An Introduction* (New York: Knopf, 1986), pp. 65–85, 154–155.

23. Céline Cyr, "La Formation d'une communauté rurale en Nouvelle-France: Beaumont, 1672–1740," in *Peuplement colonisateur aux XVIIe et XVIIIe siècles*, ed. Jacques Mathieu and Serge Courville, Cahiers du CELAT, no. 8 (Québec: CELAT, Faculté des lettres, Université Laval, 1987), pp. 267–269.

24. Jacques Saint-Pierre, "L'Aménagement de l'espace rural en Nouvelle-France:

les seigneuries de la Côte-du-Sud," ibid., pp. 146, 149. In the Montréal region, common pastures existed, but were allotted to and maintained by individuals. By the early eighteenth century, they were disappearing in favor of individual property. See Dechêne, *Habitants et marchands*, p. 311.

25. John Dickinson, "La Conception populaire de la tenure en Normandie et en Nouvelle-France," in *Evolution et éclatement* (see n. 21 above), pp. 166–170.

26. See, for example, Allan Greer, *Peasant, Lord, and Merchant: Rural Society in Three Quebec Parishes, 1740–1840* (Toronto: University of Toronto Press, 1985), and Roberta Hamilton, "Feudal Society and Colonization: A Critique and Reinterpretation of the Historiography of New France," in *Canadian Papers in Rural History*, ed. Donald Akenson, 6 (1988): 17–135, also published as *Feudal Society and Colonization: The Historiography of New France* (Gananoque, Ont.: Langdale, 1988). Interestingly, this argument about the "feudal mode of production" is not made about the system of burdensome quitrents collected by the Hudson River "barons" of New York, or by landed proprietors elsewhere in the British colonies.

27. Miquelon, *New France*, p. 198. Even in France, as has been mentioned, seigneurialism was not incompatible with extensive market involvement by peasants in many regions.

28. Courville, "Espace, territoire, et culture," p. 421.

29. Paquet and Wallot, "Sur quelques discontinuités," p. 495. The term "prefabricated society" was coined by Sigmund Diamond in "Le Canada français au XVIIᵉ siècle: une société préfabriquée," *Annales: économies, sociétés, civilisations*, 16 (1961): 317–354.

30. Jacques Mathieu, *Le Commerce entre la Nouvelle-France et les Antilles au XVIIIᵉ siècle* (Montréal: Fides, 1981), pp. 33–72.

31. Saint-Pierre, "L'Aménagement de l'espace rural," p. 156.

32. Mathieu, "Relations ville-campagne," p. 198.

33. Mathieu, *Commerce*, pp. 25, 221.

34. Saint-Pierre, "L'Aménagement de l'espace rural," pp. 149–157.

35. Ibid., p. 160.

36. Louis Michel, "Un marchand rural en Nouvelle-France: François-Augustin Bailly de Messein, 1709–1771," *Revue d'histoire de l'Amérique française*, 33 (1979): 215–262. See also Lise St-Georges, "Commerce, crédit, et transactions foncières: pratiques de la communauté marchande du bourg de l'Assomption, 1748–1791," 39 (1986): 323–343.

37. Serge Courville, "Villages and Agriculture in the Seigneuries of Lower Canada: Conditions of a Comprehensive Study of Rural Québec in the First Half of the Nineteenth Century," in *Canadian Papers in Rural History*, ed. Donald Akenson, 5 (1986): 128.

38. Serge Courville, "Croissance villageoise et industries rurales dans les seigneuries du Québec (1815–1851)," in *Sociétés villageoises et rapports villes-campagnes au Québec et dans la France de l'Ouest, XVIIᵉ–XXᵉ siècles*, ed. François

Lebrun and Normand Séguin (Trois-Rivières: Centre de recherche en études
québécoises; Rennes: Presses de l'Université de Rennes, 1987), pp. 209–210.

39. Greer, *Peasant, Lord, and Merchant*, p. 196.

40. Jean-Pierre Wallot, "L'Impact du marché sur les campagnes canadiennes au
début du XIXe siècle," in *Société rurale* (see n. 20 above), p. 239. The relatively
high literacy rates of the first generation and the prevalence of Parisian French
in the countryside further corroborate this judgment; see Raymond Douville
and Jacques-Donat Casanova, *La Vie quotidienne en Nouvelle-France: le Canada,
de Champlain à Montcalm* (Montréal: Hachette, 1982), pp. 248–250, and Hubert
Charbonneau, "Le Caractère français des pionniers de la vallée laurentienne,"
Cahiers québécois de démographie, 19 (1990): 49–61.

41. Miquelon, *New France*, p. 203.

42. R. Cole Harris, "The Simplification of Europe Overseas," *Annals of the Association of American Geographers*, 67 (1977): 476, 478–479.

43. Barry Moody, "From the Ground Up: Re-examining the Pre-Expulsion Acadian
Experience" (paper presented at the biennial meeting of the Association for
Canadian Studies in the United States, New Orleans, 1993); Griffiths, "Long-
fellow's *Evangeline*."

44. The British controlled Acadia from 1654 to 1667, and the French did not actually
retake possession of the colony until 1670.

45. Naomi Griffiths, "Perceptions of Acadians: The Importance of Tradition,"
British Journal of Canadian Studies, 5 (1990): 105; "Acadian Identity on the Eve
of the Deportation: Distinct and Particular Communities" (paper presented at
the biennial meeting of the Association for Canadian Studies in the United
States, New Orleans, 1993).

46. The extensive network of dikes constructed by the Acadians is evidence of
their technical ingenuity. In some parts of the Annapolis Valley, Acadian
drainage techniques are still in use today.

47. Perrot, an Acadian governor, cited in Naomi Griffiths, *The Contexts of Acadian
History, 1686–1784* (Montréal: McGill–Queen's University Press, 1992), p. 22.

48. Moody, "From the Ground Up."

49. Jean Daigle, ed., *The Acadians of the Maritimes: Thematic Studies* (Moncton,
N.B.: Centre d'études acadiennes, 1982), p. 32.

50. Griffiths, *Contexts of Acadian History*, p. 20; John Reid, *Acadia, Maine, and New
Scotland: Marginal Colonies in the Seventeenth Century* (Toronto: University of
Toronto Press, 1981), p. 160.

51. Griffiths, *Contexts of Acadian History*, p. 25.

52. Daigle, *Acadians*, pp. 28, 39; Naomi Griffiths, "The Golden Age: Acadian Life,
1713–1748," *Histoire sociale/Social History*, 17 (1984): 28.

53. Andrée Crépeau and Brenda Dunn, "L'Etablissement Melanson: un site agricole
acadien (vers 1664–1755)," *Bulletin de recherches*, 250 (Parcs Canada, 1986): 12,
17; David Christianson, "Belleisle 1983: Excavation at a Pre-Expulsion Acadian
Site," *Curatorial Report No. 48* (Nova Scotia Museum, July 1984). See also

Andrée Crépeau and Brenda Dunn, "A Cultural Landscape: Archaeological and Historical Perspectives on the Settlement Pattern at the Melanson Site" (paper presented at the annual meeting of the French Colonial Historical Society, Sydney and Louisbourg, Nova Scotia, 1994), and Moody, "From the Ground Up." According to Stewart Doty, excavations of an Acadian settlement from the 1680s at Castine, Maine, have yielded similar results.

54. Griffiths, "Golden Age," p. 28. It also appears that, by the eighteenth century, significant class differences were appearing among the Acadians. Current research at the Université de Moncton on Acadian marriage patterns shows a cessation of intermarriage between the more prominent families and those with Native American blood, for example.

55. Cited in Reid, *Acadia*, p. 160.

56. Griffiths, *Contexts of Acadian History*, p. 42; "Golden Age," pp. 23–24. The Acadian representatives included members of the Melanson family, prosperous farmers with mercantile and seigneurial connections. Of mixed Huguenot, Catholic, and English origins, they had close family ties in Boston. See Crépeau and Dunn, "L'Etablissement Melanson," pp. 3–6.

57. Current research of Donald Desserud at the University of New Brunswick, Saint John.

58. Crépeau and Dunn, "L'Etablissement Melanson," pp. 10, 12; Moody, "From the Ground Up." David Christianson has pointed out that Acadian houses, although small, were constructed in a variety of styles, reflecting their builders' embrace of a broad range of European cultural traditions.

59. Daigle, *Acadians of the Maritimes*, p. 40. During this interval, the Acadian population grew from 5,000 to nearly 15,000. As for tax evasion under the French Regime, one of the best examples comes from the Melanson site in Port-Royal. Archaeological evidence has shown that, in 1707, the farm actually contained nine times more arable land than was claimed in the census of the same year. See Crépeau and Dunn, "Cultural Landscape." On resistance to French taxation, see also Griffiths, *Contexts of Acadian History*, p. 30.

60. Daniel Usner has noted that similar unwarranted accusations of laziness were made against settlers by officials of the French Regime in Louisiana. Here again the problem was less a failure to produce than a failure to let officials share the profits of the very active but feebly regulated frontier exchange economy. See Daniel Usner, *Indians, Settlers, and Slaves in a Frontier Exchange Economy* (Chapel Hill: University of North Carolina Press, 1992), pp. 246–274, 277.

61. Daigle, *Acadians of the Maritimes*, p. 146; John McNeill, *Atlantic Empires of France and Spain: Louisbourg and Havana, 1700–1763* (Chapel Hill: University of North Carolina Press, 1985), pp. 151–152; Miquelon, *New France*, p. 117.

62. For broad-based descriptions of life on Ile Royale, see Eric Krause, Carol Corbin, and William O'Shea, eds., *Aspects of Louisbourg: Essays on the History of an Eighteenth-Century French Community in North America* (Sydney: University College of Cape Breton Press, 1995), and Christoper Moore, *Louisbourg*

Portraits: Five Dramatic, True Tales of People Who Lived in an Eighteenth-Century Garrison Town (Toronto: Macmillan, 1982).

63. Moore, "Cape Breton," pp. 32, 38–39, 42.

64. McNeill, *Atlantic Empires*, p. 178.

65. Moore, "Cape Breton," p. 42.

66. Christopher Moore, "The Other Louisbourg: Trade and Merchant Enterprise in Ile Royale, 1713–58," *Histoire sociale/Social History*, 12 (1979): 96. The inhabitants of Louisbourg were likewise no strangers to cultural modernity. Books were found there in relative abundance, and although 89% of them belonged to 40% of the population, 18% of the lower classes were book owners. The most popular genres were reading primers and religious works, including many copies of the Bible and Jansenist writings such as Pascal's *Pensées*. There were also scientific treatises, works in Italian, Spanish, and Dutch, and classics of the French Enlightenment such as Voltaire's histories and Montesquieu's *Lettres persanes*. See Laurent Lavoie, "Livres, libraires, et bibliothèques à la Forteresse de Louisbourg au XVIIIe siècle" (paper presented at the annual meeting of the French Colonial Historical Society, Sydney and Louisbourg, Nova Scotia, 1995).

67. Griffiths, *Contexts of Acadian History*, pp. 89–90.

68. Daigle, *Acadians of the Maritimes*, pp. 48–49; Griffiths, *Contexts of Acadian History*, pp. 89–90, 122–127; Usner, *Indians, Settlers, and Slaves*, p. 109.

69. Griffiths, *Contexts of Acadian History*, pp. 95–96.

70. Margaret Conrad, ed., *Making Adjustments: Change and Continuity in Planter Nova Scotia, 1759–1800* (Fredericton, N.B.: Acadiensis, 1991), p. 57. The continued ideological independence of Louisiana Acadians was evident in religion as well as politics; they were noted for their anticlericalism. See Carl Brasseaux, *The Founding of New Acadia: The Beginnings of Acadian Life in Louisiana, 1765–1803* (Baton Rouge: Louisiana State University Press, 1987), pp. 150–166.

71. Usner, *Indians, Settlers, and Slaves*, p. 180 (his translation).

72. Ibid., pp. 187–189. On the reconstitution of Acadian economic prosperity in Louisiana, see also Brasseaux, *Founding of New Acadia*, pp. 121–132, 191–193.

73. The crucial turning point for the Cajuns was not the eighteenth century but the Civil War. According to Carl Brasseaux, "The Acadian community that emerged from the turbulent Reconstruction era bore little resemblance to the dynamic and highly stratified prewar society, much of which had been upwardly mobile both economically and socially and was becoming integrated into the American mainstream. The postwar Acadian community became essentially a two-tiered society in which status and wealth were polarized between a small educated and influential gentry caste and a large and growing underclass of landless sharecroppers" (Carl Brasseaux, *Acadian to Cajun: Transformation of a People, 1803–1877* [Jackson: University of Mississippi Press, 1992], p. 150).

74. Liliane Plamondon, "Une femme d'affaires en Nouvelle-France: Marie-Anne Barbel, veuve Fornel," *Revue d'histoire de l'Amérique française*, 31 (1977): 181.

75. Michel, "Un marchand rural," p. 260.

76. Greer, *Peasant, Lord, and Merchant*, pp. 141–146.

77. Among the many works on this subject, see Serge Courville, "L'Habitant canadien dans la première moitié du XIXe siècle: survie ou survivance?" *Recherches sociographiques*, 27 (1986): 177–193, and R. M. McInnis, "A Reconsideration of the State of Agriculture in Lower Canada in the First Half of the Nineteenth Century," in *Canadian Papers in Rural History*, ed. Donald Akenson, 3 (1982): 9–49. For an older and more pessimistic view of rural Québec in this period, see Fernand Ouellet, *Economy, Class, and Nation in Quebec: Interpretive Essays* (Toronto: Copp Clark Pitman, 1991).

78. Dechêne, "Observations sur l'agriculture," p. 196; Greer, *Peasant, Lord, and Merchant*, p. 217. Although the English plow did not catch on around Montréal, agronomists belatedly conceded that it was ill suited to that region's heavier soils.

79. Serge Courville, "La Crise agricole du Bas-Canada: éléments d'une réflexion géographique," *Cahiers de géographie du Québec*, 24 (1980): 201, 204; W. H. Parker, "A Revolution in the Agricultural Geography of Lower Canada, 1833–1838," *Revue canadienne de géographie*, 11 (1957): 190.

80. Dechêne, "Observations sur l'agriculture," pp. 195, 198.

81. J. I. Little, *Crofters and Habitants: Settler Society, Economy, and Culture in a Quebec Township, 1848–1881* (Montréal: McGill–Queen's University Press, 1991), p. 178. See also Gilles Paquet and Jean-Pierre Wallot, "Crédit et endettement en milieu rural bas-canadien," in *Famille, économie, et société rurale en contexte d'urbanisation (XVIIe–XXe siècle)*, ed. Gérard Bouchard and Joseph Goy (Chicoutimi: SOREP; Paris: EHESS, 1990), p. 259, and George Bervin, "Aperçu sur le commerce et le crédit à Québec, 1820–1830," *Revue d'histoire de l'Amérique française*, 36 (1983): 550–551.

82. Serge Courville, "Esquisse du développement villageois au Québec: le cas de l'aire seigneuriale entre 1760 et 1854," *Cahiers de géographie du Québec*, 28 (1984): 25.

83. Yves Otis, "Dépopulation rurale et structures socio-professionnelles dans trois localités de la plaine de Montréal, 1861–1901," in *Les Chemins de la migration en Belgique et au Québec du XVIIe au XXe siècle*, ed. Yves Landry, John Dickinson, Suzy Pasleau, and Claude Desama (Louvain-la-Neuve: Editions Académia, 1995), p. 128.

84. Léo-Paul Hébert, *Le Québec de 1850 en lettres détachées* (Québec: Ministère des affaires culturelles, 1985), pp. 34–36. See also Jean-Claude Robert, "Un seigneur entrepreneur: Barthélemy Joliette, et la fondation du village d'Industrie (Joliette)," *Revue d'histoire de l'Amérique française*, 26 (1972): 375–396.

85. Courville, "Villages and Agriculture," p. 128.

86. Gilles Paquet and Jean-Pierre Wallot, "Structures sociales et niveaux de richesse dans les campagnes du Québec, 1792–1812," in *Evolution et éclatement* (see n. 2 above), pp. 243–244.

87. Gilles Paquet and Jean-Pierre Wallot, "Stratégie foncière de l'habitant: Québec (1790–1835)," *Revue d'histoire de l'Amérique française*, 39 (1986), 559; Paquet and Wallot, "Crédit et endettement," p. 265; and Wallot, "L'Impact du marché," p. 235.

88. Normand Séguin and Françoise-Eugénie Petit, "La Marginalité rurale au Québec et en France, XIXe et XXe siècles," in *Evolution et éclatement*, p. 263.

89. Dechêne, "Observations sur l'agriculture," p. 199.

90. Roger Le Moine, "La Franc-maçonnerie sous le régime français," *Les Cahiers des Dix*, 44 (1989): 121–122, 133. According to Masonic historians, a French-Canadian lodge existed as early as 1721, but its registers can no longer be located.

91. Cited ibid., p. 119.

92. Ibid., pp. 122–126, 130.

93. Wallot, "Religion and French-Canadian Mores," p. 53.

94. Paquet and Wallot, "Sur quelques discontinuités," p. 502.

95. Allan Greer, *The Patriots and the People: The Rebellion of 1837 in Rural Lower Canada* (Toronto: University of Toronto Press, 1993), pp. 203–204.

96. Wallot, "Religion and French-Canadian Mores," pp. 53, 75.

97. Greer, *Peasant, Lord, and Merchant*, p. 143.

98. Brian Young and John Dickinson, *A Short History of Quebec: A Socio-Economic Perspective* (Toronto: Copp Clark Pitman, 1988), p. 149.

99. Greer, *Patriots and the People*, p. 341.

100. Ibid., p. 191 (his translation).

101. On Marie Antoinette, see Lynn Hunt, "The Many Bodies of Marie Antoinette: Political Pornography and the Problem of the Feminine in the French Revolution," in *Eroticism and the Body Politic*, ed. Lynn Hunt (Baltimore: Johns Hopkins University Press, 1991), and "Pornography in the French Revolution," in *The Invention of Pornography*, ed. Lynn Hunt (New York: Zone, 1993).

102. Greer, *Patriots and the People*, pp. 210–212. On the American experience, see Mary Beth Norton, *Liberty's Daughters: The Revolutionary Experience of American Women, 1750–1800* (Boston: Little, Brown, 1980), pp. 166–168.

103. Wallot, *Société rurale* (see n. 20 above), p. 12.

104. Cited in Brian Young, *George-Etienne Cartier: Montreal Bourgeois* (Montréal: McGill–Queen's University Press, 1981), p. 102.

105. Young and Dickinson, *Short History of Quebec*, p. 156.

106. Cited ibid., p. 152 (their translation). The specific law in question gave full legal recognition, for the first time, to the property rights of the Sulpician order. Wellington's comment was also made in reference to this legislation.

107. Young, *George-Etienne Cartier*, p. 106. This transformation is less surprising when one considers that the Sulpicians had been cautiously moving to accommodate the new economic order for quite some time. According to Corinne Beutler, they had already reduced their seigneurial claims earlier in the century as a result of their involvement in "the industrial transformation of Montréal."

Another factor in the reduction may have been an awareness by the order "of the increasing difficulties that it would encounter on the political plane, in the exercise of its seigneurial rights." (Corinne Beutler, "Le Rôle des moulins banaux du Séminaire de Saint-Sulpice à Montréal entre la campagne et la ville, 1790–1840," in *Evolution et éclatement*, pp. 176, 180).

108. Young and Dickinson, *Short History of Quebec*, pp. 161–165.

109. Young, *George-Etienne Cartier*, p. 121; R. D. Francis, Richard Jones, and Donald Smith, *Destinies: Canadian History Since Confederation* (Toronto: Holt, Rinehart, and Winston, 1988), pp. 131–132.

110. Cited in Francis, Jones, and Smith, *Destinies*, p. 41 (their translation).

111. René Hardy and Jean Roy, "Mutation de la culture religieuse en Mauricie, 1850–1900," in *Evolution et éclatement*, pp. 397–413. See also Little, *Crofters and Habitants*, pp. 202–218.

112. Young and Dickinson, *Short History of Quebec*, pp. 155–156.

113. Courville, "L'Habitant canadien," pp. 177, 192–193.

114. Paquet and Wallot, "Sur quelques discontinuités," p. 511.

115. Young, *George-Etienne Cartier*, pp. 17, 18, 24, 64.

116. Hugh Allan (1810–1882) came from a family with international shipping interests, as opposed to merchant connections in the Richelieu Valley. In the second half of the nineteenth century, he parlayed those interests into "an integrated financial, transportation, and manufacturing empire," becoming in the process "one of Canada's first monopoly capitalists." (*Dictionary of Canadian Biography*, 11:14). By the 1870s, Allan's spin-off enterprises included Canada's second-largest bank; telephone and telegraph companies; warehousing, elevator, station, bridge, and tunnel companies; insurance companies; textile, shoe, iron-and-steel, tobacco, and paper mills; western ranches; fisheries; and coal mines; see ibid., pp. 5–14.

117. Young, *George-Etienne Cartier*, pp. xii, 134–135.

118. Normand Séguin, "L'Agriculture de la Mauricie et du Québec, 1850–1950," *Revue d'histoire de l'Amérique française*, 35 (1982): 537, 545.

119. Consolidation was particularly pronounced after the opening of the American market in 1849. In the 1830s, average farm size had been a mere 60 arpents. See Courville, "Crise agricole du Bas-Canada," p. 400, and Little, *Crofters and Habitants*, p. 30.

120. Bruno Ramirez, *On the Move: French-Canadian and Italian Migrants in the North Atlantic Economy, 1860–1914* (Toronto: McClelland and Stewart, 1991), pp. 24–26.

121. Courville, "Crise agricole du Bas-Canada," pp. 391, 410.

122. On the timing and composition of the rural exodus, see Ramirez, *On the Move*, pp. 21–49; Little, *Crofters and Habitants*, pp. 27–41; and Otis, "Dépopulation rurale," pp. 123–141.

123. Gérard Bouchard, "Co-intégration et reproduction de la société rurale: pour

un modèle saguenayen de la marginalité," *Recherches sociographiques*, 29 (1988): 284, 291.

124. Ramirez, *On the Move*, p. 84.

125. Jean Hamelin and Yves Roby, *Histoire économique du Québec, 1851–1896* (Montréal: Fides, 1971), pp. 66–67, 163–164.

126. On emigrants to the United States, see Ramirez, *On the Move*, pp. 111–137, and Yves Roby, *Les Franco-Américains de la Nouvelle-Angleterre (1776–1930)* (Sillery: Septentrion, 1990). On those who chose Montréal, see Ramirez, *On the Move*, pp. 86–87, and Jean-Claude Robert, "Urbanisation et population: le cas de Montréal en 1861," *Revue d'histoire de l'Amérique française*, 35 (1982): 523–535.

127. For example, about half of the French-Canadian immigrants in Lewiston, Maine, arrived there from colonization parishes; see Yves Frenette, "La Genèse d'une communauté canadienne-française en Nouvelle-Angleterre: Lewiston, Maine, 1800–1880" (doctoral diss., Université Laval, 1988), pp. 170–171.

128. This point has been made most forcefully by Gérard Bouchard, although he does not consider the initial peopling of New France; see Gérard Bouchard and Serge Courville, eds., *La Construction d'une culture: le Québec et l'Amérique française* (Québec: CEFAN, Presses de l'Université Laval, 1993), p. 40.

129. For a more detailed comparison between British and French colonial migrations, see Leslie Choquette, "French and British Emigration to the North American Colonies: A Comparative View," in *New England/New France, 1600–1850*, ed. Peter Benes, The Dublin Seminar for New England Folklife Annual Proceedings, 1989 (Boston: Boston University Press, 1992).

130. Robert Ramsey, *Carolina Cradle: Settlement of the Northwest Carolina Frontier, 1747–1762* (Chapel Hill: University of North Carolina Press, 1964), p. 203.

131. David Souden, "English Indentured Servants and the Transatlantic Colonial Economy," in *International Labour Migration: Historical Perspectives*, ed. Shula Marks and Peter Richardson, Commonwealth Papers, no. 24 (Hounslow: M. Temple Smith, Institute of Commonwealth Studies, 1984), p. 24.

132. Bailyn, *Peopling of British North America*, p. 20. See also John Wareing, "Migration to London and Transatlantic Emigration of Indentured Servants, 1683–1775," *Journal of Historical Geography*, 7 (1981): 356–378.

133. Hal Barron, *Those Who Stayed Behind: Rural Society in Nineteenth-Century New England* (Cambridge: Cambridge University Press, 1984), p. 133. On competency as a value of earlier New Englanders, see Virginia DeJohn Anderson, *New England's Generation: The Great Migration and the Formation of Society and Culture in the Seventeenth Century* (Cambridge: Cambridge University Press, 1991), pp. 131–176. On seaports, see Christine Heyrman, *Commerce and Culture: The Maritime Communities of Colonial Massachusetts, 1690–1750* (New York: Norton, 1984).

134. Ralph Vicero, "L'Exode vers le Sud: survol de la migration canadienne-française vers la Nouvelle-Angleterre au XIXe siècle," in *Situation de la recherche sur la*

Franco-Américanie: actes du premier colloque de l'Institut français, Assumption College, ed. Claire Quintal and André Vachon, special issue of *Vie française* (1980): 6. See also Yolande Lavoie, "Les Mouvements migratoires des Canadiens entre leur pays et les Etats-Unis aux XIXe et XXe siècles," in *La Population du Québec: études rétrospectives,* ed. Hubert Charbonneau (Montréal: Boréal Express, 1973), p. 78.

135. Greene, *Pursuits of Happiness,* p. 207.

Index

Acadia, 19, 224, 252; volume of emigration to, 2, 21, 279; population, 4–5, 38, 251, 253, 279; emigrants to, 17, 29, 112, 170, 171; religion, 130, 132, 136; settlement, 250, 254, 260, 262; economic and political life, 287–291. *See also* Cape Breton; Ile Royale; Ile Saint-Jean

Acadian diaspora, 291–293

Adultery, 144

Age distribution of emigrants to Canada, 151–158

Agriculture (Canada), 263, 281–282, 283–290, 292, 294–296, 300–302, 305

Agriculture (France), 102, 183, 202, 226; *plaine* and *bocage*, 36, 43, 52, 55, 61; Center-west, 44, 79–81, 83–85; North, 48; Northwest, 57–58, 63–64, 66–67, 70–76, 207; Southwest, 87–89; Paris Basin, 90–91; harvest failures, 163–164; grain prices, 165, 167–168, 177–178

Allan, Hugh, 301

Alps (France): emigration to Canada, 29, 31, 36, 41, 42, 45, 77, 94–95, 107, 108, 154, 165, 172, 243–245; women's emigration, 46, 48, 50, 53, 99; migratory traditions, 222, 243–245. *See also* Dauphiné; Savoy

Alsace, 30, 32, 47, 94, 124, 127, 134, 171, 235

Angoumois, 30, 32, 42, 44, 47, 85, 98, 125, 133–134, 169, 221

Anjou, 17, 57, 74, 75, 83, 90, 220; emigration to Canada, 30, 32, 42, 47, 70–73, 76, 99, 125, 126, 169, 203, 215–217, 218, 263; economy, 70–73; migratory traditions, 215–217

Antilles, 72, 133, 198, 220, 222, 225, 226, 247, 253, 286. *See also* Caribbean and West Indies; Martinique; Saint-Domingue

Army. *See* Military

Artisans: recruitment of, 56, 268–270, 276; in France, 68, 74, 91, 102, 104; in emigration to Canada, 101–107, 109, 110, 113, 115–116, 119–122, 126–128, 155, 173, 204–205, 216–217, 234, 239, 256, 263, 305; in military emigration, 116–118, 194, 268–269; in Protestant emigration, 135; migrations of, 187–194, 196, 205, 209, 218, 223, 226, 228, 230–232, 234, 241–242, 246, 277; in Canada, 295. See also *Compagnons*

Artois, 30, 32, 47

Atlantic economy, 3, 36, 43, 44, 48, 54, 56, 58, 63, 67, 71, 83, 165, 177–178, 276–277, 300, 303

Aunis, 17, 261; emigration to Canada, 30, 32, 42, 47, 78–82, 125, 126, 169, 173, 204; economy, 44, 78–82, 89; women's emigration, 96, 98, 124; Protestant emigration, 133–134; migratory traditions, 220–223

Auvergne: emigration to Canda, 30, 32, 45,

Auvergne *(continued)*
47, 95, 109, 231, 237, 239–242, 270;
economy, 95; migratory traditions, 108,
126, 231, 233, 239–242
Avranches, 65, 66, 208

Bardet, Jean-Pierre, 110, 207
Bayonne, 12, 13, 36, 136, 140, 192, 264;
emigration to Canada, 44, 88, 138–139,
178, 225; economy, 170
Béarn, 30, 32, 44, 47
Beauharnais, Governor, 274, 275
Bédard, Marc-André, 132, 133, 134
Belgium, 33, 47, 89, 196
Berry, 30, 32, 47, 127, 184, 228, 237
Bigamy, 7, 144
Bigot, Intendant, 282
Bois, Paul, 74, 105
Boleda, Mario, 16, 20, 21, 23, 112, 161, 163
Bordeaux, 7, 12, 36, 79, 88, 104, 123, 136,
138, 140, 264, 266; emigration to Can-
ada, 44, 86–87, 108, 109, 144, 225–232;
migratory traditions, 45, 127, 185–186,
191, 192, 197–198, 225–232, 240, 241,
242, 245; commerce, 70, 71, 86, 107,
125, 167, 170, 177; population, 85, 105,
279
Boston, 288, 289
Bouchard, Gérard, 302
Bourbonnais, 30, 32, 45, 48, 95, 126, 184,
270
Bourgeoisie. *See* Social class
Bourgeoys, Marguerite, 143
Bourget, Ignace, 300
Bourrachot, Lucile, 223, 226
Brandeau, Esther, 137–140, 224
Braudel, Fernand, 1
Brest, 58, 60, 168, 190, 192, 204, 228
Brittany, 27, 28, 61, 74, 82, 99, 170, 207,
210, 214, 215, 220, 225; seasonal migration to Canada, 22, 33, 59–60; emigra-
tion to Canada, 30, 31, 32, 42–43, 47,
54, 55–60, 67, 98, 108, 123, 124, 125,
126, 166–168, 201–206; economy, 56–59,
70–71, 169; migratory traditions, 190,
201–206, 209 122, 221, 222, 235, 237–238
Brunschwig, Henri, 5

Bunle, Henri, 195, 198, 199
Burgundy: emigration to Canada, 30, 32,
47, 48, 54, 93–94, 111, 124, 127, 216,
235, 270; migratory traditions, 184, 193,
236–237

Cabantous, Alain, 177
Campeau, Lucien, 131
Canada. *See* Acadia; Emigrants to Canada;
Emigration to Canada; Newfoundland;
Québec
Cape Breton, 12, 38, 208, 291. *See also* Ile
Royale
Capitalism (Canada), 293–294, 296,
300
Capitalism (France), 3, 59, 67, 76, 85, 89,
90, 99, 277; Brittany, 59; Normandy, 64;
Perche, 69; Anjou, 70; Maine, 75; Poi-
tou, 83
Caribbean and West Indies, 5, 247, 258,
282, 285, 288, 290, 304; French emigra-
tion to, 86, 159–160, 197–198, 201, 205,
211, 217, 221–223, 225, 226. *See also* Antilles; Martinique; Saint-Domingue
Cartier, George-Etienne, 299, 300–301
Cartier, Jacques, 277
Catholicism (Canada): in New France 129–
130, 132, 142–149, 249, 251; after the
British conquest, 297–300. *See* Hospitalières; Jesuits; Sulpicians; Ursulines
Center-west (France), 45, 135, 171, 172;
emigration to Canada, 29, 31, 40, 41,
42, 43, 44, 46, 48, 53, 54, 77–82, 106,
107, 109, 111, 122, 125, 127, 133, 153,
154, 158, 165, 169–170, 175, 220–225,
227; economy, 78–81; migratory traditions, 219–225, 243. *See also* Angoumois; Aunis; Poitou; Saintonge
Champagne: emigration to Canada, 30, 32,
47, 54, 93–94, 97, 122, 124, 127, 158,
171, 204, 216, 235, 237, 239, 243; migratory traditions, 193, 236–237
Champlain, Samuel de, 121, 130
Charbonneau, Hubert, 4, 8, 16
Châtelain, Abel, 18, 19
Chaunu, Pierre, 178
Chennevières, marquis de, 27, 28

Chronology of emigration to Canada, 159–178

Cities and towns: role in emigration to Canada, 37–45, 51–52, 134, 202–206, 218, 219, 224–225, 226–232, 234–239, 243–246; role in French migrations, 184–194, 219–222, 225, 233–234

Clark, Peter, 246

Class. *See* Social class

Colbert, Jean-Baptiste, 142, 146, 175, 252, 264, 270–273

Commerce (Canada), 146, 281, 285, 287–290, 294–296; fur trade, 143, 251

Commerce (France): emigrants engaged in, 13, 114, 116, 121, 135, 155, 202; with Canada, 57, 78, 126, 132, 137, 167, 169, 192, 201, 207, 227, 257; in the Northwest, 58, 62, 65–66, 67, 74, 213; Atlantic, 81, 86–90, 99, 125, 160, 177–178, 261, 270, 284; in the Center-west, 82, 83; with Spain, 241; in indentured servants, 256–260

Communauté des Habitants (Canada), 252, 254, 257, 258

Communications: role in channeling emigration to Canada, 64, 69, 72, 73, 76, 80, 82, 87, 93, 98, 99, 234

Compagnie d'Acadie, 258

Compagnie de l'Ile Saint-Jean, 170

Compagnie des Cent Associés, 130, 251–253, 254, 257, 258, 261

Compagnie des Indes, 168, 247, 253, 258, 270

Compagnie du Nord, 258

Compagnonnage, 188–194, 200, 216, 217, 224, 228, 230. *See also* Tour de France

Compagnons, 118, 120, 127, 188–194, 203, 204–205, 216, 223, 224–225, 226, 228, 229–230, 234, 246

Comtat, 32, 48

Conquest (British), economic and political effects of, 282, 291–295, 297–298, 302

Conseil de Québec, 132, 252, 257

Convicts. *See* Emigration to Canada; Prisoners

Coornaert, Emile, 191

Corvisier, André, 14, 116, 117, 118, 122, 123, 135, 171, 229, 264

Côté, Cyrille (Agricola), 298

Courcelles, Governor, 145

Courgeau, Daniel, 185

Courville, Serge, 286, 295, 300

Dardel, Pierre, 177

Dauphiné, 30, 32, 45, 47, 95, 122, 124, 134, 243, 244

Dawson, Nelson, 136

Debien, Gabriel, 11, 197, 199, 205, 221

Dechêne, Louise, 283, 284, 296

Delasselle, Claude, 236

Departmental origins of emigrants to Canada, 33–36, 48–51

Depauw, Jacques, 202

Dickinson, John, 284

Dieppe, 6, 11, 61–62, 63, 66, 86, 98, 197, 237

Duchesneau, Intendant, 281

East (France): emigration to Canada, 29, 31, 40, 41, 46, 48, 53, 89–91, 93–94, 97–98, 106, 122, 124, 153, 154, 171, 232, 234; migratory traditions, 190, 205, 222. *See also* Alsace; Burgundy; Champagne; Franche-Comté; Lorraine; Lyonnais; Nivernais

East Indies, 3, 5, 168. *See also* Ile de Bourbon; Ile de France

Emigrant recruitment, 247–277; in Perche, 69; in Anjou, 73; of soldiers, 122–124, 264–269; responsibilities for, 249–254; in La Rochelle, 255–261; role of merchants in, 255–260; role of seigneurs in, 260–263; role of the state in, 263–276

Emigrant sample, 4, 16–17, 19, 22–23, 29, 31, 33, 37, 45, 51, 59, 91, 101–102, 110, 112, 114, 133, 134, 135, 151–152, 156, 160, 203, 210, 223, 226, 234–235, 242

Emigrants to Canada: provincial origins, 29–33; departmental origins, 33–36; urban/rural distributions, 37–45; women, 45–53, 95–99, 110–111, 113–114, 124–125, 135–136, 156, 158, 175–177, 235–237, 271–273; recruitment, 69, 73, 247–277; social origins, 101–111; occupations, 112–127; religious backgrounds, 129–150; age

Emigrants to Canada *(continued)*
    distribution, 151–159; prior migrations,
    203–205, 210–211, 214–215, 215–217,
    223–225, 226–232, 235–239, 242–245
Emigration to Canada: numerical esti-
    mates, 2, 20–22, 198, 279; military, 13–
    14, 19, 112, 116–118, 122–124, 135, 168,
    169, 174, 248, 253; forced, 15, 101, 112–
    113, 118, 124, 253, 273–276; seasonal,
    temporary, and permanent, 18–20; re-
    turn rates, 19, 21; from northwestern
    France, 55–76, 165–167, 200–218; from
    central-western France, 77–85, 169–170,
    220–225; from southwestern France, 85–
    89, 170–171, 225–232; from northern
    and eastern France, 89–94, 171–172, 232–
    239; from the Massif central, South, and
    Alps, 94–95, 172–173, 239–245; familial,
    96, 98, 108, 113–114, 118, 124–125, 152,
    177, 223, 263, 274–275; chronology of,
    159–178
Engagés, 11, 19, 21, 197, 215, 217, 222, 256,
    257. *See also* Indentured servants
England, 5, 232, 249, 288–289, 291; French
    emigration to, 8, 68, 195, 213, 239; emi-
    gration to New France from, 33, 47;
    economy, 76, 89; colonial emigration
    from, 198–199, 246, 305

Faillon, Abbé, 280, 303
Families: role in emigration to Canada, 96,
    98, 108, 113–114, 118, 124–125, 152, 177,
    223, 263, 274–275
Farming. *See* Agriculture
Ferland, Abbé, 280, 303
Filles du roi, 236, 237, 271–273. *See also*
    Women
Flanders, 30, 32, 47, 48, 89, 124, 172, 235,
    239, 283
Foix, 30, 32, 44, 48, 134, 196
Fournier, Marcel, 17, 22
France. *See* Alps; Center-west; East; Ile-de-
    France; Loire; Massif central; North;
    Northwest; South; Southwest
Franche-Comté, 30, 32, 47, 48, 122, 127,
    193, 204, 235, 242, 270
Frontenac, Governor, 146, 267, 289

Galenson, David, 156
Gascony, 30, 32, 33, 47, 54, 88, 125, 126,
    127, 134
Germany, 33, 47, 134, 195, 196, 209, 239,
    289
Giffard, Robert, 69, 115, 168, 213, 214, 215,
    261, 262
Godbout, Archange, 17, 29
Goubert, Pierre, 37, 90
Gradis, Abraham, 137, 192
Grand Dérangement, 287
Granville, 65, 66, 208, 209, 210, 227
Great Britain. *See* England
Great Confinement, 276
Greene, Jack, 305
Griffiths, Naomi, 292
Guernsey, Isle of, 33
Guyana, 198, 291
Guyenne: emigration to Canada, 30, 32,
    47, 86–88, 125, 126, 127, 133, 134, 210;
    economy, 86–88, 89; migratory tradi-
    tions, 184

Hamilton, Louis, 28
Harris, R. Cole, 287
Hauser, Henri, 190, 193
Hébert, Louis, 20
Hémon, Louis, 302
Henri IV, 249, 250
Henry, Louis, 20, 185
Hocquart, Intendant, 274, 275
Holland, 33, 68, 195, 197, 239, 239, 283,
    287. *See also* Netherlands
Hospitalières (Dieppe), 6
Hospitalières (La Flèche), 148
Huguenots. *See* Protestants

Ile de Bourbon, 198. *See also* East Indies
Ile de France, 198 *See also* East Indies
Ile-de-France (Paris region): emigration to
    Canada, 29, 30, 31, 32, 40, 41, 42, 46,
    47, 53, 54, 91–94, 96–97, 98, 106, 111,
    122, 124, 126, 153, 154, 158, 165, 171,
    196, 210, 216, 222, 224, 227, 234–235,
    238 243; economy, 164, 172; migratory
    traditions, 184, 233–234
Ile de Ré, 81–82, 84

Ile Royale, 137, 254, 269, 285, 287; emigration to, 12, 167, 201, 265, 266, 268, 275; economy, 290–291. *See also* Cape Breton; Louisbourg

Ile Saint-Jean, 38, 137, 170, 174, 254, 260–261, 287, 290, 291. *See also* Prince Edward Island

Illegitimacy rates, 144

Immigration. *See* Emigration to Canada; Migration

Indentured servants: in Canada, 11, 12, 19, 101, 114, 135, 155–156, 159–160, 174, 251, 253, 254, 264, 270, 273; in French colonies, 86, 133, 197, 205, 221; from La Rochelle, 255–261. See also *Engagés*

Indentured servitude, 1, 10–11, 13, 17, 152, 197, 215

India, 33

Indians. *See* Native Americans

Ireland, 33, 47, 232

Italy, 33, 195, 196, 197, 235, 239, 243

Jersey, Isle of, 33

Jesuits, 93, 148, 252

Jetté, René, 17

Jews (Canada), 197; in New France 129, 136–142, 149, 150; after the conquest, 294, 297

Joliette, Barthélemy, 295

Journeymen. See *Compagnons*

Juchereau, Jean and Noël, 69, 168, 212, 213, 214, 215, 261, 263

Kaplow, Jeffrey, 104, 233

La Dauversière, Jérôme Le Royer de, 73, 143, 169, 215, 260, 261–262, 263

La Flèche, 73, 143, 148, 169, 215–217, 262

La Hontan, baron de, 143, 144, 272, 282, 283

Lanctôt, Gustave, 146

Languedoc, 29, 122, 126; emigration to Canada, 30, 32, 44, 47, 50, 109, 133, 134; Regiment of, 170, 238

La Puisaye, Joseph de, 214

La Rochelle, 7, 36, 70, 71, 83, 84, 86, 131, 139, 140, 219, 269; passenger lists, 11–

12, 198; economy, 78, 80, 81, 107, 167, 169, 178; emigration to Canada, 78–79, 82, 109, 132, 134, 138, 142, 147, 148, 159, 222–225, 244, 253; migratory traditions, 160, 192, 197, 204–205, 217, 220–223, 230, 231, 240; role in emigrant recruitment, 170, 255–262, 270

Laurier, Wilfrid, 300

Laval, Bishop, 131, 132, 142, 145–146, 271

Lavoie, Yolande, 8

Le Caron, Joseph, 131

Lefebvre, Georges, 90

Le Havre, 57, 61, 65, 66, 79, 177, 248, 264, 266

Le Jeune, Paul, 147, 148, 149, 263

Le Moine, Roger, 296

Léon, Pierre, 104

Le Pesant, Michel, 210

Lescarbot, Marc, 130

Lévy, Claude, 185

Limousin: emigration to Canada, 30, 32, 45, 47, 126, 241–243, 270; migratory traditions, 108, 190, 221, 233, 239–241

Literacy, 121, 230

Little, J. I., 295

Loire (region): emigration to Canada, 29, 31, 46, 94, 97, 106, 125, 154, 165, 171–172, 232, 234. *See also* Berry; Orléanais; Touraine

Lorraine, 5, 127, 172, 190; emigration to Canada, 30, 32, 47, 48, 122, 171, 235, 237, 243

Lortie, Stanislas, 29

Louis XIII, 257

Louis XIV, 5, 13, 146, 198, 248, 249, 252, 253, 254, 258, 281

Louis XV, 191, 194, 198

Louisbourg, 9, 13, 136, 305; population, 38, 146; emigration to, 158, 167, 178, 243; economy, 285–286, 288, 290–291

Louisiana, 198, 273, 279; Acadians in, 291–293

Luxembourg, 33

Lyon, 93, 95, 191, 193, 237, 239, 240, 241, 279

Lyonnais, 30, 32, 47, 48, 93, 187, 204, 235, 239

Maine (France), 67, 70, 72, 83, 90, 220; emigration to Canada, 30, 32, 42, 43, 47, 74–76, 126, 127, 166, 169, 203, 215–217, 218, 263, 267; economy, 73–76; migratory traditions, 215–217

Malta, 33

Mance, Jeanne, 169

Mandrou, Robert, 159, 160, 164

Marche: emigration to Canada, 30, 32, 45, 47, 126, 238, 239–241, 243; migratory traditions, 190, 221, 233, 239–240

Marie de l'Incarnation, 148

Marseille, 8, 94, 191, 192, 279

Martinique, 237

Massé, Ennemond, 73

Massicotte, Edouard-Zotique, 29

Massif central: emigration to Canada, 29, 31, 36, 41, 45, 46, 48, 50, 77, 99, 108, 153, 154, 165, 172, 224, 227, 235, 238, 239–243, 244, 245; economy, 84, 85, 88; migratory traditions, 94, 126, 190, 196, 221, 222, 231, 239–243. See also Auvergne; Bourbonnais; Limousin; Marche

Mathieu, Jacques, 223, 285

Ménétra, Jacques-Louis, 191–193, 230

Menou d'Aulnay, Charles de, 260, 262, 263

Mercantilism, 282–283, 288

Mercier, Sébastien, 92, 187

Merle, Louis, 205

Midi. See South

Migration: definitions of, 17–18; sexual specificity of, 45, 246

Migrations (France): short-distance, 182–183; middle-distance, 184–186; to towns, 184–185, 186–187; long-distance, 186–199; interurban, 187–194; of compagnons, 188–194; of soldiers, 193–194, 196, 238, 245, 246; foreign and colonial, 195–199, 241; in the Northwest, 200–218; in the Center-west, 220–225; in the Massif central, 221–222, 231–232, 239–243; in the Southwest, 225–232; in the North and East, 232–234; in the South and Alps, 243–245

Military: emigration to Canada, 6, 13–14; settlement in Canada, 19, 21, 276; presence in Louisbourg, 38, 290–291; emigrants, 112, 116–118, 133, 135, 152, 202, 203, 204, 240, 241, 242; recruitment, 122–124, 168, 169, 170–171, 172, 173, 174, 248, 253, 264–269; role in migration, 188, 194, 195–196, 203, 218, 229, 234, 245–246, 303

Miquelon, Dale, 287

Moheau (early populationist), 195, 197, 198

Monaco, 32, 48

Montréal, 4, 140, 293, 298, 299, 300, 301, 302; recruitment and settlement, 21, 73, 147, 149, 169, 174, 176, 260, 262; population, 38; mores, 143–145, 146, 280–281; development surrounding, 285, 286, 294, 295, 296, 302. See also Ville-Marie

Monts, Pierre Du Gua de, 130, 250

Moore, Christopher, 290

Moulin, Marie-Anne, 240

Nantes, 7, 10, 58, 62, 70, 71, 79, 82, 86, 138, 168, 220, 264, 279; economy, 56–57; emigration to Canada, 56–57, 59, 60, 202–204, 266, 267; Edict of, 131, 136, 223; migratory traditions, 190, 191, 192, 193, 202–206, 230; emigration to colonies, 197

Native Americans, 143, 146, 147–149, 282

Netherlands, 196, 204, 287. See also Holland

New Brunswick, 291

New England, 2, 5, 23, 27, 280, 282, 284, 289, 290, 293, 302, 305; population, 253. See also Boston; Thirteen colonies

Newfoundland, 4, 19, 56, 65, 208, 251, 267, 268, 290, 305

New France. See Acadia; Emigrants to Canada; Emigration to Canada; Québec

Nivernais, 30, 32, 47, 216

Nobles. See Social class

Normandy, 17, 20, 27, 28, 72, 99, 172, 212, 240, 257; emigration to Canada, 30, 32, 33, 42, 43, 54, 61–67, 108, 122, 125, 126, 133, 134, 153, 155, 166–167, 206–211, 238, 239; women's emigration, 47, 52, 98, 111, 124, 148; economy, 61–67, 89, 90; migratory traditions, 182, 187, 196,

203, 206–211, 215, 222, 233, 235, 236, 237, 245

North (France): emigration to Canada, 29, 31, 40, 41, 42, 89–91, 93–94, 106, 154, 165, 172, 232, 234; women's emigration, 46, 48, 53; economy, 89–91, 124; migratory traditions, 190, 232, 233, 236. *See also* Artois; Flanders; Picardy

Northwest (France), 44, 45, 77, 85, 109, 170, 171, 172, 219, 220; emigration to Canada, 29, 31, 36, 40, 41, 42, 43, 54, 55–76, 106, 107, 125, 126, 154, 158, 165–169, 200–218; women's emigration, 46, 53, 98, 111, 175; economy, 55–76; migratory traditions, 200–218, 221, 222, 223, 224, 227, 243. *See also* Anjou; Brittany; Maine; Normandy; Perche

Nova Scotia, 250, 291. *See* Acadia

Occupation of emigrants to Canada, 12–13, 101, 112–128, 155–157, 174–175, 202, 274–275

Ontario, 214, 296

Orléanais, 30, 32, 47, 54, 97, 124, 203, 204, 215, 235, 242

Orry, Comptroller General, 273

Paquet, Gilles, 283, 285, 296

Paris, 5, 64, 65, 67, 68, 75, 104, 118, 164, 171, 193, 203, 213, 214, 244; emigration to Canada, 20, 27, 36, 78, 91–93, 97, 107, 109, 121, 123–124, 125, 126, 234–239, 243, 265, 266, 274, 275; women's emigration, 51, 96–97, 271–272; social geography, 91–92; migratory traditions, 185, 187, 190, 191, 204, 205, 216, 217, 219, 222, 228, 230, 232–239, 240, 241, 243, 245

Parkman, Francis, 280, 303

Pays basque, 88, 225, 227

Pays d'Auge, 61, 63–64, 65, 66, 98, 206–207, 211

Pays de Caux, 61–63, 64, 65, 98, 132, 206, 211

Peasants. *See* Social class

Peltrie, Madame de la, 148–149

Perche, 70, 71, 72, 73, 74, 75, 182; emigra-

tion to Canada, 30, 32, 42, 43, 47, 67–69, 76, 96, 99, 124, 127, 166, 169, 213–215, 261, 263; economy, 67–68; migratory traditions, 183, 211–213, 217, 218

Perdiguier, Agricol, 7–8, 189

Pérouas, Louis, 135, 159, 220

Perrot, Jean-Claude, 187

Petit, Françoise-Eugénie, 296

Picardy: emigration to Canada, 30, 32, 47, 54, 94, 97, 124, 172, 210, 216, 235, 237, 238, 242; migratory traditions, 236, 237

Plamondon, Liliane, 294

Poitiers, 84, 127, 191, 224

Poitou, 27, 57, 79, 81, 90; emigration to Canada, 30, 32, 42, 43, 47, 52, 82–84, 98, 109, 125, 126, 127, 134, 169–170, 203, 262, 263, 270; economy, 82–84; migratory traditions, 133, 184, 221

Population: New France, 4–5, 38, 253, 279; New England, 253; thirteen colonies, 279

Port-Royal, 38, 250, 288, 289

Portugal, 8, 33, 197, 239

Poussou, Jean-Pierre, 2, 37, 41, 79, 85, 86, 89, 104, 177, 181, 183, 185, 186, 221, 223, 226, 228

Poutrincourt, Jean Biencourt de, 250

PRDH, 16, 20, 29–30, 31, 33, 114

Prévost, Intendant, 167–168

Prince Edward Island, 38, 170, 292. *See also* Ile Saint-Jean

Prisoners: deported to Canada, 15, 101, 112–113, 116, 118, 124, 253, 264, 270, 273–276; in the military, 266, 267

Prostitution, 143–144, 146

Protestant diaspora, 68, 129, 195–196

Protestants (Canada), 5, 6, 8, 31, 129, 130–136, 149, 150, 204, 223, 249, 250, 251, 282, 296

Protestants (France), 125, 192, 257, 258, 259

Provence, 30, 32, 47, 125, 134

Provincial origins of emigrants to Canada, 29–33, 45–48

Québec (city), 4, 37–38

Québec (province): emigration to, 2, 17, 20–22, 29, 69, 73, 112, 133, 136–137, 140, 197, 198, 268–269, 279; population,

Québec (province) *(continued)*
4–5, 38, 251, 253, 279, 301–302; historical records, 4–10, 16; commercial ties, 56–57, 65, 259; Catholicism, 142–150, 299–300; agriculture and trade, 283–287, 293–296, 301; seigneurial system, 284–285; village growth, 286–287, 295–296; liberalism, 296–298; industrial capitalism, 300–301; emigration from, 302, 305

Raudot, Jacques, 281
Razilly, Claude and Isaac de, 260, 261–262, 263
Rebellions of 1837 and 1838 (Québec), 293, 297–298
Recruitment. *See* Emigrant recruitment
Regional origins of emigrants to Canada, 55–100, 122–127, 303
Rétif de la Bretonne, 90
Richelieu, Cardinal, 5, 31, 130–131, 251, 252, 254, 257
Rivard, Adjutor, 29
Robert, Normand, 18
Roche, Daniel, 233
Rochefort, 80, 81, 119, 191, 192, 204, 219, 220–221, 224, 225, 240, 264, 266, 269
Rouen, 7, 10, 36, 46, 64, 65, 66, 67, 75, 76, 89, 104, 108, 169, 220; emigration to Canada, 61–63, 78, 98, 109, 134; social geography, 62; commerce, 107, 132, 167, 177–178, 207, 237, 252; social structure, 110; migratory traditions, 164, 191, 207–208, 230
Rousseau, Jean-Jacques, 189
Roussillon, 30, 32, 44, 47, 170, 265

Sack, Benjamin, 140
Saint-Domingue, 217, 273, 291
Saint-Malo, 59, 65, 66, 138, 191, 193, 204, 264; economy, 57, 58, 167–168, 201–202, 227; emigration to Canada, 57, 60, 62, 78, 123, 167–168, 203; migratory traditions, 205
Saintonge, 79; emigration to Canada, 30, 32, 42, 44, 47, 85, 98, 125, 126, 133, 134, 140, 169, 210, 224; migratory traditions, 221

Saint-Pierre, Jacques, 285
Saint Pierre and Miquelon, 160, 289
Salone, Emile, 281
Sample. *See* Emigrant sample
Savoie. *See* Savoy
Savoy, 32, 45, 47, 50, 95, 184, 233, 244, 270
Séguin, Normand, 296
Social class of emigrants to Canada, 101–111, 116–119, 134–135, 155–156, 173–174, 208, 256, 260, 262–263, 303
Soldiers. *See* Military
Souden, David, 246
Sources (Canada), 4–5; ecclesiastical, 5–8; census, 8–9; notarial and judicial, 9–10
Sources (France): exit documents, 10–13; military, 13–14; official correspondence, 14–15
South (France): emigration to Canada, 29, 31, 40, 41, 42, 46, 53, 77, 94–95, 99, 107, 108, 154, 165, 172, 219, 222, 227, 243–244; migratory traditions, 243–244. *See also* Comtat; Languedoc; Provence
South Africa, 195, 282, 287
Southwest (France), 12, 234; emigration to Canada, 29, 31, 36, 40, 41, 44, 46, 53, 54, 77, 85–89, 99, 106, 108, 122, 125, 126, 154, 165, 169, 170–171, 224, 225–232; economy, 85–89; migratory traditions, 81, 219, 221, 222, 225–232, 241, 243. *See also* Béarn; Foix; Gascony; Guyenne; Roussillon
Spain, 2, 8, 33, 108, 196, 197, 239, 241, 289
Subsistence crises (France), 164, 173
Sulpicians, 93, 272, 297, 299
Surnames, 188, 229
Switzerland, 184, 195, 196, 239; emigration to Canada, 33, 47, 133, 134, 235, 265; emigrants to Bordeaux, 127

Talon, Jean, 9, 247–248, 270–273, 281, 286
Tanguay, Cyprien, 28
Thirteen colonies, 22, 131, 195, 304; population, 253, 279; emigration to, 305. *See also* Boston; New England
Touraine, 30, 32, 47, 125, 134, 196, 215, 216, 262

Tour de France, 122, 188–189, 190–194, 200, 204–205, 215, 216, 217, 218, 224, 227, 228, 229, 230, 234, 245. See also *Compagnonnage*

Trade. *See* Commerce

Transvestism, 137–140

Trois-Rivières, 38, 127, 171, 275

Trudel, Marcel, 17

Ursulines, 148, 149

Usner, Daniel, 292

Ville-Marie, 73, 143, 280. *See also* Montréal

Wallot, Jean-Pierre, 283, 285, 287, 296, 297, 298

Weber, Eugen, 304

West India Company. *See* Compagnie des Indes

West Indies. *See* Antilles; Caribbean and West Indies

Women (emigrants to Canada): regional origins, 45–53, 95–99, 124–125, 235–237; social and marital status, 110–111, 113–114; religion, 135–136; age distribution, 156, 158; chronology of emigration, 175–177; recruitment, 235–237, 271–273